IMAGINING LONDON
Postcolonial Fiction and the
Transnational Metropolis

Imagining London

Postcolonial Fiction and the Transnational Metropolis

John Clement Ball

UNIVERSITY OF TORONTO PRESS
Toronto Buffalo London

© University of Toronto Press Incorporated 2004
Toronto Buffalo London
Printed in Canada

ISBN 0-8020-4496-4

Printed on acid-free paper

National Library of Canada Cataloguing in Publication

Ball, John Clement, 1960–
Imagining London : postcolonial fiction and the transnational
metropolis / John Clement Ball.

Includes index.
ISBN 0-8020-4496-4

1. London (England) – In literature.   2. City and town life in
literature.   3. Postcolonialism in literature.   4. Commonwealth fiction
(English) – 20th century – History and criticism.   5. English fiction –
20th century – History and criticism.   I. Title.

PR9084.B34 2004   823.009'32421   C2003-907151-0

University of Toronto Press acknowledges the financial assistance to its
publishing program of the Canada Council for the Arts and the
Ontario Arts Council.

This book has been published with the help of a grant from the Canadian
Federation for the Humanities and Social Sciences, through the Aid to
Scholarly Publications Programme, using funds provided by the Social Sciences
and Humanities Research Council of Canada.

University of Toronto Press acknowledges the financial support for its
publishing activities of the Government of Canada through the
Book Publishing Industry Development Program (BPIDP).

Contents

Acknowledgments

This project began with the support of an Isaak Walton Killam Postdoctoral Fellowship at the University of British Columbia. Although the two-year fellowship gave way after just six months to a tenure-track position across the country, it provided an invaluable foundation. I am grateful for the fellowship committee's endorsement and the support, friendship, and intellectual kinship of Bill New and Patricia Badir during my time at UBC. Subsequently, at the University of New Brunswick, a new faculty research grant financed travel to London and Toronto, and Roger Ploude, John Rowcroft, and John McLaughlin offered timely moral and practical support. Jennifer Bronson, Colleen Hymers, and Al Tepper were excellent research assistants. By making his office available to me during my sabbatical, Wayne Donaldson provided a much-needed private space to write; in the microgeography of the UNB campus, it was like moving away while staying home and enjoying the benefits of both. I am especially grateful to my departmental colleagues Jennifer Andrews, Tony Boxill, Randall Martin, and Mary Rimmer, who gave generously of their time to read the draft manuscript.

Andrea Sella's flat in Notting Hill was an exceptionally welcoming home base for my researches in London, as was Greg Sinclair and Kateri Lanthier's house in Toronto. For smoothing research paths I am grateful to the helpful staff at the Commonwealth Institute Library, the University of Birmingham Library Special Collections, the CBC Archives, the University of Toronto's Robarts Library, and UNB's Harriet Irving Library. For incidental research leads and general enthusiasm, I thank John McLeod, James Procter, and Ian Dieffenthaller in the United Kingdom and, in Canada, Chelva Kanaganayakam, Ted Chamberlin, Linda Hutcheon, Jim Howard, Jude Seaboyer, Margery Fee, Tracy Ware, Michel

Pharand, Tony Tremblay, Philip Mingay, Linda Warley, Douglas Ivison, and many colleagues and students at UNB.

Work in progress was presented at several conferences: CACLALS (1995, 2001, 2002, and 2003); Literature of Region and Nation (1996); Competing Realities: Fifty Years of South Asian Literature (1997); ASNEL (2000); and ACCUTE (2001). Early versions of some ideas explored in the book have appeared in articles and conference proceedings, though they are thoroughly reworked. Substantial portions of two articles are recognizably intact as they appear here: 'The Semi-Detached Metropolis: Hanif Kureishi's London' in *ARIEL* 27.4 (1996), and 'Spaces of Postimperial Dwelling: Metropolitan Life and Colonial History in Kate Pullinger's Fiction' in *Essays on Canadian Writing* 73 (2001). I am grateful to the editors for their permission to reprint.

Permission to quote from *Caribbean Voices* scripts and from Henry Swanzy and Gladys Lindo's correspondence was granted by the BBC; special thanks to Jeff Walden of the Written Archives Centre for help at various stages. Greene & Heaton Ltd gave permission to quote from a commentary written for *Caribbean Voices* by the late Arthur Calder-Marshall.

The University of Toronto Press staff has been unfailingly helpful and encouraging; I am particularly indebted to my editor, Siobhan McMenemy, for her good counsel, keen intelligence, and firm but gentle way with deadlines. Frances Mundy and Judy Williams were meticulous and gracious throughout the production process.

Lisa Alward has lived with this project since its first appearance as an inchoate gleam in a graduate student's eye. Throughout, her love of London and of literature proved infectious, and her belief in the book was unwavering. She and our children, Hilary, Jack, and Peter, were very understanding of my habitual relocation to mental elsewheres and occasional trips to geographical ones.

Long before I ever thought of writing a book about London my parents told me their stories about it. My mother, a child of the Raj, grew up in India and non-metropolitan England. My father was a Canadian with Loyalist forebears. Born and raised in faraway (ex)colonial places and with strong family links to empire, they both had vivid impressions of a metropolis they first visited as young people. My father, particularly, spoke often of his excitement as a small-town Canadian on leave in London during World War Two, hardly believing he was in the famed city, amazed when he ran into someone he knew from back home. Experiences similar to his or my mother's would sometimes echo through my literary visits to the city over the last few years. This book is dedicated to the memories of Alison Davison and Jack Ball, who introduced me to London through stories and travel.

IMAGINING LONDON

chapter one

Introduction:
The Key to the Capital

Through books alone we learnt to love the London of English literature.

R.K. Narayan

The city and the urban sphere are thus the setting of struggle; they are also, however, the stakes of that struggle. How could one aim for power without reaching for the places where power resides, without planning to occupy that space and to create a new political morphology.

Henri Lefebvre

The task of decolonization must be taken to the metropolis itself; the imperial mythology has to be confronted on its home ground.

Simon Gikandi

London and the Postcolonial Pen

In Arundhati Roy's novel *The God of Small Things* (1997), the ill-fated English girl Sophie Mol arrives in Ayemenem from London with gifts for her Indian cousins. Prominent among them are 'two ballpoint pens – the top halves filled with water in which a cut-out collage of a London streetscape was suspended. Buckingham Palace and Big Ben. Shops and people. A red double-decker bus propelled by an air bubble floated up and down the silent street' (253). The reader may go on to imagine that when Rahel or Estha takes one of these pens in hand, 'London' will accompany every twitch and loop of its movement. The ink with which it inscribes their words and pictures will flow, like an impossibly small River Thames, past the icons of a miniature metropolis.

When writers from lands that were colonized by Britain's erstwhile empire put pen to paper, a set of ideas that coalesce around the signifier 'London' often shadows their work – especially if they, like Roy and her characters, use the colonizer's language. At the height of imperial power in the late nineteenth and early twentieth centuries, London was the great metropolis, the world's largest city. 'The Heart of the Empire' (as a famous painting named it in 1904), London projected itself to the inhabitants of its pink-stained territories as the centre of the world, the fountainhead of culture, the zero-point of global time and space.[1] 'London' served as a metonym for imperial power itself: its point of origin, the place where the empire was built and around which it revolved.[2] And so, through the further subdivisions of metonymy, did those London landmarks – the Thames, Buckingham Palace, Big Ben, the Houses of Parliament, the Greenwich Meridian – that most identifiably stood for London as a city of global reach. In the words of one Asian-British writer, 'The Thames made Londinium and Londinium made England and England made Parliament and Parliament made Britain and Britain made the world. Britain also made me, for better or worse' (qtd. in Alibhai-Brown 8). The temporal and spatial largeness to which this distilled genealogy gestures is typical of invocations of imperial or postimperial London, in which the immediacy of the local here and now blurs regularly into the vast, hazy remoteness of the global there and the historical then. As a palimpsest under which millennia of material history are layered, London is an English place; as the hub of a network of global relations, it has always been a transnational space. Any postcolonial 'me' who ventures to write about contemporary London has all that expansive history and geography – which 'made' the city and the self – temptingly close at hand.

London came to include and represent 'the world' in another way during the postwar decades of formal decolonization. In the half-century from 1947 (India) to 1997 (Hong Kong), as England gradually withdrew its imperial tentacles, hundreds of thousands of former subjects went along for the ride, beginning with the arrival of 492 Caribbean immigrants on the SS *Windrush* in 1948. Over the following decades, the international citizenry of empire converged on London in a phenomenon sometimes called the reinvasion of the centre or, in the words of the Jamaican poet Louise Bennett, 'Colonizin in reverse' (33). As a result of this so-called 'New Commonwealth' migration, the metropolis that once possessed a large portion of the world now contains a transnational 'world' that is increasingly taking possession of it. With over two million non-white residents in the year 2000 (Ackroyd 715), London has been transformed; demographically it is becoming more and more global (or transnational) and less and less traditionally – that is, ethnically, racially, or even nationally – English or British. Dick Hebdige writes that as 'the British empire has folded in upon itself and the chickens have come home, ... the pressure in the cities continues to mount' and old notions of 'a racially proscribed "British" identity ... have started cracking at the seams' (142). The centre, in other words, has become decentred. As a city whose international relations and populace go back to the Roman Empire, it always was. But in recent history London's transnational decentredness has become its most visibly constitutive feature.

The multitudes of colonial and postcolonial migrants who have come to live in London during the era of decolonization have included many writers: West Indians (George Lamming and V.S. Naipaul, among many others); Indians (including Kamala Markandaya and Salman Rushdie); Africans (Buchi Emecheta and Biyi Bandele). Writers from the former invader-settler colonies, which began decolonizing much earlier, have also lived in the metropolis during this period: Canadians (Mordecai Richler and Kate Pullinger); Australians (Patrick White); New Zealanders (Janet Frame). Not surprisingly, then, London features prominently in the postcolonial imaginary. Indeed, any hyperindustrious reader who undertook to survey all English-language fiction from the postcolonial Commonwealth would find London to be the single most frequently used geographical signifier and setting.

The city's manifold appearances in postcolonial literature reflect the varied experiences of colonized peoples. It is the unimaginably distant, previously unheard-of place from which missionaries and colonizers arrive in historical novels of early contact such as those of the Australian writer Mudrooroo; based on the available evidence, the aboriginal Tasmanians in *Master of the Ghost Dreaming* (1991) create 'a myth in which [white Britons] were seen as ghosts, and London as a cold forbidding realm filled with so much suffering that a human could not survive in it' (32). Others imagine London more positively: it is the valorized destination for a migrant character seeking liberation from the restrictions of small-island societies in books such as Naipaul's *Miguel Street* (1959), Jamaica Kincaid's *Annie John* (1985), or Romesh Gunesekera's *Reef* (1994), which end with their protagonists commencing a horizon-broadening future in London. And in narratives of postindependence Africa by Emecheta, Chinua Achebe, M.G. Vassanji, and others, to be a 'London-returned' or 'been-to' is to have been made special: validated by London experience and education, ripe for elevation into a postcolonial (or neocolonial) elite.[3]

The London of such texts is largely unseen: known indirectly and by reputation. A distant, mythologized object of dream and desire, a signifier of Britain's claims to political authority, cultural quality, and centrality *vis-à-vis* the colonial 'periphery,' it is constructed from impressionistic, repetitiously circulated images. The (post)colonial subjects who come to 'know' this faraway city as a set of ideas and names may or may not get to measure their imagined London against the actual one. Most will not, limited by poverty, circumstance, or a preference for the grounding of local roots over the mobility of international routes. Some will try unsuccessfully, like the Lalani family in Vassanji's *No New Land* (1991), who plan a metropolitan stopover during their flight from Tanzania to a new life in Toronto. They feel 'they should see London, at least this one time in their lives' because for them, as for many others,

> London was not a foreign place, not really, it was a city they all knew in their hearts. To hear Big Ben chime for real, see the Houses of Parliament and London Bridge, Buckingham Palace, perhaps the Queen and Prince Philip, and Westminster Abbey where David Livingstone lies buried. London – the pussycat and Dick Whittington, nursery rhymes clamoured in their brains. (33)

These famous images are destined to stay in their brains, however; colonial history may have fostered a sense of affectionate belonging, but the Lalanis' entry is barred at Heathrow airport.

Postcolonial literature's most significant and substantial 'London' (and the subject of this book) is the composite portrait that emerges from fictions about those who do make it past the immigration desk and then spend part of their lives – sometimes the rest of their lives – dwelling in the metropolis. The London to which these first-hand witnesses testify is by definition more up close and personal, more vivid and elaborate than the 'cold forbidding realm' imagined by Mudrooroo's aborigines. But it is not necessarily more appealing. Many who travel to London perceive it as a place of struggle against overwhelming obstacles: marginalization, segregation, and solitude; an alien climate and built environment; racism, poverty, and cultural conflict. In novels by Lamming, Joan Riley, Caryl Phillips, Kamala Markandaya, and Ama Ata Aidoo, among many others, the socially and economically oppressive spaces England constructed in faraway lands are, in essence, reproduced in the (post)imperial metropolis.

Perhaps this is to be expected of a city whose 'fortunes were built on an imperial glory now departed,' as Roy Porter has demonstrated (1). In his social history of London Porter writes, 'The key to the capital is the British Empire': the city grew and prospered as the empire did (2). However, when it swelled with the peoples of empire, many migrants wondered whether they had been handed the key to the capital, been locked up inside it, or found themselves stranded on the edges of a society that would never really open its doors to them. Aidoo sardonically writes in *Our Sister Killjoy* (1977) that

> the story is as old as empires. Oppressed multitudes from the provinces rush to the imperial seat because that is where they know all salvation comes from. But as other imperial subjects in other times and other places have discovered, for the slave, there is nothing at the centre but worse slavery. (87–8)

A hope of salvation dashed by a reality of slavery: not all postcolonial representations of London employ such stark binaries. However, as Rob Shields notes, 'place-myths' are always 'subject to being amended by the uneven experiences of reality' (*Places* 32), and the lofty ideas that adhere to 'London' in colonized societies are frequently undercut by fictional and autobiographical narratives that emphasize grim disillusionment. The metropolis regularly fails to deliver the freedom, personal renewal, and worldly access that, in time-honoured big-city fashion, it is seen to promise. In many postcolonial texts, it emerges as both a site and an object of resistance.

Resisting the city may take the form of Aidoo's blunt critique, but it is more often (and more interestingly) refracted through indirection and irony, metaphor and metonymy. The satirist's techniques of diminishment inform a variety of representations that fixate on London's dirt, mess, and disorder. It is reduced to the sum of its faceless crowds, alienating streets, drab buildings, closed doors, and cold rooms (barely warmed by their ubiquitous and rapacious shilling-fed heaters). Jonathan Raban notes the difficulties involved in comprehending or representing any city as a totality; because of its 'sheer imaginative cumbersomeness,' 'its intrinsic illegibility' and discontinuity, the city 'irritates us into metaphor' (32, 242, 92). He claims further that dirt is the single feature most mentioned in writings about English cities; as such it seems to function as a 'moral synecdoche' (32). In the case of postcolonial writers, for whom London as a whole is a synecdoche of Britain's imperial adventures, the dirt can carry further moral significance by representing an object of resistance greater than urban space and life: the big mess empire made of the world.

Because the city (like the former empire) is such a vast, sprawling entity, it is sometimes resisted through a different form of reduction – a kind of descriptive downsizing. Gaston Bachelard muses in *The Poetics of Space* that 'the cleverer I am at miniaturizing the world the better I possess it' (150), and there is a strong impetus to miniaturize London in postcolonial fiction. Roy's keepsake pens are an extreme (if not especially resistant) image of a metropolis reduced to manageable – indeed, to handheld – proportions. A Canadian émigré in Margaret Atwood's *Lady Oracle* (1976) delights in noting that Big Ben is 'not so big' and that London's streetscapes look just like Toronto's only smaller, 'as though two giant hands had compressed each object and then shoved them all closer together' (145, 142). A fanciful Indian girl in Leena Dhingra's *First Light* (1988) imagines that the city is a Monopoly board, which helps her feel secure:

> Safe! Eleven years old and walking down Piccadilly on my own I felt safe. It was my first time in London, but I felt quite safe. 'I'm in Piccadilly now so I can't go to jail because the lowest the double dice can turn is two!' And so I happily walked down my real-life Monopoly board which two years earlier in India had seemed such a dream. (1)

This miniaturizing image deftly combines the quotidian insecurities of big-city life (especially for newcomers and children) with an oblique historical jibe at London-based imperial administrators' habit of throwing India's nationalist leaders in jail. Dhingra's 'Piccadilly' exists in both contemporary metropolitan space and pre-independence Indian space.

The ideologies of empire demanded that colonized people be put and kept in their place – sometimes a jail, but more often a figurative place on the lower rungs of a hierarchical racial order that positioned white Europeans above them. In the more literal contexts of space and geography, however, imperialism was about anything *but* people staying in their place. As theorists such as James Clifford and Mary Louise Pratt have ably shown, imperial culture was a culture of travel.[4] It led to the commingling of differences – the crossing of geographical, cultural, and linguistic boundaries between peoples – that travel always entails. Intercontinental travel was mostly the privilege of Europeans, of course, but just as Europeans manifestly did not stay in their physical place during the age of empire, the postimperial era has seen great numbers of once-colonized people leave their homes for the metropolis. More powerful than metonymic reductions or self-empowering fancies of a downsized

London is the resistance exemplified by that simple fact of relocation. As ex-colonials come to dwell in London and walk its streets, they appropriate it and reterritorialize it. As writers render those experiences into autobiographical or fictional narratives, they reinscribe the metropolis against their backgrounds and identities as formerly colonized subjects. The London that once imposed its power and self-constructions *on* them can now be reinvented *by* them.

A theoretical model for such resistance can be adapted from Michel de Certeau's *The Practice of Everyday Life*. For de Certeau, the appropriative use of social space is analogous to the subversive transformations colonized peoples enacted upon the cultures imposed on them. In a similar spirit to Homi Bhabha's early essays (see 85–122), de Certeau writes that Indians colonized by the Spanish may have seemed submissive but they 'nevertheless often *made of* the rituals, representations, and laws imposed on them something quite different from what their conquerors had in mind; ... their use of the dominant social order deflected its power, which they lacked the means to challenge; they escaped it without leaving it' (xiii). De Certeau's topic is not postcolonial resistance *per se* but the various ways in which cultural and social dominants are consumed or used; these uses he calls 'tactics' through which 'the weak' can 'turn to their own ends forces alien to them' (xix). A paradigmatic example is the act of walking in the city. As 'the speech act is to language' (97), he writes, so the individual journey or itinerary through city streets is to the totalized city of the map. To walk through a city is individually to reinscribe it. It is to 'transform' the city as a function of time and narrative, and thus to de-emphasize its qualities of planned and static and organizing 'place' in favour of active and spontaneously reorganized 'space' (117). It is, in effect, to take over the city: to claim it in the image of one's own story, one's own unique tour through its spaces.

A key effect of this re-placing of the city is that proper names – of streets, landmarks, even the city itself – gradually lose their old significations. As they are used, de Certeau writes, 'these words ... slowly lose, like worn coins, the value engraved on them' (104). As 'they detach themselves from the places they were supposed to define,' 'these names make themselves available to the diverse meanings given them by passers-by' (104); they then 'become liberated spaces which can be occupied' and redefined (105) – like Dhingra's 'Piccadilly.' As a form of appropriative resistance from below, the actual or literary-representational 'use' of the metropolis by new occupants borrows certain hegemonic practices – what Derek Gregory calls the '*spatial strategies*' of '*dispossession through naming,*' or writing a new land in one's own image (168, 171) – by which imperial travellers once asserted their entitlement to faraway places. For instance, just as English missionaries in Achebe's *Things Fall Apart* (1958) change the meaning of the place Igbo villagers call the 'Evil Forest' – using it as a sacred site and sanctuary by building a church, thereby undermining the authority of the indigenous name and the worldview from which it derived – so postcolonial narratives of London, by inhabiting and 'using' metropolitan spaces in new ways, begin to detach them from traditional meanings and associations: Richler's use of Hampstead Heath for a Canadian baseball game, for example, or Sam Selvon's portrait of West Indian picnickers sprawling messily and noisily across the grounds of Hampton Court.[5]

De Certeau's notion that manifestations of power can be resisted through the ways in which they are used optimistically rebuts Michel Foucault's gloomy view of power's inescapable domination of the everyday realm. 'If it is true that the grid of "discipline" is everywhere becoming clearer and more extensive,' de Certeau writes, 'it is all the more urgent to discover how an entire society resists being reduced to it' (xiv). Nonetheless, his idea that individual spatial practices such as walking, dwelling, and appropriative narrativizing constitute acts of resistance can be criticized as limitingly local, sentimentally poetic, even childishly utopian in its view of individual empowerment; it is also based on a binary view that sets totalized power (represented by the city) against dispersed resistance (enacted by the user).[6] However, as James Donald notes, even if de Certeau's resistant tactics have more impact psychologically than sociopolitically, they are not therefore without value (see 17). The girl in *First Light* uses the emotional support provided by her idiosyncratic use of metropolitan spaces to make her London more navigable and habitable. If the alternative is fear and immobility, then the benefit is clear, even if it is equally clear that neither her doing so nor Dhingra's portrayal of her doing so in a novel will materially change the city, the world, or any structures of power.

One thing that can be said of all postcolonial narratives set wholly or partly in London is that their characters, like Dhingra's, appropriate and imaginatively reinvent the city as a function of their individual and communal experiences of arriving, dwelling, walking, working, interacting, observing, responding, and describing. Moreover, their responses and reinventions are conditioned by images of home: the colony or ex-colony from which they arrived and which they continue to remember and imaginatively inhabit. The metropolitan city becomes textually reinscribed through an Indian or Canadian sensibility; it becomes newly interlinked with Trinidadian or Nigerian spaces and lived realities to which, as imperial capital, it has long been related, but at an oceanic distance. In many postcolonial narratives of London, that distance is figuratively and conceptually reduced, even eliminated. London not only includes the people of empire but, as it becomes subsumed into their postcolonial consciousnesses, it becomes overlaid with and complexly linked to faraway landscapes and cultures. Beyond any enactments of resistance, this study will argue, it is the fascinatingly varied ways the transnational, world-shrinking relations between metropole and (former) colony are imagined in postcolonial London texts that constitute this body of work's most compelling feature.

Postcolonialism: From Resistant to Transnational

Resistance is a vexed concept in postcolonial literary and cultural theory, and some extravagant claims have been made in its name. Not unlike de Certeau's attribution of resistance to the uses 'the weak' make of the structures produced by hegemonic power, postcolonial thinking typically begins from a presumption of counter-hegemonic resistance inherent in colonized people's uses of the colonizer's tools. For instance, the colonized employ the liberal humanist and Christian doctrines the colonizer teaches them to attack the legitimacy of his rule; or they slyly subvert the premise of hierarchical difference on which his identity and authority are based by unnervingly mimicking him. They appropriate and transform his language and some of his cultural practices, combining them with their own. They reread and rewrite his canonical texts; they reshape and re-place his literary forms, adapting them to local content. The use of European languages and genres to tell non-European stories is commonly seen to be therapeutic and culturally affirming. From Raja Rao's desire 'to convey in a language that is not one's own the spirit that is one's own' (vii) to Chinua Achebe's wish to 'teach my readers that their past – with all its imperfections – was not one long night of savagery from which the first Europeans acting on God's behalf delivered them' (*Hopes* 30), countless testimonials stress the individual and societal benefits provided by the enlistment of literature's mimetic and referential properties to postcolonial ends. When writers use the novel to convey local (or national) stories from a local (or national) point of view, it is assumed, formerly subordinated cultures and people feel (and are perceived to be) legitimated – brought out from the shadow of Europe's longstanding dominance of cultural and representational spheres.

As with de Certeau's everyday tactics, however, it is questionable whether the benefits of cultural affirmation and individual empowerment such appropriative uses offer add up to a form of resistance worthy of the name. The influential first major survey of postcolonial theory, Ashcroft et al.'s *The Empire Writes Back*, suggests, as its title implies, that all acts of writing by colonized or formerly colonized people in English (a language they simultaneously appropriate and abrogate) are instances of postcolonial resistance against imperialism (see 38–9). There are two major limitations to this theoretical model. First, it risks homogenizing the diverse peoples and texts of the postcolonial Commonwealth into a common agenda – a shared differentness from an imperial centre that remains front and centre. It can therefore be seen to encourage a narrow and even Eurocentric hermeneutics; Arun Mukherjee remarks that when postcolonial theory 'focuses only on those texts that "subvert" or "resist" the colonizer, it overlooks a large number of texts that speak about ... other matters' (6). Second, this model positions resistance as something performed by texts rather than people. Leela Gandhi casts a sceptical eye on postcolonial theory's reduction of the colonial encounter to 'a narrative of competing or contesting textualities' in which 'all colonial texts are seen as repressive' and 'all postcolonial/migrant texts are invested with radically subversive energies' (154). The result: 'In a move which effectively replaces politics with textuality, such theory delivers a world where power is exclusively an operation of discourse, and resistance a literary contest of representation' (156).[7]

Postcolonial fictions of London, if read too zealously for resistance, are vulnerable to both criticisms, and especially to the first since they are by definition fixated on the centre. Texts that negotiate postcolonial subjectivity in the city most steeped in imperial history may fit the 'empire writes back' model quite neatly, but as with other text-based resistances to empire, no matter how convincingly they interrogate or oppose London's power, they may be reinforcing it. As W.H. New writes, 'one of the paradoxes of postcoloniality' is that an 'act of resistance is an act of recognition – even, potentially, of ratification' (*Land* 18). Simon Gikandi articulates a similar conundrum: 'Is it possible to promote a system of knowledge that simultaneously acknowledges the constitutive power of empire at home and abroad and yet devalorizes its totalizing claims?' (*Maps* 6). Beyond postcolonial debates, Jamie S. Scott and Paul Simpson-Housley make much the same point about cities, arguing that to represent the city discursively may be to recapitulate and therefore sustain the very urban conditions (and their ideological underpinnings) that the writer would critique (see 339–40). The prevalence of London-based novels in Commonwealth literatures undoubtedly provides evidence of the continuing hold of London, and the empire it spatially concentrates, on the postcolonial imagination. But just as postcolonial theory has moved increasingly away from binary models of resistance and identity in order to embrace more ambivalent, multilateral resistances and more transnational, syncretistic conceptions of postcolonial identity, it is important to recognize the complexities of the resistance to London and empire that postcolonial fictions proffer as well as the transnational models of identity the world city of London uniquely enables them to explore. It is important, in other words, to view London as a decentred centre: a metonym not just of the empire that once controlled the world but also, increasingly, of the world that the empire once controlled.

In a recent study of postcolonial resistance, Anuradha Dingwaney Needham embraces models that articulate 'the complexities and ambiguities' in 'performances of resistance' by addressing '"the mutual contamination" of the dominant and the subordinate, colonizer and colonized' (9). Needham's emphasis on mutuality draws on postcolonial theory's aforementioned move away from binary oppositional models. Jane M. Jacobs observes that as 'the nexus of power and identity within the imperial process has been elaborated, so many of the conceptual binaries that were seen as fundamental to its architecture of power have been problematised. Binary couplets like core/periphery, inside/outside, Self/Other, First World/Third World, North/South have given way to tropes such as hybridity, diaspora, creolisation, transculturation, border' (13). Similarly, Christian Moraru argues that 'the *postindependence* postcolonial' be recognized as passing through 'two distinct moments': 'The first is the "nationalistic postcolonial." It issues forth [from] the national liberation movements and takes up a radically antinomian, antiimperalist, more often than not classical Marxist rhetoric.' It is followed by 'the "transnational" or "postmodern" postcolonial' (174). This 'second moment,' he insists, does not dispense with local voices or national struggles of resistance, but encourages the parties involved in the historical encounter 'to rethink critically both their particular positions and the historical and geographical backdrop against which they are bound to cut their figures' (174). Gandhi likewise examines the impact of a 'postnationalism' that, by emphasizing 'indeterminacies in the colonial encounter,' seeks 'to bridge the old divide between Western and native through a considerably less embattled – if more politically amorphous – account of colonialism as a cooperative venture' (124).

Homi Bhabha has been influential in these developments, with his call 'to think beyond narratives of originary and initial subjectivities and to focus on those moments or processes that are produced in the articulations of cultural differences' – on the '"in-between" spaces' where individual and communal identities are negotiated (1). And beyond the colonizer/colonized relationship, parallel arguments have been made concerning the formation of racial, cultural, and national identities. Paul Gilroy's *The Black Atlantic* proposes that the in-between space of the Atlantic Ocean, together with the ships that perpetually criss-crossed it, be considered the central and defining location of historically embedded black identities whose definitive quality is fluid diasporic mobility. (Gilroy's notion will prove very applicable to London novels by West Indian writers, in which oceanic imagery repeatedly infiltrates urban narratives.) Stuart Hall also emphasizes transformation, viewing black cultural identities – or any cultural identities – as originating in history, but insisting that 'far from being eternally fixed in some essentialized past, they are subject to the continuous "play" of history, culture, and power' ('Cultural' 212–13). Because the past is 'always constructed through memory, fantasy, narrative, and myth,' Hall says, cultural identities are best understood as 'unstable points of identification or suture' and thus as processes of '*positioning*' rather than ways of being (213). For Hall, then, while it was once strategically useful to construct 'black' and 'white' as binary opposites in need of 'reversal,' it is important to follow that process through with a 'second phase' that dismantles the binary in favour of more complex models of black identity as 'a site of problematic conjuncture' (Baker et al., 'Representing' 7). Hall also supports a parallel departure from insular conceptions of ethnicity, which can feed 'the most viciously regressive kind of nationalism or national identity,' towards a notion of ethnicity that is 'not necessarily armor-plated against other identities' and 'not tied to fixed, permanent, unalterable oppositions' ('Minimal' 118, 119).

Hall, Gilroy, and others have been tireless in their efforts to theorize 'black' ethnicities as constitutive elements not just of the geopolitical entity called Britain but of the cultural and national identities that attend it: 'Britishness' and 'Englishness.' While they strove to open up these identities and make room for the migrant subjects who have, over the past several decades, made ever more visible and audible claims to Britishness and Englishness, a corollary body of work has sought to show how notions of Englishness had already been unsettled by imperial activity abroad. Gikandi (in *Maps of Englishness*) and Ian Baucom (in *Out of Place*) begin their books from a similar premise: that 'Englishness was itself a product of the colonial culture that it seemed to have created elsewhere' (Gikandi x); that the empire 'is less a place where England exerts control than the place where England loses command of its own narrative of identity' (Baucom 3). These studies convincingly contest the spatial imaginary by which empire construed England (and especially London) as the source from which power flowed – out from the core to the periphery, from the English colonizer to the non-English colonized.[8] If, as Gikandi and Baucom suggest, the national cultural identities of colonizing peoples are as unsettled and altered by imperialism as those of the colonized, then what Frantz Fanon called the 'irreconcilable antinomies' of subjugation and resistance must themselves be resisted so that colonialism can be understood as a complex process of *mutual* exchange, influence, and transformation (Gikandi 17).

On this basis, London may still be seen by postcolonial migrants as a symbolic site representing England's former imperial hegemony (and therefore an object of resistance), but it can also be a kind of postimperial contact zone. Mary Louise Pratt's 'contact zone' names the in-between space where different cultures that met because of imperial activity encountered and influenced each other (*Imperial* 6). Even though the balance of power was invariably lop-sided, influence and power were not one-sided, and Pratt's concept, like the various models of cultural inter-face sketched above, departs from static views of the colonizer's power opposed by resistance from the colonized. Like the interactive, relational identities theorized by Hall, Gilroy, Bhabha, and others, the meeting of cultures is seen by Pratt as a dynamic and fluid exchange that she calls 'transculturation' (6). As London is 'colonized in reverse' by migrants from former colonies, it becomes a particularly complex contact zone where transcultural encounters exist as present-day challenges but also carry overtones of the legacy and burden of past encounters in faraway contact zones. Some physical spaces in London – the Thames, Big Ben – are constant reminders that it is both a local and a global site and that the time with which it is encoded is both present and past time. But other spaces – a West Indian nightclub, a Pakistani shop – point to a future into which the old London (with all of its baggage) is being perpetually

ushered by the transformative uses of its 'New Commonwealth' inhabitants (with all of theirs).

If that London is becoming postcolonial, the emphasis must remain,
as in all uses of that much-debated theoretical term, on *becoming*: on a
process that is always underway and never complete. Anne McClintock
has influentially critiqued the term 'postcolonial' as 'prematurely
celebratory' in its implication of a break from colonialism, which she
rightly argues has continued in various forms throughout the period of
formal political decolonization (12). But 'postcolonial' as it is actually
used and theorized by its leading practitioners makes no claims to a
break; the 'post' is understood to be a marker of continuity as much as
transcendence. As Peter Hulme argues, 'If "postcolonial" is a useful
word, then it refers to a *process* of disengagement from the whole colonial
syndrome, which takes many forms and probably is inescapable for all
those whose worlds have been marked by that set of phenomena'
('Including' 120). Ato Quayson similarly suggests 'that postcolonialism
has to be perceived as a *process of postcolonializing*. To understand this
process, it is necessary to disentangle the term "postcolonial" from its
implicit dimension of chronological supersession ... [and] to highlight
instead a notion of the term as a process of coming-into-being and of
struggle *against* colonialism and its aftermath' (9). Quayson endorses
the view of Peter Childs and Patrick Williams that postcolonialism is
'an anticipatory discourse, recognizing that the condition which it
names does not yet exist, but working nevertheless to bring that about'
(qtd. in Quayson 9).

It is only by thinking of 'postcolonialism' in this way – as an ongoing
process of anticipating and striving for truly decolonized future realities,
identities, relations, freedoms, and spaces – that the narratives of London examined in this study (all but one of which were published between 1950 and 2000) can be called postcolonial. Whether or not they
examine London from a temporally pre- or postindependence perspective, none of them represents London from a fully 'postcolonial' perspective if being postcolonial requires them to be informed by a
consciousness unaffected by colonialism and its aftermath. Nor does any
of them represent the city itself as completely postcolonial (or
postimperial) in the sense of being uninfected by traces of the imperial
past over which it presided. Cumulatively (and often individually) these
novels occupy a spectrum of positions. At one end of the spectrum
London is *historically* continuous with and redolent of empire; here
'empire' means the rule Britain imposed on others abroad over several

centuries. At the other end of the spectrum London is *geographically* or *spatially* continuous with and redolent of empire; in this usage 'empire' means those peoples from once-colonized lands all over the world who have converged on, inhabited, and transformed the metropolis. The further the historical empire recedes into the past, the more the spatial empire infiltrates the city and the fictions that represent it. As London undergoes a political, demographic, and discursive 'processes of postcolonializing,' it becomes a transnational city: the less it is constituted by its imperial past, the more it is constituted by a 'world' to which it formerly reached out and which is now grabbing hold of it.[9]

These changes in the demographic and narrative constitution of London during the period of decolonization parallel the developments in postcolonial theory. London's affiliation with 'empire' has shifted from a historical to a spatial-geographical axis during the same decades in which postcolonialism has moved from historically oriented models of grievance and resistance to geographically oriented models of diaspora, migrancy, transnationalism, cosmopolitanism, and ocean-spanning relationality. As Gayatri Spivak writes, 'the migrant as paradigm is a dominant theme in theorizations of postcoloniality' (221), and indeed migrancy (with its attendant body of travelling theory) has increasingly provided *the* dominant theme and paradigm as postcolonialism has moved from what Moraru calls its first to its second 'moment.' Not all critics are happy with this development. Revathi Krishnaswamy, for one, laments the rise of a postcolonial aesthetic increasingly identified with a privileged class of deterritorialized, rootless migrants such as Salman Rushdie and the postmodern fictions of displacement that they write. She regrets the fading away of more rooted realist and nationalist narratives associated with an earlier postcolonial era (see 'Mythologies'). London, this study will show, lends itself to narratives from both the resistant-realist-nationalist and the migrant-transnational-postmodern 'moments.' The degree to which one moment or the other dominates depends on which 'empire' (historical or geographical) is seen to have the most presence and influence and, correspondingly, whether a given text imagines transnational London to be an elusive, unrealized dream or a present and visible reality.[10]

As both a concretely local place known in the here and now and a global/symbolic space continually blurring into various theres and thens, London as a subject of fictional discourse is an ideal site against which to test the possibilities of what Moraru seeks in a renewed postcolonialism:

such a model should allow the local to 'ride' the late twentieth-century transnational flow of values and identities to intervene in the postmodern conversation by opening up the possibility of the global without yielding to its traditionally totalizing, imperial pressure. What I am envisioning, in other words, is a 'discrete' globalism, fraught with 'difference,' discontinuity, and transiting subjectivities ... – a globalism where former centres burst with hybridity and (also formerly) marginal subjects. To summarize, I am envisioning an updated postcolonial paradigm, able to build on the 'classical' postcolonial critique as well as to evolve and address head-on the dynamic of transnational exchanges. (176–7)

Postcolonial subjects writing about London (and the metropolitan migrants who inhabit their narratives) must negotiate the materially local urban reality in which they live at the same time as they respond to the ways in which metropolitan space and everyday life signify the global histories and geographies that underlie and transcend the local. Whether that transcendent aspect is signified by an encounter with white racists or by a London building reminiscent of imperial architecture in India, London life can never be simply material and local in scale. By the same token, the local can never evaporate under the pressure of the global perspectives that London so uniquely accommodates. The city as physical fact must be locally lived in; the city as a cluster of global-scale associations must be mentally processed, imaginatively inhabited, metaphorically and metonymically translated into text and narrative.

This rich combination of spatial scales (local and global), temporal contexts (past, present, future), and postcolonial positionings (from resistant to transnational) also suggests that narratives of London by postcolonial/migrant novelists can offer more than the rarefied textuality whose subversive influence Gandhi questions. Edward Said writes in *Orientalism* of the ways knowledge of largely unknown peoples and places is produced and circulated as 'imaginative geography' (55). While the texts he examines in that book are largely non-literary, his *Culture and Imperialism* shows how geographical imaginations (and the knowledges they produce) are also nurtured by novels: 'Just as none of us is outside or beyond geography, none of us is completely free from the struggle over geography. That struggle is complex and interesting because it is not only about soldiers and cannons but also about ideas, about forms, about images and imaginings' (*Culture* 7). Moreover, insofar as the novel is an 'inherently geographical' literary form that imagines lives lived in various spaces and places, 'any one novel may present a field of different, sometimes competing, forms of geographical knowledge' (Daniels and Rycroft 460).

Novels and other sorts of representational imaginative texts may be particularly helpful in generating images and knowledges of places that are unknown or inaccessible, including the cities in which one lives. James Donald notes that 'we never experience the space of the city unmediated' because it is 'always already symbolised and metaphorised' by prior cultural representations (17). Urban dwellers need those representations to make sense of the city's innate illegibility and discontinuity. The unbounded, heterogeneous chaos of a city – especially one as vast and diverse as London – can be known only through 'metonymic images and fleeting events' (Donald 121). As a totality, the city will always be beyond reach and comprehension. For instance, Donald suggests, a writer like Charles Dickens helped teach nineteenth-century readers how to read – i.e., understand, interpret, respond to – the urban world of London in a century during which it burgeoned with growth and change (see 1–3). The city may have been a baffling, disorienting physical environment, but it was also a set of representations constituted through the spatial and temporal orderings of narrative; the experience of the one could be filtered through the orientation provided by the other. Narrative representation may therefore be as crucial to understanding a directly accessed world like one's own city as it is to comprehending a distant place of which one has no direct, grounded experience, and as influential on the images and expectations one brings to it. Texts and images in their way constitute the cities we live in as much as planners and builders and politicians and users do. Furthermore, since novels are by one definition 'possible worlds,' they can imagine narratives not only of the city as it was and is but as it could be. As Walter Benjamin once wrote, 'reading the urban text is not a matter of intellectually scrutinizing the landscape; rather it is a matter of exploring the fantasy, wish-processes and dreams locked up in our perception of cities' (qtd. in Tajbakhsh 24). As postcolonial writers imaginatively render transnational Londons (however partially or imperfectly realized), their texts, like those of Dickens in his time, help constitute and mediate a London that is rapidly changing. They become frames through which the disorderly, ungraspable material city can be mentally and imaginatively perceived.

Imagined Cities

As an object and field of literary representation, 'the city' has historically received mixed press. In what Burton Pike calls 'the bifocal vision of

Western culture,' the city has come to represent both 'corruption' and 'perfection' (8). In Christian tradition, the city was alternately heaven (*civitas Dei*) and hell (*civitas Diaboli*); hopes for the future may have been crystallized in the idealized New Jerusalem, but stories from the past figured the city as prideful (Babel), corrupt (Babylon), or wicked (Sodom and Gomorrah). Raymond Williams begins *The Country and the City* by observing that 'on the city has gathered the idea of an achieved centre: of learning, communication, light. Powerful hostile associations have also developed: on the city as a place of noise, worldliness and ambition' (1). He concludes, 'In a sense, it seems, everything about the city – from the magnificent to the apocalyptic – can be believed at once' (278).

Many of the contradictory attitudes to cities and city life that hold sway today were articulated by eighteenth-century intellectuals and writers. In this period of steady urbanization, Roy Porter writes, 'The thinkers of the Enlightenment saw that the future lay with cities, and generally approved: despite ancient anti-urban prejudices, the city now seemed to promise progress, peace, profit, pleasure, and the erosion of ignorance; city man was civilized man' (160). At the same time, however, the city was maligned (by Wordsworth and Blake, among others) as an anti-human site of alienation, crime, disease, squalor, vice, oppression, and social disorder. After the rapid growth, industrialization, and modernization of cities in the nineteenth century, the city in the late nineteenth and early twentieth centuries was increasingly seen as the defining locus of modern life and consciousness. By this time, says Williams, the 'social character of the city – its transitoriness, its unexpectedness, its essential and exciting isolation and procession of men and events – was seen as the reality of all human life' (234). Malcolm Bradbury notes that for modernists the city's increasing concentration of social functions, communications, and experiences made it 'both the centre of the prevalent social order and the generative frontier of its growth and change.' It was, in other words, both past and future, both 'cultural museum and novel environment' (97).

If humanity's obsessive efforts to represent the urban and capture its ambivalent responses of 'attraction and repulsion' have turned the city into 'metaphor rather than place' (Bradbury 97), it is a metaphor 'whose referent seems to be a deep-seated anxiety about man's relation to his created world' (Pike 4). But for postcolonial migrants, while London offers a compelling instance of the city as cultural museum and novel environment, it cannot except indirectly be said to represent their 'created world.' London, for better or worse, represents the direct achievement and creation of the English who, in turn, used it as a power base from which to create many aspects of the wider world. Indirectly, however, because London was 'the beneficiary-in-chief from the British Empire' (Porter 2), growing as a direct function of imperial expansion and prosperity, it *is* a place that they and their colonized ancestors – through what they lost and produced under imperial regimes – helped create.

Indeed, as Williams remarks, imperialism reproduced on the global scale the relations between city and country that had long influenced national economies, geographies, and cultural and literary histories (see 279).[11] Intricate vectors of labour and capital, cultural dominance and political control had always been generated between British cities (especially London) and outlying rural areas; these became, in the imperial era, expanded and reconfigured internationally as a set of dynamic interactions between Britain as a whole and its colonies. The powerful city (or metropolis) was the centre of accumulation and prestige, while the peripheral, underdeveloped 'country' (or colony) was exploited by and for the benefit of the city.[12] The ambivalent, contradictory views of the city that are the legacy of this long tradition of thinking about nation-space are also the inheritance of many who come from the (post)colonial 'country' to inhabit the metropolitan city. If they have received a colonial education, they will have been exposed to that imaginative geography and will often draw on its representational traditions – its images and tropes – as they respond to their metropolitan experiences. Many therefore travel to a London they have idealized at a distance as a place of light, knowledge, empowerment, opportunity, pleasure, and access to 'the world' (or to 'the real world' they have come to believe does not exist at home).[13] As they respond to the city up close, their experiences may partly fulfil these preconceptions, but many will be prompted to appropriate equally time-honoured literary images that construct the city as bewildering labyrinth, alienating crowd, dangerous street, isolating room, or oppressive routine. These multiple and contradictory associations make frequent appearances in the postcolonial novels examined in this study.

In addition to images associated with 'the city' in general are those that have come to adhere particularly to London. Its huge and largely unplanned growth through the eighteenth and nineteenth centuries gave rise to some colourful metaphors; the metropolis was deemed 'a "polypus", a stain, a fungus, a mighty carbuncle, a marching giant, a facial blemish (Cobbett's "great wen")' (Inwood 5). Daniel Defoe called it 'the monstrous city,' a view echoed by a character in Tobias Smollett's

Humphry Clinker, who complains that 'the Capital is become an over-grown monster; which, like a dropsical head, will in time leave the body and extremities without nourishment and support' (118). Although this somatic image seems tailor-made for extension to the imperial capital draining its colonial extremities, the only postcolonial London fiction to feature a monster is the Canadian expatriate Kate Pullinger's little-known first novel, *When the Monster Dies* (1989); here the dying monster is the former empire as witnessed in and exemplified by a declining, postimperial London.[14]

The young Friedrich Engels offered a famous outsider's response to nineteenth-century London, writing in 1845 of the effect of London's 'colossal centralization' around the trading activity of its river:

> I know nothing more imposing than the view which the Thames offers during the ascent from the sea to London Bridge. The masses of buildings, the wharves on both sides, ... the countless ships along both shores, crowd-ing ever closer and closer together, until, at last, only a narrow passage remains in the middle of the river, a passage through which hundreds of steamers shoot by one another; all this is so vast, so impressive, that a man cannot collect himself, but is lost at the marvel of England's greatness before he sets foot upon English soil. (47)

'But,' Engels continues, to achieve such greatness 'Londoners have been forced to sacrifice the best qualities of their human nature' (47). The urban conditions that increased industrialization and trade have pro-duced cause 'indifference' and 'the unfeeling isolation of each in his private interest'; the result is a 'social war' of mutual objectification and exploitation and a growing divide between a few wealthy capitalists and 'the weak many, the poor' (48). The city that is so inclusive, so all-embracing – for J.M.W. Turner, 'the great world itself was ... contained within the city and its river' (Ackroyd 544) – is paradoxically also an unaccommodating city in which vast numbers are marginalized, desti-tute, and alone.

Increasing popular fascination and concern with London's poorest people led to a vogue among Victorians for books anatomizing them, some of which extended the idea of London as a world unto itself by making analogies between subjected but threatening classes at home and subjected but threatening races abroad. In *In Darkest England and the Way Out* (1890), William Booth writes, 'As there is a darkest Africa is there not also a darkest England? ... May we not find a parallel at our own doors, and discover within a stone's throw of our cathedrals and palaces similar horrors to those which Stanley has found existing in the great Equatorial forest?' (qtd. in Danahey 179). Booth's politics differ from those of Engels: the 'horrors' he locates in Africa are not those created by the imperialist system (as Engels's local horrors are by the capitalist one); they are simply 'found' by imperial agents. Booth's contemporary, Joseph Conrad, another keen observer of colonial 'horror,' does make the connection, however ambiguously. *Heart of Darkness* (1902) suggests strong continuities between the Thames and the Congo – between the 'brooding gloom' of twilit London, which historically 'has been one of the dark places of the earth,' and the 'immense darkness' of Africa beyond (7, 111).

The respondents to London in many postcolonial fictions offer their own versions of the links between the metropolis and distant colonized space; many also replicate Engels's combination of awe at London's size and power with dismay at its dehumanizing and isolating exclusions. Sam Selvon's classic West Indian novel of the 1950s, *The Lonely Londoners*, is exemplary in its ambivalence. For one of Selvon's metropolitan green-horns, London as a place of spectacle, pleasure, and new opportunity is stimulating in its absorptive concentration: where Engels noted that 'a man may wander for hours [in London] without reaching the beginning of the end' (47), Selvon's strolling Galahad locates 'the beginning and the ending of the world' in Piccadilly Circus (74). However, what capitalism has wrought on the everyday lives of Engels's ordinary mid-nineteenth-century Londoners, the legacy of imperialism and its divisive ideologies has brought to bear on the West Indians who populate Selvon's narrative: isolation and economic hardship. Nonetheless, even as Selvon's characters complain that London 'divide up in little worlds, and you stay in the world you belong to and you don't know anything about what happening in the other ones' (58), they do form communal bonds among themselves and, apparently, with 'the [white] Working Class' (59). Selvon's narrative, more than any other from its era, manages to convincingly balance an embrace and a critique of the metropolis. In its portrayal of spatial practices such as dwelling, walking, working, and riding public transport, it shows the enabling and disabling aspects of West Indian metropolitan life.

This is as it should be, because for all the bad press cities receive as alienating, oppressive places full of uncaring strangers, they are also inevitably places of social mixture and encounter. This makes them sites of possibility: of spontaneity and surprise, of renewing the self or transforming one's milieu through interactions with others. Henri Lefebvre writes, 'The form of the urban, its supreme reason,' is 'simultaneity and encounter': 'As a place of encounters, focus of communication and information, the *urban* becomes what it always was: place of desire, permanent disequilibrium, seat of the dissolution of normalities and constraints, the moment of play and the unpredictable' (*Writings* 129). Jane M. Jacobs articulates a similar point through a postcolonial lens: 'Precisely because cities are sites of "meetings", they are also places which are saturated with possibilities for the destabilisation of imperial arrangements' (4). Cities, that is, may concentrate and exemplify forces to be resisted – capitalism, imperialism, globalization, atomization, mechanization, social inequity – but by gathering people and prompting spontaneous interaction, they also provide the space to resist those forces. As such, the city can be an ideal site for a resistant or oppositional 'first moment' postcolonialism. But, as Jacobs goes on to say, 'This [destabilization] may manifest through stark anticolonial activities, but also through the negotiations of identity and place which arise through diasporic settlements and hybrid cultural forms' (4). Here she gestures to both the first and second postcolonial 'moments'; the second is a function of the cultural and national differences those 'meetings' and 'encounters' increasingly involve in the big cities of the contemporary world. London, which for two millennia has been a crossroads where diverse people have met, and which today includes more worlds of difference than ever, exemplifies this social hybridization and creolization.

Richard Sennett, in books such as *The Uses of Disorder* and *The Conscience of the Eye*, celebrates this aspect of cities: the creative impurity and interpenetration of differences they prompt. He argues against impulses towards 'purity,' 'order,' segregation, or group or class solidarity that lead those designing, planning, and using urban space to erect spatial and psychological boundaries. We need, he says, 'the freedom to accept and to live in disorder' (*Uses* xviii); we should not resist the city's power to break down 'the self-contained qualities of the various ethnic groups' (56). Iain Chambers also valorizes the disorder generated by the 'cultural complexity' of 'the modern metropolis – and that includes Lagos as well as London': 'It is a reality that is multiformed, heterogeneous, diasporic. The city suggests a creative disorder, an instructive confusion, an interpolating space in which the imagination carries you in every direction, even towards the previously unthought' (189). It is this quality of cities that leads an exemplary 'second moment' postcolonial writer and thinker like Salman Rushdie to embrace big cities as settings and symbols. Bombay in *Midnight's Children* and *The Moor's Last Sigh*, London in *The Satanic Verses*: through Rushdie's wide-ranging imagination, these vast metropolises come to represent the multiplicity and impurity – 'Bombayness,' as Saleem Sinai calls it (*Midnight's* 301) – that form the cornerstone of his sociopolitical and aesthetic principles. Not all postcolonial writers share Rushdie's ebullient worship of 'hybridity' and multiplicitous 'hotchpotch' (*Imaginary* 394). But as this study hopes to demonstrate, postcolonial novels of London all show an awareness of the city's potential (however frustratingly unrealized it may be) for productive disorder and intermixture, and for stimulating the imagination to roam in both familiar and 'previously unthought' directions.

Global/Local Relations

The contemporary Western metropolis has become a cultural crucible, the definitive site in which groups of people once divided by geography, ethnicity, race, or nationality are kaleidoscopically rearranged and concatenated. By the last decades of what Rushdie has called a 'century of displaced persons' – of migrants 'who root themselves in ideas rather than places' and are therefore 'free of the shackles of nationalism' (*Imaginary* 124) – it had become necessary to radically rethink the relation between place and identity. Rushdie is overzealous in severing migrants from nationalism and rootedness; both members of diasporas and assimilated immigrants can be fiercely attached to nations, whether of origin or of arrival or both. Diasporas may be, as Khachig Tölölian argues, 'the exemplary communities of the transnational moment' (qtd. in Clifford, 'Diasporas' 303), but theorists of diaspora agree that the multiple affiliations of diasporic peoples usually involve a strong communal attachment to a remembered or longed-for homeland and solidarity with others dispersed from it.[15] As diasporic peoples negotiate their identities and affiliations through what Gilroy calls 'the tension between roots and routes' (*Black* 133), old ideas of home, nation, and homeland must be perpetually revisited. As Robin Cohen notes, diasporas 'involve dwelling in a nation-state in a physical sense, but travelling in an astral or spiritual sense that falls outside the nation-state's space/time zone' (135–6).

This phenomenon presents a substantial challenge to nation-states, whose identities are often premised on congruence between the land their boundaries enclose and a relatively homogenous racial, cultural, ethnic, and/or linguistic group historically identified with it. The multiplication of loyalties, affiliations, roots, and routes entails what Vijay Mishra calls 'a shift away from homogeneous nation-states based on the ideology of assimilation to a much more fluid and contradictory definition of nations as a multiplicity of diasporic identities' (7). Indeed, Cohen notes that in the most mobile and diverse contemporary societies,

> There is no longer any stability in the points of origin, no finality in the points of destination and no necessary coincidence between social and national identities. ... What nineteenth-century nationalists wanted was a 'space' for each 'race,' a territorializing of each social identity. What they have got instead is a chain of cosmopolitan cities and an increasing proliferation of subnational and transnational identities that cannot easily be contained in the nation-state system. (175)

As Cohen suggests, the city, the main locus of diasporic gatherings, is the privileged microcosm of these new transnational and transcultural nations. But as such, cities, like nations, can find their identities destabilized as they recognize themselves at once geographically within and culturally in excess of their nation's traditional domain. For some cities this recognition is more traumatic than it is for London, which has always exceeded an Englishness that has traditionally been located in the countryside more than the capital. London has always contained and been linked to worlds of difference: through its immigrants, its economy, its imperial history, and through the global scale of its patterns of cultural absorption and projection. The English capital has long been a place of intimate and multifarious interconnections with distant elsewheres and the others who live in (or come from) them. 'Worldliness' is so intrinsic to London's historical identity that postcolonial narratives, as this study will show, frequently refer to it as a world (or 'the world') and regularly incorporate distance-shrinking images of condensed elsewheres or microcosmic worlds within it.

However, in a world that since the 1980s has become increasingly interlinked through a process of 'globalization,' London's 'world city' (or 'global city') identity takes on some new and more specific theoretical meanings. As an international economy involving nationally based firms and individuals and 'closely regulated by sovereign nation-states' is transformed into a global economy dominated by corporate oligopolies that 'span national boundaries but are only loosely regulated by nation-states' (Knox 3), London has emerged by academic consensus as one of three leading world cities. According to this mainly economic model

London, together with New York and Tokyo, is one of the dominant 'basing points and control centres for the interdependent skein of financial and cultural flows which, together, support and design the globalization of industry' (6). As a 'nexus of decision-making and interaction' (7), London is one place where 'a quite disproportionate part of the world's most important business is conducted' (P. Hall, *World* 1) because, under globalization, 'the world economy may have become more decentralized, but it is not necessarily becoming *decentred*' (A. Amin and N. Thrift, qtd. in Knox 8). This latter point seems a useful corrective to some views of globalization as an equalizing or homogenizing phenomenon. It reminds us that as global forces gather in and redefine the local, they do so selectively. Some locales are more 'global' than others. If it can be said, 'by way of metaphor, that historically, the world has increasingly become one large, interdependent city,' it is also important to note that the 'flows between its various component parts are immensely uneven' (King, *Urbanism* 2). A city like London, by a corollary metaphor, may be increasingly 'becoming' that large, interdependent 'world,' but capitals like Rangoon, Tirana, Luanda, or Ulan Bator remain largely isolated from the globalizing world that London concentrates. For many postcolonial migrants, moving to London is a way of accessing a 'world' from which they otherwise feel cut off.

London's position in the trinity of foremost world cities may be based on quantifiable economic factors such as its leading role in the '*production of financial and producer services*' (Friedmann 29), but Anthony King reminds us of 'the fact that "world city" is essentially a *cultural construct*' ('Re-presenting' 216). In an article examining the world city 'as a cultural space' (215), he pursues questions that are among the central ones this study asks of postcolonial authors' culturally constructed Londons. King asks, 'What is the significance of such a world city as a real or potential site for the construction of new cultural and political identities, or for processes of cultural transformation in general? And what relevance might it have, either for the persistence or modification of existing local, regiona', or national identities and cultures, or alternatively, for the construction of new transnational ones?' (215). Beyond economic data, world cities are demographic phenomena, and King, following Ulf Hannerz, identifies 'four categories of people who play major roles in the making of contemporary Western world cities: the transnational management class, Third World populations, expressive specialists (or cultural practitioners), and tourists' (216). Of these four groups, members of the latter three (but rarely the first) populate most

postcolonial fictions of London; it is they who 'make' the city as a
discursive and lived space. The 'expressive specialists' – the writers – who
represent London as it is experienced, perceived, and reterritorialized
by Commonwealth migrants construct it as a 'world city' based not on its
present-day economic role but on its historical and ongoing relations –
political, social, economic, architectural, literary, cultural – to the parts
of the world they know. London began unevenly 'globalizing' its own
urban spaces and the spaces of the world centuries ago, and the local
'worlds' it influenced are those that have recently come to reconstruct it
and represent it through their own cultural and national lenses.

The world city's 'local' is therefore interfused with a 'global' that is
actually a network of loosely connected, far-flung other locales, nations,
and regions. London exceeds its local spaces and boundaries through its
global relations in more (and more obvious) ways than most cities.
However, as the cultural geographer Doreen Massey has influentially
argued, it is important to see the identities of *all* places and locales as
constituted not by what they contain within putative boundaries but by
the networks of relations that extend in complex, interactive ways beyond them:

> In this interpretation, what gives a place its specificity is not some long
> internalized history but the fact that it is constructed out of a particular
> constellation of relations, articulated together at particular locus. ... The
> uniqueness of a place, or a locality, in other words is constructed out of
> particular interactions and mutual articulations of social relations, social
> processes, experiences and understandings, in a situation of co-presence,
> but where a large proportion of those relations, experiences and under-
> standings are actually constructed on a far larger scale than what we
> happen to define for that moment as the place itself, whether that be a
> street, a region or even a continent. Instead, then, of thinking of places as
> areas with boundaries around, they can be imagined as articulated mo-
> ments in networks of social relations and understandings. And this in turn
> allows a sense of place which is extra-verted, which includes a consciousness
> of its links with the wider world, which integrates in a positive way the global
> and the local. ('Power-Geometry' 66)

Massey's theory reflects what Georges Benko calls the geographer's 'meth-
odological double vision: he or she must keep one eye on the immediate
place of observation, and the other on the frontiers of its external
influence' (26). Henri Lefebvre similarly asserts that studying any space

in detail – a house, a city – breaks down its 'image of immobility' and fixed solidity and reveals it to be 'a nexus of in and out conduits' (*Production* 93). Enclosing boundaries create 'an appearance of separation between spaces where in fact what exists is an ambiguous continuity,' he maintains: '*Social spaces interpenetrate one another and/or superimpose themselves upon one another*' (87, 86). But for Massey, the conjoining of internal and external is not just a professional challenge for scholars. It is experienced in any act of dwelling in a place and coming to know its complexities.

The identities of places are therefore as relational as Hall and Gilroy insist the identities (racial, ethnic, cultural) of groups and individuals are. Postcolonial novels reflect the relational aspects of place-identity by representing London not as a discrete, stand-alone place but as a site intimately linked to and filtered through images of (former) colonial landscapes. In many cases, these external frames of reference represent home and childhood, and thus prove essential to making the metropolis inhabitable, comprehensible, and sometimes just plain bearable for the postcolonial migrant. In other cases, images of elsewhere make metropolitan life more confusing and disorienting as boundaries of difference and resemblance are constantly thrown into question. In all cases, individual identity emerges out of the entwined relations between old and new selves, between those selves and various others, and between present and distant (or past) places. Other places can overlie or infuse London in any number of ways. In Anita Desai's *Bye-Bye Blackbird* or Amitav Ghosh's *The Shadow Lines*, London's built spaces materialize ideas of London and of empire learned in India. In Jean Rhys's *Voyage in the Dark*, Joan Riley's *Waiting in the Twilight*, and David Dabydeen's *The Intended*, memory prompts imaginary trips back to a Caribbean childhood, thereby making the West Indian migrant feel more psychologically complete in a metropolis that fragments identity. In several Canadian novels, including Robertson Davies's *A Mixture of Frailties* and Catherine Bush's *The Rules of Engagement*, metropolitan experience prompts actual and imaginative trips back home, through which a protagonist's individual identity and Canada's national identity are beneficially reexamined.

For the protagonists of postcolonial novels, therefore, metropolitan living is never simply a matter of dealing with present-day local conditions. It always involves manoeuvring among the multiple spatial scales the city's history, social reality, cultural associations, and built space evoke. Life in London involves a dynamic inhabitation and negotiation of a spatial spectrum that extends from the most local inhabited space, the body, outwards through the home, the neighbourhood, the community, the city, the nation, and beyond to the most global inhabited space, the world. The migrant's cultural and national bifocality requires him or her to inhabit these various spatial realms flexibly and often simultaneously through a combination of material and imaginative (or virtual) dwelling. Urban migrants live neither globally nor locally but transnationally in Michael Peter Smith's sense of the word. For Smith, 'transnational urbanism' is a cultural and geographical rubric under which binary oppositions such as global and local, routes and roots, domination and resistance can be mediated. Building on Massey's notion of relational place-identity, he argues against scholarly and popular constructions of a dichotomy between a global realm of corporate flows – which transcend local and national boundaries while dominating their spaces – and the local or national realm as a discrete space of authenticity and resistance to globalizing forces. City-dwellers, Smith insists, develop '*interstitial*' identities 'between such dominant discursive venues as the "nation-state," the "local community," the "ethnoracial formation," and the "new world order"' (142). In the 'transnational' cities in which they live, everyday local experience is informed by phenomena and networks that 'defy easy boundary-setting' (117). The local, in other words, because it is not a stable and contained realm, is always already transnational, and to live locally (as everyone does) is also to live at the larger spatial scales that inform the local and are informed by it. The transnational social relations that constitute any locality are '"anchored in" while also transcending one or more nation-states'; Smith therefore 'insists on the continuing significance of borders, state policies, and national identities even as these are often transgressed by transnational communication circuits and social practices' (3).

Smith advocates moving away from the 'global cities' or 'world cities' concept, implicated as it is in a process of economic globalization that is seen to weaken nation-states in favour of nationless capital:

> Instead of pursuing the quest for a hierarchy of nested [global/world] cities arranged neatly in terms of their internal functions to do the bidding of international capital, it is more fruitful to assume a less easily ordered urban world of localized articulations, where sociocultural as well as political-economic relations criss-cross and obliterate sharp distinctions between inside and outside, local and global. (67)

For Smith, then, the identities and agencies of metropolitan dwellers are transnational, as are the cities where they live and act. Stuart Hall implies a similar understanding of 'transnational' when he comments, in a forum called 'Reinventing Britain,' on

> all those movements, contradictory, or not, which are above and below the level of the national, which are intrinsically transnational. When using the term transnational, I am very much against the notion that what is being constituted is a set of open co-eval spaces around the world, a kind of cultural homogenisation which will make it easier for us to move smoothly and fluently between one cultural language and another. ... I think the site on which the redefinition of England or Britain is going to occur, is now irrevocably transnational, irrevocably open at the ends, porous and unable to close its borders and its mind. (43–4)

By unhooking the term 'transnational' from the realm of deterritorialized, globalized corporate power in which it, like 'multinational,' is sometimes positioned,[16] Smith's 'transnational urbanism' and Hall's transnational Britishness combine with Massey's theory of relational places and with diaspora theory to provide a valuable framework for interpreting postcolonial narratives of London. Postcolonial migrants cannot see London as simply local or national; to do so would be to deny its historical and present-day overseas linkages, to suppress the ways its buildings and people constantly transport one elsewhere. Nor can they see London as a 'world city' made placeless – severed from its traditional identity – by what Manuel Castells calls the '*space of flows*' that dominates the postindustrial and postmodern globalized economy (169); to see the city that way would be to deny the urban landscape's power to evoke its own history and its links both to British national and (post)colonial identities.

London as a setting for postcolonial fiction is 'transnational' because of the unique ways it confounds global-local binaries and accommodates new forms and narratives of relational identity, and also because of its inclusion of people from many nations and diasporas. Those residents are physically detached but psychologically and culturally attached to non-English places and national identities, through which their experiences and portrayals of London are constantly processed. Their city is an imagined transnational community that writers – whether they imagine it as a distant prospect or a current reality – can encourage others to 'read' or see as such. Benedict Anderson's famous discussion of the nation as an 'imagined community' proposes that one important way

nations come to be is through their inhabitants' experiences of reading
the same books and newspapers; this shared experience enables people
who will never meet each other to develop an 'imagined linkage' to a
collectivity whose togetherness they mutually construct and constantly
redefine (33). Postcolonial narratives of London in all their variety and
plenitude collectively imagine an alternative to the nation on behalf of
people negotiating complex and often confusing conditions of multiple
national belonging and non-belonging in that interstitial, oceanic limbo
where both/and continually shades into neither/nor. They imagine a
transnational city that can be its own space of community outside of
those problematic national constructs. Hanif Kureishi, London-born
son of a Pakistani father and an English mother, writes, 'I'm no Britisher,
but a Londoner' ('Some' 133). Yasmin Alibhai-Brown, after a detailed
polemic on Britain's continued exclusion of minority citizens from narratives of national identity, writes in frustration at the end of *Imagining
the New Britain,*

> It is astonishing to hear pundits and politicians speaking of the 'four
> nations' of Britain. *Windrush* and its aftermath is not even an afterthought
> in this discourse. So when Scotland has got kilted up and the English have
> established their homelands far away from the Welsh and Irish, where do
> we, the black Britons go? Perhaps we can put in a bid for London, please?
> (271)

Transnational London becomes a potential replacement for attenuated,
compromised, conflicted, undesirable, or unreachable spaces of national belonging. It becomes a locus for the construction of emergent
sensibilities that are both transnational (in the spatial sense of inhabiting
multiple geographic scales) and postcolonial (in the temporal sense of
wrestling with the influence imperial history exerts on present-day life).

As such, London is experienced as a place and a space. The differences between these two terms have been the subject of long and complex academic debate, but the most useful distinction for the purposes of
this study is the simplest: that 'places provide an anchor of shared
experiences between people and continuity over time. Spaces become
places as they become "time-thickened"' (Crang 103). As Yi-Fu Tuan
explains this relationship, '"Space" is more abstract than "place." What
begins as undifferentiated space becomes place as we get to know it
better and endow it with value' and as it thereby 'acquires definition and
meaning' (6, 136). Paradoxically, a Commonwealth migrant arriving in

London for the first time can be expected to encounter the city as both space and place. It will be a space insofar as it is unfamiliar and not yet marked by personal experience of its streets and buildings. Over time, the city (or at least parts of it) will gradually come into focus as a time-laden, meaningful 'place' of deep acquaintance. In another sense, the new arrival comes to a city that is too much a place: layered with received values, meanings, and images that have accumulated on 'London' over centuries of imperial, cultural, and literary history. To satisfactorily dwell in this burdensomely familiar place, the migrant will need to come to terms with its history-soaked associations. She or he will have to dismantle, appropriate, exploit, or imaginatively re-present those associations in order to get past the colonial power relations they signify and open up the city as an enabling space. As Tuan writes, space typically symbolizes freedom and opportunity:

> Space lies open; it suggests the future and invites action. ... Open space has no trodden paths and signposts. It has no fixed pattern of established human meaning; it is like a blank sheet on which meaning may be imposed. Enclosed and humanized space is place. Compared to space, place is a calm center of established values. Human beings require both space and place. Human lives are a dialectical movement between shelter and venture, attachment and freedom. (54)

As for the humans who negotiate this dialectic in postcolonial fictions of London, the degree to which they either thrive or flounder in their efforts to appropriate and reinvent the city depends on their success at transforming abstract space to meaningful place and reinscribing oppressive place as liberating space. The more they do so, the more they are able to inhabit an actual rather than just imaginary – an existing rather than merely hoped-for – transnational and postcolonial London. The literary texts that narrate their metropolitan lives and struggles contribute to the discursive making and imagining of that desired space and place.

London Then ...

In a recent book entitled *The Promise of the City*, Kian Tajbakhsh assesses the new complexities of urban life at the turn of the millennium: 'For many transnational, diasporic migrant communities, in contrast to those of the nineteenth century, individual and community identities are structured across multiple, sometimes contradictory spaces in complex patterns of imaginary representations and memory that suggest the need for a reconceptualization of identity and consciousness' (8). The sheer scale of global migration to Western cities and the rapidity of demographic change are undoubtedly greater than ever before. The causes of such change include advances in technology (especially world-shrinking transportation and communications systems), decolonization and its troubled aftermath, and the increasing integration of the world economy under processes of corporate globalization. The effects of these large movements of people, typically from 'the East' to 'the West' or 'South' to 'North,' include the creation of 'new patterns of cultural, ethnic, linguistic, and religious heterogeneity that are now challenging the integrative powers of the nation-state to assimilate, within fixed national boundaries, the increasing presence of diasporic, transnational identities structured around noncontiguous spaces' (Tajbakhsh 5).

London, which has always been known for its heterogeneity, is arguably better prepared than most cities to meet such challenges. The transnationalism that characterizes the city and its current arrangements of people has important precedents: throughout history, London has often appeared to be a new and uniquely inclusive kind of social space. Peter Ackroyd begins his 'biography' of London, for instance, by remarking that 'London is so large and so wild that it contains no less than everything' (3); the synchronic history that follows sets about demonstrating that this hyperbolic claim is at least figuratively true. In the nineteenth century, he writes, 'It was often said that all England had become London, but some considered London to be an altogether separate nation with its own language and customs. For others London corresponded to the great globe itself or "the epitome of the round world"' (589). Its seeming spatial inclusiveness was matched by a temporal inclusiveness, through which it was seen to the 'the climax, or the epitome, of all previous imperialist cities,' including Babylon (575). Beyond that city of multiplicity and confusion, nineteenth-century London 'seemed to contain within itself all previous civilisations. Babylon was then joined with other empires' (577).

A century earlier, London was already well established as a 'city of immigrants' and even, in some constructions, a 'city of nations'; Ackroyd quotes Addison writing in the mid-eighteenth century that 'when I consider this great city, in its several quarters, or divisions, I look upon it as an aggregate of various nations, distinguished from each other by their respective customs, manners, and interests' (701). In Book VII of

The Prelude, Wordsworth conveys this sense of London as a global pot-pourri of national identities:

> Among the crowd all specimens of man,
> Through all the colours which the sun bestows,
> And every character of form and face:
> The Swede, the Russian; from the genial south,
> The Frenchman and the Spaniard; from remote
> America, the Hunter-Indian; Moors,
> Malays, Lascars, the Tartar, the Chinese,
> And Negro Ladies in white muslin gowns.
>
> (233–5; lines 221–8)

It is not surprising that Wordsworth pays special attention to the 'Negro Ladies.' The only members of his catalogue to get a whole line and some visual description, these women would have been part of a very visible and increasingly prominent sub-group of late eighteenth-century London society. As Gretchen Gerzina writes in her fine history, *Black London*, by 1768 there were probably fifteen thousand blacks in London, mostly former slaves or their children (see 5). Only recently, however, has the existence of black Londoners prior to World War Two entered the popular imaginary, prompted by a spate of historical and literary publications such as Gerzina's, Peter Fryer's *Staying Power*, Caryl Phillips's anthology *Extravagant Strangers*, and new editions of writings by eighteenth-century black Londoners Ignatius Sancho, Olaudah Equiano, and Ukawsaw Gronniosaw. Postcolonial authors have been eager to explore the period through black eyes; notable novels include J.M. Coetzee's *Foe* (1986), which brings its Friday, like *Robinson Crusoe*'s, to the capital, and David Dabydeen's *A Harlot's Progress* (1999). In the latter, the slave boy Mungo is sold in early eighteenth-century London; his first impression of the city is of the abject 'dilapidation of poor people's quarters,' and he is 'overpowered by the stench of offal and ashes littering the street' (159). Near the end of the century, as London's oldest black resident, he tells his story to a committee of abolitionists.

These novels explore the treatment of individual black men by London's white society but do not create the sense of a black community that the black, British-born writer S.I. Martin does in *Incomparable World* (1996). Martin vividly recreates a 1786 St Giles neighbourhood full of black people; his major characters are recent émigrés from America, where they 'escaped bondage to enlist in the British Army and take up arms'

against their rebelling masters (10). Though they were promised freedom and pensions as a condition of service, 'as they boarded the troop-
ships that would take them to exile in London none of the black fighters
could have imagined the so-called freedom to which they would be
doomed' (10). Employment opportunities in the metropolis are restricted by guilds, and many refugees end up on the streets as beggars,
thieves, and scam artists. Their ability to settle is compromised not only
by poverty and racism but also by a rumoured repatriation scheme that
would 'sweep us from the streets' and transport them to Sierra Leone
(120). But Martin offsets these soul-breaking negatives through a sense
of rough-and-tumble camaraderie in a community rich with characters,
intrigues, and conflicts. He even appropriates the British class divide in
the story of the beautiful freeborn schoolmistress Charlotte, who defies
the snobbery of her black writerly friends (including Equiano) when she
forms a romantic relationship with the illiterate and recently imprisoned
Buckram.

As they take over British spaces such as alehouses, apartments, and
streets, and as they assume their place in the heart of the British city and
the centre of Martin's narrative, black men and women reterritorialize a
late eighteenth-century London that is incipiently transnational. Indeed, along with many 'African-looking people, there were a number of
East Indians and South Sea Islanders' on the streets, and even 'a Mohawk'
(40). In a passage layered with ambivalent irony, Martin takes advantage
of his contemporary perspective to impute to Buckram an anticipatory
vision of a future black Britain:

> Apart from a small, nervous-looking group of Hussars surrounding the
> pub, there was not a single white face to be seen. Buckram had never been
> amongst so many anxious, agitated, black men in one spot in his life.
> Hungry black men were everywhere.
>
> Suddenly he was seized by a delirious vision of this land, this London, in
> time to come, teeming with generation after generation of his kinfolk,
> freedmen, English-born and bred; transforming this wet, cold island with
> African worship and celebration. Imperial orphans in communion with a
> fractured past – his present – leading Albion's hag-masses to a greater,
> more wholesome dance of life. And would they, like him, still be hovering
> by closed doors, waiting for scraps from the master's table? And would they,
> like him, still be able to rely on the kindness of curious suburban strangers?
> God willing, death would find him before either of those futures came to
> pass. (40)

Buckram's questions are clearly an invitation and a challenge to the reader to assess present-day conditions for black Londoners in light of their forebears' lives over two centuries ago. How has the city's culture been transformed by its black communities? To what degree do black Londoners continue to be disenfranchised by racism and broken promises? Martin's novel adds moral authority to the claims of entitlement made by contemporary black Britons, showing through a vivid and sympathetic narrative how their own compromised states of belonging can be contextualized by a two-hundred-year-old history.

Of course, the black presence in London does not just go back to the eighteenth century; it has been continuous since the arrival in 1555 of five Africans 'to learn English and thereby facilitate trade' (Gerzina 3). Slaves soon followed, and by 1596 there were enough Africans in London to prompt Queen Elizabeth to complain in a letter to civic authorities that 'there are of late divers blackamoores brought into this realme, of which kinde of people there are allready here to manie' (qtd. in Fryer 10). In 1601 a royal proclamation ordered them to leave, but, as Ackroyd notes, 'like all such proclamations touching upon London and London's population, it had little effect. The imperatives of trade, particularly with the islands of the Caribbean, were more powerful' (711).

Furthermore, even before the rise of empire and overseas trade in the sixteenth century, a black presence can be traced as far back as Britain's own colonization by Rome, as Peter Fryer reveals (see 1). Inspired by Fryer's book (as its acknowledgments note), the most recent novel to portray a historical London through black eyes goes back further than any of its predecessors. Bernardine Evaristo's verse novel *The Emperor's Babe* (2001) wittily portrays Londinium in AD 211 as the adopted home of Sudanese migrants who have 'elevated' their daughter, Zuleika, through marriage to a Roman nobleman (13). The ancient city's international flavour is repeatedly emphasized. Zuleika's father 'employs all sorts' in his shops: 'a Syrian, Tunisian, Jew, Persian, // hopefuls just off the olive barge from Gaul, / in fact anyone who'll work for pebbles' (4). The market sells goods from 'Kenya, ... Arabia and Ethiopia' (40), and a brothel owner boasts about the racial and national diversity of his women: 'I 'ave a Woppy, a Chinky, a Honky, a Paki, / a Gingery, an Araby, now all I need is a Blackie' (45). Though such passages hardly point to a model transnational community, *The Emperor's Babe*, like Martin's *Incomparable World*, enables its historical society to anticipate a contemporary black London. Its chief strategy for looking ahead is a hybrid, anachronistic diction that layers names and social realities from later Londons, like a linguistic palimpsest, over its Roman foundation; as John McLeod notes, everything from 'Latinate terminology' to 'streetwise skaz' inflects Zuleika's playful tongue (Rev. 61). As the novel wittily jumbles up past and present, he adds, 'The implication is that London today is not too different to the Londons (or Londiniums) of yesterday: bawdy yet violent, full of merchants and traders noisily plying their wares, a home to migrants from Asia Minor and Africa, an ambivalent place of refuge to those fleeing conflicts in other lands' (61). As heroine and narrator, Zuleika emerges as the precocious precursor of a postfeminist black woman of twenty-first-century London. Navigating along the triangular transnational axes of her British, African, and Mediterranean cultural worlds, she saucily critiques and daringly undermines the paternalistic structures of power and desire that constrain her.

... and Now

Novels such as those by Evaristo, Martin, and Dabydeen correct the portraits of London as a white city that dominate English history and the literary canon. They also provide a valuable counter-narrative to constructions of Englishness or Britishness limited by skin colour or ethnicity by depicting the historical roots of Commonwealth migrants' postwar claims to these identities – or to hyphenated versions of them, or simply to a 'Londoner' status that goes beyond geographical *being there* to signify some form of *belonging*. As such, these novels add depth to the composite portrait of a transnational postwar London that emerged in postcolonial and 'black British' fiction during the last half of the twentieth century. It is to a detailed examination of that portrait – of the contemporary city as experienced and inscribed by diasporic and expatriate migrants – that this study will presently turn.

Although London novels have been written by authors from many once-colonized nations and from every region, the focus here is on the three literatures that have contributed the greatest number and variety of narratives since World War Two: Canada, the West Indies, and India.[17] A final chapter examines some recent London narratives by the 'black British' children of immigrants from Asia, Africa, or the West Indies. Each chapter analyses several novels in detail, showing how recurring themes and concerns of a national or regional culture are thrown into relief by the metropolitan experiences of migrants. My chapter titles (e.g. London North-West) are designed, through their compass-point and postal-district echoes, to playfully reinforce the global/local multi-dimensionality of these migrants' Londons and cultural identities. At the same time, they indicate the direction from which each chapter's protagonists have typically travelled and to which their homing instincts collectively point. Some representations of the transnational metropolis do evoke the whole world, but many of them extend London's local spaces most significantly into one specific overseas place such as Canada (which is home to Mordecai Richler and his protagonist), Guyana (home to David Dabydeen and his), or India (home to Anita Desai and hers).

This bipolar orientation – in which the metropolitan 'here' is linked primarily or exclusively to an originary 'there' that is the same across adjacent texts within a chapter but different between chapters – implicitly relies on and reinforces Michael Peter Smith's definition of the transnational as including rather than superseding or diminishing the nation-state. The retention and privileging of discrete national/regional focuses for each chapter also implies that the most fully, deeply, and broadly transnational London is not the city as it appears in any one novel or regional group. It is, rather, a composite of the similar-but-different cities portrayed in the dozens of London novels that reflect a diverse mix of regional preoccupations, cultural influences, personal experiences, and postcolonial sensibilities. In the readings of those novels, particular attention is paid to how spatial practices such as dwelling, walking, travelling, and observing contribute to the portrait of metropolitan life and the transnational city. By studying the ways spaces and places are encountered, inhabited, imagined, remembered, desired, appropriated, transformed, and represented by characters and narrators – and how they are related to other spaces and places – I hope to show the variety of ways London has functioned as a key signifier in the development of postcolonial consciousness and transnational community through the era of decolonization, mass migration, and postimperial decline.

The topic, like the city itself, is seemingly boundless, and beyond literary novels a dizzying array of films, television shows, songs, festivals, photographs, installations, performances, magazines, detective novels, and other forms of popular culture have contributed to the imagining of transnational London. In the literary realm, there have also been poems, plays, and short stories. I have kept my focus primarily on literary analysis as a reflection of my training and in order to contain the sprawling possibilities available in the category of 'urban text' in the era of contemporary cultural studies. And I have limited the literary field almost entirely to novels as these are the most plentiful and widely read London

texts; they also offer, as a group, the most extended and varied representations of the transnational city. I have, nonetheless, included discussion
of two films (scripted by Hanif Kureishi) and one radio program (the
BBC's influential *Caribbean Voices*); in both cases, these texts anticipate
and help contextualize the concerns of later novels. I also depart from
my usual focus on postwar novels with postwar settings to include Susan
Swan's *The Biggest Modern Woman of the World* (published in 1983 and set
in the nineteenth century) and Jean Rhys's *Voyage in the Dark* (published
in 1934 and set twenty years earlier). Both novels make notable use of
their metropolitan settings and bear important similarities to the contemporary narratives examined in their respective chapters.

The texts selected for discussion are those that offer the most substantial portraits of London and of metropolitan life from the perspective of
migrants and/or the children of migrants. Not included are novels in
which the experience of London represented is that of characters who
are white British (as in Naipaul's *Mr Stone and the Knights Companion* or
E.R. Braithwaite's *Choice of Straws*) or whose racial, ethnic, and/or national origins are indeterminate (as in Vikram Seth's *An Equal Music* or
Bidisha's *Seahorses*). In the spatially oriented readings that follow, the
focus is on what one group of British critics has called 'axial writing'
(qtd. in Blake et al. 5). In this kind of writing, London emerges as one
point in a multicentred network of transnational axes across which
people, things, ideas, and representations move in a constant flow of
traffic. As such, it tends to reveal at least as much about the originary
cultures from which the capital is approached and to which it constantly
points as about the British culture it nominally symbolizes – as much
about the (post)colonial seers as the (post)imperial scene.

chapter two

London North-West:
The Broader Borders
of Metropolitan Canadianness

One may easily sail round England, or circumnavigate the globe. But not
the most enthusiastic geographer ... ever memorised a map of London.
Certainly no one ever walks round it. For England is a small island, the
world is infinitesimal amongst the planets. But London is illimitable.

Ford Madox Ford

Here, There, and Everywhere

In 1965 Northrop Frye made the influential statement that the sensibility
informing Canadian literature 'is less perplexed by the question "Who
am I?" than by some such riddle as "Where is here?"' (222). While Frye's
thematic thumbnail appeared to abandon a question of identity for one
of place – turning from psychology to geography – it actually served to
link the two, as he and the critics he inspired made clear in their
paradigms: 'the garrison mentality,' 'isolation,' 'survival.'[1] Frye's questions are therefore best understood not preferentially but relationally:
conflated into something like 'Who am I (now that I'm) here?' or 'How
does being here affect who I am?'[2] Their relational dimensions are also
apparent in the familiar dualities they call to mind. 'Where is here?'
implies recognition of a 'there' to which 'here' is coupled and compared; as the one word contains the other, a proper coming to terms with
'here' inevitably requires an awareness of its relations to one or more
significant 'theres.' Similarly, understanding the personal or cultural 'I'
– the self – always occurs in relation to personal or cultural 'others,'
some of whom are within the self's national society and some of whom
are outside it.

For several Canadian novelists, London has provided fertile ground for an exploration of personal and national identity, typically through the story of a young Canadian taking up residence in the (post)imperial metropolis. For Canadians as with other Commonwealth writers and characters, London's history and world city status make it a uniquely overdetermined 'there' and point of access to others: a place from which the Canadian 'here' (nation and society) and the Canadian self (individual subject and national citizen) may be newly imagined. The list of London-leaning authors includes Susan Swan, Robertson Davies, Margaret Atwood, and Mordecai Richler, as well as the emerging writers Kate Pullinger and Catherine Bush.[3] As a group, their novels feature a recurring narrative in which the British capital represents an enabling space of access, opportunity, and broadened horizons where an expatriate Canadian, between nineteen and twenty-five years old and most often female, can escape something limiting or unpleasant in Canada. Arriving on the cusp of adulthood – at or close to the traditional age of majority – the protagonists in these novels reinvent themselves and come of age in what one of them calls 'the big wide world' of London (Pullinger, *Last* 23). Some, like Swan's Anna or Davies's Monica, move with the sanction of institutional support, good connections, and a clear purpose, whereas the young women in novels by Atwood, Pullinger, and Bush all move there spontaneously, secretly, and in response to a traumatic event at home. They pursue more or less successful careers, typically as writers or performing artists, and enter into romantic relationships; through the education in culture, loyalty, and morality these experiences provide, each character arrives at a reinvigorated understanding of the ways the Canadian past contributes to her (or his) identity and worldly agency. London becomes most interesting for the ways the worldly experience it provides both clarifies and complicates notions of identity that originate in and persistently return to Canada. As migration transforms London into a 'here' from which to observe Canada's 'there,' the metropolis becomes one node in a set of transatlantic relations, reversals, and substitutions. These become increasingly multifaceted in the most recent novels – those written in the current era of increased global interrelatedness. As a version of the world, London for younger Canadian writers is transformed from a there to a here to a version of everywhere.

That London should prompt a reinvigorated awareness of self and nation is not surprising. Its imperial past and multicultural present make it a city defined by its intimate relations to a wide variety of elsewheres and ethnic 'others,' and it is this aspect of London that makes it such a rich site for writers of the postcolonial Commonwealth. That Canadian authors in particular should be drawn to it is also not surprising. It was the Canadian theorist Marshall McLuhan who coined the phrase 'global village' to describe the world-shrinking and linking effects of new communications media (*Gutenberg* 31). In *Borderlands: How We Talk about Canada,* W.H. New sees McLuhan's ubiquitous concept as 'not a techno-logical *universal* but a remarkably *Canadian* metaphor, a way of seeing the connection between the local and the large, and of constructing the border between them as a field of negotiated relationships' (51). Urban theorists who describe London as a 'world city' or 'global city' speak to a quality that writers from across Britain's former empire have observed: London is itself a kind of global village. But London is also a location and a centre, whereas McLuhan's oxymoron speaks primarily to the decentred dis-location of multiple connections between, say, speaking voices in one place and listening ears in many others. So London earns the 'global village' designation not just as a specific place but as part of a web of relations to elsewheres, including Canada. And, as New's remarks may be extended to suggest, it does so in a special way for Canadians, whose fragile sense of national identity is profoundly relational.

Constructions of Canada, according to New, are indebted to 'various forms of boundary rhetoric' and references to borders – as geopolitical facts and as metaphorical figures (*Borderlands* 5). The borders that para-doxically both divide and connect different places – liminal spaces that force us to think both in terms of *either/or* and of *both/and* – are central to Canadians' self-constitution. 'For most of its history,' New writes, 'Canada has been an Atlantic and an American society, looking east to Europe and south to the States for imperial roots and continental desires – so much so that ... these two borders came to seem *normative* angles of cultural disposition' (6). Ian Angus also uses the border as the control-ling metaphor for his study of Canadianness, *A Border Within.* 'English Canadian identity,' he writes, 'has been predicated upon a need to maintain the border between one's own and the Other. Its most distinc-tive philosophical theme is thus the explication of this notion of the *border*' (111). Borders, with their connotations of in-betweenness and mutual exchange, have emerged as central figures in contemporary cultural theory, but for Canadians borders provide a special focus for anxieties about difference and sameness. Seeking to define what makes them distinct from those other North Americans across the longest undefended border in the world, Canadians will often contrast their history of political gradualism and evolution into nationhood with the revolutionary past of the United States. For Angus, this difference is 'a main reason why [English Canada] has a weak national mythology'; it affects 'the temporal and spatial dimensions of English Canadian identity' *vis-à-vis* both the United States and Europe:

> The temporal dimension of the [Canadian] nation suggests continuity and gradual pragmatic evolution, unlike the focus on temporal break and new foundation in the republican tradition, for example. Thus it has tended to articulate its difference from Europe through a relation to the geography of the new land. In revolutionary traditions, time suggests discontinuity and thus difference from Europe. Space, geography, land, may then be perceived in a European way as a storehouse of resources without this continuity becoming threatening to identity. In the English Canadian case, by way of contrast, geography becomes important for identity where history has failed to provide it. (114)[4]

It is Canadian writers' traditional obsession with this sense of spatial difference from Europe that led to Frye's 'where is here?' question and the geographical orientation of the thematic critics' paradigms for Canadian literature.

When Canadians think of a border, they are much less likely to picture the Atlantic Ocean between them and their former European colonizers than the long line – metonymically dubbed the forty-ninth parallel – that both separates them from and joins them to the neo-imperial superpower to the south. That border has been described by a Canadian diplomat as 'a typically human creation; it is physically invisible, geographically illogical, militarily indefensible, and emotionally inescapable' (qtd. in McLuhan, 'Canada' 226). Emotionally inescapable it certainly is, and in no small part because it marks proximity rather than the Atlantic's vast distance: wherever it isn't dividing up inland waterways, the Canada-US border separates two identical pieces of adjacent territory that nonetheless represent enormous differences in economic power, international influence, and national self-esteem.[5] Canadians find the United States harder to ignore than Europe, and in popular political discourse the national anxiety is voiced through figures of speech such as 'sleeping beside an elephant.' When literary critics think comparatively, they either reinforce the sense of Canadian identity as weak – for Stanley Fogel, American identity is distinctive and 'cathectic' as opposed to Canada's ill-defined and 'anorectic' identity (9) – or they recognize more neutrally that Canada's sense of national self is inescapably relational and oriented to the south: T.D. MacLulich writes that 'most assertions of the Canadian identity are still comparative rather than absolute: Canadians habitually define their country's identity by contrasting it with the United States' (13).

McLuhan, too, recognized the primacy of the US border. His wittily titled essay 'Canada: The Borderline Case' briefly acknowledges Canada's lengthy coastline as 'the frontier for Europe on one side and the Orient on the other' (244), but his focus is on the forty-ninth parallel and the ways that, in Richard Cavell's paraphrase, Canada is 'defined by its interfaces rather than by an essence' (200). Defining a border suggestively as 'an interval of resonance,' McLuhan constructs Canada's poorly defined but 'flexible' national identity as a benefit: a positive function of its 'multiple borderlines, psychic, social, and geographic' ('Canada' 226, 227, 244). In an age of boundary-crossing 'electric information' (246), he sees Canada's 'low-profile' and decentred identity as an advantage compared to 'lands long blessed by strong identities [which] are now bewildered by the growing perforation and porousness of their identity image in this electronic age' (247). With hindsight, McLuhan's optimism seems rather utopian. It was Canada that insisted on exempting 'culture' from the Free Trade Agreement of 1989 and the subsequent North American FTA, fearing a loss of cultural sovereignty and a diminished national identity if the US increased its domination of Canadian cultural industries. The porous border continues to cause anxiety and ambivalence in Canada today.[6] Still, McLuhan's vision of the border as a figure for a relational Canadian identity characterized by 'interval,' 'interface,' and '"between-ness"' (233), and of the Canada-US border as the boundary of choice in discourses of Canadian identity, concurs with the views of many who have scratched the itch of the national-identity question.

Big Apple Dreaming

Given these geopolitical preferences, it is perhaps fitting that one of postwar Canadian literature's chronologically earliest representations of London subordinates it to New York. Susan Swan's *The Biggest Modern Woman of the World* (1983) makes its London narrative a sideshow to a mainstage allegorizing of Canada-US relations in the nineteenth century. The novel is loosely based on the life and career of Nova Scotian giantess Anna Swan (1846–1888), whose forty-two years of life were

exactly bisected by Confederation in 1867. That moment, in the year
during which twenty-one-year-old Anna would traditionally come of age,
is tellingly absent from the text: the moment of transition from colonies
to nation, of (partial) independence from the mother-country, passes
without mention, despite the obvious allegorical possibilities. The reason for this absence is that the novel's playful interrogation of national
identity is more interested in the US than England. For Susan Swan, it is
Canada's conflicted responses to America – responses of desire and
resistance, self-assertion and self-doubt, independence and dependence
– that define its hesitant, fitful stumbling into modernity and nationhood. She constructs national identity as a function of international
relations allegorized through marital/sexual ones. Anna's three major
relationships are to a Canadian, an American, and an Australian; Britain
is not included. As Smaro Kamboureli notes, by allegorizing 'national
difference' through 'sexual otherness,' Swan demonstrates that 'the idea
of the nation is defined in correlation to other nations, alterity thus
becoming the only measuring device of national identity' ('*Biggest*' 10).
National identity, in other words, is relational.

The most important and nuanced of these allegorical relationships
involves Anna's American show-business career and her marriage to the
Kentucky Giant, Martin Bates. As Anna explains it,

> I feel I am acting out America's relationship to the Canadas. Martin is the
> imperial ogre while I play the role of genteel mate who believes that if
> everyone is well-mannered, we can inhabit a peaceable kingdom. That is
> the national dream of the Canadas, isn't it? A civilized garden where lions
> lie down with doves. I did not see the difference until I married Martin. We
> possess no fantasies of conquest and domination. Indeed, to be from the
> Canadas is to feel as women feel – cut off from the base of power. (273–4)

Critics offer various interpretations of the novel's view of Canadian-US
relations, but for all their differences, they tend to agree that its vision of
Canadian nationhood hinges on this relationship more than any other.
They typically locate the novel's intertwined sexual and national allegorical narratives in a state of unresolved tension between domination
and mutuality, acquiescent absorption and feisty independence.[7] The
border-zone that Canada's relational identity inhabits is given a material
location through the novel's imagery of grotesque bodies. A Bakhtinian
conception of the grotesque as an image of boundary-crossing exchange
between realms informs Swan's view of Canada and its 'body politic.'[8]

Anna's body is regularly displaced from literal fact to metaphorical figure, associated variously with animals and plants, land and landscape, nation, world, and even the universe. Through the play of substitutions between the body as private and as public space, the sexual/national allegory constructs Canadian identity as a function of the nation's contradictory responses to the penetration by other nations of geographical and political boundaries figured as bodily ones.

Britain and London do have a presence in *The Biggest Modern Woman*, and the representation of them is filtered through the same preoccupation with size that dominates the novel's central allegorical gestures – big and small people, big and small countries. (In the latter case, the adjectives apply to Canada and Britain differently depending on whether the reference is to physical size or to population and power.) When the novel depicts major cities and their built space as national symbols, it employs a rhetoric of diminishment that appears frequently in Canadian narratives of London. Anna's first such downsizing is of New York, her narrative's most prominent city, in a chapter called 'A Dream of Smallness in Central Park.' Her lover Angus has visited her, disliked New York, and left, insisting she can have him only if she moves to Cape Breton. Anna, torn between her American career and her Canadian lover – between the future offered by the city and the past associated with the 'country' – realizes that 'I am not going to get everything I desire' (133–4). In a dream, she takes an imagined revenge on 'the city which has ruined my fairy-tale romance, ... willing New York to shrink with all the magic energy I can summon' (134):

> The city, from Fifth Avenue to Battery Park, dwindles to the size of a tourist trinket whose inner workings are plainly visible in Manhattan's clear river light. I can make out the tiny, rugged stone façades and the streets with the amusing traffic congestions, the needle-sized spire of St. Paul's, a minute city hall colonnade, and the uninspiring little geyser of the Croton Water Fountain. Angrily, I reach down and pick up the miniature town and in a long, ladylike toss, pitch New York as far as I can out into the Atlantic Ocean. (134)

The liminal, inter-national space of the Atlantic Ocean serves as the site of resistance to the US in another important scene. On board the ship taking them to Britain, Ingalls, Martin, and Anna act out the 'hymeneal' performance that poetically crystallizes the novel's national and sexual allegory and, in 'Anna's Answer True,' provides Anna's response to the

American designs upon Canada that are equated with his designs upon her: 'I'll be damned, Martin, / if I'll be crammed / on the seat of your / imperial fantasy' (183). But like the downsizing of New York, this second strong statement of resistance is compromised by its origins in the imagination – as a dreamed or performed enactment of desire. Reality takes different turns: Anna stays in New York after imaginatively shrinking and disposing of it; and shortly after resisting Martin's 'hymeneal' overtures, she marries him.

The Atlantic continues to be a politically ambiguous space when Anna-as-Canada – now vowing she is 'through with' New York and planning to 'make London my home' (185) – loses her voice upon arrival in London, a condition that persists during her wedding to Martin there and throughout her stay. For Kamboureli, this development signifies Anna's 'loss of independence' on becoming married, but also 'allegorizes the colonial status of her already dwarfed Canadian identity' in relation to Britain ('Biggest' 13). Silence can signify resistance too, however, and Anna's muteness in Britain can alternatively be read as a complement to various statements of diminishment and disappointment associated with Britain, London, and their people. Anna is initially impressed with London's built environment and, tourist that she is, visits many of its famous monuments. Admiring 'the sixteenth-century architecture' of Trafalgar Square, she writes in a note to Martin, 'I belong among these civilized people who have the sense to design on the grand scale' (189). Martin, presumably because he is American, rejects her easy association of large New World self with large Old World buildings, especially since the English people are smaller than he is. After viewing Nelson's column, he competitively contrasts his relation to the monument with Britons' relation to himself: 'He [Nelson] towered 162 feet above us who look down on the limey head and I [Martin] asked: "Monument to monument, my dear, do you think I have the old warrior beat?"' Anna's odd reply – 'Martin, you should be grateful to appear small in the eyes of your God!' – upbraids his uppity heightism and indirectly seems to associate either Nelson or the 'limeys' with God (189). Later, however, her disillusion with Britain makes those people the target of her downsizing accusations. 'For a nation that would fit inside a Canadian lake,' she writes, 'the Brits are an arrogant people' (229). And far from the architectural grandeur of London's monuments is Anna and Martin's 'honeymoon chamber which turns out to be a shabby cubicle facing the wall of the hotel stable' (205). These changes in perspective show Anna (as Canada) shifting from an affiliation with

Britain that distances her from Martin (as America) towards a deflation of Britain that associates her more closely with his views. As post-Confederation Canada detaches itself from Britain, it nudges closer to America.

Most significant, though, is the novel's diminishment of Queen Victoria, who presided over nineteenth-century Britain's vast imperial growth from her throne in London. Her empire may be gigantic, but Victoria herself is 'a tiny, melancholic figure' only four feet eight inches tall. When Anna meets the 'miniature monarch' at Buckingham Palace, she realizes that the queen is 'just another normal' – and an insecure, eccentric one at that (193). Victoria regrets that her 'midget' frame is 'no height for a queen' but cheers herself up by manoeuvring Anna into letting her walk, in full, tiara-topped regalia, under Anna's five-foot-long legs (195). Anna is horrified at being exposed, especially in her 'brazen' undergarments, but Victoria, after offering some fashion advice, pronounces herself thoroughly satisfied with Anna's help: 'Miss Swan, you have amused me and thus done the Empire a great service' (196, 197). This memorably outrageous scene is the London equivalent of Anna's shrinking of New York, but as an actual rather than imagined event within the fiction of the novel, it works towards several thematic ends. As in many Commonwealth narratives, it makes London the place where the (post)colonial subject becomes aware that her identity is enmeshed in and constructed by imperial power relations. The dumb giantess is reduced to a spectacle for Victoria's eyes and a playground for her body, allegorically and parodically signifying the large, spectacular, and largely silent Canadian landscape as it revealed itself and gave pleasure to European explorers and colonizers. As Victoria penetrates Anna's skirts, private space is redefined as the public space of 'Empire.' But if Victoria has the power to command a performance *in* the scene, Anna, voiceless within it, has the power of representation *over* it; she controls the narration, which includes a full report of the childlike imperial queen acting her size: making a display of Anna but also of herself. Victoria and the empire in whose name she acts both appear diminished and thereby resisted. In tandem with the other downsizing representations of London, this scene moves Anna away from her initial identification with Englishness and closer to the bigger-is-better detachment (though without the arrogance) of her American husband.

The London section thus helps to clarify the novel's central allegorical relation. Anna's decision to return to the US (where she will live out her life) is prompted by the failure of her British experience and the evolution of her views from hope and awe to disillusion and diminishment.

She more fully resists British imperialism's sideshow than the mainstage America to which she is repeatedly drawn. She remains 'wed' to America, in the form of Martin, until her death, even if Susan Swan undercuts the relationship through Martin's impotence, the dead babies fathered by Ingalls, and Anna's remark at the end of her life that 'I do not fit in anywhere' (332). Through the relative proportions of its geographical settings, and through the omission of Confederation, Swan implies that Britain is not as significant to Canada's quasi-colonial identity as its more proximate American partnership. Moreover, as a principal narrator who outgrows the temporal boundaries of her historical life by speaking both to her time and ours,[9] Anna Swan reinforces the centrality of Canada-US relations to Canadian identity not just in the Victorian era but across two centuries of Canadian nationhood.

From Pumpkin to Centre

Jonathan Kertzer, prompted by the Hegelian idea that a nation's character (or 'genius') may be personified as an individual person in a heroic narrative, remarks that Canada is 'harder to personify' than, say, the US (as Uncle Sam) or Britain (as John Bull). He does note, however, that

> Canada and its literature are commonly characterized through a 'lexicon of maturation' ... , by which the country is pictured as an irresolute youth striving for maturity. ... For example, the land is 'young' but eager to prove itself; or it suffers from an identity crisis as it matures from colony to nation; or it remains 'a highschool land / deadset in adolescence.' ... If Canadian history is not an epic, it is at least a *Bildungsroman*. (44)

Coral Ann Howells makes a related point: '[The] coincidence of similar problems of self-definition in nationalist and feminist ideology would go some way to explain why so much attention is being paid to women writers in Canada at the present time, for their stories seem the natural expression of the insecurity and ambitions of their society and in many ways they provide models for stories of Canadian national identity' (26). *The Biggest Modern Woman of the World*, with its foregrounded national allegory, would seem to fit both of these models, yet it also presents Anna's life as a parodic fairy tale starring an 'OLYMPIAN CINDERELLA' so large that, in Anna's words, 'Mr. P.T. Barnum likes to say that if I left a slipper on the stairs of a palace, he would be hard pressed to find a prince to fit it' (4, 2). The (ironic) Prince Charming who elevates this

Cinderella from a Nova Scotia farm to fame and fortune is an amalgam of Barnum, Martin Bates, and the America they both represent. The next significant representation of London in Canadian fiction, chronologically speaking, is Robertson Davies's *A Mixture of Frailties* (1958); it too, as Clara Thomas notes, is 'a Cinderella story' (184). In this book, it is not New York but London that serves as the necessary location for elevating a disadvantaged but exceptional Canadian girl beyond what Canada could provide. Like Swan's novel, Davies's is at least as much *Künstlerroman* as *Bildungsroman*, and it too, though less overtly, presents a national allegory that casts Canada as a Cinderella needing rescue by a foreign prince.

For twenty-one-year-old Monica Gall, London is the place to escape the limiting circumstances of her Ontario town, her family, her job at the local Glue Works, and her obscure religion in order to become a singer. Supported by an eccentric Salterton woman's trust fund, she gains top-drawer education in music, European languages, and life. She loses her virginity in the process to one of her teachers, the bohemian composer Giles Revelstoke, eagerly celebrating her new-found sexuality as a release from the limiting moral code of her background. Professionally, Monica moves from strength to strength; though initially hampered by her lack of 'general cultivation' (123), she learns well and blossoms quickly into a talented singer who, after three years in London, is on the brink of a promising career. She also seems about to marry Sir Benedict Domdaniel, the famous conductor whose protégé she has been, though Davies coyly withholds closure on this point. A man thirty-two years her senior, Sir Benedict at one point refers to Monica as being from 'Pumpkin Centre' (333); of the three male teachers who play Pygmalion to her Galatea, it is he who finally also plays the prince to her emergent Cinderella.

Here London assumes what Raymond Williams describes as the city's time-honoured literary identity; by moving from the 'country' of provincial Canada to the 'city' of London, Monica progresses from birth to learning, innocence to experience, the past to the future – from simplicity and backwardness to worldliness and ambition (Williams 1).[10] The novel largely endorses these traditional binaries; not only is 'jolly old London' perceived by everyone in the novel as *the* place to go for such transforming professional and personal development (although sexual initiation wasn't in the sponsors' plan), but the city does indeed fulfil that role (77). The place the jejune Monica initially associates with 'her great dream of life' – a musical career she had thought impossibly out of reach – turns out to be the very place to realize that dream (59). After crossing the Atlantic 'determined' that London will 'transform her' from provincial Monica Gall into the diva Monique Gallo, 'to whom London and all the capitals of the world would seem like home,' she is indeed transformed (84, 87).

Davies reinforces this overarching narrative of constricting circumstances traded in for expanded possibilities through the spatial details of Monica's movement from Salterton to London. At her farewell party, Monica feels 'stifled and cramped in this atmosphere' (79); the metaphor is then literalized when her seasickness en route keeps her confined to her cabin. On arrival she sees little, either on the 'boat-train' or in London itself, because of fog and rain; she spends her first days stuck in a small, smelly room with nothing to do, frustrated that her expectations of 'the new world which she had decided to make her own' have been so poorly met (121). But as this description suggests a desire to possess the metropolis – the Old World paradoxically cast as the New World by this Canadian reinvading the centre – she overcomes her confinement by walking and thereby, as Michel de Certeau would say, performs a 'pedestrian speech act' in which she lays claim to the city and inscribes it with her personal narrative (97). Eventually she will see landmarks such as the Albert Hall and Hyde Park, but her first impression of outdoor London does not lead to awe or reverence: she notices the 'sour, heavy smell' of Marylebone Road and feels what she sees there is, 'in other respects, not greatly unlike Toronto' (87). Once her formal and informal education gets underway and she gains confidence and maturity, Monica's mobility continues to increase. Soon she is moving freely through London's rarefied social worlds and venturing to Paris, Wales, and eventually Venice, where she sings in an opera that Giles wrote and she helped finance through her trust account. With London serving as threshold to the world, the gradual expansion of Monica's metaphorical horizons that the city enables is matched with an expansion of her spatial horizons beyond those initial narrow limits.

Her travel includes two return trips to Salterton that accentuate for Monica, her family, and the reader just how much she has been transformed. Some aspects of the return are liberating; Monica rejoices in being able to breathe 'the cool, clear air, which had not been breathed and re-breathed by everybody since the time of Alfred the Great' (253); after a London repeatedly described as bad-smelling, close, and dirty, this contrast seems to locate openness in Canada. Or does the Canadian air signify emptiness and absence compared to London's history-saturated richness? To some degree Davies does complicate his Salterton/

London binary and its assumptions about nationality and identity, mainly through the variety of ways Monica is forced to interrogate her Canadianness. But even as he does so, he reinforces a sense of division. Three scenes will serve as examples. Early on, Monica realizes she has instinctively 'edited' her past for consumption by London acquaintances, asking herself, 'Was it something about England, which made real truth and real revelation impossible? Had that dreadful week on the Atlantic really drawn such a broad line between herself and her past?' (89). With this metaphor, the Atlantic is figured not only as a spatial and cultural borderline marking unbridgeable difference, but as a temporal divide between 'herself' (the desired self of her present and future) and 'her past' (her former, embarrassing self). Identity is not so much the product of mutual relations between selves and the places in which they are based as it is a graduation from one place-identity to another, better one. Later, in the Christmas week after losing her virginity, a newly self-confident Monica again edits her Canadian past, this time by romanticizing her home culture with idyllic images of winter sports she has never played and exotic dishes her mother cannot cook, and by not mentioning her religion and the Glue Works. However, this ingratiating performance for Giles's family trips her up. Attempting to link her Canadianness with the Britishness she admires in them, she claims Loyalist ancestors, but 'this fell rather flat, for nobody present seemed to know what United Empire Loyalists were' (181). After explaining, she feels justly 'rebuked' by Giles's dismissal of loyalty as too modest a virtue to be worth admiring (182). Her lesson: even a laundered version of Canadian identity will be put in its place in Britain. Much later still, Monica finds she cannot identify with publicly sanctioned romantic stereotypes of Canadian identity. After three years in London she sees 'a poster which urged settlers to move to Canada' in which 'a young man in shirt-sleeves stood in a field of wheat, his bronzed face split with a dazzling grin. I suppose he represents my country, thought Monica, though I've never met anybody like that in my life. Odd that he should be so young, and that I feel so old' (334–5).[11] Monica, now twenty-four, is not old, but in the Old World she has matured and, Davies implies, outgrown her place of birth. In the process of being transformed (and transforming herself) into a musician she has become 'a Londoner now in her own estimation' (347) and no longer the 'irresolute youth' of Kertzer's national persona. That process involves leaving Canadianness behind and learning to think and live more broadly – independent of the prescribed opinions and attenuated codes of conduct she learned in her youth.

Significantly, the process begins during an encounter with some ur-Canadians in London. In a novel that often mocks Canadian smallness, Davies saves his fiercest satire for Lorne and Meg McCorkill, Albertans living in South Wimbledon in a house called Beaver Lodge. Nationalistic to the point of absurdity, these proud 'Canuck' expatriates import Canadian food and appliances, criticize anything British, and fret about every Cockney phrase their daughter picks up (114). Sharing the narrator's bemusement at these lonely, bunkered 'exiles,' Monica concludes that they are simply 'uprooted, afraid, and desperately homesick' (119). She finds her ability to judge them beneficial to 'her self-esteem, which had been badly bruised during her five months in London' (119): she enjoys her 'new freedom' not to agree with her elders, realizing that 'if it was to be fight between England and Canada for the love of Monica Gall, ... England would win' (120). Here is an early sign that in this novel, maturity will be equated with outgrowing the limitations of Canada and Canadianness, however comically portrayed.

Davies reinforces this equation through his choice of narrative mode. Most discussions of *A Mixture of Frailties* remark on a split between its trivializing representation of Salterton society in the first three chapters – dominated by the broad 'burlesque,' 'slapstick and caricature' of the trilogy's earlier novels – and the more expansive and empathetic comic realism of Monica's London narrative (Peterman 105). This is seen both negatively as a flaw of structure and craft – 'needing a kitchen for his Cinderella, Davies resorted to the very kind of writing he was seeking to avoid' (Peterman 104; cf. Thomas 195) – and positively as a sign of developing artistry (see Grant 369).[12] But this divided mode has another effect: it reinforces the thematic associations of the geographical split and the progressive model of identity formation it helps organize. The novel is structured by several hierarchical binaries: London versus Salterton, expansive future versus confining past, Sir Benedict's Eros ('people who are for life') versus Thanatos ('people who are against it'), and realism versus satire (102).[13] Provincial Canada, these overlaid pairings suggest, is a place of anti-life worthy of satire, whereas complex characterization and realism belong in London. In a novel whose original title was 'Water Parted' (Grant 366), Davies draws his own 'broad line' longitudinally through the Atlantic to mark his preferences. And in the McCorkills, the sole instance of satire to intrude on the comic realism of his London narrative, he makes both Canadian nationalism and satire seem out of place in the more refined London world.

The satire is tempered during Monica's two return visits to Salterton, but Davies continues to contrast her two worlds as he explores her geographically divided conscience. At the beginning of her first visit, Monica agonizes about 'keeping two sets of mental and moral books – one for inspection in the light of home, and another to contain her life with Revelstoke, and all the new loyalties and attitudes which had come with Molloy, and particularly with Domdaniel. To close either set of books forever would be a kind of suicide, yet to keep them both was hypocrisy' (251). This passage suggests a relational moral identity, but Monica's irresolution is only temporary, as it becomes clear that rather than continue negotiating within herself, she will substitute one set of books for the other in the interests of personal growth and progress. Similarly, during the visit home she realizes that 'her manner of speech, her clothes, her demeanour were all at odds' with 'the stuffy little house' (264). Her dying mother protests that she is 'talkin'' 'funny' and says, 'You ain't Monny!' (264); but Monica realizes that she 'could not go back to the speech of her home, for the new speech had become the instrument of the best that was in her mind, and heart.' To abandon it would be a 'betrayal' of her teachers and of 'all the poets and musicians who stood behind them in time' (265). As goes her speech, so go her morals: if the big city has performed one traditional role by elevating Monica into the company of 'poets and musicians,' it has performed another by corrupting her. Paradoxically, that corruption is seen as elevating. When her mother insistently asks if she is 'a good girl' and Monica says yes, she knows she is being 'disloyal to home' – even a liar – because by her mother's code of conduct she has not been good (264, 266). But according to her new codes, 'She was a good girl. Chastity is to have the body in the soul's keeping; Domdaniel had said it, and everything in her own experience supported it' (266). The rigid morality of her mother, and of her own youth, is supplanted by the worldly one she has learned in London.

Davies clearly endorses this model of the self expanded and beneficially transformed in an elevating environment. And part of the narrowness of his satirized Canadians is their inability to fully comprehend such changes. On a second visit home, Monica's new identity baffles her sister Alice: 'It was inconceivable to Alice that what had been learned, and thoroughly digested, could become more truly one's nature than the attitudes and customs of the family into which one had been born.' Monica, with her 'high and mighty ways,' is simply 'sticking it on,' according to Alice (347). But 'nature' can be transformed by culture, and Davies suggests that what Alice and other Saltertonians fail to understand – hewers of wood and drawers of water that they are – is that Monica's old self was just raw material, a natural resource needing refinement at the centre. The author's sympathies are clearly with Monica and the process she undergoes; his narrative suggests that integrity of self can be maintained and even enhanced in a movement from country to city, birth to learning, that abandons the backwardness of the former for the transformative possibilities of the latter. As she moves from the old New World to the new Old World, Monica outgrows her natal culture, becoming the new person she could not have become in the mother-land of Canada.[14]

A Mixture of Frailties is less obviously a national allegory than The Biggest Modern Woman of the World, but as a Künstlerroman with a Cinderella intertext, it is both more straightforward and more problematic in its implications for Canadian identity. Swan's novel employs both the fairy-tale allusions and the Künstlerroman generic model parodically, under-cutting them through the unidealized reality of Anna's professional and romantic achievements and through the questionable artistry of her work as freak-cum-spieler-cum-actor. The complexities of the relations that structure its combined sexual and national allegory complicate the vision it presents of Canada's relational identity vis-à-vis the US and Britain in ways that speak fruitfully to Canada's ambiguous nationhood. Davies, for all his comic ironies and resistance to romance,[15] largely embraces the Cinderella model and writes a much more conventional Künstlerroman. However, the binaries that structure his narrative of matu-ration and re-placement imply that, since virtually all his representations of Canada and Canadian society emphasize limitations, Canada can become most fully realized not simply by developing closer ties to Lon-don and the world but by ceasing to be everything that defines it as Canadian. That, of course, is impossible. The implication is either the abandonment of faith in the nation or, perhaps, a warning to the critic about the perils of allegorical reading.

Off in All Directions

Monica's sense of doubleness – of choosing between two different people she could be, two mutually exclusive identities available to her – leads to a process of self-fashioning that is less relational than what might be called substitutional: a re-placing of the self. This notion of alternate selves for different locations is one of many intriguing correspondences between Davies's novel and Margaret Atwood's Lady Oracle (1976). In the early 1960s, Atwood's Joan Foster migrates from Toronto to London at age nineteen to escape her mother, who has stabbed her in the arm during an argument. Like Monica, Joan is the beneficiary of an eccentric woman's will; her Aunt Lou leaves her $2,000 on the condition that she lose one hundred pounds. She does so, gaining a new bodily self, and uses the money to cross the Atlantic in search of further reinvention: 'I wanted to have more than one life,' she says. 'I was the right shape, but I had the wrong past. I'd have to get rid of it entirely and construct a different one for myself, a more agreeable one' (141). Whereas Monica initially fixates on London's dirt and smells, Joan remarks on its visual disappointment: she too finds it not unlike Toronto, but smaller, 'as though two giant hands had compressed each object and then shoved them all closer together' (142). Her first stop is Canada House because she feels homesick; only then does she venture into a depressing city full of 'squat people with bad teeth' and greasy, unpalatable food (143). Like Monica she makes pilgrimages to the famous sights: she mocks Big Ben (it's 'not so big') and calls the Lake District 'the Puddle District' (145). The rhetoric of diminishment in this novel seems to reflect a left-over colonial insecurity, a youthful, knee-jerk nationalism compelled to bring London's (and Britain's) ancient grandeur down to size by emphasizing, as in Swan's novel, physical size rather than historical and cultural stature.

Atwood's consistently ironic (and self-ironizing) characterization of Joan makes it hard to know what authority to grant these negative representations of the metropolis. Indeed, the belittling gestures amount not to a general critique of London but to a minor qualification of the city's otherwise enabling role. London expands Joan's prospects as it does Monica's; it sets her on the course to a more adventurous and mature adulthood than her troubled home life could have provided. Although her progress is more haphazard, unidealized, and comically portrayed than Monica's, Joan too is sexually initiated by an older male artist who then helps her begin her own artistic career – in this case, as a writer of historical romance novels. In London she also meets Arthur, the Maritimer she later marries back in Toronto. Joan – like Monica – returns home because of her mother's death;[16] by the time Arthur finds her and marries her, she is well established as a person with two distinct identities, names, bank accounts, careers, and passports: one for each city. She manages to keep her romance-novelist identity hidden even from Arthur: 'I was two people at once,' she says (214). Later, as her entanglements grow, she worries that 'my dark twin, my funhouse-mirror reflection ... wanted to kill me and take my place' (252). When things close in on her further, she does kill off one self, faking its death so she can fly off as the other self to Italy.

With its narrative similarities to Davies's novel, Atwood's suggests the same rather ominous national allegory. In both, Canada as young woman is ushered into adult worldliness through sexual and professional initiation by an older male Londoner. Her transformative coming of age and transcendence of her Canadian self's limitations are signalled by her cultivation of a new identity and by the death of her mother – allegorically the motherland. Despite the ironic brush with which he paints some aspects of London life, Davies positions Monica's progress in a way that largely supports such an interpretation. Atwood, while echoing the general narrative, subverts the allegory in several ways. First, London plays a much smaller part in *Lady Oracle*; its London scenes comprise only one-tenth of the whole. Second, the men in Joan's life are not British, like Monica's, but Polish and Canadian. Third, the fugitive and serendipitous nature of Joan's progress is a far cry from Monica's carefully managed career-building and self-fashioning; despite her success, Joan's transformation is at best a reduced, ironic, picaresque version of Monica's. Fourth, although London is a springboard to new identities and experiences for Joan, it isn't positioned as the obvious or only place where these could be achieved as it is in *A Mixture of Frailties*. One can imagine Joan's London narrative happening in New York or Vancouver in a way one can't imagine Monica's. And fifth, after Joan trades her London life in for a one-way ticket to Toronto following her mother's death, she never returns. London is only an interim stage in a continuum of identity constructing and career building, not a final or inevitable destination.

Mordecai Richler also explores a self through *alter-ego* doubles in *St. Urbain's Horseman* (1971), a novel set in London with flashbacks and imagined peregrinations to various *alter loci*. The crisis precipitated by Jake Hersch's appearance at the Old Bailey on trumped-up sex charges becomes an opportunity for self-appraisal; Jake reevaluates his life and aspects of his identity by examining his psychologically and morally complex relations with cousin Joey (the Horseman) and sometime friend Harry, with whom he is on trial. As his entanglements with other selves cast Jake's character into relief, the inclusion of other places (especially Canada) within a London-based narrative frame renders the metropolis as a place that in various ways – through Jake's consciousness, Richler's narrative structure, and its own international networks – contains the wider world.

London is actually Jake's third urban destination after leaving Montreal at age twenty-one. His first choice is New York, which 'had always been their true capital. Ottawa? Quebec City? Those were bush league towns.... They were the places the regulations came from, not life's joys. ... New York was quality, top quality' (97–8). Jake's dreams of the Big Apple are foiled by an American immigration officer who mistakes him for Joey, a political undesirable, and refuses him entry. He goes instead to Toronto and modest success directing for television, but he and his friend Luke see Toronto as 'ugly' and 'provincial,' a 'farm club' from which they plan to graduate: 'Luke swore his first stage play would have to be good enough to open in London or New York. Or not at all' (149, 150). Viewing 'Toronto's approval as a stigma,' they focus their ambition on England (156). Finally, in 1955 when Jake is twenty-five, 'He and Luke set out to conquer' (177). The reverse imperialism implied by the verb 'conquer' is subtly reinforced in the description of their exhilaration 'as they slid out of Quebec City into the broadening St. Lawrence' (177). This passage inverts Northrop Frye's famous description of early Europeans' fearful experience of entering the St. Lawrence 'like a tiny Jonah entering an inconceivably large whale ... ; to enter Canada is a matter of being silently swallowed by an alien continent' (219). Refusing to be swallowed by Canada's cultural narrowness – constricted, one might say, by its *strait*-jacket – Jake and Luke head for the expansive opportunities symbolized by a widening watercourse. That Richler's narrative then elides the Atlantic and the journey across it, hopping immediately to 'sooty Liverpool' and the London 'boat train,' may be taken to represent the complete break Jake wants to make by leaving Canada's 'cultural desert ... to nourish himself at the imperial fountainhead' (177, 178). As these binary metaphors imply, Jake is not yet ready for the relational sense of place-identity that the Atlantic's waters would represent among this cluster of images.

Despite Jake's enthusiasm, the London that Robertson Davies, Monica Gall, and Saltertonians regard as the number-one destination for an artistic career is clearly a back-up choice – one Jake questions and regrets even after twelve years there (see 175–6). Its main attraction seems to be that it is not a minor-league Canadian city, but in itself London has little appeal. Jake's boyhood associations with England make for a conventional catalogue – Big Ben, fog, Churchill, the blitz, a 'distorted' 'literary experience' of 'decency, wit, political maturity' from Jane Austen – but despite these impressions 'he had never been drawn toward it' (177, 176). His first days in London comprise a narrative of discomfort, disappointment, and doubt. He and Luke freeze in 'bone-chilling damp' hardly ameliorated by 'a spill of shillings down the gas meter.' Venturing outdoors, 'They made the required, wearying pilgrimages to the British Museum, the Tate, and Westminster, scornfully avoiding (though they were both desperate to see it) the changing of the guard' (178). The ambivalence conveyed by such ritualized activities – both the submission to the tourist's 'required' routes and the resistance to them are conventional – affiliates Richler's novel with numerous postcolonial narratives of first arrival in London, including Sam Selvon's and Anita Desai's (examined in later chapters), and Davies's and Atwood's discussed above. Even more than Atwood's Joan, Jake diminishes London through grotesque images of disgust. He finds its 'girls' to be

> depressingly lumpy, all those years of bread-and-dripping and sweets and fishpaste sandwiches having entered their young bodies like poison, coming out here as a mustache, there as a chilblain, and like lead through the teeth. ... London, he came to believe, was no more than a gum-gray, depressing city. Where the workers were short with black teeth and the others were long and pallid as forced asparagus with a tendency to stammer. (178)

The architecture is also unwelcoming: the first streetscape Jake sees is defined by 'bow windows on either side of the road, dressing tables shoved against them from within to shut out the obtrusive sun. Should it appear' (178).

Nonetheless, he stays, like the ambivalent Commonwealth migrants in many other novels, and like Richler, whose own impressions of London at age twenty provided the basis for Jake's.[17] Jake remains in London for reasons beyond his careerist preference for an imperial headwater over a colonial desert. He also has vague hopes of finding Joey, the older cousin who fascinated him as a boy and who has led a peripatetic existence in various countries since leaving Montreal in 1937. Jake, who romanticizes Joey, tells his Montreal family before leaving for London 'that he was bound to come across Joey somewhere, in England, where he was last heard from, or Israel, possibly' (159). He never does, but in both England and Israel Jake meets women with whom Joey has had relations (and who relay experiences that temper Jake's romantic view of his cousin). In London, Jake's own relation to Joey is emphasized in a second instance of mistaken identity: at Canada House he is given mail for J. Hersch that turns out to be for Joey. It is significant that the two scenes in which Jake is thought to be Joey occur in liminal spaces between nations and therefore outside any singular national identity: an immigration office at the Canada-US border and the Canadian High Commission in London. Various critics have described how these scenes foreground Joey's role as *alter ego* and foil, but as important to the establishment of Jake as psychologically a function of Joey is the construction of this pairing geographically and temporally. Insofar as the Jake-Joey duality is located anywhere, it exists in the politically indeterminate geography of international boundaries and of Jake's intinerant mental wanderings. All such unfixed spaces are spaces of relation – between governments, between identities. Even the liminal space of the Atlantic is retrospectively invoked in the opening sentence of the London scene: 'The very day of Jake's arrival, as the pavement continued to heave up at him like the deck of a Cunarder, he went to Canada House, in Trafalgar Square, to inquire about mail' (179). Spatial in-betweenness here corresponds to temporal in-betweenness: 'The very day of Jake's arrival' marks a transitional time, hence the seasick feeling, just as, in another way, Jake's aborted attempt to move to New York also occured at a time of transition: the age of twenty-one.[18]

Attending to these geographical and temporal aspects of Jake's complex affiliations to Joey enables London to be seen as a particularly apt, rather than merely convenient, setting. Prior discussions of the novel have ably shown how Jake's idealization of his cousin as an avenging Horseman marks his search for moral certainties. He constructs Joey as an imagined, romanticized Golem figure righting various international wrongs, most notably those of the Holocaust.[19] Jake's growth into self-knowledge involves demystifying Joey as a 'false god' (Ramraj 93) and recognizing his image of Joey as a product of his own self-doubt: 'What if the Horseman was a distorting mirror and we each took the self-justifying image we required of him?' he wonders at the end (433). As for Jake's relationship to his other *alter ego*, the pathetic, vicious Harry Stein is typically seen to be 'an exaggerated image' of Jake as 'defiant failure'; Harry counterpoints Joey, an image of Jake as heroic success (Davidson 155). The process of discovering a sustainable self between (and finally autonomous from) these outsized characters reveals Jake as, in Arnold Davidson's words, 'a midcentury man caught in various middles' (162): middle age (his father dies as his own third child is born); an ethical middle between selfless heroism and selfish weakness; a religious middle between German-hating fanaticism and laissez-faire secularism; and a generational middle that makes Jake and his contemporaries 'young too late, old too soon' to participate in the century's great conflicts – 'ever observers, never participants,' 'his generation was now being squeezed between two raging and carnivorous ones' (*Horseman* 80, 81).[20]

Davidson's spatial metaphor can be extended further by considering the geographical and temporal 'middles' Jake's relational identity invokes. Geographically, Jake's place-identity falls between those of Harry and Joey. Harry, 'a Londoner born, a Londoner bred,' has never left the metropolis except for a brief evacuation as a child during the war (57). Joey, born in Yellowknife and raised in various parts of Canada, leads a spatially indeterminate existence. His luggage stickers and postcards signal his free movement from continent to continent. Jake's imaginings of him repeatedly idealize Joey's purposive transnational mobility, which contrasts so starkly with his own dubious purpose (a film director being paid not to work) and restricted mobility (on criminal trial):

> The Horseman. Right now, Jake thought, maybe this very minute, he is out riding somewhere. Over the olive-green hills of the Upper Galilee or maybe in Mexico again. Or Catalonia. But, most likely, Paraguay. (30)

> Out there, he had thought, resuming his place in the dock. Out there, riding even now, St. Urbain's Horseman. ... Galloping, thundering. Over the olive-green hills of the Upper Galilee. Or possibly already in Paraguay. Out on the steaming flood plains of the Paraná, ... searching the savannas below for the unmarked track that winds into the jungle, between Puerto San Vincente and the border fortress of Carlos Antonio López, where the *Doktor* waits, unaware. (64)

Jake, born and raised in Montreal, has lived in Toronto and London and travelled to Israel and Germany. His place-identity therefore falls in the 'middle' of Harry's and Joey's, and he is drawn towards both the rootedness that Harry represents and the rootlessness of Joey. Temporally he can also be located between a Horseman identified with a romanticized past and a Harry associated with a future of uncertain appeal.

Specifically, Jake's Horseman fantasies associate Joey with historic causes (the Spanish Civil War, the Arab-Israeli conflict, the Holocaust), and Joey's equestrian pursuit of the Nazi '*Doktor*' Mengele turns him into 'an old-fashioned hero' modelled after comic books and cowboy movies (Osachoff 39). He seems to exist not only in a nebulous place but a misty, nostalgic time – 'Still yesterday,' as Asunción time is called in Jake's early-morning dream (3). Harry, first described in connection with the blitz – an event that puts him, however unheroically, at the centre of a 'Jewish War' from which Jake was safely distant – emerges more importantly as representative of a future-looking 'swinging London' that Jake is tempted by but continually rejects (19, 217). As Stephen Inwood writes in his history of London, the city's image was made over in the late 1960s with the help of an influential *Time* magazine article that constructed '"Swinging London"' as '"a city steeped in tradition, seized by change, liberated by affluence." "In a decade dominated by youth, London has burst into bloom. It swings; it is the scene"' (867). The article's emphasis on the new – youth culture, pop music, fashion – 'did something to displace the foggy Dickensian image which had previously dominated international impressions of London' (Inwood 867). It reoriented the city's image from the past to the future.[21] In the 1960s, however, 'swinging' also connoted loosening sexual mores. While Harry embraces such swinging – it is his escapades with Ingrid that lead to the trial – Jake resists sexual temptation, not only with Ingrid but with others: he fails to enjoy an orgy (see 10–11), and while he feels his 'constancy' with Nancy is 'onerous' in light of the broken marriages and 'reprobate's license' of various friends, he remains monogamous (278). Indeed, in the same month the *Time* article was published, April 1966, Nancy buys them a house (see Inwood 867; *Horseman* 263).

Jake therefore falls in the middle: where Harry and other friends enjoy the new promiscuity available in swinging London, Jake is conservative and domestic. Where Joey is a political radical involved in historic events, Jake accepts that he is a political 'liberal' whose work 'had no importance other than the intermittent pleasure it gave him. ... After all the posturing, the assumed moral stance, he was ... no more than a provider' (283). But once he realizes that Harry and Joey are both charlatans loyal to no one but themselves, he can start to accept these aspects of his own middle-of-the-road ordinariness. In Jake's gradual, hesitant acceptance of a middling moral and ethical position, therefore, Harry and Joey become foils not just through the ways their complementary characteristics clarify his relational identity, but through the geographical and temporal 'middles' in which they help locate him.

This process of relational self-discovery tends to be extended by critics from the realm of personal psychology to that of Jewish historical identity: Jake's moral middle results from a fraught working out of his ethical responsibilities as a Jew, and he settles in the end for a kind of ambivalence. His middle position is also, however, an aspect of his Canadianness that he can recognize only by being in London. Canada, the middle power that negotiates its identity and cultural boundaries in relation to the United States and Britain, is put into perspective in London in ways that affiliate national anxieties about inferiority, absence, and weak identity with Jake's personal anxieties. He and Luke may have brought over from Canada an awareness of 'the cultural thinness of their own blood,' but in the world city they come to see this inheritance relationally:

> Adrift in a cosmopolitan sea of conflicting mythologies, only they had none. Moving among discontented commonwealth types in London, they were inclined to envy them their real grievances. South Africans and Rhodesians, *bona fide* refugees from tyranny, who had come to raise a humanitarian banner in exile; Australians, who could allude to forebears transported in convict ships; and West Indians, armed with the most obscene outrage of all, the memory of their grandfathers sold in marketplaces. What they failed to grasp was the ironic truth in Sir Wilfred [*sic*] Laurier's boast that the twentieth century would belong to Canada. For amid so many exiles from nineteenth century tyranny, heirs to injustices that could actually be set right politically, thereby lending themselves to constructive angers, only the Canadians, surprisingly, were true children of their times. Only they had packed their bags and left home to escape the hell of boredom. And find it everywhere. (182)

The sense of historical injustice that Jake's Canadianness fails to provide his Jewishness does – hence his need to identify with a mythic avenging Horseman. As the gentle irony in the depiction of young 'commonwealth types' implies, injustices are not always 'set right politically.' In one of his essays Richler provocatively says of Canada, 'We are, above all, a nation of injustice collectors. In an adolescent society, where the verities come in convenient halves only, and absolutely nobody is responsible for his own failures, round and round we go. It's a dizzying and depressing time, this country, like Stephen Leacock's famous horseman, riding off in all directions' ('O Canada' 266–7). One wonders whether Richler was thinking in this 1983 essay of a certain 1971 novel: Jake's maturation, after all, is achieved partly through his abandonment of a sense of injustice collection focused on a horseman who rides off in various directions pursuing justice. The parallels are intriguing and reinforce the idea that Jake's Canadianness is a key aspect of his identity.

Even as Jake flirts vicariously with agency through his Horseman dreams, his ambivalence about 'injustice' is apparent in the contrasting tones of two passages in which he imagines his London home invaded. In the first, 'Jake's Jewish nightmare,' 'extermination officers seeking out the Jewish vermin' raid his Hampstead house and brutally murder his three children (67). In the second, Jake is not the imagined victim of horrific injustice but the sardonic observer of 'injustice-collectors' from the 'outer, brutalized world' who he expects will someday disturb his domestic peace: 'The concentration camp survivors. The emaciated millions of India. The starvelings of Africa. ... The demented Red Guards of China are going to come, demanding theirs, followed by the black fanatics, who live only for vengeance. The thalidomide babies, the paraplegics. The insulted, the injured. Don't bother barring the door, they'll spill in through the windows' (81–2).[22] These two imaginary invasions draw on aspects of London's relatedness to the world mentioned in the novel: wartime London as a victim of Hitler's bombs during the blitz; and postwar London invaded by Commonwealth migrants armed with historical grievances they identify with the city's imperial links. Taken together, these contrasting passages express a very Canadian ambivalence in Jake about his identity (is it secure or insecure?) and his relationship to perceived 'injustice' (is he a direct or indirect victim of persecution?).

After twelve years in London, Jake has altered his view of the city and, in an introspective passage worth quoting at length, he revises his view of Canadianness based on his ambivalence towards London:

> London was almost Jake's home now, but he had mixed feelings about the place. For if the city he had come to know was no longer Big Ben, Bulldog Drummond, and the anti-Zionist fox hunters of his childhood dreams, neither could it be counted the cultural fountainhead he had sought so earnestly as a young man. Slowly, inexorably, he was being forced to pay the price of the colonial come to the capital. In the provinces, he had been able to revere London and its offerings with impunity. Fulminating in Montreal, he could agree with Auden that the dominions were *tiefste Provinz*. Scornful of all things home-baked, he was at one with Dr. Johnson, finding his country a cold and uninviting region. As his father had blamed the *goyim* for his own inadequacies, mentally billing them for the sum of his misfortunes, so Jake had foolishly held Canada culpable for all his discontents. Coming to London, finding it considerably less than excellent, he was at once deprived of his security blanket. The more he achieved, feeding the tapeworm of his outer ambitions, the larger his inner hunger. ... He would have been happiest had the capital's standards not been so readily attainable and that it were still possible for him to have icons. (281)

Here Jake's conception of place (Canada and London) is relational –
each is comprehended in relation to the other – and so is his implied
conception of nationality: Canadianness looks different in London than
it does in Canada.

In various ways, then, London proves to be uniquely qualified as a
location for Jake's conflicted exploration of his individual, ethnic, and
national identity and for the cluster of ambivalent 'middles' his mid-life
crisis prompts him to recognize. One synonym for 'middle' is 'centre,'
and throughout London's imperial past and cosmopolitan present, those
features of the metropolis that make it a centre – hub of power, cultural
source, magnet for global migrants – are a function of its position in the
middle of a multidirectional web of relations to other places, whether
through imperial administration and trade or contemporary travel, finance, and culture. London, in other words, is both central and in-
between. Robert Young offers a compelling image of the Greenwich
Observatory and the meridian that runs through it as a symbol of
London's paradoxical role as both consolidating centre – the 'zero
point' of global time and space – and heterogeneous alterity: by dividing
the world into East and West, Young argues, Greenwich symbolizes the
in-betweenness of a city 'inalienably mixed' and 'inscribed with the
alterity of place' (1–2).

In very different ways and for different reasons, Canada too is characterized by in-betweenness. Its insecure, conflicted identity is most
often defined in terms of its ambivalent relations to more assertive
(neo-)imperial nations, its essence found in the borderline interstices
and 'middles' of those relations. Psychological theories of identity formation emphasize 'crisis' and comparative peer relations as important
stages towards 'identity achievement' through the in-between time of
adolescence.[23] It is tempting therefore to read the mid-life crisis depicted in Richler's novel as allegorizing the identity crisis of an 'adolescent society' anxiously negotiating its identification with larger-than-life
others and eventually settling for an ambivalent middle ground ('O
Canada' 266). In the absence of New York (and the United States it
represents), London (and therefore Britain) serves primarily as a larger
'other' with a more defined – in psychological terms, more 'achieved' –
identity, as the Horseman and Harry do for Jake. Secondarily London
serves Richler's narrative as a place undergoing a mid-life (or post-
retirement?) crisis of its own, as Commonwealth migration prompts it to
rethink its identity as a function of its (post)imperial relations.

Allegorical readings of novels can be dangerously reductive, and insisting on this one would risk oversimplifying Richler's narrative. Nonetheless, what it distils and therefore helps to clarify are the overlapping layers of signification made available to the reader. Unpacking the novel's intricate vision of relational identity means coming to terms with Jake as an individual, a Jew, a Canadian, and a Londoner. This entails considering the involvements through which each of these aspects of his identity emerges and the relations between the aspects themselves – Jake as Jewish Canadian, Jake as Canadian Londoner, and so on. Richler offers many points of intersection in this quintessentially relational novel.

The Big Wide World

St. Urbain's Horseman plays a pivotal role in this chapter's selective genealogy of Canadian literary Londons. The only novel to probe metropolitan Canadianness through the story of a young man rather than a young woman, it looks 'back' to the London narratives of Swan, Davies, and Atwood in the ways it (allegorically or otherwise) thematizes national identity through individual self-fashioning.[24] Like Davies, Richler portrays London preferentially, as a place where an artistic career not possible in Canada may be pursued, though he is more inclined to qualify the binary view. His novel anticipates more recent books by Kate Pullinger and Catherine Bush in its retrospective rendering of the expatriate experience. Like Jake, the thirtysomething protagonists of Pullinger's *The Last Time I Saw Jane* (1996) and Bush's *The Rules of Engagement* (2000) have been in London for at least a decade and recall earlier experiences in Canada and London through memory-based flashbacks. All three novels portray London as a point of relational access to 'the world'; the city's worldly dimensions provide a necessary framework for the ethical self-investigation of the central characters. While for Davies's Monica London provides a springboard to a worldly education and international experience, 'the world' in this context means Europe, and Davies's 1950s London is still quite unproblematically English. Similarly, Atwood's Joan uses London as a springboard to an international existence that takes her back to Toronto and onwards to Spain. The London of Richler, Pullinger, and Bush, however, is much more fully and multiply linked to the world; it is also more visibly multicultural. It is a transnational space that in various ways – demographically, historically, imaginatively, politically – includes and engages with numerous elsewheres.

Doreen Massey's relational model of place captures this aspect of London. Massey, as noted in the previous chapter, argues against a

concept of place as 'bounded, ... as singular, fixed and unproblematic in
its identity' and defined against 'the other which lies beyond' it; instead,
she advocates a view of places as 'open and porous,' their identities
defined 'through the specificity of the mix of links and interconnections *to* that "beyond"' (*Space* 5). Because 'the social relations
which constitute a locality increasingly stretch beyond its borders,' she
writes, 'it seems that you can sense the simultaneous presence of everywhere in the place where you are standing' (162). But while some
theorists (and regular citizens) find the fluidity and multiplicity of
our increasingly globalized and multicultural places disorienting, Massey opposes 'reactionary' efforts to shore up more stable and bounded
place-identities (162). She shows how a relational, 'extra-verted' view
of place can be enabling as it integrates 'the global and the local'
('Power-Geometry' 66). Michel Foucault makes a comparable point in
his essay 'Of Other Spaces':

> We are in the epoch of simultaneity: we are in the epoch of juxtaposition,
> the epoch of the near and far, of the side-by-side, of the dispersed. We are at
> a moment, I believe, when our experience of the world is less that of a long
> life developing through time than that of a network that connects points
> and intersects with its own skein. (22)

But if Foucault (like many theorists) implies that space and time are
separate, Massey argues that we must think of space as 'four-dimen-
sional' – as constituted by and impacting on the dynamic changes of time
– and 'insists on the inseparability of time and space, on their joint
constitution through the interrelations between phenomena; on the
necessity of thinking in terms of space-time' (*Space* 261, 269).

While Massey and Foucault are writing about places and spaces in
general, London is especially suited to being envisioned as a global
locality, a hub in a weblike network of spatial and temporal relations.
Moreover, by the 1990s, when Pullinger's and Bush's novels are set,
London was much more conscious of and comfortable with its own
transnational identity than it had been in the 1960s. The immigrants so
often resisted in the 1950s and 1960s as a threat to white Englishness
were, as their numbers and cultural influence grew, beginning to be
recognized as contributors to a multicultural identity that was the city's
imperial inheritance. A revised sense of what it meant to be 'British' or a
'Londoner' emerged as a function of changes not only in London but
internationally. Post–Cold War shifts in national boundaries and influ-

ence, combined with an increasingly mobile global populace, meant that throughout the world traditional place-identities were becoming destabilized. According to the editors of *Space and Place: Theories of Identity and Location*, 'The presumed certainties of cultural identity, firmly located in particular places which housed stable cohesive communities of shared tradition and perspective, though never a reality for some, were increasingly disrupted and displaced for all' (Carter et al. vii). Describing this phenomenon theoretically requires the assertion of 'a more fluid and relational notion of difference' and 'identity' (x).

Another way to express this idea, following Paul Gilroy, is by reorienting identity away from the static metaphor of *roots to* places and towards a more dynamic focus on *routes among* places – a more pluralized and relational concept of place-identity (see *Black* 133; cf. Crang 171–2). As David Morley and Kevin Robins succinctly put it, ever-larger numbers of people are 'facing the question not so much of where they are from, as of where they are between.' Morley and Robins argue, quoting Alexander Lisser, that 'in the context of centuries of imperialism and cross-cultural contact, we would do better to think of human societies as open systems "inextricably involved with other aggregates, near and far, in weblike, netlike connections"' (129). One logical culmination of such views is the submergence of 'place' entirely by what Manuel Castells calls 'a *space of flows*' that has emerged 'as the logic of dominant organizations detaches itself from the social constraints of cultural identities and local societies through the powerful medium of information technologies' (6). However, the teleology of a world of porous boundaries and places evacuated of social meaning that a pure 'space of flows' would create is resisted by theorists who seek to preserve a role for place.[25] Erica Carter and her coeditors assert that 'if places are no longer the clear supports of our identity, they nonetheless play a potentially important part in the symbolic and psychical dimension of our identifications' (xii).

London was, of course, only one place whose traditional identity altered as it became more multicultural and more aware of itself *as* multicultural in the 1980s and 1990s. Canada went through such changes as well, and Toronto, which has adopted 'The World within a City™' as its official tourism slogan (Toronto), shares with London the distinction of being among the most multicultural cities in the world. As emplaced identities formerly available in cities and other locales were challenged by global movements, Canadians, too, were rethinking their collective identity as a society. In Morton Weinfeld's words, 'Canada [in the 1990s] is becoming a microcosm of the planet, blessed with a growing roster of ethnic and cultural groups contributing to the ever-elusive Canadian identity' (120). For Reg Whitaker, such local and global changes lead Canadians to an enhanced sense of relational identity:

> In a traditional world, we are rooted, placed, located; our identities are ascribed, not achieved. In modernity, we shape and reshape ourselves in interaction with others. There is great promise here, but great insecurity and anxiety as well. We recognize ourselves as we are reflected in the eyes of others. In other words, our recognition of ourselves lies in our recognition by others. (77)

Canadian philosopher Charles Taylor, in his influential essay 'The Politics of Recognition,' shows how relational (or 'dialogical') conceptions of personal identity underlie contemporary demands for cultural recognition (32). Such demands have prompted Canada's Multiculturalism Act and more complex ways of conceptualizing Canadian identity than the old 'two solitudes' model of English and French Canada allowed. Indeed, for Ian Angus, 'Multiculturalism as a social ideal requires that the plurality of ethno-cultures be seen as a *key content of a shared national identity*' (144). It also, logically, entails de-emphasizing the old model of relational identity – which positioned an implicitly homogeneous Canada in relation to the United States and Britain – in favour of a national identity characterized in terms of relations *to* many elsewheres and relations within Canada among peoples originally *from* many elsewheres. For Angus, multiculturalism should be seen not as a threat to national identity (as it is sometimes seen to be), but its foundation (see 166–7).[26]

It is within these contexts that Pullinger's novel extends the incipiently transnational London of Richler. *The Last Time I Saw Jane* articulates London's spatial and historical connectedness as a quality of access to 'the world' that the city stimulates in a reflective consciousness. Audrey Robbins, like Pullinger herself, initially moves to London from British Columbia at twenty or twenty-one, an age when 'she longed for the big wide world out there, she was waiting to put an ocean between herself and that place' (23). In that image of the ocean as an in-between space that both separates and connects distant places – and across which the transformations of imperial power and postimperial migration happen – Pullinger establishes her controlling metaphor for the London of this novel. The city may be, for Audrey, 'a place she could sink deep into, sink everything, and yet not drown' (4), but her London is more than a place to be immersed *in*. Through the fluid movements of consciousness and narrative, this is also a London to be transported *from* – a city that, like Conrad's Thames, like Audrey's mind, and like Pullinger's ocean-crossing and transhistorical plot, continually spills beyond urban space to connect with the wider world.

Audrey goes to London 'to get away from my family, from people who thought they knew who I was' (39). On arrival, she is smitten with 'city-love, and a love affair so true and strong she felt the city embrace her, she clutched it to her breast' (132). Her spirit of exuberant possession – 'this city is mine! Mine' (132) – is qualified by a sense of partial exclusion:

> She arrived in the city expecting to find herself inside the beating heart of everything, but instead found there were large parts of city life that she couldn't find a way into. There were tensions and divisions. She opened her mouth to speak and was transfixed by her own difference. It was like discovering that she had been adopted. (157)

Nonetheless, although 'some people complained that Britain was a small country, cramped, dark, too full,' Audrey 'found large-ness, largesse, in London she discovered the world. The city seemed enormous, uncharted, and in some ways, unnavigable, a place of real mystery. She launched herself upon its wide sea, swam the depth, and found something that belonged to her, something that made her feel she belonged' (158). In keeping with the ocean metaphor, however (fluid and metamorphic, oceans 'belong' to many nations but to no single one), Audrey disturbs that sense of easy belonging: 'London is a place for unbelonging,' she says and then offers a mediating thought: 'Everyone hovers somewhere between belonging and homelessness' (158). The same ambivalence applies to her Canadian affiliations. As a child, Audrey 'was determined never to feel at home' in Victoria after her family moved there (58); as an adult Londoner, 'Canada was home, she thought, dousing herself in irony' (115).

Her uncertain belongings lead her alternately to assert and to question her national identity: 'she was a Canadian – that said it, right there. She was her nationality. Wasn't everybody? Who is English, who is British, she wondered, of all the people I see in these streets, who is foreign, and what does it mean?' (157). As Rosemary George writes in *The Politics of Home*, 'Imagining a home is as political an act as is imagining a nation' (6); the imagined nation in *The Last Time I Saw Jane* is not Britain, however, but Canada. After several years of dwelling in London, Audrey insistently pulls her narrative temporally and spatially beyond present-day London, seeking links with Canadian pasts whose relations to her

metropolitan life she glimpses only dimly at first. The narrative repeatedly criss-crosses the Atlantic, into and back out of Canadian spaces to
which her life in London becomes linked through an intricate web of
recurring images and narrative patterns. The most important of these
involve attachments to friends, lovers, and family (with themes of loyalty
and betrayal), race (with images of skin, blood, and miscegenation),
and water (with scenes of bathing, swimming, and drowning). Pullinger
weaves this web through several plot lines, between which her narrative
shuttles and through which she articulates her vision of the expatriate
metropolitan Canadian as an in-between, transnational, oceanic kind
of self.

The narrative segments set in London focus on Audrey's sexual relationship with Jack, an African American film producer, and her friendship with Shereen, a lawyer raised in Calcutta, with whom Jack also
becomes involved. Both seem to be more psychologically settled in London than Audrey, though Jack's non-committal view – 'too lazy' to move,
he says, 'I'm as at home here as I am anywhere' (54) – epitomizes his
rootless, detached, postmodern approach to metropolitan dwelling. He
likes London's 'fluidity' (54); Shereen also images her attachment to
London through water, describing her arrival there at seventeen as 'my
real Western baptism' (37): 'I held my breath and slipped into the
stream like a fish, like a mermaid' (37–8), she says, claiming to be 'good
at jumping cultures' (38). But although she says, 'London is my home,'
she 'repeated the sentence as though to reassure herself' and still recognizes the primacy of her natal culture: '"My mother thinks she has to
keep me Bengali," she continued. "She doesn't realize that despite the
veneer ... there isn't anything else I could possibly be"' (38). These
statements may suggest a simplistic binary of authentic versus performed
identity – by 'veneer,' Shereen means her London hair and clothes – but
Pullinger reverses the alignment in Audrey's case: 'Sometimes Audrey
thought her own sense of herself as Canadian had become anglicized,
romanticized. She could become Ur-Canadian when the need arose,
displaying national characteristics like a performing dog. Yes, I can ski, I
can paddle a canoe, I speak French badly, "oot and aboot," I adore ice
hockey' (25). Beyond the clichés (reminiscent of Monica Gall's performances), Audrey's national identity becomes a subject of serious narrative exploration, prompted in part by the more nuanced use Pullinger
makes of another 'veneer' that becomes an identity marker – skin.

Images of skin recur in Audrey's relationship with Jack. The idea of
'his skin against hers, their flesh together ... turned her on'; while this

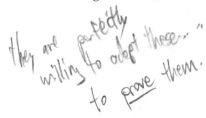
they are perfectly willing to adopt those... " to prove them.

description seems to slip rhetorically from an image of black and white skin as separate and contrasting to an image of racial blending, the next sentence invokes such blending only to deny it: '"It's the kiddies I worry about," she could hear her father saying. Well, there are no kiddies, there would be no kiddies, and anyway, what if there were?' (25). Audrey, who often writes about 'racial politics' for women's magazines, intrigued by 'that intersection of cultures that London provides' (22, 21), indirectly suggests the racial blending that the oceanic crossings of empire and migration have enabled in another image of blended skin: when African American Jack begins sleeping with Indian Shereen, the jilted Audrey imagines the 'love-slick' of their 'creamy brown skin-tones poured together' (136). The novel is full of domestic scenes mentioning Jack's or Audrey's wet skin or body in a shower or bath, sometimes echoing references to larger bodies of water in separate narrative lines. In one scene, Jack's skin is stained blue by a rain-soaked shirt, 'the dye fading without disappearing altogether' even after a bath (44). Through these various passages, Pullinger brings skin and liquidity together to suggest intermingling and metamorphosis in contexts ranging from the substantial (sex and miscegenation) to the trivial (stained skin). The significance of these links is not fully apparent in the emotionally muted, low-stakes world of Audrey's London affairs, but Pullinger capitalizes on their resonances as figures for hybrid, 'mixed blood' identities (103) in a separate plot line involving James Douglas, the Hudson's Bay Company official who married the half-Native Amelia Connolly and later became the first governor of British Columbia.

Audrey studied Douglas at university and now, years later, is drawn back to his 'cross-bred world, a place struck at the brink of modernity' (18). Thinking that Douglas is 'sending her messages, oblique and personal, from another century' (15), she has a series of dreams narrating the life story of a Scot so transformed by the New World that, after settling 'as far west as he could go without falling off the land-shelf into the Pacific,' he eventually became 'entirely remade, not one inch of his skin, not one hair on his head, of his former self would remain' (5). Audrey's dreams focus on Douglas's complex imbrication in the politics of miscegenation. Douglas is horrified when Amelia's father, William Connolly, repudiates his marriage to Suzanne Pas de Nom, the Cree woman whom he wed à la façon du pays, and disowns the children of that marriage, including Amelia. Connolly claims that his first marriage was 'never properly sanctified, a country marriage, a bush marriage, of the forest not the city' (102–3), and moves on to wed a white woman in

Montreal. For Douglas and Amelia, Connolly has 'repudiated the very thing upon which they were building their lives, mixed blood, the very thing that ran through their veins' (103). Douglas remains loyal to Amelia, and, in a late section of the novel entitled 'Between' (195), Pullinger recreates Douglas's childhood world in order to provide a psychological accounting for that steadfastness.

Following recent biographers, Pullinger proposes that Douglas, born in British Guiana, was a quadroon, the son of John Douglas, a Scot, and Martha Ann Ritchie, the Barbadian daughter of a freed slave and a white planter.[27] The narrative describes the trauma of six-year-old James as he is wrenched from the mixed world of the Demerara River, which 'sheltered a great herd of nations' (204–5), across the Atlantic and away from his mother forever once his father abandons his own 'bush marriage' to wed a white woman in Scotland. John Douglas, like William Connolly, elects to keep his two worlds and wives separate, 'across the Sargasso Sea' from each other: 'North. South. Old. New. Empire and colony' (213, 214). The punctuation here suggests both separation and connection, and the reference to the Sargasso Sea implies, as in Jean Rhys's *Wide Sargasso Sea*, the dangerous entanglements that a nineteenth-century British–West Indian marriage could involve if relocated to Britain; by compartmentalizing his lives and his wives, John Douglas avoids the fate of Rhys's Rochester character. But what for John is a clean and easy break is not so for James, whose Scottish childhood involves both separation from and continuity with his former life:

> At the age of six, James Douglas made the long Atlantic crossing, south to north, west to east, a distance much greater than its mileage could indicate. In Scotland James began to unlearn his mother, to forget her and, in the act of forgetting, remake himself.
>
> But, for a while in that Lanarkshire boarding school, he did long for his mother, transfixed by the ice which formed in swirling patterns on the river in winter. He longed for the soft and sudden changes of the Demerara air, his mother's hand on his brow. Years later, when he reached Vancouver Island, his 'Eden,' he woke one summer morning with the uncanny sensation of having returned to his mother's house. (214)

His loyalty to Amelia emerges as a reaction against their shared experience of having been the children of mixed-race families broken up by the racial politics of their times and places. James refuses to do what both of their fathers did – abandon a 'country' marriage for a 'city' one – and he and Amelia emerge in Audrey's dreams as pioneers of a particular kind of modernity – of New World newness.

Pullinger establishes many correlations between her nineteenth-century 'country' narrative and her late-twentieth-century 'city' one – through the juxtapositions of her crosscutting stories, through their shared racial themes, through the likelihood that Douglas was Audrey's ancestor, and through Audrey's detachment from her own father (who accidentally kills her mother in the novel's first scene). A further intriguing connection can be seen in these narratives' shared structures of triangulation. Conflicted relationships among interracial threesomes – Jack and his two lovers, Connolly and his two wives, John Douglas and his two wives – not only echo each other but are also echoed in the geographical triangulation of Douglas's story: British Guiana to Scotland to British Columbia. Audrey writes at one point that 'sometimes it feels as though all colonial history, all of modern British history, somehow leads back to slavery. The very fabric of the cities in which we live' (217); like the triangular, ocean-spanning structure of slavery's 'middle passage' (Europe, Africa, the Americas), the Douglas story has a spatial, oceanic fullness that the narrower London-Victoria-Toronto axis of Audrey's contemporary narrative lacks. Indeed, as the reader shuttles between two centuries and their similar-but-different triangular relationships, it is hard not to think that, while Audrey's urban entanglements are an echo of Douglas's global ones, they offer a faint, reduced, lower-stakes version. Reviewers of the novel certainly found them so, calling Audrey and Jack's affair 'a dysfunctional modern equivalent' of James and Amelia's 'loving relationship' (Stead) and complaining about Audrey's 'coolness and detachment' (Carey) and 'dulled responses' (Boddy). Understanding what these contrasts of emotional and spatial scale might imply about the novel's vision of London, Canada, and postimperial dwelling requires attending briefly to two further plot lines.

The first involves Shula Cronin, a maverick Toronto professor for whom Audrey works as a research assistant at the British Library. Cronin attracts controversy by arguing against Quebec nationalist ideology:

'Those nationalists – at their most extreme – believe in racial purity. They think the Québécois are a race. They do – believe me. I am going to write a book that shows how those people, that race, from Samuel de Champlain onward, are descended from mixed blood – the blood of the English as well

as the French, the Algonquin, Huron, Iroquois, Mohawk ... the blood of the
French empire – West Indian, Vietnamese, Haitian ... and that their notion
of racial purity is as backward and ill-informed as that of the Ku Klux Klan.'
(118–19; ellipses in the original)

Cronin also claims that Quebec's land belongs to its indigenous people,
if anyone; moreover, 'same goes for the water, the right to sell hydro-
power to the Americans' (119). Her desire to push Canadian history and
identity beyond the 'two solitudes' model and towards a three-way (or
more) intersection of French, English, and Native peoples is validated to
a degree by the Douglas narrative; presumably, even the 'white' Audrey
has traces of Cree and African blood if she descends from Douglas and
Amelia. Cronin's linking of water to questions of national property and
international exchange is of interest in a novel saturated with images of
water as a signifier of in-betweenness, metamorphosis, and transnational
connection; her account of a plane crash that she survived, in which one-
third of the passengers drowned in a British Columbia lake, is also
significant. 'The plane,' Cronin says, 'rested too deep to salvage but they
tell me that on a clear day if you fly north of Fort St James, over Stuart
Lake, you can see the outline of the wrecked plane down in the water,
like a shadow of the one you are in' (187–8). The lake, containing the
trapped people and the wrecked stuff of history, eerily duplicates and
'shadows' the present – not unlike the shadowing of Audrey's London
narrative by Douglas's historical one.

Cronin's escape from drowning connects this story to the second
additional narrative interwoven with the Audrey-Jack and Douglas-Amelia
stories: Audrey's account of her teenage friendship with Jane and their
secret relationship with a teacher, David, at his seaside house. Although
not interracial, this threesome resembles the novel's other triangular
liaisons in several ways. Audrey's unlikely friendship with Jane overcomes
vast differences between them: in their looks, their social cliques, their
success at school, their ambitions. Audrey, initially the third-wheel witness of David and Jane's transgressive affair, later sleeps with David
herself; when Jane finds out, she says to Audrey, 'You betrayed me' (232).
The Jane plot culminates near the end of the novel in two successive
scenes that involve bodies of water and the disappearance of bodies *in*
water. In the first scene, the two friends have a nighttime swim in a
British Columbia lake. Audrey asks herself, 'what lay beneath the blackness of the surface? She imagined she could see down through the clear
water as she swam – dead trees decaying on the bottom, swaying water

weeds, fish, sunken debris' (228). When she brushes against Jane, her friend's skin feels 'rubbery and cold, dead' (228), and after surfacing from a deep dive Audrey can't see Jane and panics that she has 'disappeared' (229); it turns out that Jane is huddled on the shore, convinced that Audrey herself has disappeared, 'swum away' and left her behind (230). Later, of course, Audrey will 'swim away' to London's metropolitan 'sea,' but by then Jane will have disappeared for real. The next scene describes Audrey's last sight of a 'heavily pregnant' and unhappy Jane (231), who – after bitterly accusing Audrey of betrayal with David – mysteriously vanishes. They are crossing the Georgia Strait on a ferry in foggy, rough conditions; after their conversation, Audrey sees Jane on the outside deck heading for a handrail, but then 'a great wave washed over the prow' and Jane disappears: 'It was as though the sea had opened up and swallowed her, taken her away' (233). Although she searches for Jane without success, Audrey at her most emotionally detached tells no one what she saw and never inquires if Jane is still alive. That evening she decides to move to London, and over a decade later she has no further knowledge about Jane's fate.

An intriguing contrast emerges from this scene: Jane, pregnant by an unappealing man and doomed to live a dull, limited life in British Columbia, apparently drowns, while Audrey expands her spatial and cultural horizons by crossing the Atlantic to live in London, the 'wide sea' on which she can swim the 'uncharted' 'depth' (158) 'and yet not drown' (4). Pullinger, who has written of her interest in 'the complexities of belonging and identity, the shifting and cross-cultural experience which has become common to many people as we move about on the planet' (Introduction), does not unequivocally valorize the migrant subject in this novel; to do so would be to favour John Douglas and William Connolly over their less physically and socially mobile first wives. But through the stories of Audrey and James Douglas, and the cross-referencing among her various triangular plot lines, a relational model of expatriate identity emerges as a privileged form of (post)imperial dwelling. Audrey's Canadianness becomes an important part of that identity – one that increasingly helps to reflect and inform her London life – but it is only one node in a multiply located being, an aspect of her identity that is alternately submerged and afloat in her consciousness. For Pullinger, the self is most fully equipped to swim, not sink, when it is most aware of its syncretic dimensions – its multiple and hybrid connectedness across oceans of spatial, temporal, cultural, and racial distance and difference.

Here the novel reflects some postcolonial thinking. Robert Young shows how the concept of hybridity, a nineteenth-century physiological concept tied to race, has 'in the twentieth century ... been reactivated to describe a cultural' phenomenon (6), and theorists such as Homi Bhabha, Stuart Hall, and Paul Gilroy have been painstaking in their investigations of cultural hybridity, syncretism, and impurity in both European cities and colonial contact zones. By using the ocean – along with smaller bodies of water from lakes to bathtubs to raindrops – as a controlling metaphor connoting transformation, life and death (swimming and drowning), the fluid mingling of races and cultures that empire and postimperial migration enable, and distance and connectedness across time and space, Pullinger creates her own version of the global in-between space that Gilroy invokes in *The Black Atlantic*. For Gilroy, the Atlantic is *the* space of black history; for Pullinger, the sea is the space of an expatriate identity fully conscious of and enhanced by its 'unbelonging' and in-betweenness.

Well suited though this metaphor of a watery, fluid city may be for the contemporary migrant's London – recall Richler's Jake 'adrift in a cos-mopolitan sea' (182) – it has also been used to describe much earlier incarnations of the city. The historian Roy Porter writes that as Tudor London expanded outside City walls it became 'lapped by a turbulent metropolitan sea' into which poured a 'tidal wave of migration' (54, 58). Joseph McLaughlin, in his study of *fin-de-siècle* representations of Lon-don, quotes Sherlock Holmes's sidekick, Dr Watson, describing London as 'that great cesspool into which all the loungers and idlers of the Empire are irresistibly drained' (2). As McLaughlin interprets this century-old image, it sounds incipiently postcolonial and entirely com-patible with Pullinger's relational metropolis:

> In the sanitary metaphor of Dr. Watson, what is crucial is not whether he accurately portrays London as the festering effect of Britain's imperial activities during the preceding centuries and, in the process, ignores London's role as empire's enlightening agent and first cause; instead, it is his evocation of an empire imagined as one vast plumbing network in which London is neither beginning nor end, but rather a location – a 'pool' – into which things flow, and out of which things ooze and bubble. This difference in the spatial imagination is crucial. As absolute geographi-cal difference (a world of us versus them) gives way to a world that is increasingly without boundaries (a world of us *as* them), personal identity becomes a matter of epistemological uncertainty and anxiety. (2–3)

This is an early version of the 'impurity' and 'mongrelization' Salman Rushdie has influentially valorized in our nomadic and diasporic world (*Imaginary* 394) and the oceanic decentring impulse of Gilroy's 'black Atlantic' paradigm.

For Pullinger, the metaphor of London as a sea from which the self can become linked to spatial and historical elsewheres – through travel and memory, through ancestry and nationality – emphasizes the city's transoceanic associations with empire and figures the metropolis itself as an in-between, transnational space. Her London is more important for the global, century-crossing, immaterial connections that its imperial history and international citizenry prompt than for its own material identity. This preference is signalled by the novel's vagueness about location. Apart from public spaces such as the British Library, the reader rarely knows where in the 'colossal and embracing' metropolis this narrative is taking place (48). When Audrey rides the Underground, no lines and stations are mentioned; when buildings are described, details are either absent or generic. This nebulousness suits Pullinger's conception of London's relatedness as a function of its ability to prompt the mind to transcend the city's spatial and temporal limits in order to access 'the world.' It becomes a city of the imagination.

There is a tension, nonetheless, in this image of London. It is a tension of scale and depth made apparent through the constantly expanding and contracting movements of Pullinger's narrative shuttle and through the differences between the literal and the metaphorical oceans and journeys she invokes. If London is a 'sea' in the sense that it provides access to 'the big wide world' (including the Canada from which it initially invites escape), then, in keeping with the city's physical smallness compared to that world (and also its diminished stature since its imperial heyday), the triangular narrative that it houses seems to be smaller, shallower, ethically and emotionally of less moment than the larger, imperial-era Douglas story. Perhaps, with 'the world' having collapsed in on London as a function of the empire's 'reinvasion of the centre,' this shrinking of scale is appropriate: Audrey's love life may reflect the 'time-space compression' that David Harvey associates with postmodernity (*Condition* 284), with the mix of reduction, simultaneity, and supersaturation that his concept implies. And even though, as the *TLS* reviewer notes, 'the novel is less interested in celebrating postmodern rootlessness than in charting the search for home and history' (Boddy), the history it pursues puts Audrey's London life into perspective in a way that both expands her consciousness through imaginative engagements and casts into sharp relief the smaller scale of her actual romantic entanglements. Fittingly, the novel ends with an image of a watery London that is both cozily small and evanescently boundless: Audrey and Shereen in Audrey's sitting room 'tucked up on a wet night with the city all around us' (247). To dwell intelligently in Pullinger's London is to know the city and the self as surrounded and extended by the fluid waters of (post)imperial space-time.

Duelling and Dwelling in Toronto and London

Setting her novel in and between two places that are both more visibly multicultural than they once were, Pullinger uses London to contextualize Canada. One reason the young Audrey goes to London is her boredom with British Columbia, where everyone seems 'basically the same' and which sees itself as 'a white British place' despite its Asian and European immigrants (126, 127). Audrey wants a change from this perceived homogeneity: 'Her parents' friends were all white, and that seemed ordinary'; 'she craved difference' and seeks it in London (127, 157). The 'difference' she finds there is described in ways that tellingly complicate the word's racial associations: 'When Audrey first came to London she was amazed by how black the city could be,' but it is when 'she opened her mouth to speak' that she became 'transfixed by her own difference. It was like discovering that she had been adopted' (157). This passage suggests that difference *out there* is visible (more 'black' people than expected), but the difference she discovers *in herself* begins as audible (her different accent) and then acquires a racial dimension in the reference to adoption. This is confusing: to whom does Audrey feel suddenly unrelated? The implied answer is the British, the people of the 'mother country,' but why? Because of London's surprising blackness (a visible, racial difference), or because of the different voices in which British and British Columbian people speak (an audible, national/cultural difference)?

The categories of race, nation, and culture have a long history of being conflated, and Pullinger's oblique blurring of them resembles more direct instances of category confusion in two other Canadian London novels. Robertson Davies's Monica, after the deflating reception her performative Canadianness garners in Wales, is advised by the American John Ripon to conceal her nationality:

'Why don't you try passing as white? You know about the light-skinned Negroes in the States, who move North and live among whites as one of themselves? The only way to get on in peace with the people over here is to conceal as well as you can that you're not one of themselves – pass as white. Minimize the differences; don't call attention to them. This country's full of Canadians, Australians, New Zealanders, yes and Americans, all passing as white, because if they let it be known what they are, the natives will patronize the living bejesus out of them.' (184–5)

Monica is white, and so presumably are the settler-colony nationals to whom Ripon refers. But even in a novel whose only other foregrounding of race is Domdaniel's Jewishness – and in a 1950s London represented as traditionally white and English – the implication is that the descendants of English colonials who settled the New World and the antipodes are not, somehow, as 'white' as the English. Ripon does not say the expected 'pass as English'; what begins as an analogy (with blacks in America) becomes a state of being. A colonial background equals false or inauthentic whiteness. Monica's success depends on abandoning her Canadianness; she outgrows Salterton's limited cultural outlook and moral principles, becoming more English, more worldly, and, apparently, more 'white.' Davies's non-racial themes of colonial inferiority and metropolitan education are confusingly couched in the language of race. Pullinger's less obvious race/nation/culture blending, by contrast, is linked thematically to her use of London as a space of difference from which to explore questions of racial, national, and (multi)cultural identity back in Canada.

Arcadia Hearne, the Canadian narrator of Catherine Bush's *The Rules of Engagement*, also expresses national difference in the lexicon of race. She remarks that shortly after arriving in London she could 'pass as English' by imitating British speech, dousing her *London A–Z* map-book in the bathtub 'to make it look more weatherworn,' and having an English-sounding name (39).[28] Despite the reference to 'passing,' however, 'whiteness' is not mentioned; the London in which Arcadia lives is, like Pullinger's and unlike Davies's, a city defined by its transnational connections to national and racial others. Arcadia, like Audrey, has lived in London for ten years since she aborted her undergraduate degree at age twenty-one and fled Canada secretly 'to escape the past' (38). Two young men with whom she was romantically involved fought a duel over her in a Toronto ravine, an event she witnessed but did not stop; without knowing whether the man who was shot would live, and without leaving a note for her family, she vanished across the ocean. 'I burned with desire,' she says, 'for transformation, to create a new life' (39); 'I wanted a blank slate. No traces. *Terra nullius*' (38). As that metaphor suggests, Bush's

novel, like Pullinger's, is steeped in geography. Moreover, its probings of
the migrant subject's relationship to her own past and the wider world to
which the 'vast metropolis' connects her (71) are similarly figured through
images of urban space, racial/national 'others,' and bodies of water.

Arcadia moved to London as a safe 'haven' and assumed she would
never return (13). But ten years later she is drawn out of isolation
through experiences that force her to reconsider her own agency –
specifically, her willingness to intervene at sites of conflict, whether in
interpersonal affairs or international ones. Her refusal to prevent the
duel continues to haunt her, yet her life in London parallels that earlier
detachment. She works for a think-tank called The Centre for Contemporary War Studies, where she theorizes about military intervention
from a secure position of non-involvement far from any war-zones. In her
office, she is both protected and connected:

> These rooms are our shell, the carapace that hides the telecommunication
> lines and fiber-optic cable and complex binary codes that store our infor-
> mation and connect us to each other, to colleagues, and to conflicts around
> the globe. We cross borders with ease this way, even though the computers
> are chained to bolts in the floor. (15)

As these spatial metaphors make clear, the border crossing is only virtual.
It exists in the abstract space of McLuhan's global village or Castells's
space of flows rather than in a material world of real, separate places.
The 'white cocoon' of Arcadia's flat contains an old-fashioned, low-tech
version of that same virtual connectedness: one wall is covered with
'maps dotted with pins and pencil lines to demarcate the world's rest-
lessly new and shifting borders' (13). These are the hot-spots to which
she and London are connected but from which, she believes, they are
protected. Arcadia glibly excuses herself from more tangible links: 'The
work I do is perfectly valid. I'm a theorist. I hardly need to race about the
globe. Besides, I value safety. And here in London I've found a sort of
safety' (27). Her views are anachronistic, recalling an old idea of London
as a place linked to and acting upon foreign territories while remaining
safely untouched by their distant events and retaining a hermetically
'English' identity. Just as that idea has been challenged – by scholars'
insistence that London and Englishness were not just creators but products of empire, by relational models of place, and by the city's postwar
'invasion' by its erstwhile empire – Arcadia is forced to reconsider her
avoidance of risks and real border-crossing. In doing so, she wrestles with

some of the urgent questions that David Morley and Kevin Robins ask in *Spaces of Identity*: 'How do we position ourselves within the new global cultural space? How do we reconcile our cognitive existence in hyperspace, in the virtual space of electronic networks, with our bodily existence in localised space?' (38). Arcadia is prodded into reassessing these aspects of her London life when the outside world converges upon her and punctures her cocoon. It does so in the form of Basra Alale, the Somali refugee she is asked to assist, and Amir Barmour, the Iranian who forges passports for refugees and makes Arcadia an unwitting participant in this work. Through her involvements with Basra and Amir, Arcadia learns over the course of the novel to rethink her avoidance of risks and her self-oriented obsession with 'safety.' At the end of the novel, she is about to begin participating more actively and altruistically in zones of international friction.

Arcadia's renewed perspective on the relations between self and world is also prompted by her revisiting, through memory and a return visit, the scenes and states of paralysis her younger self inhabited at the time of the duel. As with Pullinger's Jane plot, the narrative of her former Canadian romances is spliced in as memories prompted by her current involvement with a racial and national other (Amir) in the world city of London. Bush's narrative shuttles back and forth between London in 1996 and Toronto in 1986, with the parallels between political and personal intervention – and between wars and duels – clearly drawn and reinforced. Arcadia's fascination with duels has led directly to her interest in war studies and the book she is writing on military intervention. She has read enough on the history of duelling that she 'could have drawn up a duelists' map of the city of London' (77); she views the city as a palimpsest that both conceals and reveals its violent past, observing that in London 'a history of war was mapped upon the city as scars are mapped upon a body. ... I lived in a city saturated by war culture' (84). Present-day Toronto is similarly laid over its violent past; walking at the Yonge and College intersection, Arcadia recalls a duel there in 1817, musing that there is 'blood under our feet somewhere' (223). These layerings are described as physical, if hidden, urban presences. In the immaterial realm of the mental map, Arcadia's Toronto and London also hide and reveal each other: half-asleep one morning in Toronto, she imagines that under its streets, 'like a ghost stratum, lay London, remembered, conjured London' (165).

The Rules of Engagement is a tale of two cities, each physically overlying its own history and imaginatively underlying the other through Arcadia's experiences in them. They are further linked through resemblances between Toronto's ravines and London's canals. Arcadia compares them explicitly, and both are described in separate passages as spaces of wildness and difference where people mysteriously appear and disappear; walking in these heterotopic sites is 'like entering border country' and 'leaving the rest of the city behind' (17, 69). Here Bush, like Pullinger, uses watery spaces to represent in-betweenness and transformation. The ravine where the duel takes place corresponds to the canal where Arcadia confronts Amir about his passport forging and implication of her in it; in both scenes, Arcadia poises on the brink of involvement and uninvolvement, risky intervention and safe neutrality. In the canal scene, Amir overtly challenges her penchant for detachment; he asks, 'What are the risks that you'd be willing to take?' but she later remembers the question differently: 'what I heard was not only *risks*, but *What borders are you prepared to cross?*' (146, 151). Bush's prose is peppered with references to borders and border crossing – as literal facts and as metaphors for processes of transformation (of the self, of the lives of others) that always involve a moral imperative. As Amir challenges her, Arcadia plunges from his boat into the canal; she flees from him and then, without telling him, traverses the watery border of the Atlantic to Toronto. Once there, however, haunted by both the recent conflict on the canal and the decade-old one in the ravine, she does not remain detached. As she revisits the sites and tries to find the people involved in the duel, she also helps Amir stay safe in her London flat, and she goes out of her way to find Basra in Toronto to 'make sure she's safe' (206). When Arcadia crosses the Atlantic again to return to London, it is with a new resolve resulting from her visit to Basra (and her acceptance of a passport-smuggling mission to Kenya) and also from what she has learned about the consequences of her inaction before the duel. She has come to believe that if she is going to put herself in the same category of expatriate border crossers and 'continent jumpers' as Amir (126) – who fled Iran illegally and now helps others doing likewise – and if she is going to claim expertise in global military intervention, she must leave her cocoon and attach herself more tangibly to the world.

In this novel, London can provide temporary escape, anonymity, and seclusion, but eventually its cosmopolitanism will not only enable access to the wider world but enforce engagement with it. If you are living in a place as spatially, politically, demographically, and historically connected as London, Bush implies, you cannot forever shut out the world or the past, or retain only virtual connections with them. Watering and weeding your tiny backyard garden is not enough of a way to make a haven. Larger bodies of land and water must be taken on; other selves must be made safe. In the sanctuary of Arcadia's childhood bedroom was a *trompe l'œil* ceiling with painted stars and moon; like her office at the think-tank, this is one of many images of enclosure that juxtapose safe containment with a virtual openness to the outside.[29] After Arcadia's departure, that painting was eventually erased – a symbol of her growing up and moving out into the 'real' world beyond her bedroom walls. A decade later, as her childhood home begins to seem 'eerily permeable' (191), Arcadia develops a more mature and expansive ethical position by, in effect, erasing her false image of the world outside London (and outside the walls of her flat) as a *trompe l'œil.* London long ago outgrew its walls and became elaborately related to the outer world; Arcadia begins to do the same.

Her new resolve implicitly involves a more realistic assessment of her own situation in London. Arcadia's sense of safety and security there has always been self-deceiving. She is highly aware of the city's permeability to violence from Irish outsiders: 'I learned to fear not rockets or sniper fire but suitcases, briefcases, brown paper packages. Domestic war. Phone booths. Rubbish bins. Letterboxes. Buses. Cars' (84). Because she lives in London 'illegally' she is 'gripped by the temporary. I could not shake my fear that at any moment the life I'd fashioned could be taken away' (39). She is, in T.F. Rigelhof's words, 'a refugee of sorts' (221). Becoming willing to help 'other' refugees is a way of acknowledging her own vulnerability – her kinship to them as well as her privileged state of dwelling relative to theirs.

Rigelhof also mentions Bush's debt to modernist writers such as Conrad and Thomas Mann. Her rendering of the city certainly begins in the manner Raymond Williams associates with modernist writings, in which the city becomes a function of the consciousness inhabiting and perceiving it (see Williams 239, 243–4). Modernist influences are also apparent in the ways her London and Toronto are places of chance encounters and miscellaneous strangers, about whom Arcadia speculates with an idle detachment. 'Out of curiosity,' she writes on the novel's opening page, 'I tried to imagine' how people she sees on the Underground 'would look transformed by anger' (3). In his 1903 essay 'The Metropolis and Mental Life,' which influenced modernist representations of the city, Georg Simmel wrote that the individual's greater bombardment by external stimuli and 'differences' in the city (compared to the small town or rural dweller) leads the city dweller to a less 'sensitive,' more 'matter-of-fact,' and 'intellectualistic' attitude (325, 326). 'Instead of reacting emotionally' to the environment, Simmel writes, 'the metropolitan type responds primarily in a rational manner' and so 'creates a protective organ ... against the profound disruption with which the fluctuations and discontinuities of the external milieu threaten' to unsettle the self (326). This person's 'unrelenting hardness' is caused by a 'blasé attitude [and] an indifference toward the distinctions between things' (326, 329).[30] Arcadia may be more emotionally engaged than Simmel's 'metropolitan type,' but she is similarly self-contained and intellectualizing in her perceptions of the city and her life in it. The trajectory of Arcadia's story moves her and her vision of London towards an awareness of the connectedness of self and place that Simmel also moves towards to offset his vision of indifferent detachment:

> The most significant aspect of the metropolis lies in this functional magnitude beyond its actual physical boundaries.... A person does not end with [the] limits of his physical body or with the area to which his physical activity is immediately confined but embraces, rather, the totality of meaningful effects which emanates from him temporally and spatially. In the same way the city exists only in the totality of the effects which transcend their immediate sphere. (335)

Here, almost a century earlier, is a version of the 'relational' model of place and individual place-identity that Massey and others advanced in the 1990s. This is what Arcadia is beginning, at the end of the novel, to embrace – a concept of the self and the city as no longer securely bounded.

Transnational London, Postnational Canada?

Bush's vision of London and of an ethically responsible form of metropolitan dwelling affiliates her narrative most closely of all Canadian London novels to Michael Peter Smith's notion of 'transnational urbanism.' As outlined in the previous chapter, Smith theorizes the 'transnational locality' as a corrective to models of globalization that, in his view, create a binary schism between, one the one hand, a dynamic 'global' realm of transnational capital and communication flows and, on the other, a static 'local' domain constituted by 'embedded communities' that collectively resist globalization (102). Such thinking opposes the grounded and bounded authenticity of the local 'within' to the spatially dispersed 'outside' of a transcendent global sphere that threatens the integrity of locales and nations and is accordingly resisted by individuals and groups seeking to shore up 'communities' and threatened place-identities. To break down this binary, Smith argues that 'the "local" itself has become transnationalized' (110). He critiques the theories not only of David Harvey and Manuel Castells but of Henri Lefebvre and Michel de Certeau, whose writings on the everyday uses of space also, he believes, identify 'the local' with a space of opposition to structures of domination that exist in the global realm. 'In transnational cities,' Smith writes, 'people's everyday experiences are affected by a wide variety of phenomena, practices, and criss-crossing networks which defy easy boundary-setting' (117). Human dwelling and agency in the contemporary world occur not in valorized local spaces beleaguered by global machinations but among

> processes whereby *networks of power*, subsisting at every point from the most 'local' to the most 'global,' are formed, related to each other, and transformed. Since human agency operates at many spatial scales, and is not restricted to 'local' territorial or sociocultural formations, the very concept of the 'urban' thus requires reconceptualization as a social space that is a cross-roads or meeting ground for the interplay of diverse *localizing* practices of national, transnational, and even global-scale actors, as these wider networks of meaning, power, and social practice come into contact with more locally configured networks, practices, and identities. (127)

Even the populist mantra 'Think globally, act locally' overly dichotomizes the two realms, and Smith recommends three alternatives: '(1) thinking locally while acting globally; (2) living bifocally, i.e. thinking transnationally while acting multilocally; and (3) thinking and acting simultaneously at multiple scales' (158).

By the end of *The Rules of Engagement*, Arcadia has begun to do all three, and it is the focus on her nascent political agency that distinguishes Bush's transnational London from those of Richler and Pullinger. In their novels, London is transnational in two related ways: first, because of its multicultural residents and the imperial history of which they serve as a visible reminder; and second, through the international border crossings Jake and Audrey undertake from London in the immaterial realms of dream and memory. But these two forms of transnationalism are not connected through any *realpolitik*; agency is either vicarious fantasy of worldly political action (Jake's Horseman dreams), low-impact textuality (Audrey's articles, Jake's screenplay), or limited to the personal and domestic realm (Jake's self and family, Audrey's romances and friendships). Jake and Audrey act locally. Identity in their stories may be complicatedly relational and stretched over multiple spatial scales, but it is so within a sphere of imaginative awareness and understanding. In Bush's novel it also inhabits a sphere of worldly activity. Even when Arcadia is simply walking – which she does constantly, in both cities – the implications of that activity transcend the local, individual act of resistance that de Certeau would see in it.

However, what Bush's novel appears to lack that the earlier novels possess (including those of Davies and Swan) is a thematic engagement with Canada as a sociopolitical entity and Canadianness as an aspect of identity. Though Toronto has a substantial presence, Canada as a polity, culture, or source of national identity is more elusive. Of all the London novels by Canadians, *The Rules of Engagement* conforms most thoroughly to Frank Davey's description of the postnational Canadian novel in *Post-National Arguments*. Reading a group of sixteen novels published within a quarter-century of Canada's Centennial, Davey discovers and implicitly laments that the nation's importance as a field of activity has diminished. Indeed, he writes, 'There is usually little faith or interest offered, even in the social and political processes by which communities are constituted or modern states constituted and maintained. As well, in the imaginary geographies the novels construct for their characters to inhabit, the Canadian home-ground is more often part of a global field than of any inter-regional Canadian one' (253). Nationalism has gone AWOL, replaced by 'various discourses of intimacy, home, and neighbourhood, together with others of global distance and multinational community. Between the local and the global, where one might expect to find constructions of region, province, and nation, one finds instead voyages, air flights, and international hotels' (258–9). Although the novels he examines are all set partly or entirely on Canadian soil, he finds that in many, 'neither the text nor its protagonists inhabit any social geography that can be called "Canada." They inhabit a post-national space, in which sites are as interchangeable as postcards, in which discourses are transnational, and in which political issues are constructed on non-national (and often ahistorical) ideological grounds' (259). Of the novels discussed in this chapter, only *The Biggest Modern Woman of the World* is among Davey's sixteen – Davies, Atwood, and Richler are represented by different novels – but all of them fit his criteria in the main. Those prior to Bush may more overtly address 'Canada,' but Davey would doubtless regret that all of them, like most in his group, emphasize 'individual salvation' rather than 'the possibility of a participatory politics' (253).

Bush's Arcadia begins with exactly this bias, of course, but her narrative journey is entirely about a movement towards political agency. That agency is both postnational in Davey's deprecatory sense (it doesn't occur on a national field or pursue nationalist goals) and transnational in Smith's favourable sense (it links global and local fields in multiple ways). Davey's analysis is pervaded by a sense of nostalgia for a more nationalist, sovereign Canada whose loss was heralded by the 1989 Free Trade Agreement, to which he devotes a contextualizing chapter and which Ian Angus would later identify as a watershed moment in the decline of a postwar 'left-nationalist' 'consensus' in which 'the national pole of identification held sway over other social identities' in Canada (27, 23). Davey's own left-nationalism leads to a binary split between the national and the postnational or transnational (which he uses interchangeably). As in the localist discourses that Smith critiques, the nation is seen as the appropriate sphere for political commitments and identifications that will strengthen it against encroachments of multinational, transnational, or continentalist forces.

Bush's novel has no interest in a nationalist mode of political agency, but in its only direct comment on Canadian identity it points to a thematic reconciliation between national and transnational spheres. Arcadia remarks that Canadian passports are highly desirable among forgers and people-smugglers because 'traveling as a Canadian is perhaps the easiest way to find safe passage. In a crisis, everyone wants to be one of us. We're known globally for our innocuousness, our apparent harmlessness' (154). Arcadia initially personifies this national stereotype: she values invisibility, passivity, detachment from aggression, safe and risk-free observation. But her reluctance to cross physical and ethical borders, she comes to realize, has the potential to be harmful to others in cases where intervening could help. Since the novel is steeped in references to military intervention in 1990s hotspots like Bosnia and Somalia – places in which Canadian peacekeepers participated – an allegorical reading is inviting. In the aftermath of the debates, in Canada and globally, over the value and timing of military intervention leading up to the recent Afghanistan and Iraq wars, it is even more inviting; those developments give Bush's political themes even more currency than when her novel was published in 2000.

The anxieties that inaugurated the new millennium – global insecurity, border-crossing threats, terrorist enemies of unfixed nationality –

gave urgent new contexts to old debates about the Canada-US border, continental integration, and especially Canada's willingness to intervene in international conflicts. Indeed, a month after the events of 11 September 2001, William Thorsell argued in the *Globe and Mail* that 'Canada needs to leave its teenage years behind' and embrace its transnational responsibilities. The era of our 'free-riding posture on security and its sometimes preening stance on morality' with respect to the militarily 'impetuous' United States was over: 'Canada needs to temper its often self-serving idealism in world affairs with more credible commitments to share the burdens of war-making and prevention through stronger counterintelligence and security establishments.' A renewed national identity, in other words, will be a function of Canada's willingness to act in diverse capacities – to intervene – on the multiple spatial scales of the transnational while remaining firmly (if less distinctively) independent in its nationhood and military policies. The national soul-searching that accompanied the Afghanistan and Iraq campaigns gave new impetus to longstanding debates over Canada's most appropriate international role: as fighters, peacekeepers, mediating diplomats, intelligence gatherers, providers of aid to the less fortunate, or some combination of these and other activities? Arcadia, having failed to keep peace in the duel, now seems on the brink of a new role gathering intelligence, mediating between distant nations, and providing a new, subversive form of international aid in the form of a false Canadian passport – a compromised but useable symbol of the national identity she is implicitly remaking as she attaches herself more actively to the world. It is among the transnationally engaged people of London that Arcadia begins her journey to renewed agency and identity, and it is notably in the airspace between nations that, at the end of the novel, she confirms it.

For the protagonists of the six Canadian novels examined thus far, reinventing the self in London is a function of several kinds of engagement: sexual engagements with national and sometimes racial others; ethical engagements necessitated by the surprising ways those relationships develop; professional engagements and career building; imaginative engagements with the Canadian past that put it in a new and beneficial perspective; and a more engaged awareness of and agency within 'the big wide world' to which London provides access and which it comes to represent. Looked at as a group, these novels also trace an interesting arc in their ways of positioning Canada and London. London remains a unique place to Canadian writers; special kinds of stories can be set there that would suit no other city so well. But the differences are important. If, for Davies, Canada is a marginal place to be left behind and transcended in favour of London as worldly centre, for the later writers London is more dynamically and complexly interlinked with Canada. London may represent a larger and more expansive 'world' than the Canadian home, but as such London transcends its own national space. London in these novels is decentred; no longer an easy symbol of British culture, it becomes most significant for the other places it enables its young Canadian migrants to go, both literally and metaphorically, and for the other people and other times to which it draws them. The narratives of Swan, Atwood, Richler, Pullinger, and Bush move comfortably through and beyond London. London figures most importantly in their novels as an international contact zone that ultimately leads its residents elsewhere: into an absorbing past, back to a newly understood Canada, out into the real 'world.' As they criss-cross and periodically inhabit the various border-zones to which London leads them, these Canadian expatriates continually rethink and reconstruct their identities. In doing so, they engage with the ethically and emotionally loaded ideas of exile, home, race, nationality, and transnationality that are increasingly urgent as London, the world, Canada, and Canadian literature become ever more transnational.

Power Failure: A Postscript

In a footnote to *Post-National Arguments*, Frank Davey remarks that he has not included among his sixteen novels important books by Nino Ricci, Rohinton Mistry, and M.G. Vassanji. The reason: they 'contain few if any significations of Canada or of Canadian polity' (7). Kate Pullinger's first novel, *When the Monster Dies* (1989), had a much lower profile than their award-winning ones, but if Davey knew it he excluded it for presumably the same reason. Set entirely in a late-1980s London littered with rubbish and layered with reminders of empire, Pullinger's novel has almost no representations of Canada. While it does feature a young Canadian expatriate, he is one of six main characters, and the few details of his former life in Canada seem intended more as texture than as an opportunity to explore Canadianness. Though marred by some first-novel awkwardness, Pullinger's ambitious text constructs a compellingly original version of a metropolis inextricably related to its local and overseas histories and paradoxically both renewed and disempowered by its resident 'others.' Indeed, four of its six major characters are Commonwealth migrants (Canadian, Australian, and West Indian) and another is a London-born black, so the novel has important points of comparison with those discussed in subsequent chapters. Moreover, by viewing London almost entirely through a specific neighbourhood in Vauxhall, *When the Monster Dies* renders a street-level London that is more grittily material – more architectural and more archaeological – than that of any other Canadian novel.

Pullinger's young characters – Australians Karl and Irene, Canadian Finn, West Indian Charlotte, and two native Londoners, Mary and Michael – muse obsessively on the past and on their own ambiguous states of belonging to 'a huge city, monolithic and all-encompassing' (15), a place that both accommodates and excludes them. For Mary, London is 'a multi-cultural city, although it did not like publicly to admit that. A city full of people from everywhere imaginable' (17); Finn thinks of his and his friends' occupation of London as 'like colonisation backwards or something' (163). However, the city's international citizenry does not mean that 'all previous notions of Englishness ... have been rendered obsolete,' according to Mary: 'The English clung to some indefinable past, a past of their own imagining, of an Englishness or, in some cases, Britishness that somehow excluded India, Ireland, the West Indies, Canada, Africa, Australia, despite the fact that those places have long been part of Britain's sociological and political map' (17). Ian Baucom has shown how conceptions of a stable national identity – of Englishness or Britishness – were unsettled by imperial activity, by slippages and contradictions caused by the perceived location of 'Englishness' in the spaces of an 'imperial beyond' and a 'national within' (6). By bringing characters from the Commonwealth beyond to the metropolitan within and having them struggle, together with lifelong Londoners, to interrogate and conceptually renovate the metropolis, Pullinger complicates old notions of Englishness and excavates London's time-infused spaces.

The novel literalizes its preoccupation with dwelling and renovation in the act of squatting. Both Charlotte and Mary squat their houses and work constantly to fix the plumbing, wiring, and guttering despite the constant threat of eviction; they behave like homeowners, investing in houses to which they have no secure claim. These activities may offer a compelling metaphor for metropolitan dwelling, but, by making her squatters a black West Indian and a white Londoner, Pullinger complicates the expected identification of the squatter's invasive, precarious state of inhabitation with the uncertain belonging of London's Commonwealth migrants. It is notable, nonetheless, that Mary has squatted the same house for several years without eviction, whereas the bailiff has turfed Charlotte out of several places in the same time. And when Charlotte reveals that 'I always have nightmares after I get evicted.... I dream about big white men who smash down my door and come after me with sledgehammers' (23), she describes the metropolitan present – in particular, the aggressive unhousing of squatters under Margaret Thatcher – in ways that echo the un-settling violence of colonial invasion.

One telling conversation reveals the different political and emotional stakes of the two women in their domestic spaces. Charlotte says,

> 'I need to feel I have a home somewhere, you know, even if it is under siege.'
>
> 'It's not so much the idea of "Home" that I like,' said Mary. 'It's more basic than that. Shelter. Territory.'
>
> 'No,' said Charlotte, shaking her head as she sipped her coffee. 'For me it is definitely "Home" that I need. I never feel like I fit in anywhere else.'
>
> 'Basically,' said Mary, 'I think we all want to be homeowners but without having to buy the house. We're house-stealers somehow ...'
>
> 'I have never stolen anybody's house – nobody wants these bloody wrecks except us.'
>
> 'Yes, but that's not what I mean. It's like we pretend to be homeowners – we knock down walls and do the garden and generally behave as though the houses are ours, outraged when anyone says anything to the contrary ... Anyway, have you ever thought about going back to St. Vincent?'
>
> 'Back to St. Vincent? No, I don't really remember ever having been there anyway. St. Vincent is like a folk memory to me, something I know only through my family. It's their home, I suppose, not mine.' (23–4; ellipses in original)

The authors of *The Empire Writes Back* observe that 'the construction or demolition of houses or buildings ... is a recurring and evocative figure for the problematic of post-colonial identity' (Ashcroft et al. 28), and Rosemary George shows how the idea of 'home' shifts fluidly between signifying a private, domestic space and a public, national one (see 11–13). In *When the Monster Dies*, Charlotte's relentless determination to make a home for herself in London is qualified by her ambivalent affiliations to the metropolis as a British space. After she reinvades the boarded-up house from which she was recently evicted, ready to make it liveable again, she uses spatial, architectural language to muse on her identity: 'While homelessness in London is a chronic problem, to Charlotte it was a state of mind that occupied the part of her soul that felt neither West Indian nor English but something empty, boarded-up, inbetween' (35–6). Her state of non-belonging is confirmed in a later passage: 'British by passport, she thought the question of her nationality was unimportant and uninteresting. She did not belong anywhere' (66). Mary, by contrast, insists that London is 'where I belong': 'I can't imagine living anywhere else' (62). Nonetheless, despite their different origins and degrees of at-homeness, and despite the different meanings that they attribute to their squatting and DIY renovating, Mary and Charlotte inhabit London in similar ways. In the paradox of Charlotte's search for home in a place to which she does not belong, and in Mary's insistence that squatting is as close as she wants to get to home ownership in a place to which she does belong, Pullinger characterizes London as a place best inhabited ambivalently, as an in-between, balancing commitment with detachment.

This ambivalence is a function of a historic transition that Pullinger's characters see London as undergoing: out of the detritus of its imperial past and into a questionable newness. Finn is drawn nostalgically and 'aesthetically' to London's architecture on his arrival in 1982; the city's spaces 'appealed to Finn's bright Canadian eyes, previously accustomed to the new and somewhat shiny cities of North America, as old-fashioned and from another time' (16). By the end of the 1980s, however, 'A lot of that had changed. The city was being forced very quickly out of the past and into some warped view of the future. The Americans were marching in, their businesses transforming the West End. But the grime still remained and, in fact, the amount of litter and street rubbish was increasing' (16). The implication here that London was being partially made over in the image of an increasingly dominant neo-imperial America is given only minimal direct attention in the narrative. But through some complicated plot connections and interrelated images, Pullinger indirectly links this postmodern, neo-imperial transformation both with a much older vision of London as a Roman colony and with London's own nineteenth-century imperial might. The city's spaces reveal the material histories of several empires.

Pullinger flirts with images of Gothic horror as she connects London's visible decay and filth with its diminished power. Finn suggests that he and his Commonwealth friends 'came here out of morbid fascination for the decaying empire' (62). Similarly, the Australians Karl and Irene 'had not come to London to be part of a movement but to chronicle the movement's decline, to watch it die. To them, Britain was like an ancient and handsome aristocratic vampire tied to a lamppost somewhere in Piccadilly, forced to watch the sun rise over the rest of the Empire' (93). This bizarre image of disempowered imperial monstrosity is echoed in Mary's 'sense of London as a living entity, heaving itself through history' (85), and especially in the metaphor that gives Pullinger her title. According to the black, British-born Michael,

> It's like the British Empire is some kind of monster, a terrible beast that is now dying as it shelters itself beneath consumption ideology. We've all come to crowd around and watch its grotesque death-convulsions. Its power to subordinate people in their own countries is growing weaker by the minute, is already weakened beyond repair, so now it's as vicious as possible to those still within reach. But this monster is not dead yet and its last blows are ever more cruel and ruthless.... Instead, it will police itself into submission, it will bash its offspring over the head in an attempt to split skulls so that we all die with it, so that we all go down with the dying monster. (163–4)

His point is put more idealistically, if less vividly, by Mary: 'In a better world,' she says, 'London would love its foreigners. It would revel in its own multi-ethnicity and diversity, embrace the foreign and make it its own' (163).

Despite these complaints about London's aggressive exclusions, Pullinger's characters are more inclined to chat and spin metaphors than to take action against monstrous oppression. The emphasis on watching in the above passages suggests that the death throes of empire are a spectacle to be observed and suffered rather than a danger to be fought. However, the novel does contain one rather capricious act of resistance against the city as symbolized in one of its modern monuments, the Battersea Power Station. As Burton Pike observes, a city's 'stubborn spatiality' is 'epitomized by its monuments' (132); the geographer Jane M. Jacobs shows how 'efforts to preserve the historic built environment' of London in the name of 'heritage,' as well as some redevelopment schemes, reveal a nostalgic desire to preserve, commodify, and 'memorialise the might of empire' (40). The colossal power station – which once provided one-fifth of London's power but after 1983 was idle and falling apart – becomes a symbol of London's imperial power and subsequent decay. Described, not unlike London itself, as 'a once-mighty, now elderly person' (147), the power station is being redeveloped into 'an amusement theme park with rides and shopping and

skating' by a team that includes the two Australians (43). Although the
station has no direct link with the empire, Michael reminds his friends
that 'the money that propped up British industry came from ... the
Caribbean, Africa, India, black and Third World people, fucking slavery'
(45–6). This indirect connection is reinforced in the novel by recurring
images of brick buildings and loose bricks, among other rubbish, along
the banks of the Thames as well as by the narrator's observation that 'like
most European cities it [London] was built with the proceeds of Imperialism, its very bricks bought with blood and conflict' (101); the station,
which sits beside the Thames and looks like a fortress, is believed to be
Europe's largest brick building,[31] and the river's associations with empire are clear.

   In its renovation as a fun-fair site, the Battersea Power Station also
seems to exemplify London's American-style consumerist makeover –
the neo-imperial future as well as the imperial past – although Pullinger's
handling of this plot line confuses matters slightly. Karl sees his and
Irene's work on the project as a way to make a 'statement' about Thatcher's
Britain: 'The Vindication of the Working Classes, a blow against capitalism and the Government, retaliation for the removal of London's self-
governing powers, the repression of homosexuality, the new tax laws, the
fact that the power station has been replaced by nuclear energy, the
dismantling of the Welfare State, Art, Boredom ...' (45; ellipsis in original). This is a somewhat inchoate but clearly political list; however, when
Michael encourages Karl to 'say you're doing it on behalf of all of us
immigrants and the children of immigrants, Australian, Canadian, West
Indian alike. The Empire goes Disney,' Karl upbraids him: 'We are
looking to make an artistic statement here,' he says. 'I never said anything about politics. Art transcends politics' (46). Given his preceding
catalogue, this statement seems disingenuous, but when the novel reaches
its strangely anticlimactic climax – after months of working on the power
station, Karl and Irene plant a bomb and blow up part of it – none of the
characters seems to know what kind of statement has been made by their
vandalism. Even though the explosion takes place immediately after
Michael's speech about the empire as a dying monster, when Karl ushers
his friends out to silently witness the spectacle its status as an act of
violent resistance against that old monster (or the new American one) is
unclear. For Mary, 'It's like a metaphor for something, but I can't think
what' (169); Finn agrees, suggesting that their confusion reflects a general loss in 'our powers of interpretation,' though he does liken the
event to 'a military coup or something. An unsuccessful uprising' (170).

Henri Lefebvre writes that monuments have traditionally provided societies with 'a collective mirror' of societal 'consensus' – 'a generally accepted Power and a generally accepted Wisdom' (*Production* 220) – but that, when such consensus breaks down, monuments lose their prestige and become vulnerable to 'sudden eruptions of violence' (223). Anthony King, after citing several instances of terrorism against high-profile buildings, notes dryly 'the extent to which the world city's "signature architecture" has upstaged the state's (and the world's) more sober debating chambers as the appropriate site to conduct an alternative international politics' ('Re-presenting' 218–19). Pullinger's would-be radicals may have a politics of resistance in mind, but it is not at all clear what form it would take. And her choice of the power station as her central symbol of empire – London's 'signature architecture' – is odd: as a modern industrial building, it lacks the cultural associations and history of, say, the British Museum or Big Ben, which is described in the novel as 'a father reassuring his children,' ringing out 'across the Thames and ... broadcast across the world' (84). Furthermore, by treating the blowing up of the power station as a capricious and questionable act – as if the explosion has taken on the reduced scale and trivial associations of the fun-fair itself – Pullinger undermines her bomb plot's potential to represent an important theme: the crumbling of national consensus apparent in London's transformation into a postimperial world city whose empire has imploded as formerly colonized people put pressure on old notions of Britishness.[32]

It may be, however, that Pullinger deliberately refuses clear symbolism so that her characters' uncertainty may reflect the multiplicity of London's imperial connections. Earlier in the novel, Mary imagines Martians coming to Britain and finding 'a colonised country.' She is thinking of the Americanization of Britain, though she wonders whether these Martians would 'know the difference between the grime of Old Britain, the buildings and alleyways coated in caked-on centuries of coal-dust and city filth, and the cheap plastic charm of New Britain, brightly lit American restaurants and chain-stores' (67). She locates this fanciful invasion, fittingly, in Piccadilly Circus, where Karl and Irene will later describe the British Empire as a tied-up vampire. But Pullinger is less interested in examining the linear transition from traditional British imperialism to American corporate neo-imperialism than in exploring London as a palimpsest whose layers of dirt, bricks, dust, and built space accumulated over two millennia prompt a more transhistorical, spatially dense view of multiple empires. As Mary muses just before her Martian fantasy, 'The

Britons in Ireland, the Americans in Britain, the Romans in Britain,
there is nothing new in this world' (67). By rhetorically equating these
three very different imperial relationships, Pullinger indexes an intricate set of relations among London's various imperial identities, all of
which are readable and relatable through the city's material spaces.

In the opening scene, Mary uncovers a Roman bath while transplant-
ing a lilac bush in her garden; she promptly reburies it, fearing that
archaeologists will swoop in and unhouse her from her Vauxhall squat.
The implied links between the dispossession of invaded peoples by
ancient empires and the eviction of squatters by contemporary bailiffs
are reinforced in a whimsical later scene:

> Mary dreamed she was a Roman dressed in full metal armour. She was on
> the train from Rome to London returning to inspect the Baths. Annoyed
> to discover a house and garden on top of the structure she had built in
> the boggy ground of Londinium, she quickly nailed an official Roman
> eviction notice to the front door of the building, without sympathy for the
> occupants. (54)

The dirt pile in the garden later seems to have been tampered with, and
Pullinger connects its hidden mysteries with two further narrative lines.
Mary, a painter, works throughout much of the novel on an abstract that,
like Dorian Gray's picture, begins to change on its own. During the
above dream, it becomes 'a bit darker, slightly more angry' (54), and
later its 'red slashes [become] more blood-like, deeper, more real' (74).
As it gets progressively more hideous, Mary decides to hide it – initially in
the cellar and finally by burying it in the garden over the bath. She starts
a second painting, of her garden, but, after a 'faint outline' of a Roman-
looking figure appears where she has painted the lilac bush, she covers
the whole image with black paint (129). She then starts a new painting, a
cross-section of the garden from ground level down, revealing 'the Romans who still remained undetected underneath her garden' and 'the
Baths, steaming, crowded and fully functioning ... at their most foggy
and decadent' (148).

By imaging the city through urban and artistic palimpsests and through
the eruption of the invisible past in the visible present, Pullinger renders
a London eerily infused with its history. And she connects different
empires two millennia apart by linking the modern Battersea Power
Station to Roman Londinium through Mary's consciousness: 'The moon
hung between the chimneys of Battersea Power Station. Mary remarked

to herself silently that the same moon had hung over the Romans while they practised their ablutions in her garden' (28). Elsewhere the station is described as 'a grand ruin like Stonehenge' (132). Both the bath and the Disneyfied power station become associated with decadent pleasure, and, while the partial destruction of the station represents (if anything) a minor act of insurgency against both American neo-imperialism and the vestiges of the British Empire that this 'grand ruin' still embodies, Pullinger offers a further set of connections through images derived from an outdoor 'fun-fair' in Vauxhall's Kennington Park (110). Like the one in the power station, this contemporary event is an attenuated version of a 'permanent summer-long fairground' that occupied Vauxhall Spring Gardens from 1660 to 1859 (25). One night Mary dreams that she is standing at her front door in nineteenth-century clothing; she sees and hears a fair in the distance but awakens too soon to visit it. She then goes into the garden, where 'the night was misty, as if the Romans were producing steam in their baths down below and it was rising up through the dirt' (99). In the novel's final scene, after the explosion at the power station and its ambiguous aftermath, Mary completes the earlier dream, standing amid a richly imagined, detailed version of the nineteenth-century fair; then, apparently now awake, she feels the ground heave in her garden, exposing the bath 'as though her garden was imploding with the weight of history. The ruins were coming to the fore, the remainder of an Empire made feeble by excess' (173).

Through these interrelated images and plot lines, *When the Monster Dies* presents a heady vision of a London burdened with and haunted by its multiple imperial attachments. Pullinger implies that a fully engaged form of postimperial dwelling, whether by native Londoners or by Commonwealth migrants, involves recognizing and responding to London's past and present imperial relations, imaginatively and through lived practice. Cerebral to a fault, the novel is weakened by its overwrought intellectualization and a consequent failure to communicate its ideas as emotionally felt realities in the lives of its characters. Still, their mental mappings are rewarding. Supersaturated with London's temporal and spatial abundance, the novel summons up both material and immaterial history in a way comparable to Sigmund Freud's conception of the 'Eternal City' of Rome in *Civilization and Its Discontents* (15). From the premise that relics from all stages of Rome's past are still evident, Freud says, 'let us make the fantastic supposition that Rome were not a human dwelling-place, but a mental entity with just as long and varied a past history: that is, in which nothing once constructed had perished, and all the earlier stages of development had survived alongside the latest' (17). He acknowledges the physical impossibility of his concept: 'If we try to represent historical sequence in spatial terms, it can only be done by juxtaposition in space; the same space will not hold two contents' (18). But his point is analogical; he is using this historically spatialized city as a metaphor for the ways in which all previous memories may or may not be present in the human mind.

Pullinger's version of a city laden with what Massey calls 'space-time' – or 'four-dimensionality' – comes close to being purely a construction of the mind (*Space* 264). But in its obsessive combing of the local – from garden dirt, rubbish, and bricks to houses, streets, and monuments – it grounds its cerebral musings in the tangible material of inhabited space and offers a more tactile and visual rendering of London than any other Canadian novel. As in the other books, but to a greater degree, Pullinger's narrative substitutes private, domestic space for public, national space; it dwells on personal residences to suggest insecure states of social belonging. Moreover, through the narrative democracy of an ensemble novel, Pullinger endeavours to represent a multicultural London that Davies and Atwood ignore, Richler observes in passing, and the more recent novels by Pullinger and Bush render through the single perspective (and the bilateral relationships) of a white expatriate from Canada. By giving voice to West Indian, Australian, 'black British,' and Canadian 'others,' *Where the Monster Dies* raises some of the racially infused dimensions of metropolitan dwelling that will dominate the texts examined in the following chapters. The real protagonist – the central subject – of Pullinger's unusual novel, however, is London itself: the metropolis in all of its transhistorical, multicultural, richly ambiguous, and messy complexity.

chapter three

London South-West: Caribbean Fiction and Metropolitan Life

Wat a devilment a England!
Dem face war an brave de worse,
But me wonderin how dem gwine stan
Colonizin in reverse.

Louise Bennett

'London Calling the West Indies': A Prologue

It has become a commonplace of Caribbean literary history to locate the 'explosion' of the region's writing during the 1950s in London. Kenneth Ramchand wrote in 1970 that since most West Indian novels of the previous two decades had been published in the metropolis, and since most of the novelists were living there, 'London is indisputably the West Indian literary capital' (*West* 63). More recently, the editors of *The Routledge Reader in Caribbean Literature* have identified London as 'the "literary capital" of the West Indies' (Donnell and Welsh 206), and Louis James writes in a book published in 1999 that the postwar '"phenomenon" of West Indian literature ... was created not in the Caribbean, but in London' (90). As truisms these statements are all perfectly valid. London did accommodate much of the West Indian literary activity of the 1950s; many of the well-known writers associated with the early 'flowering' of West Indian literature – to use another metaphor of that heady time – were based in the English capital, where they found print and broadcast outlets for their work that didn't exist at home (see Swanzy, 'Islands' 350). Besides the three small magazines *Bim, Kyk-over-al,* and *Focus,* which printed only shorter pieces, there were no literary publishers in the West

Indies in 1950; as for broadcasting, George Lamming writes in *The Pleasures of Exile* that commercial radio in the region was a 'Dead End' for literature. 'Corpse-Land,' he calls it: 'So it was London, or nothing' (67). London also brought a community of West Indian writers together and enabled a sense of collective regional identity and cultural mission to emerge, all of which would have been virtually impossible in the isolation of disparate island communities. Sam Selvon's remark that 'my life in London taught me about people from the Caribbean, and it was here that I found my identity' is typical ('Finding' 37). It can be convincingly argued that without the gathering and processing of the 'harvest' of writers and writing in London (Swanzy, 'Islands' 351), early West Indian literature would not have burgeoned and reached its international audience to anything like the extent it did.

However, there are ironies involved in this assignment of a necessary, enabling role to the former heart of empire – ironies not lost on the aforementioned writers and critics. The idea of gathering and processing resources in the centre for export back to the margins is a familiar one from imperialist economics; London is privileged once again as a site of power and source of cultural goods. But can a phenomenon as diverse as West Indian writing really have a centre? If London is the 'centre' or 'capital' of early West Indian literature, the place where it was 'created,' where does that leave writers who did not move to London, such as Derek Walcott and V.S. Reid? What does it say about the groundedness of a literature whose original appeal was based in part on its vivid sense of the local? Before examining the manifold representations of London in West Indian fiction, it is worth pursuing the implications of this London-centrism in order to reconsider the place (or places) of early West Indian literature. The archival records of the BBC radio program *Caribbean Voices* provide an important resource in which to explore the question. From 1945 to 1958 *Caribbean Voices* was integral to the early development of a viable regional literature; since its structures were a microcosm of those in the wider sphere of writing and publishing at the time, and since it was produced in the English capital, looking at the program's pivotal contribution is one way to rethink London's place in West Indian literary history.

Caribbean Voices was broadcast on the BBC Overseas Service (later the World Service) from London to the British West Indies every Sunday night at 7:30 Caribbean time. The program's benevolent intention was both developmental and pedagogical: to help foster a distinctive regional literature and an audience for it, and to provide appropriate standards and guidance towards the betterment of West Indian writing. Material was solicited from across the region and selected in London by Henry Swanzy, the producer and host from 1946 to 1954; he worked closely with Gladys Lindo, a Jamaica-based agent hired by the BBC who did initial gathering and culling of manuscripts. Poems, stories, and sketches accepted for broadcast were recorded in London and then, as Austin Clarke recalls, 'our "voices" [were] pelted back to us on the BBC' (*Passage* 15; cf. 9). As Lamming wrote in 1971, the program was structured like a colonial sugar economy in which the raw material is 'cut, sent abroad to be refined, and gets back [to the colony] in the finished form' (qtd. in Donnell and Welsh 215). Some episodes included analysis of recent work – often quite harsh and imperious in tone – at first by English writers Arthur Calder-Marshall and Roy Fuller, and later by West Indians such as Alfred Mendes and V.S. Naipaul. Panel discussions with London-based Caribbean writers, as many as fourteen in one show, were also occasionally broadcast. London provided the incipient literature with infrastructure, intellectual capital, and quality assurance. The filters through which West Indians could look at themselves, and the voices through which they spoke to each other, were in London. *Caribbean Voices* was premised on the cultural authority of the metropolis.

The show was undeniably paternalistic in structure and sometimes in tone. Here is the opening announcement from a 1945 program: 'Hello, West Indies, it's always pleasant to turn again to these Sunday programmes of your own poetry and prose' (18–19/3/45; Box 1).[1] Another early show includes this linking segment: 'And now for our prose reading. We have selected a little story by R.L.C. Aarons of Jamaica' (8–9/4/45; Box 1). Such language, combined with the 7:30 timeslot and the use of a lullaby for the signature music, is strongly reminiscent of parents reading to children at bedtime.[2] The essays by Calder-Marshall are a fascinating mixture of condescension and encouragement, as seen in this passage from his first, broadcast in 1948:

Generalising wildly, I should say that at the moment your writers are rather like men on a dark moonless night trying to find their way with torches; and as far as the torch throws its light things are clear and distinct; and from the deep shadows sometimes comes the most distant flash of an animal's eyes caught in the light; but all round is darkness.

Every poem and short story that you write which is original and fresh pushes back the frontiers of darkness a little further and a little further. You yourself sitting at home in your own room, in your own town on your own

island may not see this. But here in England, at this distance, I can see it;
like someone standing on the top of a hill looking down over a city; like
Laventille for example looking over Port of Spain as night falls and the
lights flash on one by one with reflected light. I can see the West Indies
beginning to glow as a poet here, a short story writer there succeeds in
kindling his fire. (1/2/48; Box 3)

Calder-Marshall then tells West Indian writers what they require to
progress: knowledge about their past (so they can illuminate that particular darkness), writing that is rooted in the local soil (so they can
render their world in their own words), and a sense of community (so
they can transcend their island differences and cultivate a regional
identity). Those are worthy and necessary goals, but Calder-Marshall also
implies through his metaphorical flights that West Indians require metropolitan guidance to help them see what they, myopically enshrouded
in darkness, cannot, but that he from the Olympian heights of the
metropolis, with his long-range vision, can. Later critiques by Calder-
Marshall were often scathing in their dismissal of individual stories,
ridiculing authors and their writings in the manner of a schoolmaster
hectoring a recalcitrant student.

His metaphors evoke a familiar legacy of colonialism, and in the early
days of the program they probably seemed *de rigeur* to many in this still-
colonial era. Swanzy could be direct in his criticism too; although he and
Lindo were selective, the work broadcast was uneven, he felt, writing in
an early letter to her, 'We don't want to give the impression that because
a poem or short story is broadcast, it is necessarily altogether good' (13/
8/46).[3] For *Caribbean Voices* to raise the standard of the region's writing,
Swanzy wrote, criticism must be broadcast and also, where possible, sent
directly to the authors. Lindo agreed, saying she felt sure the authors
wouldn't 'resent' the feedback (14/9/46). Indeed, the first one with
whom Swanzy corresponded, Harold Telemaque, was gushing in his
appreciation of Swanzy's response to his work: 'Your service to West
Indian artists is enormous,' he writes in a letter, 'and it will be the means
of much West Indian uplift soon' (11/6/47). Swanzy's role becomes that
of a generous but tough guide. Indeed, Philip Nanton argues that
Swanzy did not simply reflect the developing West Indian literature but
helped mould it: he 'provided an identifiable intermediary role which
gave shape and direction well beyond what might be expected of a radio
programme' (12).

The implied relations of parents and children or of imperial teachers guiding colonial pupils may have seemed inevitable to many on both sides of the Atlantic, but they were not unchallenged. Swanzy himself clearly felt uncomfortable about his outsider's role, agonizing about it in letters and on the air. Two years after taking over as producer, his script for one episode reads as follows:

> *Some of* You must have got rather tired by now of hearing my ~~didactic, Oxford~~ *unCaribbean* voice poking its slightly supercilious nose round the treasures of your Caribbean foreshore, and not yet openly nipped by a good, sound, Caribbean native, I mean a crab. But I hope (for I am afraid of crabs) that there may perhaps be less of it, I mean ~~this cultural ant eating~~ *the Oxford* voice, less of it in 1948. (11/1/48; Box 3; strikeouts in the original; handwritten amendments shown in italics)

The edits in this bizarrely worded script convey Swanzy's sense of the delicacy of his position: how much should *Caribbean Voices* include of his voice – his metropolitan opinions, aesthetic tastes, judgments – at the expense of West Indian voices? In 1949, he acknowledged the limitations of producing the program 'at a distance of 4,000 miles' from the 'soil of every day life' in which the literature was properly 'rooted,' and he noted that the program had been 'rather severely criticised' for its 'remote and patronising' commentators. While it could usefully aim to provide encouragement and money, he said, 'Why should the BBC set up as a critic at all ... ?' (21/8/49; Box 5).

In an article published in *Caribbean Quarterly* the same year, Swanzy called himself a 'temporary caretaker' of Caribbean literature: someone filling a need created by the paucity of outlets for cultural exchange in the region and the isolation of its scattered writers ('Caribbean' 23). He hoped, he said on air in 1949, that the program would nurture a self-sufficient literary community with its own 'first-class literary review with money and an alert public to back it, or even a regional wireless station building its own literary tradition' (21/8/49; Box 5). In other words, the show's finest achievement would be to make itself redundant. What happened instead was that numerous writers moved to London and formed a community there in collaboration with Swanzy and his program. They were hired as on-air readers and commentators, and they continued to contribute new writing. In effect, they gradually took over. This did allow the program to develop a more West Indian identity in the 1950s, but it still privileged the metropolis. The writers who came to be most closely identified with *Caribbean Voices* were those in London, and the actual voices heard on the radio, though now more West Indian than before, were still speaking from there. Moreover, when Trinidadians like Mendes and Naipaul took over the commentator's seat from Calder-Marshall, they often adopted the same scathing tone, giving the impression that West Indian literature was still being condescendingly judged from lofty metropolitan heights.

Swanzy agonized about this, too. Even as he was arranging for writers to meet and gathering them on Thursday evenings at his home, and even as he was helping them find publishers and pay their bills, he worried that the centre of gravity of West Indian literature, and of his program, was shifting too much to London. He discouraged Sam Selvon from even coming, given the difficulties of finding work. And he fretted in a letter to Frank Collymore in 1950 that 'the West Indian literary colony in London is increasing at a fast and almost alarming rate' – alarming because of the difficulty of apportioning reading duties and fees among them all (16/5/50). Even after he spoke enthusiastically in a 1952 program about the gathering of Caribbean authors at the London premiere of Walcott's play *Henri Christophe*, and of the 'West Indian literary rebirth' that this event signified, he worried that 'the drain of aspiring writers to London' may cause 'those remaining faithful to their islands' to feel that *Caribbean Voices* 'is becoming purely European.' Unlike the far-sighted Calder-Marshall, he acknowledged that 'a clear view' of West Indian literary and cultural trends may be 'somewhat obscured for us here,' although he reassured his listeners that most contributions to the program still came from the region (10/2/52; Box 8). Four years later, however, by which time Swanzy had left the show and Naipaul was hosting it, the scales had tipped further. Naipaul questioned the show's *raison d'être*, saying on air in 1956, 'It is getting more and more anomalous that this programme, meant to be an outlet for isolated writers in the Caribbean, should have nearly half its contributors in London' (16/9/56; Box 17). Naipaul left *Caribbean Voices* later that year and was replaced by Edgar Mittelholzer. In April 1958, by which time several writers had published successful novels and new outlets for West Indian writing had emerged, the show was cancelled; as a BBC director recalls in a 1998 radio documentary, by then 'the children had outgrown the patronage of the parent' ('What').

What are the implications of these developments in the program, and the sense of a newly consolidated, metropolitan West Indian community that it helped create, for London's position in the region's literary history? Undoubtedly, as Alison Donnell and Sarah Welsh argue, the show's location in London 'perpetuated notions of literature happening "elsewhere"' and constructed an 'ex-centric' image of Caribbean literary production (216). But even in the early years of the program, where colonial structures were most obvious, the West Indies was not oppressed or erased. Caribbean voices – Caribbean texts – were the primary material (the point of origin), and Caribbean listeners the audience (the final destination). Anne Walmsley calls *Caribbean Voices* 'in effect a fledgling school in creative writing, and a broad-based literary club' that not only helped writers capitalize on a postwar British publishing boom but also brought West Indian writing to a 'far wider' Caribbean audience than *Bim, Focus,* or *Kyk-over-al* reached (11, 9). In *The Pleasures of Exile,* Lamming describes the show's reception among writers in the region:

> these writers would look forward to that Sunday evening at half-past seven. It was their reprieve. Moreover, 'Caribbean Voices' enabled writers in one island to keep in touch with the latest work of writers in another island. ... The programme was intended to 'encourage' local talent; and it was a most salutary change when, under Henry Swanzy's direction, I'm sure, Fuller and Calder Marshall became astringent. And Calder Marshall, whose sincerity was beyond question, could be very rough.
>
> The West Indian writers would meet in the same house and listen to these programmes. Then ... the writers, furious or elated according to the critics' recent judgment, would ramble to Down Town Port-of-Spain: George Street, Marine Square, harbouring for a while with the rats in Auntie's Tea Shop. And all the way they were tearing Fuller and Calder Marshall to pieces.
>
> 'Who the hell he think he is ... ?' 'Is all right for him sitting up there talking 'bout we don't take more time ...' 'Is what we got to get is a native critic ...' And so on. ...
>
> But you see the magic of the B.B.C. box. From Barbados, Trinidad, Jamaica and other islands, poems and short stories were sent to England; and from a London studio in Oxford Street, the curriculum for a serious all-night argument was being prepared. These writers had to argue among themselves and against the absent English critic. (*Pleasures* 65–6; third, fourth, and fifth ellipses in original)

Clearly the show helped gather a West Indian community and cultural identity not just in London but in the islands. As such, it provoked engagement, argument, and resistance, as metropolitan power does on a broader scale.

Even at this early stage, then, London was only partly a monolith imposing itself. In important ways it was already partly decentred: whether in terms of production or reception or both, the show can be seen as a link in a network that began and ended in the Caribbean. As many West Indian writers consolidated their sense of community and identity in London, the city accumulated a small measure of additional power, authority, influence, and cultural capital. But this enhanced prestige was offset by the ways the city was destabilized and transformed. 'This is London calling the West Indies' the program began, but over time it became more like the West Indies calling the West Indies, with London simply as a point of access, a conduit in a web of interconnections. 'London' spoke increasingly in a Caribbean accent – a Caribbean voice – especially once Naipaul took over as host. This changed what 'London' came to signify: the London that called the West Indies on *Caribbean Voices* became, over time, less hegemonic, more thoroughly decentred, more like a node in an intricate web of transnational relations than a place from which power emanated. The original associations with parents and children, light and darkness, teachers and pupils gradually disappeared, and London's cultural authority was increasingly hybridized.

Donnell and Welsh write that Swanzy and his program 'formed a network between writers in (and from) different islands based in London and in the Caribbean' (214). To see *Caribbean Voices* as a network – as a complex set of dynamic relations among a multicultural London and many different West Indian islands – is to complicate not only traditional views of London as the centre or capital of West Indian literature, but the very idea of there being a centre at all. One way to reconceptualize the place of early West Indian literature is to follow the lead of Paul Gilroy, for whom the Atlantic Ocean is *the* space of a decentred black history. In *The Black Atlantic*, Gilroy suggests that cultural historians 'take the Atlantic as one single, complex unit of analysis in their discussions of the modern world and use it to produce an explicitly transnational and intercultural perspective' (15). The Atlantic waters hug the shores of Europe, Africa, the Americas, and the Caribbean; the ships that linked those shores represent for Gilroy 'the shifting spaces in between the fixed places they connected' and point to 'the playful diasporic intimacy that has been a marked feature of transnational black Atlantic creativity' (16). Similarly, the centre of early West Indian literature, at least in its radio manifestation, is actually a *middle* located in the in-between spaces high above that same alternately calm and turbulent sea. This is where

Caribbean literature was really happening: in the air-mail through which Gladys Lindo and an array of aspiring authors sent work to London and corresponded with British and West Indian Londoners, and in the air-waves through which Caribbean voices and cultural expressions were transmitted back. It was in the open, wireless air over the Atlantic that the BBC linked distant places into one dynamically related, decentred literary and cultural space.

After the demise of the radio program, cultural phenomena such as the *West Indian Gazette* (1958–65) and the Caribbean Artists Movement (1966–72) continued to decentre the metropolitan space in which they were located. And just as *Caribbean Voices* redefined the signifier 'London' over several years, West Indian novelists have, through many decades of writing about the city, reexamined it through the lenses of Caribbean culture and the immigrant experience. There are more West Indian novels set wholly or partly in London than there are from any other Commonwealth region. Almost all of the region's major English-language novelists have written at least one London novel; the list includes George Lamming, Jean Rhys, Sam Selvon, Edgar Mittelholzer, V.S. Naipaul, Andrew Salkey, Wilson Harris, Joan Riley, Beryl Gilroy, and David Dabydeen.[4] As they negotiate the divisions and connections between metropolis and (post)colony – and between the lives these two related spaces can accommodate – their novels consistently bring West Indian cultural images and historical consciousness to bear on the metropolis. Over the years, their representations trace a path parallel to that of the BBC's implied 'Londons.' It changes from an exclusive, distant, hegemonic, and largely unseen city to a site gradually reclaimed and redefined by what Robin Cohen calls the Caribbean 'cultural diaspora' (137), finally becoming saturated with its own intimate, ocean-crossing relations to the West Indies and the wider world. According to Simon Gikandi, 'A postcolonial reading is not one that inscribes the temporal and spatial distance between metropolis and colony but one that reinstitutes their mutual imbrication at that moment of rupture (decolonization), when they were supposed to have been finally separated' (*Maps* 228). The West Indian novels of London set before, during, and after decolonization encourage and reward this kind of postcolonial reading. What they reveal as a group, through a set of recurring spatial images and intertextual correspondences, is that for West Indian migrants London is a place overdetermined by imperial history and power structures even as it shows itself to be mutually imbricated with the peoples and spaces of its (former) Caribbean colonies.

A City Barely Visible and Mostly Unseen

In 'London,' an essay first published in 1958, V.S. Naipaul laments that the metropolis is so difficult to know. 'It is a matter of climate,' he writes: 'In a warm country life is conducted out of doors. Windows are open, doors are open. People sit in open verandas and cafés. You know your neighbour's business and he knows yours.' In London, by contrast, 'everything goes on behind closed doors'; whereas 'the man from the warm country automatically leaves the door open behind him,' 'the man from the cold country closes it' (14). Dwelling upon this image, Naipaul regrets that he cannot really know a people he sees only 'in official attitudes' (15). Depressed by 'the privacy of the big city,' and by the 'barrenness' and absence of 'communal pleasures' in his life there, the young Naipaul says that London is 'not a place I can write about. Not as yet' (15, 16). In his inability (or refusal) to represent the city, together with the metonymic image of the closed door, Naipaul shares a vision of London with some unlikely bedfellows from early West Indian literature, including George Lamming and Jean Rhys. While both do write novels set in London – as Naipaul himself went on to do in the 1960s – they substantially limit their narrators' and characters' visions, knowledges, and experiences of the city. To adapt a phrase from Salman Rushdie, London in early West Indian literature is a city barely visible and mostly unseen (see *Verses* 241).

As a group, Caribbean writers were the first to produce a large body of fiction rendering the (post)imperial metropolis from the point of view of the empire's former subjects. Early West Indian narratives of London are contextualized by the immediacy of empire; in the 1950s decolonization in the region was only just underway, and the 'New Commonwealth' presence was still very new in the capital and correspondingly lacking in influence. How these early texts portray and avoid portraying the city reflects what might be called London's architecture of power. Henri Lefebvre's theory that space is the product of social, political, and economic relations (see *Production* 46–7 and 80–5), together with Roy Porter's view that 'London grew because it became the headquarters of the world's hugest empire' (1), suggests that London's spatial environment is a concrete legacy of imperialism's structures of production and power. When early West Indian writers represent London as a world of faceless buildings, closed doors, cramped interiors, limited mobility, and constrained, disconnected lives, they imply that the divisive binaries and excluding borders associated with colonialism have extended into the very metropolitan space that was supposed to offer the colonial subject expanded opportunities and a break from the past.

In his influential book *Space and Place*, Yi-Fu Tuan shows how architectural space defines and 'clarifies social roles and relations,' particularly in the ways it manages the categories of 'interior and exterior, closed and open, darkness and light, private and public' (102). Architecture's power 'to demarcate and intensify forms of social life' is a function of how such oppositions are perceived and experienced: either as distinct and mutually exclusive or as fluid and interconnected (108). 'Constructed form,' Tuan writes, 'has the power to heighten the awareness and accentuate, as it were, the difference in emotional temperature between "inside" and "outside"' (107). But while demarcating that difference is architecture's most fundamental task, Richard Sennett sees it as a regrettable binary. He argues that 'modern [Western] culture suffers from a divide between the inside and the outside' that is reflected in its architecture and that corresponds to 'a divide between subjective experience and worldly experience, self and city' (*Conscience* xii). Sennett shows how this division impedes the interactive exchange between realms that individuals, communities, and even narratives need in order to be complete. The modern Western city is designed, Sennett says, 'to wall off the differences between people, assuming that these differences are more likely to be mutually threatening than mutually stimulating' (xii). The closed door that typifies London in Naipaul's essay exhibits this quality; it separates not just outside from inside but brown West Indian from white Londoner. The imperial structures made concrete in the built environment are figured through a spatial divide that corresponds to the racial divide at the heart of imperialism.

The result is a city that cannot be fully or satisfactorily seen or comprehended. On one level, of course, this is visually and epistemologically true of anyone's experience of any city. The sheer size of cities, along with their visual and cultural diversity, defies the omniscient gaze or the inclusive narrative; an observer can see and understand only a fraction of a city at any given time. But as Kevin Lynch writes in *The Image of the City*, particular urban worlds can present widely varying degrees of coherence. For Lynch, a comprehensible and appealing urban environment is one with visual coherence or '*imageability*': that combination of 'shape, color, or arrangement which facilitates the making of vividly identified, powerfully structured, highly useful mental images of the environment' (9). Such a city, he says, will 'invite the eye and the ear to greater attention and participation' (10); its visual clarity and legibility enable its inhabitants to achieve a strong sense of orientation and conti-nuity – in other words, an understanding of how their city's diverse elements are interconnected. This imageable quality is often absent from the London of early West Indian fiction. The most extreme in-stance is George Lamming's *The Emigrants* (1954), a detailed analysis of which will establish the spatial hermeneutic framework for a compara-tive examination of Jean Rhys's earlier *Voyage in the Dark* (1934). In both novels, the circumscribed options London presents to the development of expatriate colonial identities – whether individual or communal – are conveyed through environments characterized by claustrophobic enclo-sure and a lack of visual definition.

The Emigrants is the first postwar novel about the metropolitan experi-ence of black West Indians; it was published in 1954, just six years after the SS *Windrush* inaugurated West Indian immigration as a mass phe-nomenon and four years after Lamming himself arrived (on the same boat as Sam Selvon). The newness of the subject does not, however, result in expansive description; in *The Emigrants*, visible minorities in-habit a virtually invisible city. Arriving in a 'dark' London filled with 'smoke,' Lamming's characters are swallowed into the belly of the beast without even a glance at a building or street (125). In over 150 pages of episodic London narrative, only four place-names are mentioned, all from the same area – Marble Arch, Hyde Park, the Serpentine, and Kensington High Street. The urban landscape is almost completely un-represented in the narrative; every scene takes place in a room, usually underground and behind a closed door to which attention is repeatedly drawn. Windows tend to be covered with curtains, and when they are not, it is either too dark to see outside or the view is 'abruptly blocked by houses which came up like a wall between two foreign territories' (155). Opportunities to go outside are regularly passed over by the narrator and avoided by his characters. The overall effect is of people imprisoned, barred entry to the very city they have come to inhabit. This figurative confinement is anticipated by the dominant space of the sea voyage that occupies the first third of the novel: Lamming's emigrants are usually seen not in the open air of breezy decks but in a cramped dormitory that echoes and updates the middle passage. In London, the narrator explic-itly mentions the difference between island and metropolitan life in a passage that recalls Naipaul's essay:

In another climate, at another time, [these men] would ramble the streets yarning and singing, or sit at the street corners throwing dice as they talked

aimlessly about everything and nothing. Life was leisurely. But this room
was different. Its immediacy forced them to see that each was caught in it.
There was no escape from it until the morning came with its uncertain
offer of another day's work. Alone, circumscribed by the night and the
neutral staring walls, each felt himself pushed to the limit of his thinking.
(192)

The virtual imprisonment within physical and mental interiors, contrasted with the free, outdoor movement of the island, is ironic given the
emigrants' reason for moving – to expand their horizons and opportunities beyond the limitations of island society.

Lamming's visual effacement of London is especially notable because
his account of the train journey from Plymouth to London is full of
energetic descriptions by various characters of the new landscape and
buildings, punctuated repeatedly with the imperative 'Look' (120–3).[5]
Indeed, the book is strewn with references to watching and looking:
'Gawd bless my eyesight' says someone on the train (121); 'I never
thought ah would have set eyes on England,' says another (114). On the
boat, when asked what England is like, Tornado says, 'When you get
there you'll see for yuhself. ... God give every man two eyes to see with, ...
an' as far as I can see you got two like me' (84). Eyes are associated less
often with seeing, however, than with not seeing. In a cryptic exchange
on the boat-train one passenger says, 'In the land o' de one eye the blind
is king,' to which another responds, 'You see, partner, if you can't see,
we'll all start thinkin' that's w'at we got eyes for, not to see' (116). In
London, some characters suffer delusions of being watched, and others
fail at their peril to recognize each other. Una Solomon's eyes are
described as 'two abandoned pools filling the holes under her brow'
(247), and Collis, the character most closely identified with the shadowy
narrator and with Lamming himself, finds his eyesight mysteriously deteriorating. Faces become indistinguishable to him, like 'object[s] without
any of the usual attributes' (275), and in his encounter with the Englishman Frederick (whose eyes 'had the glassy impersonal dullness of eyes
that had popped from the scarlet sockets of dead fish'), the failures of
recognition and mutuality that characterize all black-white relations in
the novel are crystallized in an optical image: 'Collis was looking for his
eyes but it seemed that he had forgotten what an eye was. He saw the
objects of dull glass evenly balanced on either side of Frederick's nose,
but he could no longer recognise Frederick's eyes' (224).

The narrative's enactment of this trope of blindness – its own myopic failure or refusal to see and represent a visually distinctive London – may be interpreted in several ways. On one level, Lamming's non-city is a realization of the fear of Higgins, on arrival in Plymouth, that beyond the 'cage' of the boat's dormitory was '*no-THING*' (105) – the void, a living death. England may, as Lamming writes in *The Pleasures of Exile*, have been perceived by its new arrivals as 'a promise and an expectation' (212), but for Higgins, whose expectation of training and working as a cook has just been snatched away, the 'space' that beckons beyond the docked ship's doors is deceptive (*Emigrants* 106). England is actually 'an extension of the ship,' 'a cage like the dormitory vastly expanded' (106). It is guarded by officials 'Caged within their white collars' who appear to view the new arrivals as 'lunatics' for leaving 'the natural relaxation' of their islands (108). Even though 'the doors remained open' for Higgins, he hesitates on the threshold in the belief that 'he could make no claim on these things' beyond the ship (106). And well he might; as James Procter notes, metaphorical and literal doorways did not always correspond in this period: 'As Britain's doors were opened to its colonies and former colonies through the Nationality Act of 1948, those doors guarding the nation's residential hinterlands were being effectively closed' ('Descending' 21). The constricting quality and closed doors of Lamming's London reflect a social reality of racism marked by the appearance of 'No Coloureds' signs on flats for rent through the 1950s and 1960s. This London is a city of segregation, of firmed-up boundaries between 'English' and 'immigrant' citizens.

A sense of division is registered narratively through an absence of street scenes and the crowds of white Britons that would have populated them. It is registered architecturally in the only substantial description of London's built environment: 'The way the houses build was that people doan' have nothing to do with one another. You can live an' die in yuh room an' the people next door never say boo to you no matter how long you inhabit that place. ... An' what all you here goin' learn for the first time is what it mean to live in yuh own own [sic] room alone without knowing a single soul in any of the other hundred. That is if you can get a room' (74–5). Spoken on the sea-journey by Tornado, who has been to London before, this speech begins with a time-honoured truism about cities as filled with people who are paradoxically both proximate (one lives beside them or passes them on the street) and distant (they remain strangers).[6] Tornado's final sentence – 'That is if you can get a room' – moves beyond these general experiences, however, to address a quality of isolation particular to black Londoners: the difficulty of claiming their own domestic spaces in the metropolis. The closed doors, walls, and curtains that dominate Lamming's settings metonymically signify the social gulf that can exist despite physical nearness – particularly when formerly distant, unseen black colonials become suddenly close and visible in the English capital. Distance in its literal and figurative senses is a concept that permeates Caribbean cultural thinking, and Lamming repeatedly emphasizes the 'enormous distance' between his major white English characters, Pearson and Frederick, and their black 'others,' even when they are in the same room (146, 158).

The novel's one positive image of interracial relations – Azi's vision of European and African mutuality resulting in 'a fantastic mix-up, a really great, constructive chaos' and 'fundamental convergence of the several bloodstreams' – remains just a passing fancy mentioned in a letter (214). The reality for Lamming is not coalescence or Rushdiean hybridity but failure, distance, and exclusion. With his characters running up against barriers to social mobility and interracial exchange, Lamming elides the urban landscape to suggest their lack of power in and knowledge of London: their tiny sliver of purchase is registered by a kind of boarded-over narrative through which sunlight barely seeps. Moreover, if knowing and feeling empowered in a city are a function of imageability – of clear seeing, especially from a panoramic height to which these base-ment dwellers never rise – urban knowledge and power are also associ-ated with walking. Raymond Williams shows how the qualities of the modern city have so often in literature been articulated and compre-hended, whether affirmatively or critically, through the figure of the lone walking individual (see 233–5). For Michel de Certeau, as noted in previous chapters, walking in the city is an appropriative spatial practice. Just as the speech act individualized language, each pedestrian enunci-ates and writes the city in the image of his or her own story – transgress-ing borders, reinscribing spaces, and resisting hegemonies through the individual choices of a unique itinerary. Not surprisingly, Lamming's text has virtually no walkers; after the constant motion and narrative continuity of the ship and train journeys, the story becomes fractured and immobile, as if it is not just myopic but paralysed.

Not walking corresponds therefore to not seeing, not knowing, and not claiming the city in Lamming's London. It also corresponds to a failure of narrative. Critics of *The Emigrants* typically find its London section fragmentary and disorienting as it jumps from group to group

and room to room.[7] Basic facts, events, and contexts in characters' lives
are omitted, and the narrative seems deliberately incomplete. This too is
a function of the novel's spatial qualities; de Certeau develops his correspondences between walking, enunciating, and inscribing into a vision
of stories as 'spatial trajectories' and narrative as a way of traversing and
organizing space. 'Every story,' he says, 'is a travel story – a spatial
practice' (115). J. Hillis Miller makes a similar point: 'Every narrative,
without exception, ... traces out in its course an arrangement of places,
dwellings, and rooms joined by paths or roads' (10). Sennett sees this
relation between place and narrative as an essential feature of good
urban design, arguing that city spaces should always be designed with
'weak borders rather than strong walls' in order to encourage 'the
narrative use of places' and 'permit space to become thus encoded with
time' (*Conscience* 196). Lamming's characters do not inhabit such spaces;
their London has strong borders – both literal and metaphorical – and
the time with which it is encoded is still the old, oppressive time of
imperial history. His novel may not be the 'exception' that proves Miller's
rule, but it unquestionably favours the stasis of rooms over the fluid
mobility and narrativity of paths and roads. The inside-outside boundaries that Sennett wants to make more porous are extremely rigid in this
novel; Lamming's city is not an enabling space for West Indian immigrants or for narrative, which can offer only a fractured account of their
struggles to live and build communities.

Furthermore, at this early stage of West Indian settlement the spatial
limitations of Lamming's migrants may enact their view of themselves as
colonial children in the motherland. Young children are spatially very
restricted – safely behind closed doors, not walking alone in the city.
Children have much less spatial awareness than adults; infants, who
begin life myopic, are for months unable to distinguish objects or to see
and comprehend spaces and spatial relations (see Tuan 19–33; Sack
121–43). Their world is severely limited in terms of motion, perception,
and comprehension – just like the London of Lamming's new arrivals.
Since his colonial characters have learned the white parent/black child
trope from the doctrines of imperial cultures – and reiterate it without
irony in several passages (e.g., 132, 191, 192) – the incorporation of
spatial limitations analogous to those imposed on children marks another way Lamming's London reflects the legacy of imperialism. Indeed,
as far as its constituting narrative is concerned, this London is no more
seen or known than it would be by colonials back on the islands. And,
Lamming implies, it will not be until West Indians stake a stronger claim,

take possession, form coherent communities, and begin to remake the city in their own image.

London's near-absence from *The Emigrants* may therefore signify a form of resistance: a refusal to substantiate or legitimize a city still steeped in the architectonics of imperial power. Dissolving the city into an unperceived immateriality, refusing to usher it into basic forms of textual representation such as expansive visual description or mobile, continuous narrative, Lamming implies that London in 1954 is not yet fully enough inhabited, known, and reterritorialized by West Indians to be suitable for visual or narrative imaging. The many references to deteriorating eyesight and non-recognition of people and objects either can be seen to reinforce this disintegration or, alternatively, may suggest that images of metropolitan life formed in the distant Caribbean must themselves dissolve when their referent is up close and concretely material. In either case, Lamming approaches the acts of perception and representation with a politically charged caution. Unlike the archetypal male imperialist newly arrived in colonial space – the imperial I/eye of colonial discourse theory, a figure whose myopia doesn't stop him from authoritatively constructing the new world as the product of his own ethnocentric vision[8] – Lamming holds back from the knowing gaze, the arrogant claim of representational authority. In this context, Lamming's virtual non-inscription of London signifies both humility and resistance. I don't know you well enough, it admits, and at the same time: But what I do know tells me you aren't worth my full attention yet.

More positively and assertively, Lamming's representational choices may signal that he is beginning to West-Indianize the metropolis at two distinct levels: writerly narration and character inhabitation. Neither of these, however, turns out to offer a positive endorsement of metropolitan life. At the writerly level, his elision of the cityscape is uncannily like the handling of the Caribbean landscape in many of the region's folktales. As Edouard Glissant writes in *Caribbean Discourse*, the setting of Creole tales is an empty, 'symbolic space' that 'becomes a pattern of succeeding spaces through which one journeys' (129):

> But it is important to realize that if the place is indicated, *it is never described.* The description of the landscape is not a feature of the folktale. Neither the joy nor the pleasure of describing are evident in it. This is because the landscape of the folktale is not meant to be inhabited. A place you pass through, it is not yet a country.
>
> ... So this land is never possessed. (130)

Lamming, who indicates but does not describe London, and who fragments it into a succession of interior spaces and disconnected scenes,
implies that the metropolis is a non-place to be passed through but not
possessed. Just as a sense of displacement, non-belonging, and alienation
from the land pervades Caribbean culture as a legacy of the region's
history of slavery and indentured labour, the London that oversaw that
history is here, in the early years of decolonization, rendered as an alien
landscape for displaced West Indians. This writerly West-Indianization of
the metropolis does not, therefore, mean it has become home – quite
the opposite.

Alternatively, Lamming's emphasis on interior inhabitation may indicate that his characters are reterritorializing the metropolis at the small-
scale level of barber shops, hair salons, and clubs. For Procter, 'the
basement represents a "pocket" or enclave that re-houses the Caribbean
within the white metropolis'; these spaces are 'private, exclusive and
exclusionary territories, West Indian strongholds, "colonized" sections
of London, unfamiliar, unknown and unwelcoming to white Londoners'
('Descending' 30).[9] Seen in this light, Lamming is anticipating such
later London narratives as Sam Selvon's *The Lonely Londoners* (1956),
Timothy Mo's *Sour Sweet* (1982), and Hanif Kureishi's *My Beautiful
Laundrette* (1986), in which small retail businesses also become microcosmic colonies or outposts of cultural autonomy and front-line resistance.
But none of those texts restricts its characters' mobility or effaces outdoor London as *The Emigrants* does. Combined with the fractured narrative and the emphasis on alienated individuals and dysfunctional
communities, Lamming's confining interiors come across less as empowering strongholds than as ghettos or consolation prizes claimed in lieu of
the larger city.

Procter does temper his optimistic reading with the observation that
the novel's 'subterranean locations are deeply ambivalent spaces, functioning as prisons (underworlds, graves, dungeons, jails); wombs (roots,
foundations, sources, embryonic sites that are invested with an imma-
nent potential for change, growth, or 'uprising') and as fortresses (en-
claves or sites of resistance)' ('Descending' 25). He glosses the second
and third metaphors positively, but these interpretations also need quali-
fying. A fortress is a sign of a hostile outside environment and can be as
restricting to its occupants' mobility and connectedness as any prison.
Similarly, a womb is not always an enabling space. Lamming describes
the women's enclave of Miss Dorking's hairdressing business as 'a womb
which the world (meaning those other than you) was not aware of. The

world passed by on the outside, intent or callous, but ignorant of the intimacy and the warmth of this house' (148). The positive aspects of the image (the womb as comfortable and safe haven) are qualified by the absence of interaction with all those 'others' that constitute 'the world.' In the same way that a womb is a healthy space of confinement for just nine months, after which the outside world must be entered, there are limits to this symbolic womb's long-term value as a sanctuary within a 'callous' white world that, in Lamming's narrative, seems destined to remain alien. Moreover, when Lamming ends his novel with a traumatic abortion, he casts the womb's associations with growth and rebirth into further doubt. Whether as prisons, fortresses, wombs, or playpens for colonial 'children,' the negative significations conveyed by Lamming's underground rooms outweigh any incipient sense of a reterritorialized metropolis.

All Exactly Alike

Jean Rhys's *Voyage in the Dark*, published twenty years before *The Emigrants* and set in 1914, begins with a similarly questionable association between rebirth and confined space. Of her arrival in England at age sixteen, Anna Morgan writes, 'It was as if a curtain had fallen, hiding everything I had ever known. It was almost like being born again' (7).[10] The novel's dominant setting is a series of inhospitable rooms, variously described by Anna as 'like being in a small, dark box' (22) and as seeming to shrink or expand as a function of her emotional condition (see 26, 29). Anna is a white Creole West Indian; her London, like that of Lamming's black migrants, is a cold, drab, and unaccommodating place, and the trajectory of her life there at ages eighteen and nineteen is a 'downward spiral' through increasingly alienating relationships and into prostitution, culminating in a near-fatal abortion (O'Connor 84). As in *The Emigrants*, this concluding event repositions the womb/room from an image of (re)birth to one of death.[11] Such associations have been previously implied by Anna's alarming perception (after reading Edgar Allan Poe) that she is trapped between 'the walls of a room getting smaller and smaller until they crush you to death' (26). Death is also implied by the two similes mentioned above: the 'small, dark box' connotes a coffin, and the curtain associated with 'being born again' falls, as Teresa O'Connor notes, 'like a guillotine, cutting off the past' and killing the former self (87).[12] At a later point in the narrative, Anna stops going out of her room and encloses herself in bed; when you 'lie in the dark and pull the sheet over your head,' she says, 'It's as if you were dead' (120, 121).

Although walls, doors, curtains, and beds dominate Anna's spatial environment, Rhys's narrative is not limited to cloistered, deathly interiors. Between rooms, Anna is seen moving through London's streets; character and narrative have greater mobility and continuity here than in Lamming's text. Still, the urban scene is minimally, repetitiously, and often disorientingly portrayed, beginning with a breathless stream-of-consciousness passage conveying Anna's impressions on arrival:

> smaller meaner everything is never mind – this is London – hundreds thousands of white people white people rushing along and the dark houses all alike frowning down one after the other all alike all stuck together – the streets like smooth shut-in ravines and the dark houses frowning down – oh I'm not going to like this place I'm not going to like this place I'm not going to like this place. (15–16)

After more than two years, nothing has changed; as if stuck in her first response like the broken record she begins to sound like here, Anna returns obsessively to both the evaluation and the images of this first description. She tells Maudie, 'I don't like London. It's an awful place; it looks horrible sometimes' (40). Individual houses continue to frown darkly: her first lover's residence is depicted in two nearly identical passages as 'dark and quiet and not friendly to me. Sneering faintly, sneering discreetly, as a servant would' (43; cf. 31).[13] Groups of houses remain indistinguishable: Anna remarks that 'all the houses outside in the street were the same – all alike, all hideously stuck together – and the streets going north, east, south, west, all exactly the same' (89). Later, she repeats this defining image of London almost verbatim: 'Everything was always so exactly alike – that was what I could never get used to. And the cold; and the houses all exactly alike, and the streets going north, south, east, west, all exactly alike' (152). The towns she travels to as a chorus girl are similarly uniform: she remarks on 'how exactly alike they were, bedrooms on tour' and regrets that 'the towns we went to always looked so exactly alike. You were perpetually moving to another place which was perpetually the same' (128, 8).[14]

This drab architectural sameness indicates that Anna's spatial awareness of the city is undeveloped. She observes little, and what she does see is indistinct, static, and uninviting; moreover, she sees it repeatedly, in minor variations, from her first arrival through her later residence.

Colours also blur together; as Elaine Savory shows in her study of the novel's colour coding, Rhys represents England and London through muted and indeterminate colours (see 85–108). As in *The Emigrants*, Anna's London lacks 'imageability': the visual clarity, colour, and distinction that affect how a city's occupants perceive themselves to be oriented and connected to their spatial environment. What Lamming suggests through elision, Rhys conveys through repetition and indeterminacy. Anna may navigate through London with the familiarity of a local (albeit in a rootless, disconnected way), but her perception of identical houses, streets, and even directions ('north, south, east, west, all exactly alike') conveys a strong sense of disorientation that speaks to the city's impact on her emotions and on the direction her life is taking. Anna, Rhys implies, is lost in ways beyond the geographical. As Kevin Lynch observes,

> To become completely lost is perhaps a rather rare experience for most people in the modern city. ... But let the mishap of disorientation once occur, and the sense of anxiety and even terror that accompanies it reveals to us how closely it is linked to our sense of balance and well-being. The very word 'lost' in our language means much more than simple geographical uncertainty; it carries overtones of utter disaster. (4)

Anna's disoriented response to the urban landscape conveys her unbalanced psychic state and prefigures the disastrous course her life there will take. At the same time, London's vaunted imperial centrality and global connectedness is turned on its head: the streets that lead in four indistinguishable directions come across not as pathways to wider worlds but as dead ends in a bewildering labyrinth.[15]

Contrasted with this London of grim interiors and foreboding, disorienting exteriors are the richly detailed descriptions of Anna's West Indian home, which is portrayed in vivid colours. She routinely escapes there, to memories and imagined journeys full of movement and expansive space. This world, unlike London, Anna really knows: one long paragraph about the road to the Constance Estate and its surrounding landscape and seascape evokes more enthusiasm, variety, detail, and connection – of spaces to each other, and of the human body to those spaces – than all of her London descriptions combined. Most crucially, this evocation of Anna's *roots* is described through a depiction of *routes*: the pathways along which she journeys and orients herself to this environment: 'The road goes along by the sea. ... And then – wait a minute.

Then do you turn to the right and the left? To the left, of course. You turn to the left and the sea is at your back, and the road goes zigzag upwards' (129). For Lynch, familiarity with paths, and an ability to picture an environment in terms of journeys along landmark-filled routes, is an important measure of a person's familiarity with and orientation to his or her environment (see 46–9). This passage's moment of disorientation is quickly and confidently dispelled, and the paragraph is filled with descriptions of visually distinct and familiar landmarks.

These contrasts – between a confining, disorienting, alienating urban British world and a spacious, rural West Indian one to which Anna is oriented and emotionally connected – are part of a larger pattern of binaries built into the novel. Most critics remark on what Savory calls Anna's 'dualist' view of the world – 'the West Indies versus England' – and read the novel in light of its evident contrasts (91). Anna establishes an oppositional framework right after the opening image of the falling curtain: 'The colours were different, the smells different, the feeling things gave you right down inside yourself was different. Not just the difference between heat, cold; light, darkness; purple, grey. But a difference in the way I was frightened and the way I was happy' (7). Here physical and visual oppositions correspond explicitly to emotional ones and, with the West Indies as the favoured place, Rhys reverses the hierarchical binaries of imperialist discourses that elevate metropolitan over colonial spaces. Anna's later comment that she 'always wanted to be black' because 'being black is warm and gay, being white is cold and sad' similarly upends imperial power's racial hierarchies (27).

However, just as imperialist binaries conceal a reality of mutual relations and reciprocity – London is built up by the empire it builds; colonizer and colonized transform each other – Rhys incorporates a relational dynamic into her novel that offsets the manifest oppositions between here and there. The curtain that purportedly hides the known past from Anna represents geographical and temporal separation only; mentally those distant spaces and times can be visualized, through acts of imaginative return that are woven fluidly into Anna's London narrative from the first paragraph to the final scene. Far from hidden, the West Indies is brightly and distinctively visible throughout; indeed, the novel's second paragraph opens up the question of which of her two 'worlds' Anna is 'really' inhabiting: 'Sometimes it was is if [sic] I were back there and as if England were a dream. At other times England was the real thing and out there was the dream, but I could never fit them together' (7–8). In a similarly relativistic spirit, Anna supplements her comment that Constance Estate is 'beautiful' with this observation: 'On the other hand, if England is beautiful, it's [i.e., the Estate is] not beautiful. It's some other world. It all depends, doesn't it?' (45). The sense of separate but substitutable worlds is reinforced by occasional passages in which London is allowed a measure of the Caribbean's enabling expansiveness and visual appeal (e.g., 25, 67, 134) and others that attribute to the island home the fears and confinement normally associated with metropolitan life (e.g., 59, 129–30).

In one important dream during her pregnancy, aspects of the two places and their characteristic images coalesce. Anna imagines she sees 'dolls of islands' from a ship 'sailing in a doll's sea'; one island resembles her home 'except that the trees were all wrong. These were English trees' (140). The doll-sized environment (inhabited by a 'boy bishop' sitting 'like a doll' in 'a child's coffin') begins, disorientingly, to get larger:

> I tried to catch hold of a branch and step ashore, but the deck of the ship expanded. Somebody had fallen overboard. ...
> I was still trying to walk up the deck and get ashore. I took huge, climbing, flying strides among confused figures. I was powerless and very tired, but I had to go on. And the dream rose into a climax of meaninglessness, fatigue and powerlessness, and the deck was heaving up and down, and when I woke up everything was still heaving up and down.
> It was funny how, after that, I kept on dreaming about the sea. (140–1)

Here a Caribbean scene acquires not only English trees but the contracting and expanding qualities of Anna's coffin-like London room. But whereas the expanding room conveyed a lifting of anxiety and regaining of control (see 29), the expanding deck – an in-between space of access to the island – adds to the dream-Anna's anxiety and powerlessness by preventing her from reaching her goal. The 'baby coffin' suggests both Anna herself – whom Vincent Jeffries calls an 'infantile' 'child' (69) – and the abortion she will soon undergo, ending her pregnancy and the morning sickness that feels 'like seasickness, only worse, and everything heaving up and down' (138).

The dream also recalls earlier scenes in which maltreatment by men is figured through images of expansion, contraction, and death by water. Shortly after Walter Jeffries breaks off their affair, Anna goes to meet him with 'a shrunken feeling just like having fever' and a feeling of intense 'fear' that 'had grown gigantic; it filled me and it filled the whole world' (82). In the middle of trying (and failing) to reestablish the relationship, she imagines herself falling into water and 'grinning up' through it, blowing bubbles as she tries to speak: 'And how do you know what it's like to try to speak from under water when you're drowned?' (84). In the next scene, Anna is recovering from an illness and free-associating on a music-hall song about blowing rings in the air and drifting; she changes the song's line 'Legions away from despair' to 'Oceans away from despair' because 'it's the sea, I thought. The Caribbean Sea' that she identifies with 'despair' (90, 91). She then recites a quotation from a potted history of the indigenous Caribs that emphasizes their vigorous resistance to British rule and their eventual near-extermination. Anna seems to be identifying her condition of exploitation and victimization by British men, and her resulting despair, with aspects of Caribbean history located across oceans of time and space. Many Amerindians died by drowning (or drowned themselves as forms of resistance).[16] Black West Indians have a similarly horrific history. Notably, the genealogical line of descent from some first-generation slaves was cut off when they died from drowning, thrown off slave ships that heaved up and down during storms; among the slaves who survived that dark voyage, some are thought to have aborted or killed their children as a way of opposing slavery.[17] Anna – who valorizes West Indian blackness over European whiteness, who is teasingly called a 'Hottentot' by British friends, and who is criticized by Aunt Hester for talking 'exactly like a nigger' (12, 56) – has an abortion as her own act of resistance against the metropolitan world of exploitative white men and women she reluctantly inhabits. During the procedure her hallucinations focus on childhood memories of Carnival celebrations, which also have a history in slave resistance. Having regained some control over her body and her future in the aftermath of the abortion, Anna is able in her final paragraph to think tentatively, and with more conviction than before, 'about being new and fresh' and 'about starting all over again' (159).

The London of *Voyage in the Dark* is overdetermined by both its oppositional contrasts with the West Indian birthplace and its intricately woven relations to it. The metropolis's complex relationality is conveyed by a narrative that fluidly and effortlessly crosses the ocean through memories, dreams, and imaginings; curtain or no curtain, Anna is never barred from this other world. The spatial boundaries of her consciousness and the first-person narrative it inscribes can expand and contract at will, alternately crossing frontiers of time and space or cowering in box-like rooms. Anna survives and begins to take control of her life as a direct function of this spatial flexibility and the cluster of interrelated images that her mobile narrative weaves together: the room that is both womb and coffin; the child who has become an adult; the death that can be a new beginning; the white woman who identifies with blackness; the here and now that merges into there and then; and the ocean whose heaving waves symbolically join these different selves and worlds. As the various images coalesce, relational and syncretic thinking – even if it is 'only' thinking – dilutes Anna's obsession with binary difference and helps ameliorate the visual sameness that, paradoxically, exemplifies what makes London's difference so disorienting and alienating.

The sea is a central image of interconnection, completeness, and mobility in Caribbean culture and history. Long before Paul Gilroy published *The Black Atlantic*, Derek Walcott was invoking the ocean as the defining space of the region's history and transcultural identity in poems such as 'The Sea Is History,' 'The Schooner *Flight*,' and *Omeros*. The synchronic vision of West Indian historical time and geographical place on which Edouard Glissant bases his influential 'poétique de la Relation,' or 'Cross-Cultural Poetics,' identifies the sea with the very essence of the region's relational identity:

> What is the Caribbean in fact? A multiple series of relationships. We all feel it, we express it in all kinds of hidden or twisted ways, or we fiercely deny it. But we sense that this sea exists within us with its weight of now revealed islands.
>
> The Caribbean Sea is not an American lake. It is the estuary of the Americas. (139)

Glissant's translator, J. Michael Dash, argues that 'the defiance of confinement, the movement away from stasis is central to the imaginative discourse of the Caribbean' as Glissant perceives it; furthermore, 'the Caribbean imagination balances on this axis of shared images of mobility.' Often, Dash adds, 'this flight from an enclosed world is expressed in the images of the ship, the spiral, the journey that recur in Caribbean art' (xli). Rhys's inclusion of relational sea and ship images in the spiral descent of Anna's metropolitan journey, obsessed as it is with questions of enclosure and openness, stasis and mobility, helps integrate scattered images and so strengthens the links and deconstructs the oppositions between her two worlds. Through its imagery and fluid narrative mode, her novel brings the West Indian world into the metropolis. In so doing, it anticipates portrayals of London as a complexly relational locale in much more recent novels by West Indians discussed later in this chapter, as well as by Canadians (Kate Pullinger, Catherine Bush) and South Asians (Salman Rushdie, Amitav Ghosh) discussed in other chapters.

Such relationality is missing from the London of *The Emigrants*, even though Lamming makes the sea and the journey central images. The transatlantic voyage of emigration that Rhys's novel omits takes up over a third of Lamming's text; this section contains many references to the sea that summon up themes of West Indian identity and desire. The most interesting ones involve a spatial imagination that, like Rhys's, figures psychological distance through increases and decreases in physical size and distance. Lamming's intermittent I-narrator, in his first appearance, recalls a recurring vision he had in Trinidad in which he stared across a valley that 'was a vast presence like the sea in this fading sunshine' (6–7). The valley seemed to shrink 'so that the space invited a leap which boys attempt without thought on the sand. ... Then everything collapsed. The gulf had widened' (7). Following a lengthy passage portraying the sea as 'dark, and sinister and suggestively horrific' (6), this image of shrinking and expanding space suggests the ambivalence with which the would-be West Indian emigrant perceives the paradoxically distant but proximate metropolis. The camaraderie among various islanders on board the ship encourages the Jamaican to assert, 'De wahter separatin' you from him ain't do nothin' to put distance between de views you got on dis life or de next. Different man, different land, but de same outlook. Dat's de meanin' o' West Indies. De wahter between dem islands doan' separate dem' (61). The group identity he articulates begins to fragment after arrival in London, and with that optimistic solidarity go the references to the water the Jamaican summoned as a metaphor for West Indian connectedness. In the London of discrete rooms, fragmented identities, stunted communities, and fractured narrative that follows the Atlantic journey, references to sea and to the West Indian past almost completely disappear. Lamming's disabling, alienating metropolis does not foster or accommodate the kind of transoceanic connectedness and relational identity conveyed by Rhys's novel. As a result, his emigrants seem more constricted than Anna does, and at the end, the prospects for most of them seem less promising than hers.

The Spin of the World

The failure of group identity and community in *The Emigrants* indirectly anticipates the fate of the West Indian Federation eight years after the novel was published. The Federation was, in Kenneth Ramchand's words, 'inaugurated with drums and colours in 1959' but formally dissolved in 1962 (Introduction xx), thereby ensuring that the islands remained more separated than integrated by their shared sea. The Federation's failure is also indirectly prophesied in Sam Selvon's *An Island Is a World* (1955). This ambitiously philosophical novel set in Trinidad, London, and the United States attempts, as its title implies, to explore through its structure and images the connections among Trinidad, the West Indies, and the wider world. However, its representations of London and of West Indian community turn out to be less relational than in Selvon's subsequent novel, *The Lonely Londoners* (1956), even though the latter is set entirely in the metropolis and contains no representations of West Indian places.

An Island Is a World introduces its vision of global and cosmic connectedness with its opening description of Foster's early-morning musings:

> The world spun in his brain, and he imagined the island of Trinidad, eleven and a half degrees north of the equator. He saw it on a globe, with the Americas sprawled like giant shadows above and below, and the endless Atlantic lapping the coastlines of the continents and the green islands of the Caribbean. The globe spun and he saw Great Britain and Europe, and Africa. The east countries, Australia. Foster imagined Trinidad as it was, a mere dot on the globe. But he saw himself in the dot.
>
> He saw himself in the dot, and he transmitted thoughts into the universe ... like how RKO introduce their films with a radio station broadcasting into space.
>
> Lying there on the double bed after his wife had got up to prepare breakfast, Foster was big and the globe was small, spinning off there in space. (1)

With its Rhys-like images of a world expanding and shrinking *vis-à-vis* the individual dreamer, together with the spinning-globe motif that recurs throughout the novel, this passage promises a relational perspective on place and identity. That promise is partly met by the novel's narrative structure; in what Clement Wyke calls the 'dance-like movement between the situations of the leading characters,' the back-and-forth plot lines involving Foster in London, Rufus in the United States, and Andrews in Trinidad contain numerous parallel and contrapuntal elements (45). Relationality is undermined, however, by the novel's themes, which locate identity in both universal and national frameworks and then resolve the apparent contradiction through a shared sense of isolation and compartmentalization.

The novel's 'universal thematic vision of life' (Wyke 25) is summarized in a conversation between Foster and Father Hope. Recognizing Foster's frustration at Trinidad's smallness, Father Hope says, 'I used to feel that this island was too small, that my mind reached the sea as soon as it began to expand.' But rather than counter this image of the shoreline as barrier with an alternative view of the sea as conduit, Father Hope opens up 'the world' only to foreclose it: '"People are the same all over the world," Father Hope said. "It does not matter where you are, you encounter sadness, happiness, love, hate. An island is a world, and everywhere that people live, they create their own worlds"' (73). The novel's title, in other words, suggests not so much local-global interrelations as a view that universal likeness need not imply mutuality. If an island is a world, then every (basically similar) world is also an island whose separation from all the other island-worlds is of little matter: 'What you want is variety,' Father Hope tells Foster. 'But you could stay in one place and have that' (73). In a similar spirit of foreclosure, Foster later locates Trinidadian identity in a global framework, showing how it exceeds its small-island limits, but he immediately rejects this expansive view for a narrower and more exclusive view of nationality. Because of Trinidad's mixed society, he writes in a letter, 'I used to think we belonged to the world, that a Trinidadian could go to Alaska and fit in, or eat with chopsticks in Hong Kong, and he wouldn't be disturbed by the thought that he belonged somewhere else' (106). Now, however, he realizes, 'You can't belong to the world, because the world won't have you. The world is made up of different nations, and you've got to belong to one of them, and to hell with the others' (107).

Foster reaches this conclusion while living in London. Meeting people who 'belong' to higher-profile nations, he envies these 'Englishmen and Frenchmen and Americans' their definition: 'Over here you don't say you come from Trinidad, because no one knows where or what Trinidad is. You have to say the West Indies, and then they take it that you are from Jamaica' (106). A stronger, clearer national identity may be a desirable antidote to obscurity, but for Foster such renewed affiliation is incompatible with belonging to the world: 'to hell with the others,' he says; worldly belonging and national belonging are mutually exclusive. London, which Foster calls 'the centre of the world' (154), may provide access to that world in the form of people from various elsewheres (including other West Indian islands), but a transnational social reality does not usher in a vision of transnational consciousness or relational identity.

The representations of London and Foster's life there reinforce this narrowing. Portrayed initially in letters from Foster to Andrews and later in a third-person-limited narrative, Foster's London emerges as a 'world' observed but only minimally engaged. The people he sees, and even most of those he meets, blend into a faceless and generic crowd not unlike the one in T.S. Eliot's 'unreal city' of London in 'The Waste Land' (65). None of the West Indians or Africans Foster meets are named or described. Conversations among them are mentioned but not reported; only an English writer named Paul and Foster's English girlfriend Julia are given names and voices. The physical city is treated with similar vagueness. Foster's perception of the crowds' movements as alternately purposive – 'Why must they always be moving, going some place, all these people' (152) – and 'aimless' – 'a general movement to nowhere' (154) – is more a reflection of his own confusion and alienation from the crowd and the London it represents than a reliable analysis. 'Everyone else [in London] is unconcerned with the spin of the world,' he claims to know (118), but since 'you couldn't know anything about anybody in the restless sea of movement' (131), how can he tell? Solipsistic and 'indescribably lonely' (131), the epistolary Foster offers a largely abstract, cerebral, and detached representation of London. Andrews finds him a frustratingly monologic, non-interactive correspondent (see 114); the metropolis Foster presents to him and the reader is strikingly devoid of engaged relations between the self and 'the world.'

Indeed, Foster's existential questioning, and his failure to find answers or fulfilment in London, cause a retreat into the self: 'The one thing to be done then was to try and live in a state of acute consciousness of being. ... The world spins, and somewhere on that globe you are, a microscopic dot in a land mass, with the oceans of the world flowing about you, existing because you exist, existing as long as you exist' (129). This man not only lives on an island; he *is* an island. The oceanic crowd that flows around him – 'the restless sea of movement' – inspires feelings not of connection but seclusion. His isolation is projected onto his portrayal of West Indians in London; their aimless anonymity seems to prevent them, too, from taking possession of the metropolis or from turning its relational promise into strong transnational communities:

In and out of the frenzied bustling of London, threads of West Indian lives ran. Sometimes he lost track of them, they were swallowed up and disappeared behind a million white faces. There were those who worked at anything they could get, the railways, factories; living in cheap dirty rooms, meeting the boys now and then for a game of rummy or poker. Out of the frying pan into the fire. No sense of gain or loss, no backward glance. No hope of making progress in the old 'Brit'n,' but it was better than living on the 'rock.' Here and there they slouched about the streets, men without future or hope or destiny, lost in London, fooling themselves into a way of life because there were so many people and they seemed to be doing the same thing. (153)

This passage from the final days of Foster's two-year stay in London undercuts the more optimistic vision of his first letter. There he suggested that the West Indians brought together in a London hostel were forming a collective identity: 'inter-island feelings and differences are minimised, as would be expected: we are all birds of a feather, fighting against the injustices of the Mother Country' (95). Two years later, that incipient solidarity has dwindled into cheerless card games and atomized drift, so uninspiring that neither Foster nor the narrator feels compelled to individualize the group portrait with faces or names.

As in *The Emigrants*, the inability of transnational West Indian communities to convincingly gel in London anticipates the later failure of the West Indian Federation movement. Andrews notes in *An Island Is a World* that the movement's 'headquarters' are in London: the British government, he says, has proposed federation as a deliberately divisive and stalling 'compromise' response to West Indian demands for self-government. For Andrews, federation will not be viable until governments and polities are strengthened at the national level: currently, he says, 'our own administration is corrupted and dishonest, each individual seeking his own ends' (147). His pessimistic outlook on both federation and nation corresponds with Foster's withdrawal – from a transnational sense of 'belonging to the world,' then to West Indian-regional and Trinidadian-national 'belongings,' and finally, when these more local attachments fray, into his aimless, unattached self.

More disillusioning than inspiring, more disabling than enabling, London – and the one significant relationship it spawns – is abandoned by Foster after two years. Once he has left Julia and London for Trinidad, Foster realizes that his former faith in the nation – 'you've got to belong to one' – has been damaged by his metropolitan experiences:

He had nothing. He had been brought up as a Trinidadian – a member of a cosmopolitan community who recognised no creed or race, a creature born of all the peoples in the world, in a small island that no one knew anything about. The world, in reality, consisted of the continents – the world was London, New York, Paris, and the big cities one read about every day in the newspapers. Who was interested in a few thousand people living on an island, when in one big city there were millions constantly moving to and fro, cheering the royal family, watching the bus fares rise, feeding the pigeons in Trafalgar Square? Of what material loss would it be to the world if the island suddenly sank under the sea? (211–12)

London in this novel provides the site for a working-out of questions of identity and political affiliation that have their origin and end in the West Indies. Despite the promise of Trinidadianness as a form of transnational belonging, living in London has made Foster feel detached from anything larger than himself. Even when, in the book's final scene, Andrews offers hope for the nation in the form of a royal commission that will 'purge' its corrupt administration, Foster is unable 'to shake off the despondency he felt. He could see the world spinning ahead of them. It was as if they were going towards it, but it kept its distance, they were never nearer. Somehow it didn't seem to matter any more' (236, 237). On this bleak note of individual alienation and national irrelevance, the novel ends.

Selvon's most famous London novel, published one year later, recapitulates several themes introduced in *An Island Is a World.* The metropolis of *The Lonely Londoners* is replete with alienating and restless crowds, aimless drifters, and reminders that blackness is a liability. The narrator speaks of 'a kind of communal feeling with the [white] Working Class and the spades' based on shared hardships and poverty, but offers no representations of such an interracial community (and only sketchy ones of white people) (59). West Indians can offer occasional fellowship, but Moses warns the newly arrived Galahad that 'every man on his own. It ain't have no s— over here like "both of we is Trinidadians and we must help out one another"' (21). Even after ten years, Moses finds London 'a lonely miserable city' where the English withhold acceptance and West Indian friends are scattered and easily lost (114). The narrator recalls the London of Lamming, Rhys, and the earlier Selvon when he laments that

it have people living in London who don't know what happening in the room next to them, far more the street, or how other people living. London is a place like that. It divide up in little worlds, and you stay in the world you belong to and you don't know anything about what happening in the other ones except what you read in the papers. (58)

As in the earlier novels, rooms are ambiguous spaces. Moses's flat brings a fragile but sustaining community of West Indian 'fellars' together occasionally 'to talk about things back home' (114). But the room's enclosure and privacy make Moses, like Lamming's Tornado and Rhys's Anna, fear death in a way he did not in the open-air Caribbean: 'look how people does dead and nobody don't know nothing until the milk bottles start to pile up in front of the door. Supposing one day I keel off here in this room? I don't take milk regular – I would stay here until one of the boys drop round. That is a hell of a thing to think about, you know' (115).

Still, despite its forthrightness about London's depressing realities, its wholly metropolitan setting, and its more negative-sounding title, *The Lonely Londoners* achieves a more upbeat and expansively relational vision of London than *An Island Is a World*. It does so through aspects of style, characterization, and setting. Stylistically, the innovative use of dialect that made Selvon the first author to render London entirely in West Indian diction and speech-rhythms has the paradoxical effect of integrating and pluralizing his narrative. Considered by many critics to be the novel's greatest achievement, its dialect narration creates what Frank Birbalsingh calls a 'wholly original language, an invented dialect incorporating linguistic elements from a number of West Indian territories' ('Samuel' 154). Ramchand writes that by drawing 'expertly upon the whole linguistic spectrum available to the West Indian writer,' Selvon 'expresses the sensibility of a whole society' ('Song' 229). Wyke analyses this narrative voice in detail, showing how changing registers of diction, tone, and syntax move the dialect constantly among a variety of speech-modes (see 34). What all three critics imply is the transnational, relational nature of this language. Using Trinidadian Creole as a base – which itself is influenced by English, Spanish, and French, as well as Indian, African, and indigenous languages – Selvon further cross-pollinates his language by incorporating elements of the dialects of other islands and of various classes. In the process, just as white people are largely excluded, both Standard English and London dialects such as cockney are shunted aside. London is represented entirely through an imported, hybrid language.

Selvon individualizes the generic crowd of his earlier London novel by populating *The Lonely Londoners* with distinctive immigrant characters, all with their own idiosyncratic stories, voices, and metropolitan survival strategies. As Moses, Galahad, Tolroy, Tanty, Cap, Bart, Daniel, Lewis, Big City, Five Past Twelve, and Harris make their picaresque way around the metropolis, they inhabit it more vividly and convincingly than Foster's anonymous West Indians. Both as well-delineated characters (in both senses of the word) and as a tenuous but vital transnational community (with Moses as unofficial leader), the cast of *The Lonely Londoners* moves Selvon away from the glum solipsism of Foster. This novel largely abandons the earlier one's obsession with the question that Glissant calls 'meaningless' to Caribbean culture – 'Who am I?' – for what he sees as the more relevant question 'Who are we?': 'In what way does a community influence the individuals who make it up? Or vice versa?' (86).

That Selvon's individual emigrants draw sustenance from a continuation of their West Indian affiliations is clear from the portrayal of 'the boys'' informal gatherings at Moses's flat, and it is enhanced by aspects of setting. The novel's opening scene represents Waterloo Station as a gateway for West Indians, an in-between 'place of arrival and departure' that prompts 'nostalgia' in Caribbean Londoners: 'It have some fellars who in Brit'n long, and yet they can't get away from the habit of going Waterloo whenever a boat-train coming in with passengers from the West Indies. They like to see the familiar faces' (9, 10). Most of the rest of the novel is set in 'the Water,' the Bayswater Road neighbourhood that becomes a West Indian colony (9). While both Waterloo Station and Bayswater Road metonymically signify 'London,' linguistically they signify 'water.' The water that geographically and historically relates Britain to its colonies, and that envelops the Caribbean islands, is by chance evoked through the names of the metropolitan conduits that bring those distant peoples into London and closer to each other.

Moreover, the place names and landmarks so conspicuously absent from earlier West Indian novels of London are important elements in what Ramchand calls the 'fulfilling romance of the city' in *The Lonely Londoners* ('Song' 230). Offsetting the sombre recognition of isolation and poverty are heady passages that convey the immigrant's reverie: his discovery of the city's wonders and pleasure at being part of it. Familiar place names that once signified London's unreachable importance now indicate nearby sites that can seen and entered. For Galahad, 'when he say "Charing Cross," when he realise that is he, Sir Galahad, who going there, near that place that everybody in the world know about (it even have the name in the dictionary) he feel like a new man' (68). The narrator shares his euphoria:

Oh what it is and where it is and why it is, no one knows, but to have said: 'I walked on Waterloo Bridge,' 'I rendezvoused at Charing Cross,' 'Piccadilly

Circus is my playground,' to say these things, to have lived these things, to
have lived in the great city of London, centre of the world. To one day lean
against the wind walking up the Bayswater Road (destination unknown), to
see the leaves swirl and dance and spin on the pavement (sight unseeing),
to write a casual letter home beginning: 'Last night, in Trafalgar Square ...'
(121; ellipsis in original)

Such passages, which have no counterpart in Lamming or Rhys, suggest
both a colonial's awe at famed metropolitan places and an incipient
postcolonial claim to inhabitation and possession: London as 'my playground.' The delicate balance between these attitudes parallels the balance Selvon achieves between a city that circumscribes and controls
immigrant lives, erecting barriers to prosperity, happiness, and community, and a place that offers liberating feelings of proximity, access, and
pleasure. Complementing these countervailing views is the balance of
indoor and outdoor spaces represented in the narrative. Once again, the
physical stasis and mobility associated respectively with interior and
exterior settings reflect sociopolitical and psychological conditions, but
the narrative mode of *The Lonely Londoners* establishes an ease of movement between inside and outside that Lamming eschews and Rhys achieves
mainly through Anna's border-crossing imagination.

The novel's only notable female character, Tanty, exemplifies its ambivalent balance. On one hand, Tanty can reterritorialize the metropolis:
when she bullies a white shop-owner into offering credit, she is West-
Indianizing a London space, effecting a take-over of his business practices and making the shop a model of resisted and transformed
metropolitan space. But as forceful a presence as she is in her
neighbourhood – 'Everybody in the district get to know Tanty so well
that she doing as she like' (63) – her influence is limited to the Harrow
Road area because of her reluctance to take public transport. The rest of
London is *terra incognita*. When circumstances force her to make a
journey alone by tube and bus, finally traversing the wider city she has
avoided, her triumph in conquering unfamiliar space is comically tempered by her fear that the double-decker bus 'would capsize' and her
consequent refusal to 'look out of the window and see anything' (66,
67).[18] Tanty's combination of taking charge and taking refuge, of mobility and myopia, exemplifies the differences between Selvon's metropolis
and that of his predecessors. His lonely Londoners are inhibited by the
city but can still inhabit it. His episodic narrative shifts fluidly between
inside and outside, stasis and movement; it dips gracefully in and out of

scenes in a way Lamming's never does, reflecting its characters' greater mobility and command of urban space.

The Caribbean *Flâneur*

Despite Tanty's defining role, it is Selvon's male narrator and predominantly male characters, 'the boys,' whose ambivalent responses to London life give the novel its bittersweet flavour. The metropolis may disappoint their expectations of 'streets paved with gold' (25); they may be reduced to an atomized class of 'hustlers, desperate' to eat and stay warm in the face of increasingly clear signals that white English 'don't like black people' and 'don't like the boys coming to England to work and live' (8, 23); but for all these many reasons to return (and even Moses flirts with the idea), Selvon's migrants all remain to stake their claim. At the end of the novel, four years after Galahad's arrival and ten years after Moses's, the narrator describes 'the boys coming and going, working, eating, sleeping, going about the vast metropolis like veteran Londoners' (122). The emphasis here on fitting in and quotidian getting by implies a qualified victory; the boys' routinized activity suggests joyless conformity to the city's regimens, not the creatively appropriative and resistant spatial practice of Michel de Certeau's urban pedestrian. However, when Selvon tightens his narrative focus from wide-angle crowd shots to close-ups of individual walkers and their ambulatory consciousnesses, his walkers enunciate metropolitan space through memorably personal itineraries. They resist (or at least temporarily ignore) London's controlling hegemonies by appropriating and reinscribing the city through their own languages and spatial stories. The spirit of intoxicated reverie with which they often do so – traversing and observing but also exuberantly romancing the city – affiliates them with an earlier and more influential model of literary walking than de Certeau's. What the nineteenth- and early twentieth-century figure of the *flâneur* does for the new city of industrial modernity, Selvon's West Indians do for the newly discovered (post)imperial metropolis of London.

As conceptualized by Charles Baudelaire, Walter Benjamin, and numerous contemporary scholars of literature, sociology, and cultural studies, the *flâneur* is a lone male walker who intensely observes and writes about the streets, crowds, and spectacles of the city.[19] Wallowing in the proliferating stimuli of urban European modernity, he is a leisurely and seemingly indolent consumer of metropolitan sights, a connoisseur of 'urban enchantments' (Ferguson 37; cf. Shields, 'Fancy' 61). The stroll-

ing *flâneur* 'reads the city as he would read a text – from a distance'
(Ferguson 31). His detachment and keen attentiveness make him 'a
stand-in for the artist' or poet (23), but he is also a 'detective' figure who
expertly scrutinizes and differentiates the city's multifarious people (Benjamin 40). Enraptured with public spaces in which he can, as Baudelaire
puts it, 'take a bath of multitude' (a multitude that paradoxically affords
him 'solitude'), the *flâneur*-poet merges with the crowd while remaining
apart from it (qtd. in Tester 3) – 'at the centre of the world,' Baudelaire
writes, but 'hidden from the world' (qtd. in Mazlish 50). In Keith Tester's
words, he 'is the centre of an order of things of his own making even
though, to others, he appears to be just one constituent part of the
metropolitan flux' (3). As the *flâneur*'s stance oscillates between elite
observer and 'man of the crowd,' mastery and discovery, analysing spectator and delirious reveller, he emerges as a politically ambivalent figure.
His consumption and celebration of the city's kaleidoscope of visual
inputs mean that he responds to urban modernity largely on its own
terms. But *flânerie* can be seen as an early instance of postmodernism's
complicitous critique; hence its appeal to contemporary theorists.[20] The
flâneur's ostentatious slowness and seemingly purposeless drifting can be
read as critiques of capitalist modernity with its emphasis on accelerat-
ing speeds and specialized, economically purposive labour (see Gleber
25–6). Through his peripatetic observations, the *flâneur* not only *reads*
(or consumes) the city but creatively *writes* (and textually produces) it.

    In the figures of Galahad and the anonymous narrator, Selvon adopts
the *flâneur* model while adapting it to a distinctly postcolonial, West
Indian vision of the metropolis. Galahad grows into *flânerie* after beginning with its antithesis. In his comically disastrous first outing, he refuses
Moses's offer of guidance and immediately gets lost; reluctant to ask
directions of busy-looking strangers, he is rescued by a policeman and
then by Moses, who takes him to the Employment Exchange. His 'drift' is
just an embarrassing 'walking stupid,' not a pleasurably independent
tour (26); rather than enabling him to observe the city, his disorienting
venture just shakes his confidence and delays his purposive journey – to
enter the very labour market that a *flâneur* should rise above. After a
short time, however, Galahad is an old hand at consuming and delight-
ing in the city's pleasures. Dressing up in fancy clothes (like the dandy
that was the *flâneur*'s more conspicuous cousin), he ventures out 'cool as
a lord,' enthusing that 'this is London, this is life oh lord, to walk like a
king with money in your pocket, not a worry in the world' (71). In
Piccadilly Circus he, like the *flâneur*, savours the 'marvelous show' the

city lays before him, regarding its images each time 'with a renewed sense of amazement, ... as if for the first time' (Ferguson 31; Gleber 4). Here Galahad's consciousness positions itself as a hub at the centre of the world, with an intoxicating mix of visual delights swirling around him on all sides:

> Always, from the first time he went there to see Eros and the lights, that circus have a magnet for him, that circus represent life, that circus is the beginning and the ending of the world. Every time he go there, he have the same feeling like when he see it the first night, drink coca-cola, any time is guinness time, bovril and the fireworks, a million flashing lights, gay laughter, the wide doors of theatres, the huge posters, everready batteries, rich people going into tall hotels, people going to the theatre, people sitting and standing and walking and talking and laughing and buses and cars and Galahad Esquire, in all this, standing there in the big city, in London. Oh Lord. (74)

This increasingly breathless paragraph replicates the connoisseurship of public spaces, monuments, crowds, and spectacles associated with *flânerie*, and its obsession with consumer commodities and the posters that trumpet them renders postwar London as a version of the new city of nineteenth-century modernity. Anke Gleber argues that *flânerie* emerges at times when large-scale social and economic changes destabilize the city and prompt its occupants to see it anew (see 31). Londoners in the 1950s were starting to stretch their capitalist and consumer legs again after two decades of depression, war, and postwar rationing, and for the West Indian immigrant, of course, everything *was* new.

That newness included the increasingly conspicuous presence of him and his fellow islanders. 'Mummy, look at that black man!' says a child pointing at Galahad (71). Echoing a famous passage by Frantz Fanon,[21] this remark makes Galahad a part of Piccadilly's spectacle – the observer observed – and the narrator notes that while earlier such an incident would have caused Galahad to decry his blackness, 'at this stage Galahad like duck back when rain fall – everything running off' (72). He feels aristocratically above judgment: elevated out of his racial and socioeconomic marginality by the urban spectacle's inspiring high. Indeed, on meeting his date, Daisy, even the idea that 'people in the tube station must be bawl to see black man so familiar with white girl' seems remote: 'Galahad feeling too good to bother about the loud tones in them people eyes' (74). He joins Daisy immediately after the orgasmic reveries of the above-quoted paragraph; a movie and dinner later, he takes her home for his 'first time with a white number' (77).

With Daisy's entrance at the pinnacle of Galahad's *flânerie*, Selvon makes a thematically significant departure from the traditional *flâneur*, for whom women were not companions but urban objects to be enjoyed and visually consumed. From Elizabeth Wilson's feminist perspective, the *flâneur*, 'a man of pleasure,' is an 'embodiment of the "male gaze"'; as he 'takes visual possession of the city,' he 'represents men's visual and voyeuristic mastery over women,' and his freedom to wander is a masculine freedom ('Invisible' 65). Selvon's male characters do objectify 'white pussy,' and even as Galahad strolls with Daisy he thinks of her as a 'piece of skin' (74, 75). But Galahad needs that white female skin at his side in a way the nineteenth-century Parisian *flâneur* did not. This city is not his in the same way; he cannot assume such things as freedom of movement or gendered mastery because his maleness is qualified by black West Indianness. As they stroll through Piccadilly, Galahad points out the times-of-the-world clock to Daisy: '"What time it is now in Trinidad?" Galahad look at the big clock, watching for Trinidad; the island so damn small it only have a dot and the name. "That is where I come from," he tell Daisy, "you see how far it is from England?"' (75). Galahad needs Daisy beside him not only to make him feel good, but to close that distance, shore up his maleness with borrowed whiteness, and validate his presence in London. Ignoring the stares that would tell him a mixed-race couple is a 'black mark' on the urban spectacle enables him to further reinforce the tenuous sense of belonging Daisy provides.[22]

As an exemplar of *flânerie*, Galahad is compromised in other ways. He may feel and convey the lofty, leisured superiority of a 'lord' or 'king' – the *flâneur* as 'self-proclaimed and self-believing monarch of the crowd' (Tester 4) – but only when he is not doing 'night work' (*Lonely* 70). Although he is free when others are working, Selvon makes it clear that Galahad's idleness is time-sensitive and labour-market-dependent. And while Galahad conveys the *flâneur*'s impassioned spectatorship, he does not offset his euphoria by becoming an 'aristocratic critic and judge,' wittily dissecting the capitalist (or postimperial) city through his writings, which Bruce Mazlish considers an essential element of traditional *flânerie* (50). Galahad is not a writer, and his rants against London tend to be comic rather than trenchant. If, as James Donald writes, the *flâneur* combines 'the passionate wonder of childhood with the analytic sophistication of the man of the world,' Galahad tips the balance towards wonder (45).

The most complete *flâneur* in *The Lonely Londoners* is not Galahad but the narrator. Not only does this figure experience and textually render his own occasions of euphoric urban strolling, but he also depicts the grim realities of London life for its West Indian denizens. An 'insider' who is apparently one of 'the boys,' the narrator never emerges into a name, a defined character, or a distinct set of relations and circumstances. He never speaks or is spoken to in dialogue; he has no specific liaisons with other characters. He remains outside, an anonymous composite who invisibly inhabits the urban scene on which he presents the controlling and subsuming point of view. With his omniscient perspective – his thorough knowledge of the boys and their doings – he emerges as a *flâneur*-detective expert at revealing and differentiating metropolitan phenomena, most importantly its people in all their quirky (and not always becoming) individuality. Because he is a notional rather than flesh and blood person, the narrator's leisure, freedom of movement, and access are infinite; he is, however, in an important way self-limiting. The people on whom his fluid narrative dwells are not 'Londoners' writ large, or even just the 'lonely' ones. The narrator's attentions are focused on West Indian lives; white people without exception come across as generic types of interest only for their relation to his cast of black immigrants.

Even at its most inclusive and mobile, then, the polydialectical narrative voice of this novel observes a very specialized subset of the metropolitan scene. In his choice of details, this pan-Caribbean *flâneur* sees London through a deliberately blinkered gaze. The passage in which Selvon's narrator most adventurously suggests the *flâneur*'s leisured freedom, ubiquitousness, and enthralment by urban rituals is a sprawling stream-of-consciousness sentence that begins

> Oh what a time it is when summer come to the city and all them girls throw away heavy winter coat and wearing light summer frocks so you could see the legs and shapes that was hiding away from the cold blasts and you could coast a lime in the park and negotiate ten shillings or a pound with the sports as the case may be or else they have a particular bench near the Hyde Park Corner ... (85–6)

and ends, nine pages later, in a less celebratory vein:

> ... oh it does really be beautiful then to hear the birds whistling and see the green leaves come back on the trees and in the night the world turn upside

down and everybody hustling that is life that is London oh lord Galahad say
when the sweetness of summer get in him he say he would never leave the
old Brit'n as long as he live and Moses sigh a long sigh like a man who live
life and see nothing at all in it and who frighten as the years go by
wondering what it is all about. (93–4)

For all its roaming diversity, the experiences and impressions of the city
that this long passage captures are specifically those of a regional, racial,
and gendered group. While superficially it suggests a mobile, all-inclusive gaze – the 'perambulating Panopticon' that Baudelaire's *flâneur*
resembles (Mazlish 50) – it also manages to convey (and to replicate)
something of the drifting aimlessness and the unfulfillingly limited sphere
of activity and observation in which the 'fellars' are stuck. Combined
with the pan-Caribbean language, the partiality of the narrator's gaze
and narrative choices throughout the novel conveys an ambivalent view
of the metropolis as both an enabling space of free, pleasurable movement and a restricting space of social isolation and low economic ceil-
ings. The text both romantically celebrates and realistically critiques
metropolitan life.

The narratorial *flânerie* of *The Lonely Londoners* is an important measure of its difference from other early West Indian novels of London.
Neither the wide-ranging walking nor the attentiveness to urban stimuli
that *flânerie* requires is possible in Lamming's disjointed, indoor, visually
impaired narrative. The only *flâneur*-like figures in *The Emigrants* are the
men who 'would ramble the streets yarning and singing' back on the
islands; in a passage quoted above, their 'leisurely' walking is explicitly
contrasted with the solitary confinement of London rooms (192). Rhys's
narrative may have greater mobility, and Anna more inclination to walk
and describe the streets, but whereas the *flâneur* makes astute differentia-
tions among urban phenomena, Anna sees London's streets, buildings,
and even certain people as disorientingly alike. As for Selvon's earlier
rendering in *An Island Is a World*, it shows Foster obsessively scanning and
meditating on the London crowds, presumably while strolling among
them, but with no sense of pleasurably engaged connoisseurship and no
attempt to distinguish or describe details.

Two minor West Indian novels that appeared soon after *The Lonely
Londoners* also severely limit London as an object of narratorial percep-
tion and site of expatriate dwelling. In this regard, Edgar Mittelholzer's
A Tale of Three Places (1957) and Andrew Salkey's *Escape to an Autumn
Pavement* (1960) resemble Lamming's novel more than Selvon's; their

male protagonists do walk through outdoor London but with little attentiveness to its people or cityscapes. Both novels are inclined to 'place' their characters on London's streets by naming landmarks rather than responding to visual details: 'Trafalgar Square. The Strand. Aldwych. Kingsway. Bloomsbury' (Salkey, *Escape* 170); 'There was London, waiting to be explored. The National Gallery, the Albert Hall, Hyde Park – all were within his reach now' (Mittelholzer 157). To the extent that Mittelholzer's Alfie does 'explore' London, he mostly confirms its resemblance to images he formed in Trinidad: 'In the Strand, London looked like the London he had dreamed about. The red double-decker buses were exactly as he had expected them to be. And the crowds on the pavements, and the buildings, drab and solid-looking, all fell into the pre-conceived pattern' (157). Still, his first excursion undermines that incipient visual mastery; as it conveys Alfie's alienation, it seems to follow a pre-conceived pattern of its own – one borrowed from Mittelholzer's literary predecessors:

> He stood on the pavement in Oxford Street and gaped at the crowds. Streets seemed to lead off in so many different directions that he was baffled to know which way he should go. He just strolled.
>
> After a while, he began to feel disconcerted and disorganised, as though all purpose had vanished from his movements. He looked about in some panic at the cold, detached faces that flashed past him. (158)

After this derivative beginning, Mittelholzer does not give Alfie a chance to develop into a discriminating *flâneur*; he lets him escape every weekend to a country house. The rural landscape enables a pleasurable 'wandering' and 'enchantment' that London never provides, and it is described in far greater (and more loving) detail (170, 171). Alfie's metropolitan life becomes equated with 'a stuffy room when the window had to be closed. The strangeness and discomfort of it all dismayed him for an instant. Then he told himself that he would soon accept it without a thought. One got used to everything in time' (166). Despite these reassuring platitudes, Alfie never embraces London as he does the countryside, and the vague, generic descriptions of the metropolis simply reinforce the non-engagement and sense of drift that he, like Selvon's Foster, never stops feeling: 'I'm just going along pointlessly,' he complains, 'meeting strangers, eating in cafés and restaurants, seeing the sights of London, and asking myself where it's all leading to – and I never know the answer' (171).[23]

Salkey's *Escape to an Autumn Pavement* is set entirely in London and mostly, despite its title, indoors – in flats, stairwells, a 'West Indian night club' (23). In his rare outdoor rambles, the Jamaican émigré Johnny occasionally goes beyond naming districts to provide an evocative image: 'Piccadilly Circus was a grey whore of lights, an open, cold storage' (206). There is an extended scene in 'Oxford Street with its squeaking silences under shutters' (34). Both of these images render streetscapes through oxymoronic metaphors: open but enclosed and static, silent but squeaking. Like Lamming, Salkey resists writing expansively about London. Johnny, for all his sardonic confidence, never seems convincingly at home in the metropolis, and by the end he has lost faith in what he once believed: 'that London's that big cinema of a city where trees are banks and money plus freedom is as easy to come by as leaves on an autumn pavement' (206). His friend Larry is more negative: 'I am ... going to pieces in this man's town. ... I am almost suffocating,' he says (202). Larry's and Johnny's most significant spatial insights do not involve the physical city; they emerge from two human encounters on the street. In one, they count the 'Spades' they see; though there are many, Larry says, 'They look obvious like they don't belong on this landscape' (176). In the other encounter, the two black men are handed a racist pamphlet, which reads in part,

Avoid disease – avoid contamination – avoid mongrelism. Send them back to their place of origin – get them out. Keep W.11 white – keep Notting Hill white – be wise. European people generally mix well with us and add something to our life. They are welcome if they do not make worse the housing and unemployment problems. But it is no good bringing coloured people who are very different to ourselves. Oil and water will not mix. (118)

Through these two street-level encounters, Larry and Johnny are reminded that London both includes and excludes them. In a narrative peppered with anti-miscegenation propaganda, with a plot that involves a troubled interracial affair and outright enmity between Johnny and his Indian neighbour, Salkey represents London as a place of divides to which the black West Indian can have at best an ambivalent attachment.

For both Mittelholzer and Salkey, London is an unromanticized backdrop to romance. It is a convenient setting, minimally sketched in broad and conventional strokes, against which their protagonists can play out the sexual-romantic entanglements and narratives of self-discovery that are the authors' real interest. In *The Lonely Londoners*, by contrast, the most sustained and compelling romance is with the city itself. Through its unique adaptation of *flânerie* to a specific group's experience and sensibility, this most enduring of West Indian London narratives manages – without donning rose-coloured glasses or blinding itself to hardships – to present the most vivid, expansive, and hopeful vision of the metropolis in early West Indian fiction. The vitality and detailed originality with which it responds to the urban environment and the migrant's experience bring its London into the sharpest focus. As a direct function of its narrative attentiveness and individuation, it comes closest to portraying a city that West Indians can call their own.

The City of Magical Light

The emergence of the *flâneur* in the nineteenth century coincided with new technologies of lighting that improved the visibility of city streets. According to Stephen Inwood, with the introduction of oil-burning street lights in the eighteenth century, 'London, which had been regarded as one of Europe's darkest capitals, now gained a reputation as its most well-lit' (365). Still, it was dark by comparison with the city after 1807, when gas lamps began more thoroughly to illuminate the cityscape (see 366). Other European cities followed suit and so, Anke Gleber writes, 'flanerie becomes imaginable as an all-day pursuit' of increasingly visible exteriors and people (31). As gas lamps give way to electric lighting, which in turn becomes supplemented with neon and other new forms of commercial illumination, 'each innovation in lighting brings about states of increased disturbance and shock that correspond to new intensities of light and exposure in the public sphere' (32). Changes in lighting, in other words, shake up the urban pedestrian's perceptions: of people, of exterior spaces, and of one's own visibility as part of the spectacle. These periodic jolts into ever-brighter modernity make the city seem constantly renewed, ready for rediscovery and creative reinscription by the *flâneur*, whose aesthetic sensibilities are galvanized by 'the new experiential economy of space and sight' (33).

When V.S. Naipaul writes about London in *The Mimic Men* (1967), he does so through the eyes of a would-be *flâneur*.[24] Ralph Singh is a connoisseur of urban light, and his unsuccessful search for the city's enchantments is obsessively focused on its qualities of natural and artificial illumination. Writing his memoirs in London as a political exile from the Caribbean island of Isabella, Singh registers his disenchantment with the metropolis as the culmination of a process of savouring its shifting conditions of light:

> So quickly had London gone sour on me. The great city, centre of the world, in which, fleeing disorder, I had hoped to find the beginning of order. So much had been promised by the physical aspect. That marvel of light, soft, shadowless, always protective. They talk of the light of the tropics and Southern Spain. But there is no light like that of the temperate zone. It was a light which gave solidity to everything and drew colour out from the heart of objects. To me, from the tropics, where night succeeded day abruptly, dusk was new and enchanting. I would sit in Lieni's basement room, in the clutter, and study the light, not willing to risk losing any gradation in that change. Light was slowly withdrawn; a blueness remained, which deepened, so that before the electric lights began to make their effect the world seemed wholly aqueous, and we might have been at the bottom of the ocean. Then at night the sky was low; you walked as though under a canopy; and all the city's artificial lights, their glow seemingly trapped, burned intensely; and sometimes the wet streets threw up their own glitter.
>
> Here was the city, the world. I waited for the flowering to come to me. The trams on the Embankment sparked blue. The river was edged and pierced with reflections of light, blue and red and yellow. Excitement! Its heart must have lain somewhere. But the god of the city was elusive. ... In the great city, so solid in its light, ... in this solid city life was two-dimensional. (18–19)

This passage, reinforced by many subsequent laments that 'the city of magical light' proves so ephemeral, establishes a multivalent defining metaphor for Singh's London (229). By suggesting that the artificial light of evening creates an enveloping 'canopy,' it suggests interiority in outdoor space. Gleber notes that an important development in the cultural history of *flânerie* occurs when artificial lighting reaches sufficient intensity to transform streets into 'veritable living spaces.' 'In this new light,' she remarks,

> the public sphere is perceived as an interior space in the street. ... The imaginary outdoor 'ceiling' of such artificially lit interiors would be assumed to be above the first floor where the shine of light emanating from the lower row of windows disintegrates into the darkness of the night skies. The 'walls' that surround this space on both sides are shaped by the

material walls of the houses that line the street, the façades and windows that surround it. (33–4)

Singh's rendering of outside as a virtual inside provides an intriguing variation on a now-familiar theme. London disappoints and constrains him for quite different reasons than it does earlier fictional migrants, but for him too 'the anguish of London' is captured by images of enclosure: 'the mean rooms, the shut door, the tight window, the tarnished ceiling, the over-used curtains, ... the rigged shilling-in-the-slot gas and electric meters' (56). Singh, however, favours interiors as spaces of safety, privacy, and withdrawal; he feels most comfortable outside when it resembles inside, as he makes clear when he recapitulates the image of an interior-like street: 'The sky was low; for just a little way above street level there was light, from street lamps and shop windows. The city was as if canopied; I had no feeling of being exposed' (229).[25] Despite his discerning eye for urban visuals and portrait of himself as a sometime 'dandy, the creation of London,' Singh's characteristic spaces are not streets but 'British Council halls, art galleries and excursion trains' (50). Any potential *flânerie* is undermined by his penchant for enclosure, including his examination of the city's solid light from the stasis of 'Lieni's basement room' (18). Indeed, he writes his entire memoir from an 'unchanging' hotel room, and when he boasts of 'the gift of minute observation which has come to me with the writing of the book,' he has just finished describing the stains on his desk (244, 245).

These self-limiting aspects of Singh's narration suggest another way in which exterior scenes dissolve into imprisoning interiors in *The Mimic Men*. Critics often comment on Singh's penchant for analysis over description, telling over showing, as he relays his life and times.[26] Just as he is attracted more to illuminating light than illuminated objects, his heavily mediated narrative prefers summary to scenes, sacrificing any illusion of direct, transparent representation to an intellectualized processing that becomes suffocatingly self-contained. The narrative feels trapped inside the recirculated air of Singh's head. This dissolution of material reality before the force of the immaterial mind and word is nonetheless of a piece with what the city's light does to Singh's perceptions of himself and his world. In the passage quoted above, the light and the city it illuminates are both said to be 'solid,' but that very solidity makes 'life' there seem 'two-dimensional.' In an adjacent paragraph, Singh's illumined city reduces the proportions of 'life' even further. It highlights the dissolution of community into atomized individuals: 'We seek the physical city and find only a conglomeration of private cells. In the city as nowhere else we are reminded that we are individuals, units' (18). And it dissolves individuals into nothingness: London becomes 'the too solid three-dimensional city in which I could never feel myself as anything but spectral, disintegrating, pointless, fluid' (52).[27] But for a man seeking 'withdrawal,' who finds 'shadowless' light 'protective' (presumably because it makes him seem invisible), being isolated and insubstantial may not be wholly negative (32, 18).

Ihab Hassan has written that the city is 'intractable' but also 'immaterial,' 'a gritty structure' that is nonetheless 'invisible, imaginary, made of dream and desire, agent of all our transformations' (94). Ralph Singh's city is full of such binary paradoxes: exterior but apparently interior, solidified but also disintegrated by its light. His panegyric on urban light disrupts another significant opposition – the distinction between light and darkness. He is captivated by the gradualism and in-betweenness of a London dusk, which he contrasts with the more sudden darkening of tropical light. The *OED* defines dusk in part as 'the darker stage of twilight before it is quite dark at night,' but Singh invokes it more broadly, as a synonym for twilight in its manifold gradations and shadings. Twilight is a potent metaphor in Caribbean discourse. Temporally, it expands beyond quotidian sunsets to become, as in Derek Walcott's essay 'What the Twilight Says,' 'a metaphor for the withdrawal of Empire [on which the sun was said never to set] and the beginning of our doubt' (4).[28] Psychologically and epistemologically, twilight is identified with a binary-breaking 'creative schizophrenia' – a 'twilight consciousness' that both Walcott and Edouard Glissant see as characteristically Caribbean, and which blends the oppositions of 'light and dark, self and other' that underlie imperial discourses (Dash xxvi). In Simon Gikandi's reading, the 'twilight zone' poetics of Glissant, Walcott, and Wilson Harris poise writers between ancestral inheritance and imposed colonial structures, self and community, private and public discourses, 'break[ing] the binary oppositions that sustain such values as mutually exclusive entities' (*Writing* 13). If twilight's in-betweenness can be unnervingly fluid (hence Walcott's 'doubt'), it also represents an opportunity to rethink imperialism's legacy not as a confrontation of separate worlds but as a set of encounters and connections reaching across the gaps and binaries that its discourses policed. Neither light nor dark but an infinitely variable combining of both, twilight is a temporal equivalent of the ocean as spatial metaphor: both represent liminality, relationality, and transformation. The twilight London of Naipaul's Singh is also, notably, an 'aqueous' world reminiscent of 'the bottom of the ocean' (18). London's visual aspects figure it once again as the space of a relational imperial history defined by intertwined worlds, cultures, and identities – by shades of grey. It is not surprising, then, that the city disappoints any expectations of an absolute break. Fleeing Isabella's vacuity, its 'transitional or makeshift' disorder, Singh crosses the ocean to find only 'the greater disorder, the final emptiness: London and the home counties' (8).

Naipaul, so often criticized as a neo-imperialist binary-monger, uses twilight as a defining metaphor for London to capture an integrating and relating impulse that is sustained throughout the narrative of *The Mimic Men*. London, the seat of an empire now withdrawing, does not exhibit the stark oppositions of imperialist discourses – metropolitan light contrasted with colonial darkness. Instead it manifests both the light and the darkness and, definitively, everything in between. In this it resembles the crepuscular London of *Heart of Darkness*. Tempering the hierarchically imperialist worldview that Chinua Achebe and Edward Said have read into that novel[29] is Conrad's sense of London – and Brussels, and the European imperialism they both represent – as integrated with and implicated in colonial Africa's 'darkness.' Marlow relates his narrative in gloomy twilight, and as darkness gradually envelops London, both literally and in various figurative ways through the story he tells, imperialism's expansive connections are also figured through the final image of the Thames, London's major conduit for international relations, oceanically 'leading to the uttermost ends of the earth' (111). This metonymic image implies a one-way flow of power and influence that Conrad would not deny; Naipaul similarly recognizes London's grip on Isabella, whose politicians 'lack power' but do not realize it, through Singh's humiliating and career-destroying failure to obtain permission for the nationalization of a bauxite estate (8). However, both Conrad and Naipaul balance these evident contrasts by imaging London as a place of twilit liminality and by embedding city and colony in London-framed, memoir-driven narratives that pull distant 'worlds' together to reveal their reciprocity. Ralph Singh's back-and-forth experiences in Isabella and London – 'my two landscapes of sea and snow' (31) – reflect and inform each other in many ways; the process of narratorial sifting, analysing, cross-referencing, and cerebral refining that he applies to both worlds also contributes to a sense of their mutuality.

The key image of shipwreck, with the related motifs of drift, exile, and withdrawal, crystallizes the twilight consciousness of Ralph Singh. Living his life and pursuing his ephemeral political career in the (ephemeral) twilight time of imperial withdrawal, he comes to realize that he feels equally exiled, adrift, and shipwrecked in Isabella and in London. The two 'worlds' mirror each other. 'Shipwreck,' an image with heavy historical freight in the West Indies, central to such archetypal narratives of colonial encounter as *The Tempest* and *Robinson Crusoe*, defines the young Singh's feeling of rootless isolation in Isabella: 'I resolved to abandon the shipwrecked island and all on it, and to seek my chieftainship in that real world from which ... I had been cut off' (118). But it applies equally well to London: 'Shipwreck: I have used this word before. With my island background, it was the word that always came to me. And this is what I felt I had encountered again in the great city: a feeling of being adrift, a cell of perception, that might be altered, if only fleetingly, by any encounter' (27). Even as, finishing his memoir, he fears being 'continually washed up on this city,' Singh cultivates a state of withdrawal, anonymity, and homeless detachment there (251; cf. 247). Moreover, in two separate earlier passages he identifies 'withdrawal' with the political exile in London and then with the active period in Isabella that preceded it (32, 52). This latter (but chronologically first) withdrawal is itself inaugurated by his first period in London 'and was part of the injury inflicted on me by the too solid three-dimensional city' (52). As Singh and his memoir shuttle between his two disordered worlds, withdraw from previous withdrawals and 'escape to what I had so recently sought to escape from' (31), the correspondences between the two places become more apparent than their differences. Moreover, both are reduced to cerebral constructs; narrative continuity and an idiosyncratic cluster of motifs and images draw them together, making the isolating 'shipwreck' they both exemplify the paradoxical basis of their relatedness.

Singh's London emerges, in Timothy Weiss's words, as the site of a 'greater shipwreck': 'an exile without alternatives' in which 'neither his former West Indian colony nor the English metropolis can be a home' (93). But, as Landeg White asks, 'if London is an illusion and the possibility of escape is a colonial myth, what and where then?' (154). If the two worlds are mutually constitutive and equally conducive to shipwreck and withdrawal, what is the novel's view of London, the West Indies, and the imperial past that links them? Can Naipaul, through Singh, still be valorizing the metropolis over the colony, as his fiction and non-fiction are so often seen to do? Walcott appears to think so. He clearly has Naipaul in mind in the following passage from 'The Muse of History': 'to most writers of the archipelago who contemplate only the shipwreck, the New World offers not elation but cynicism, a despair at the vices of the Old which they feel must be repeated. Their malaise is an oceanic nostalgia for the older culture and a melancholy at the new' (7). He addresses *The Mimic Men* explicitly in 'The Caribbean: Culture or Mimicry?'; here he reads Naipaul's notion of mimicry as a 'pantomime ... based on metropolitan references' conducted before a mirror (6):

> Once the meridian of European civilization has been crossed, according to the theory, we have entered a mirror where there can only be simulations of self-discovery. The civilized virtues on the other side of this mirror are the virtues of social order, a lineally clear hierarchy, direction, purpose, balance. ... Somehow, the cord is cut by that meridian. Yet a return is also impossible, for we cannot return to what we have never been. (6–7)

Like the 'broad line' in Robertson Davies's *A Mixture of Frailties* (89), the spatial metaphors in these essays construct the ocean as a space of division. The notional meridian that severs worlds is a mirror in which the New World is but a fraudulent reflection of the Old, its inhabitants doomed to cynical malaise and nostalgia. Walcott invokes this imaginary geography in order to reject its implications: 'There was no line in the sea which said, this is new, this is the frontier, the boundary of endeavor, and henceforth everything can only be mimicry' (8). The ocean, he implies, is rightly a space of conjoining, assimilating, relating.

Walcott's reading is powerful, but Naipaul's imaging of London and Isabella as inducing similar conditions of shipwreck, drift, emptiness, and withdrawal suggests that the metaphorical cord may not be cut and that if there is a mirror, it is facing two ways, revealing both worlds to be fraudulent and unreal versions of each other. Hence London's uncertain reality: sometimes three-dimensional, solid, and real, but at other times two-dimensional, flat, and shadowless, depending on the perceived effects of the one constant, its 'magical light.' Homi Bhabha's more relational theory of mimicry – that it generates fissures in the identities of both the mimicking colonized and the mimicked colonizer unsettled by the contemplation of his '*almost the same, but not quite*' other self (86) – suggests that the London that creates colonial space and fosters part-English (but subordinate) subjects in the West Indies (umbilically constructing itself as the motherland) is not simply bolstered in stature by these acts of power. It is also – in the imperial era and after – unsettled and transformed by the images reflected back upon it of its own colonial creations, particularly when they appear, like Ralph Singh, in person. The metropolitan city, as Bhabha suggests in another essay, is the primary space in which 'the West' most directly witnesses 'the liminality of cultural identity' through the transformations effected by 'emergent identifications and new social movements of the people' (170). The 'spectral' and withdrawn Ralph Singh conveys London's newly visible identifications as a function not of its people (few of whom come into focus) but, through cross-pollinating metaphors, of the place itself as an environment and set of responses that connect it with colonial space.

Naipaul's autobiographical 'novel' *The Enigma of Arrival* (1987), published twenty years after *The Mimic Men*, reiterates and indirectly contextualizes many aspects of Singh's metropolitan experiences through the impressions of an unnamed narrator who closely resembles Naipaul.[30] His feeling of farawayness as a boy in Trinidad leads to 'withdrawal' and 'waiting' 'for life at the centre of things' (120). On arrival in England, he enjoys the 'extended dusk' he observes from the boat-train window, finding it 'new, enchanting to someone used to the more or less equal division of day and night in the tropics' (117). His focus at Waterloo Station that evening remains the light: 'The station lights gave a suggestion (such as the New York streets had already given me) of a canopied world, a vast home interior' (118). Settling in at his Earls Court boarding house, he 'rejoiced at the view from the window, some floors up, of the bright orange street lights and the effect of the lights on the trees' (118). Naipaul anticipates a London he 'knew very well' from literature, especially Dickens, describing himself in paradoxical terms as 'like a man entering the world of a novel, a book; entering the real world' (123, 119). The metropolitan world has been made more 'real' than Trinidad, he implies, by its representation in novels – by the lives he has vicariously lived there through narrative. But he finds the city he actually inhabits 'unknown,' 'strange and un-read-about' (123). The grand city he knew is being transformed and scaled down like the empire it once controlled: 'I grew to feel that the grandeur belonged to the past; ... that I had come too late to find the England, the heart of empire, which (like a provincial, from a far corner of the empire) I had created in my fantasy' (120).

For Naipaul, as for Ralph Singh, London becomes a place of disenchantment and loneliness: 'My tramps about London were ignorant and joyless. I had expected the great city to leap out at me and possess me; I had longed so much to be in it. And soon, within a week or less, I was very lonely' (121). In his solitude and disappointment at London's newness he fails to see what he later realizes was the city's real gift to him as a writer: its transformation by 'the flotsam of Europe' and the wider world (135; cf. 130). The boarding house was full of international 'drifters' who were, after the war, 'becalmed and quiet in London': 'These people's principal possessions were their stories,' but at the time Naipaul 'took them all for granted, looked beyond them' and 'noted nothing down' (130).[31] Fixated on the past, he failed to see London's future-looking contemporaneity; having inherited through his colonial education a version of what Bhabha calls England's 'pedagogical' identity, he ignored the 'performative' transformations of London's transnational populace (146):

> Because in 1950 in London I was at the beginning of that great movement of peoples that was to take place in the second half of the twentieth century – a movement and a cultural mixing greater than the peopling of the United States, which was essentially a movement of Europeans to the New World. This was a movement between all the continents. ... Cities like London were to change. They were to cease being more or less national cities; they were to become cities of the world, modern-day Romes, establishing the pattern of what great cities should be. (130)

Only later does Naipaul recognize London's gift of 'the world' to him when he was an aspiring writer. He does so by recognizing the same gift in Trinidad. Through its combination of apparent farawayness *from* the world and cosmopolitan inclusion (as a mixed society of Africans, Asians, and Europeans) *of* the world, 'the island had given me the world as a writer; had given me the themes that in the second half of the twentieth century had become important; had made me metropolitan, but in a way quite different from my first understanding of the word' (140).

Connecting the transnational 'flotsam' of postwar London with the intercontinental gathering of people that constituted Caribbean society, Naipaul suggests that the metropolitan 'world' (and a metropolitan consciousness, like a 'twilight' one) exceeds the metropolis. As in *The Mimic Men*, the heart of empire and the distant colony are related: in this case, as mutually constituting and mirroring conduits to (and from) the transnational 'world.' But even now that he can acknowledge what he missed, Naipaul continues to withdraw from London. Unlike Ralph Singh, who retreats psychologically from a city that he nonetheless remains physically within throughout the composition of his fictional memoir, Naipaul writes the memoir-fiction of *The Enigma of Arrival* from a Wiltshire country-house world that is also his main setting. London has little presence except as an initial pit-stop en route to a state of dwelling in England that has come to be obsessively and minutely focused on the countryside. It is rural England, not the metropolis, through which Naipaul wants to read the history of empire and his own self-fashioning as a migrant writer. As he walks about observing country spaces and lives in minute detail, he emerges as a discriminating connoisseur of this world's surfaces and depths – a kind of rural *flâneur*. And as Ian Baucom's fine reading shows, in his dwelling on and among rural houses, folk, and ruins, Naipaul comes to see the Wiltshire countryside as representing a vanishing object of desire and perfection that he associates with the withdrawal of empire and his own (post)colonial belatedness (see Baucom 176–89). Baucom overstates his case, however, when he links the fetishizing of past country-house glory – and the present-day human and architectural ruins that symbolize its decline – with a wholesale rejection of the metropolis and its postwar transformation. For Baucom, Naipaul's remarks about his failure to recognize the migrancy theme in the metropolitan boarding house signal not a youthful blindness but a permanent preference:

> This city, Naipaul allows, might have become his theme. The emergence, in cities like London, of a postwar narrative of English habitation and belonging might have sustained his invention of himself as an English writer. But, with admirable honesty, he admits that this is not what he wanted. 'I noted nothing down. I asked no questions.' Migrancy was not to be his theme. He rejects the image of a city of migrants, where, even after the end of empire, the imbricated narratives of imperialism and Englishness continue to be written. (187)

Naipaul is no Salman Rushdie (to whom Baucom contrasts him in this regard), nor a Sam Selvon. But he has made metropolitan migrancy a theme: in autobiographical publications such as *Enigma*'s London segments and 'Prologue to an Autobiography'; in his portraits of Michael X and his fictional counterpart Jimmy Ahmed;[32] and, most extensively, in the shipwreck of Ralph Singh. Together, *The Mimic Men* and *The Enigma of Arrival* read traces of empire and its aftermath in the English city and country: in the conditions of dwelling a (post)colonial migrant arrives at among the urban spaces of an emergent future and the rural spaces of a vanishing past.

The Locations of Resistance

The Mimic Men is the first of several West Indian fictions to link London's distance from a Caribbean island to an overtly political theme. Ralph

Singh's political career in Isabella is bracketed by his two periods in London, the second of which is an apparently permanent exile as an ousted politician and dispossessed millionaire, a victim of the unstable political culture he helped create. His sanguinity about his reduced circumstances – his lack of desire for return, restitution, or revolution – contrasts with the diverse resistances embraced by the protagonists of three novels published in the following decade, two of which intertextually allegorize the *Tempest* and *Crusoe* stories to which Naipaul's shipwreck metaphor only gestures. In George Lamming's *Water with Berries* (1971), Andrew Salkey's *Come Home, Malcolm Heartland* (1976), and Sam Selvon's *Moses Ascending* (1975), the Black Power movement that energized London's West Indians in the 1970s underlies narratives that directly interrogate the possibilities and the limitations of the metropolis as a space for political resistance. While Lamming's Teeton and Salkey's Malcolm aspire to return to the Caribbean as political subversives, Selvon's Moses tries to upend the racial order on the microcosmic level of a London house. All three men fail spectacularly, and their stories cast a sceptical eye on the prospect of being black and politicized in seventies London.

In a speech given in 1985 and published as 'Concepts of the Caribbean,' George Lamming argues that 'the Caribbean ... does not exist exclusively within the sea and at the shores that we geographically call the Caribbean. There is a Caribbean world that exists, in a very decisive sort of way, in many metropolitan centres, whether in North America or in Europe.' Cities such as London, Paris, and New York he calls 'the external frontier, and this frontier, particularly the visionary progressive elements within it, has a very decisive role to play in the future cultural and political development of the Caribbean' (9). *Water with Berries*, with its convoluted reworking of the Prospero-Caliban encounter at this new frontier, seems doubtful about the impact its visionary progressive elements might make, either in the Caribbean or in London. Still, it makes oceanic connectedness between the Caribbean and the 'external frontier' a central image of its first scene. In the London room he rents from the Old Dowager, Teeton makes curtains out of maps, to which foreboding references are constantly made: 'He glanced at the map and saw the island smile and sink under the shadows of early morning' (12); 'The Old Dowager saw the sizzling blaze of an ocean spread out on the maps' (13). Moments later Teeton, who escaped his island home of San Cristobal as a political undesirable and plans to return, seven years later, to foment revolution, 'turned to look at the maps again, inviting the island to pass some verdict on his escape. And the blue ink of ocean looked so troubled, so utterly indecisive' (19). Later still, 'he saw the map shivering against the window pane. A draught had found its way up the backside of the island. The ocean shook' (28). These increasingly ominous visions of the map-curtains portend the explosive consequences Lamming will foresee as he reinscribes the paradigmatic colonial encounter in metropolitan spaces.[33]

The map-curtains and Teeton's other eccentric decorating idea, a 'black tree trunk' he has dragged in from the garden, draw attention to binary categories only to disturb them (12). The maps that shut the room off from the urban world represent virtually its (and its occupant's) relation to a wider one; a trunk that would normally be outside is relocated within. The Caribbean seascape and landscape are symbolically present in London, just as, in the wake of large-scale West Indian migration, 'the islands were no longer behind them, on some other side of the ocean. New cargoes of men had crossed the sky; and San Cristobal had started to multiply in the heart of England' (69). Lamming's allegorical signifiers multiply there too. In *The Pleasures of Exile* Lamming writes that 'Caliban himself like the island he inherited is at once a landscape and a human situation' (118), and in *Water with Berries* Caliban is represented both as people and as aspects of landscape. The three male artists, Teeton, Roger, and Derek, are clear Caliban figures, as are the shadowy members of the Secret Gathering plotting revolution in San Cristobal. But as Shakespeare's indigene is redefined as the former colonized within the imperial home of London, the black tree trunk (echoing the firewood Shakespeare's character carries) is also a version of Caliban brought into domestic space from the half-wild, half-cultivated space of the garden/colony. The Old Dowager, Mrs Gore-Brittain, who owns the room and the garden, plays the role of Prospero as aged, weakening imperial power; she welcomes Teeton as her first-ever tenant, but initially she is reluctant to allow the tree trunk, afraid that wild 'things' within it will proliferate. Teeton insists, she relents and, after a time, grows so used to it she 'wouldn't yield an inch to anyone who wanted to dispose of it. The ordinary black portion of a fallen tree had become a necessary piece of the furniture, a natural element of the household' (12). With Prospero here as the cautiously welcoming, liberal portion of the British polity, the site of (post)imperial encounter is simultaneously Britain and several metonymic subdivisions of British space: London, the Old Dowager's Hampstead house, Teeton's room in the house, and the corner of the room in which the migrant trunk resides, with the maps as a kind of running commentary on the unsettling implications of these resettlements.

The relational in-betweenness suggested by the oceanic maps and the garden-to-room transfer is reinforced by the novel's use of Hampstead Heath. Combining wildness and cultivation in a site that is both within and outside of the urban realms, the Heath represents, like the garden and its 'thing'-infested trunk, another version of Caliban as Caribbean landscape within London. Hampstead town and heath were historically well outside London but became merged with it as a result of the suburban expansion that occurred simultaneously with Victorian England's imperial expansion. Once called 'the most convincing illusion ever created of real country brought to the heart of a vast city' (qtd. in Inwood 580), Hampstead is symbolically associated in Lamming's novel with the appropriated 'country' space of the West Indian colony. The Heath is where Teeton meets Myra, the daughter of the Old Dowager, and the latter's brother-in-law Fernando, the novel's other Prospero figure. The Heath is identified with the Caribbean further through ocean imagery associated repeatedly with it (see 56, 106, 107) and through Lamming's splitting of Shakespeare's Miranda into two characters: Myra, who was raped as a child in colonial San Cristobal by her father's overseer and now prostitutes herself on the Heath; and Randa, Teeton's wife, who slept with the American ambassador to secure her husband's escape seven years ago and has remained in San Cristobal until her recent suicide. With Shakespeare's story spread across several interrelated 'human situations' and multiply relocated in metropolitan and Caribbean spaces, Lamming's removal of his narrative to yet another locale, the North Sea island where Teeton meets Fernando and kills the Old Dowager, seems forced – as if Lamming had doubted his substitutions and thought a real rather than virtual island setting was needed to drive home the allegory. If instead the scene had taken place on the vast, sprawling Heath – in an abandoned shed or secluded grove perhaps – Lamming could have more clearly consolidated the novel's central thematic question: how does London, the former heart of empire, provoke and accommodate violent resistance to the imperial legacy?

The novel's other major acts of resistance do take place in London: Roger's rejection of the 'white impurity' he associates with Nicole's pregnancy, which leads to her suicide and his arson campaign (139); Derek's rejection of corpse roles, which leads to his on-stage rape of a white actress; and the Secret Gathering's rejection of the political status quo in San Cristobal, which prompts them to plot revolution in a London basement. They and their plan, like Lamming's narrative, never make it to San Cristobal. The Gathering's members are galvanized by

Teeton's arrest on murder charges to redirect their energies to the political landscape of London; as Lamming writes, they 'defied the nation with their furious arguing that Teeton was innocent' (249). London may therefore be the new, preferred place to undo the legacies of imperial power, as Lamming has suggested in comments on this passage,[34] but the results are not encouraging. Roger, Derek, and Teeton have lived in London as creative artists – composer, actor, and painter – but are brought to acts of destructive criminality – arson, rape, and murder. Their acts of resistance are equated with a quixotic desire to purge the new frontier of the past's racial legacies by symbolically 'burning away' colonial history and memory (247). Like the theatre that reduces Derek from playing Othello to playing corpses, the metropolis in which Caliban re-encounters Prospero becomes a place of failure and death. Lamming reinforces these bleak prospects with the images of death he repeatedly uses to describe the urban landscape. In one such description, as one of Roger's fires burns, 'The city had become a huge and foreign mausoleum where they walked. A procession of avenues marched them past the houses that rose like vaults, where everyone was asleep and shut tight in. And miles away the wave of fire rode after them with its cargo of ruins from the past' (221). Echoing the 'sizzling blaze of ocean' on Teeton's map-curtain, this merging of metropolis, fire, and the oceanic 'wave' on which the past's 'cargo' 'rode' reinforces what the novel as a whole conveys: that as a stage on which colonial legacies are to be revisited and revised, London remains an unreconstructed, damaging space.

In his essay 'Minimal Selves,' Stuart Hall writes, 'The classic questions which every migrant faces are twofold: "Why are you here?" and "When are you going back home?" No migrant ever knows the answer to the second question until asked. Only then does she or he know that really, in the deep sense, she/he's never going back. Migration is a one-way trip. There is no "home" to go back to. There never was' (115). Hall means this conceptually rather than physically, of course – the home one leaves will never be the same on return, especially once emigration has unsettled the very idea of 'home' – but his questions and answers are literalized and internalized in *Water with Berries* and Salkey's *Come Home, Malcolm Heartland*. The protagonists of both novels doubt their purpose and sense of belonging in London. Both resolve, from the first page of their respective narratives, to return 'home' as political radicals. Both fail to do so. In their final weeks in London, both become entangled in messy, high-stakes relations that turn their intended round-trips into one-way journeys.

Set explicitly in the context of the Black Power movement, Salkey's novel foregrounds the question of where the revolutionary goals of black migrants ought to be pursued: in London, in the Caribbean, or elsewhere. Malcolm is frustrated by the 'meaningless drift' of his London life, and even after twenty years and a legal career, his 'image of the Black immigrant in London' is of a large locked white door 'with the small figure of a Black man, standing in front of it and knocking softly, as if the fist he raised were made of a dab of black cloud' (46). Like Ralph Singh, he keeps coming back to such images of the urban self as ephemeral and immaterial, dwelling on 'the unreal quality' of his London experiences: 'The years were like a magic-shadow show. He had lived within a shower of shadows. He had moved around in it daily, not touching anything, not making any impression' (53). In the weeks before his planned move to Jamaica, Malcolm falls in with a group of Black Power agitators who try to recruit him and keep him in London, but he finds their visionary talk of transnational revolution empty, abstract, and destined to have no material impact. He sees the group as preferring '*the upholstery of Theoryville*' to on-site action: 'London was such an insulation against the realities of the home struggle in action; it was an excellent stage for playing the rebel-act, for acting out the padded version of the drama of the distant confrontation, and for fooling oneself that one is strong enough and ready enough, with theory and tension, to carry the fight forward elsewhere' (150, 96). His own insistence on pursuing a more hands-on agenda in Jamaica proves to be Malcolm's undoing. Mocking his new acquaintances as 'metropolitan playthings,' 'self-regarding amateurs ... playing at resistance politics,' he rebuffs their overtures and, ironically, provokes them into finally taking violent action: murdering him (179, 197). The London he has associated with theatrical artifice, fantasy, and separation from worldly impact becomes the place where Malcolm himself is proved the fantasist: regarding both the possibilities of consequential action in Jamaica – Clovis disabuses him of this dream just before killing him – and his freedom to opt out of a secretive Black Power cell once it has claimed him.[35]

In their two tragic novels of aborted return, Lamming and Salkey cast a sceptical eye on the prospects of a constructively politicized blackness in London or the West Indies. Revolution in the Caribbean homeland remains a distant and possibly deluded dream, and resistance in the 'external frontier' of London is a mug's game of futile violence and deadly talk. Malcolm Heartland (sounding again like Ralph Singh) worries throughout that he is 'locked out of the society he had chosen for his

exile: a double lock-out, in his case, both at home and abroad' (56). His
plan to alter his condition is blocked by Salkey, who finalizes Malcolm's
exile from both societies by killing him off. The two novels differ in their
contexts – Salkey's lacks the connection with colonial history that
Lamming's *Tempest* allegory implies – and in their protagonists' relation
to violence – Malcolm is victim, while Teeton, Derek, and Roger are
perpetrators. Both novels suggest, however, that a generation after the SS
Windrush the metropolis remains a place of double exile for West Indians – a place where they are cut off from the past and from the prospect
of improved conditions of belonging on either side of the Atlantic. Both
authors acknowledge the diasporic consciousness through which, as
Paul Gilroy writes, 'An intricate web of cultural and political connections
binds blacks here [in England] to blacks elsewhere' (*There Ain't* 156).
But for both, the links that exist in the realms of historical memory,
literature, and theory become destructive and obstructive in the world
of actions and consequences, and the '*homing desire*' that motivates the
transnational solidarity of diasporic peoples turns out to be fatal (Brah
193; cf. Cohen 23).

Two West Indian authors are mentioned in the text of Selvon's *Moses
Ascending*. They are, as it happens, Lamming and Salkey, who are heralded by Galahad as leading proponents of 'Black Literature, ... who
write some powerful books what making the whole world realize our
existence and our struggle' (43). At one point Moses describes himself
'kicking aside a batch of Lamming's *Water For Berries* [*sic*] that was in my
way to stand up by the window' (138). His view, unlike Teeton's, is not
blocked by map-curtains, and though Moses states no desire in this novel
to return to the West Indies – he does return in *Moses Migrating* (1983) –
and makes little direct reference to the region, Selvon's novel, like
Lamming's, uses allegory to relate the colonial past to 'human situations' in London. In his comic account of the topsy-turvy relations
between Moses, the black London landlord, and Bob, his white 'man
Friday,' Selvon invokes a canonical text that, like *The Tempest*, involves a
shipwreck, a remote island, and a paradigmatically colonialist power
structure (4). Here, of course, Selvon reverses the racial hierarchy that
Robinson Crusoe takes for granted.

Moses, like Salkey's Malcolm, becomes reluctantly affiliated with a
Black Power group; this one, at its rhetorical extreme, aspires to 'kill all
the whites and burn down the City of London' (93). Arrested in Trafalgar
Square, he is put in a prison that resembles 'the hold of a slave ship,' but
it is in the 'sinking ship' of Moses's house that the novel most strongly

shows colonialist power relations crossing the ocean and continuing in the metropolis (36, 138). Moses is less interested in the political resistance Black Power promises, which he rejects, than in resisting the racial status quo at the microcosmic level of domestic space. He does not aspire to influence a wider field; even his claim that the black worker is 'in charge of the city whilst the rest of Brit'n is still abed' – that he alone 'holds the keys of the city' – is a sanguine, if ironic, recognition of the immigrant's subordinate status (5, 6). Moses is content to be retired, apolitical, and lord of his house. Even in this limited sphere, however, he fails to maintain his power. Against his will, he is manipulated into housing a Black Power office and an illegal-immigrant operation. After getting caught in a compromising position with Bob's fiancée, he is forced to give up his penthouse for the claustrophobic 'small enclosure' of Bob's room: 'Thus are the mighty fallen, empires totter, monarchs dethrone and the walls of Pompeii bite the dust. Humiliated and degraded, I took up abode in Bobbie's erstwhile room, while he and Jeannie move in to the penthouse' (134).

This reversal of an earlier reversal reinstates an old status quo – white above subordinated, constrained black. Combined with the novel's satiric treatment of Black Power, it suggests once again that resisting the racial order that sustained imperialism and continues to prevail in London is doomed – though Selvon's comic idiom is a far cry from the ominous earnestness of Lamming and Salkey. Alternatively, just as Moses kicks aside Lamming's text, Selvon may be offering a sly subversion of their theme. Within the microcosmic society of the house it is Bob, an immigrant to London from the Midlands – 'the Black Country' (110) – who plays the illiterate native to Moses's complacent, writerly colonizer, and it is Bob, not Moses, who supports Black Power (and is even pictured on the first issue of Brenda's newsletter). In a London transformed by the 'reverse imperialism' of New Commonwealth migration, Selvon enacts a strategy of multiple reversals that destabilizes and multiplies its own allegorical referents. Favouring the playful over the portentous, and preferring comic machinations to violent *realpolitik*, Selvon's novel, like its hero, largely withdraws from London's streets. Whereas resistance in *Water with Berries* and *Come Home, Malcolm Heartland* is a tangled, angst-ridden, life-and-death business, *Moses Ascending* approaches it as a low-stakes escapade, an inconsequential lark. Indeed, even its final paragraph, in which Moses plans a further reversal that would reinstate him above Bob, suggests that the apparent failure of his resistant self-assertions, unlike those of Teeton, Derek, Roger, and Malcolm, is far from final.

Metropolitan Microcosms and the Shifting Grounds of Britishness

The fact that Moses's intermittently successful resistance to the historical and racial order takes place entirely within his house and not on the streets does not prevent it from having at least symbolic reverberations outside the domestic realm. It is a truism universally acknowledged (at least, in postcolonial critical circles) that a house in a Commonwealth novel often functions as a synecdoche, a microcosm in which conditions of possession and dispossession, belonging and unbelonging in the national sphere may be thematized. V.S. Naipaul's *A House for Mr Biswas* (1961) is the definitive West Indian example. Mr Biswas's lifelong desire to own a home is frequently read as an allegory of the disenfranchised colony aspiring to self-rule, and the dilapidated house he finally buys becomes a comment on the emergent nation. The authors of *The Empire Writes Back* read houses as politicized spaces (see Ashcroft et al. 28), and Rosemary George's *The Politics of Home* explores in detail the complex links between home and nation in colonial and postcolonial texts. But if the location of Mr Biswas's house clearly suits a Trinidadian national (or Caribbean regional) allegory, the dwellings West Indian characters inhabit in London demand a different interpretive frame. In the metropolis, the abode of a character like Moses may signify such things as his or her socioeconomic purchase, permanence or transience, or level of security and belonging in British society. But to a greater degree than in the West Indies, race becomes a key marker of identity – the one that always contextualizes and usually limits a migrant's ability to make a home in the mostly white 'mother country.' The emergence in the early post-*Windrush* years of racially exclusive room-to-let signs – on which 'No Coloureds' often had the same semiotic status as 'No Dogs' – made domestic space a notoriously contested terrain for West Indian Londoners. As James Procter notes, in narratives of black British settlement, 'it was the dwelling place, not the official point of entry, at which the regulation, policing and deferral of black settlement was to be most effectively mythologized. The British homestead took on the significance of a national frontier' ('Descending' 21).[36]

Indeed, what the *ad-hoc* racism of individual landlords accomplished in the domestic realm, amendments to public policy effected in the larger sphere of national belonging. In 1948, the year SS *Windrush* arrived, the British Nationality Bill conferred British citizenship on the inhabitants of all current and most former colonies. As Ian Baucom explains, British nationality under this legislation was based on place: the Bill's inclusive Britishness was the last reassertion of a nine-hundred-year-old legal principle of *ius soli*, or 'law of the soil,' according to which one's membership in the national citizenry was contingent on one's place of origin – in this case, British soil being defined as the lands of the United Kingdom and its Commonwealth (see 7–24). In the decades after 1948, that principle underwent a number of restrictions, culminating in Margaret Thatcher's 1981 British Nationality Act. By enshrining 'patriality' as the new basis of Britishness – defined as descent from a parent or grandparent born in Britain – Thatcher's act replaced soil with blood, place with race, as the basis of Britishness. At a stroke it removed citizenship from the majority of Commonwealth subjects, particularly those with brown or black skin who, unlike many settler-colony nationals, could not usually claim entitlement through patriality. As Baucom writes, 'Discarding nine hundred years of legal precedent that recognized a territorial principle as the sole absolute determinant of British identity, the act determined that Britain was, henceforth, a genealogical community' (8). Insofar as it maintained a reduced version of *ius soli*, the act implied 'that the territory of the United Kingdom and the territory of the colonies were not interchangeable, that the "home" soil had greater right-endowing properties than the soil beyond the sea' (13).

The shifting grounds for official belonging through this period are reflected in the microcosmic world of domestic space by the fact that West Indian Londoners in novels are much more likely to rent than to own their dwellings, and by the tendency of home-ownership, when it is achieved, to evaporate. *Moses Ascending* is the first Caribbean novel to portray a West Indian homeowner in London; those in two later novels, Joan Riley's *Waiting in the Twilight* (1987) and Beryl Gilroy's *Boy-Sandwich* (1989), share Moses's experience of losing control, but with more permanent ramifications. Both books feature elderly West Indians who live for many years in London and work hard to buy a house only to see it reclaimed for a development scheme. Like the legal Britishness extended to West Indian immigrants and later retracted, the properties that literally and symbolically represent their newly 'grounded' identities – their attachment to the soil – are withdrawn by institutional forces beyond their control. After serving for a time as sites of empowerment, possession, and belonging, the houses come to symbolize the opposite in the 1980s: disempowerment, dispossession, unbelonging. Although neither of the novels mentions the Nationality Act, it is notable that both construct a generation gap: the experience of belonging is ephemeral for older black immigrants but generally not for their children or grand-children born in London.

Riley's Adella, like many immigrants, projects her desire 'to build a better life for the children' – so they can be 'accepted' 'just like white people' – into a dream of owning a house (15). Her finances and her colour severely limit her choice, and she ends up with a 'broken-down, half-dead place in the middle of a rotting street' that is nothing like her dream-house (16). Too poor to maintain or repair it, she loses her tenants after the roof falls in, and when the house is repossessed, she moves to a government estate. She is devastated: 'They had pulled the heart out of her when they took her house'; although she knows many West Indians to whom the same thing has happened, 'that did not take away her personal failure, the shame of living in a government house' (13, 127). For Adella, the failures associated with the house are emblem-atic of larger losses: of her job, her husband, and the respect and support of her most assimilated children, who fit in, it seems, at the cost of their links to her. Her years in London are a litany of misery and disappointment, beginning the moment she arrives to find herself unex-pectedly without accommodation.

As a young woman in Jamaica, Adella was attracted by the promise of 'the Motherland' 'where the streets were paved with gold' (2); after gaining and losing her London house, she is pictured walking in icy cold 'along the wrong-way paving through the yellow brick estate' (140). If Riley is alluding here to the dreams and disappointments of *The Wizard of Oz*, the import of Adella's experience is not that tale's trite 'there's no place like home.' In *Waiting in the Twilight*, there is no place that *can* be home. Cold England has failed Adella, and while she may once have been 'happy in Kingston,' she cannot return except in memory (151). Cast adrift from both places, she is suspended in an oceanic twilight zone of in-betweenness and limbo. Her narrative conveys this condition not only in its title but in its structure, which moves, like Anna's in *Voyage in the Dark*, fluidly back and forth among the present and past in England and the earlier island past. Free-floating memory connects Adella to Jamaica, overcoming the 'endless oceans of danger' that seem to sur-round her in England (76). That metaphor is prompted by her experi-ence of attack by white youths one moonlit night; she feels as though oceans are 'dividing' her from her London house, even though it is 'less than a hundred yards away' (76). This Rhys-like image of ocean-space expanding and contracting conveys Adella's alienated distance from the

London that her house symbolizes – an alienation for which her black-ness is largely responsible. The novel's other reference to the sea – Adella the non-swimmer's 'fear of drowning' as she sails from Jamaica to London – similarly constructs the ocean as insurmountable distance from (more than bridging connection to) the West Indies (161). Once Adella has embarked on her ocean voyage to England, home, like the house that represents it, becomes an elusive and illusive dream.

In Gilroy's *Boy-Sandwich*, Tyrone Grainger's grandparents endure taunts by 'rent-a-mob racists' on the day they leave their house – to be demol-ished for a town-house development – and move into 'the limbo of a sheltered home' (2, 1). Although Grandmother has long treasured a bag of 'Island earth' and Grandfather, from whom 'words flowed ... like water,' loves talking of 'yesterdays ... across seas and oceans and in the country beyond,' Tyrone fears that the Island-based identities they have maintained for many years will be forgotten in the 'home' (13, 20, 5). The two residences together represent various facets of 1980s London in microcosm. The elder Graingers' house represents a state of belonging achieved over many years of 'dog-work' in England, overcoming preju-dice as 'deep as Atlantic Ocean' to gain a place from which they are then forcibly removed (4, 20). The unsettling environment of the 'home,' with racist staff who apparently steal their possessions, extends the sense of insecure West Indian belonging in London that their unhousing conveys. Later, a fire set by an arsonist at a house party, which kills twelve young blacks and badly burns Tyrone's girlfriend, further reinforces this association of houses with racism and precarious states of dwelling.[37] The novel's interrelated images of earth, water, and fire suggest that attachment to place is an elemental condition; like the elements, place-identity is both transforming and itself subject to transformation by exterior forces. In the wake of the fire's tragically final dispossession, together with the grandparents' eviction from their piece of British soil, a new urgency attends the possibility of returning to the home across the water that the grandmother's bag of earth represents.

When a financial windfall enables Tyrone to pay for a trip to the Island for his grandparents, parents, his recuperating girlfriend, and himself, Gilroy further complicates the ideas of home and belonging. Despite some ambivalence – the grandfather worries that leaving England after forty years is 'betraying' what blacks have suffered and achieved there (96) – the old couple does feel at home on the Island, as do Tyrone's parents and Adijah, whose burn-wounds have destroyed any feeling for London as 'home' (116). They all choose to stay on the Island, but the

London-born Tyrone responds differently. He has insisted back in London that 'I belong, regardless of those who say I don't' (30), and now the fishbowl community of Picktown makes him realize what he misses about London:

> I conclude that it is my need for anonymity. ... I have grown up with just an urban identity and come to treasure that. In Picktown I am trapped – in my family identity, the identity of my community and the identity of my opportunity. In London I had lived another life, grown other feelings, got to know myself as 'Tyrone.' ... I do not want the involvement of 'belonging' without the choice of 'not belonging.' I feel unhappy outside my harsh urban skin, unable to site myself in time and space. (110–11)

As John McLeod writes, Tyrone is prompted 'to rethink his identity in terms of unpredictable *routes* and not secure *roots*' and to reconsider London as 'a space where he can understand and nurture his difference' (*Beginning* 235, 236). The novel ends with Tyrone settling into the airplane that will take him back to London. This appropriately in-between, linking place reinforces his preference for the mobility of a 'routed' identity formed in the diasporic interstices of his Britishness and his West Indianness. Along with the original flight to the Island, it also adds a completing element, air, to Gilroy's earth, water, and fire images. Together, they help organize her novel's compelling examination of transnational place-identities and the stresses that time, tragedy, generational difference, and changes in the urban and national spheres impose on the idea of home.

Gilroy's novel ends more happily than Riley's, notwithstanding the smile in Adella's eyes as she dies. Both narratives move towards a relational vision of a London-based in-betweenness; the difference is that for the youthful and mobile Tyrone, the British identity he embraces (and which is his legal birthright) seems destined always to include a strong West Indian component. With his financial means and strong family ties, there is no reason to think Tyrone will not visit Picktown again and, as he matures, nurture his Caribbean connections as a complement to his black Britishness. He will likely grow into an inclusive sense of belonging that balances both routes and roots. By contrast, the poor, elderly, and infirm Adella, shut out materially from both British and West Indian belongings, is caught in the limbo of an excluding liminality. She can sustain only attenuated roots, and she has access to routes purely in her imagination. Still, as with Rhys's Anna, the spatial and temporal fluidity of her mental journeys (and the narrative that conveys them) is not insignificant. Her virtual routes criss-cross the ocean freely and partly offset the pain of disenfranchisement symbolized by the loss of her house.

Moreover, while *Voyage in the Dark*, *Waiting in the Twilight*, and *Boy-Sandwich* all represent dwelling places as microcosms, reflecting aspects of identity and attachment in the experience of residential space, their ocean-crossing relationality points towards a further microcosmic dimension of their setting. When a London house or room represents a site of national belonging, the city is implicitly constructed as the British capital. But for West Indian immigrants, London is just as importantly the (former) imperial capital, linked to distant colonies through complex relations of travel, trade, and administration. Metropolitan spaces are therefore potentially a microcosm of a wider global field of transnational belonging, especially as their inhabitants become ever more international in origin. Recent novels of London by West Indian authors – like many by Canadian, South Asian, and black British authors examined elsewhere in this book – figure London most importantly as a microcosm of and point of access to the wider world. Because, as the editors of a book on place-identity write, an 'easy alliance of place and identity' is not possible for diasporic people, 'if the cities are to act as locations for identity once again, they must be "reimagined" as such' (Carter et al. viii). One way London is often reimagined is as a kind of world-in-miniature. Defined by its fluid connections to global elsewheres, the metropolis becomes a virtual container of the lands and waters of empire.

Wilson Harris's typically cosmic novel *The Angel at the Gate* (1982) is set in a London full of such expansive imagery. Not only does it feature a toy 'skeleton house' with 'collapsible doors and windows,' but the house in which three-year-old John plays with this toy (sitting in a chair that resembles 'a half-sunken, half-floating boat') is a 'smouldering boat of a house cast adrift in the winter of space' (10, 34). Within that house Harris imagines intercontinental space in the most mundane corners:

> [Sebastian] did not see the crumpled sheets and blankets he had left on struggling out of bed; he did not see the miniature map and relief model those bedclothes had made as if they were ridden by a cosmic chariot, cosmic anancy plates under Africa, Asia and Europe to divide the bed into land masses and oceans, into compressed towering mountains, into descending boats and troughs, now fashioned into a geologic toy with which precocious baby John could play at continents in motion. (33–4)

The home of Father Joseph Marsden also functions as a virtual conduit to the world. Marsden is both an actual man living in London in 1981 and a transhistorical, transnational figure of empire: as the Indian Khublall says to the Jamaican Jackson in Shepherd's Bush, 'Who doesn't know Marsden of Angel Inn? Your antecedents and my antecedents were taught by him in India, the West Indies, South America, USA, Africa, everywhere. And we still feel attached to him' (91). Marsden takes Mary on a voyage to India that seems real, even though it takes place entirely in his bathtub. On 'the diminutive ocean of the bath,' in 'a boat that sails in his house,' he takes her 'through an upset sea to the continent on the other side of the bath, a map of India, where they landed' (61, 60, 62). A month later, after they have travelled to Mysore and a village two hundred miles away, 'the ship on the bath returned to dock in London' (65). *The Angel at the Gate* is saturated with further references to seas, oceans, voyages, globes, planets, and expanding and contracting space, even as it physically remains entirely set in London. However, the metaphysical and metafictional orientation of Harris's narrative, and the perplexingly slippery identities of its characters, make its rich images difficult to connect to the kind of referential portrait of metropolitan life that would most beneficially extend this chapter's analysis.

More rewarding is David Dabydeen's coming-of-age novel *The Intended* (1991), which uses its microcosmic imagery to reinforce a complex set of interrelations between the London of the narrator's adolescence, the Guyana of his childhood, and the shifting identities they jointly accommodate. The novel's most explicit small-scale virtual world within London is the World Cruise ride where the narrator works in the summer. This dark, watery tunnel offers a fifteen-minute alphabetical boat-tour of the world – from Austria to Zanzibar via Fiji, Greece, India, and Timbuktu. Guyana, significantly, has been 'neglected' (78). Here Dabydeen echoes V.S. Naipaul's view that West Indian colonies suffered decline and neglect by London after the abolition of slavery.[38] The larger allusion, however – sustained throughout *The Intended* – is to Conrad's *Heart of Darkness*.[39] The oceanic Thames that frames Conrad's African tale, an 'interminable waterway' that 'seemed to lead into the heart of an immense darkness' (Conrad 5, 111), is reduced in *The Intended* to the World Cruise's miniature indoor river. Here, water that is 'not so much brooding and mysterious as dank and still' carries pleasure-seekers and lovers on small boats past crude, two-dimensional paintings of iconic national clichés: an alpine village, the Taj Mahal, an African landscape with zebras and bare-breasted natives (77). Kurtz's ivory profiteering becomes a ticket-ripping scam by which the narrator and Shaz cheat their employer of ten shillings a day; further subversiveness occurs when Joseph paints a Kurtz-like figure into an African scene along with 'a dead elephant lying on its back, four massive feet stuck in the air like the chimney stacks of Battersea power station which lay just outside the Fun Fair and which provided the model for Joseph's artistry' (112).

London's global connectedness, a central motif of *Heart of Darkness*, is here, in the context of imperial contraction and collapse, parodically reduced to a depthless simulacrum. As in other recent novels discussed in other chapters, London contains or embraces 'the world' not just as a demographic, historical, or economic fact but as a flattened-out, shrunk-down image of virtual access.[40] Dabydeen complements the World Cruise scenes when he has Joseph begin making a film of *Heart of Darkness* in Tooting Bec Common:

> It had everything, trees, pond and clumps of bush with which to re-create a feel of the African landscape. He stood under a large tree and pointed the camera, scanning the branches, zooming closer to capture a sense of dense foliage blacking out the sky. He threw stones in the pond to create a movement in the water, which would pass for the trail of a river boat. He lay flat on his stomach and inched towards a patch of tall grass, the snout of his camera pushing through the blades, suggesting a hazardous journey through the jungle. (109)

This image of Africa is not only miniaturized and topographically incorrect but devoid of Africans – as though the *Heart of Darkness* Joseph is filming is the dehumanizing one critiqued by Chinua Achebe (see *Hopes* 1–13). (Moreover, while Achebe recommends that Conrad's novella not be read, Joseph's footage is never seen, even by himself.)

Dabydeen does include people in his other significant microcosmic image of London. After introducing himself and his friends as a 're-grouping of the Asian diaspora in a South London schoolground' (5), the narrator turns to a wider field of diasporic Indians: those whose visible presence on public transport generates a mix of empathy and embarrassment:

> as the train trundled through a dark tunnel we flashed glances at one another, each a blinding recognition of our shared Asian-ness, each welding us in one communal identity. In the swift journey between Tooting Bec and Balham, we re-lived the passages from India to Britain, or India to the

Caribbean to Britain, the long journeys of a previous century across unknown seas towards the shame of plantation labour; or the excitement with
which we boarded *Air India* which died in a mixture of jet-lag, bewilder-
ment and waiting in long queues in the immigration lounge at Heathrow –
just like back home, the memory of beggars lining up outside a missionary
church for a dollop of food from a white hand. (16–17)

'Diasporic identities,' writes Avtar Brah, 'are at once local and global.
They are networks of transnational identifications encompassing "imagined" and "encountered" communities' (196). Dabydeen's narrator figures the dark tunnel of London's Underground as a transnational and
transhistorical space where randomly encountered Indians can become
an imagined community. The momentous voyages of migration that
define the imperial and postcolonial eras are distilled down to the trip
from one tube station to another. And the psychic and material effects of
dislocation – the wrenching apart and bringing together of diverse
peoples – dwindle into the awkward, anxious glances by which strangers
form an ephemeral communal consciousness.

Where *The Intended* departs most significantly from other novels that
portray microcosmic virtual worlds in London is in its subtle and compli-
cating inclusion of similar images in Guyana. The idealistic mantras of
the narrator's grandmother make her a voice of global unity and
relationality – 'you is we, remember you is we' she tells the narrator just
before he crosses the ocean to England; 'all body on dis earth is one
God's people' (40, 39) – but she is equally worldly in body. On the
cracked soles of her feet, 'there were lines everywhere, running in all
directions, like a spider's web or a complicated map of the world tracing
roads and rivers and other routes. She was born in Albion village, had
never travelled out of the village, and would eventually die there, yet her
feet mapped all the pathways of the world' (37). The grandfather, by
contrast, is an unsavoury drunk who beats his wife, spends his grandson's
money on rum, and steals livestock from neighbours. The narrator
accompanies him on a sheep-stealing mission; in the 'semi-darkness' of
early morning they walk, wade across a pond, and bring the stolen,
exhausted animals back across the pond and home (30). The narrator is
identified with the lamb; at one point on the far side of the pond he is
separated from the grandfather and feels 'abandoned,' exhausted, and
wants 'to lie down and sleep and out of spite never wake up' (32). The
pond is here transformed into a miniature, symbolic ocean: the scene
looks both forward to the narrator's migration to England, where his

father will suddenly abandon him, and backward to the history of Africans stolen from their lands and spirited 'across the pond' to slavery and death in the Caribbean.

This historical echo is reinforced when Peter's father mysteriously disappears and the pond is searched unsuccessfully for clues. Here Dabydeen nods to Derek Walcott's image of the sea that contains wrecked slave ships and dead slave bodies as an opaque, inaccessible vault containing West Indian history.[41] When the search is called off, Peter tosses the items he has gathered as clues

> into the canal which ran the length of the village. By the time we reached his house he had discarded two buttons, one red and one blue, an empty cigarette carton, half a plastic comb, some goat dung hardened into marbles, a piece of string, four awara seeds and a dead wasp lodged in a leaf. ... The clues to his father's existence lay in this jumble which we dumped forever at the bottom of the canal. Peter pushed off the leaf with the wasp on it like a boat, and we stood watching it drift towards the centre, trembling in the fragile ripples. He took up a stone and pelted it in, the wave created tipping the wasp into the water so that fish could nibble at it. (53–4)

The wasp on its fragile 'boat' is a further miniature image of the precarious voyages of slavery and indenture, and is echoed in three later references to journeying insects. In the first, the narrator recalls ants and flies travelling along the scar in a sweet-seller's face until they get too close to his mouth and are licked up and eaten; his diction – 'a smooth path,' 'terrain,' 'headed back up-country in the direction of his nostrils' – suggests a topographic analogy (150). In the second, Joseph's bizarre collage film includes a shot of ants entering a tramp's nose and being sneezed out, which he interprets as 'the experience of immigration: the black ants were West Indians laden with suitcases landing on the tarmac of England, and the nostrils were the interrogation lounges at Heathrow' (159). Third, back in Guyana, the narrator remembers seeing ants crawl in the nose-hole of a cow's skull while flies 'drowned' in a pail of cow-dung (229).

Through an intricate web of miniaturizing images that reverberate across the ocean, Dabydeen relates his city and country worlds – London and the Guyana village whose name, Albion, is a negative appellation for England.[42] Insects represent slaves and migrants; ponds, canals, and tunnels suggest the oceans and rivers across which imperial and postcolonial journeys were made, while cracked feet, faces, and nostrils also evoke the dangerous pathways of (post)imperial routes. Recurring references to rippling water, drowning, fish, and sexuality add to the transoceanic play of these microcosmic images. And in a novel that Dabydeen, with some exaggeration, says 'is set on buses and trains,' public transport in both London and Guyana connects disparate people through their journeys together and repeatedly represents intercontinental and historical journeys (Birbalsingh, 'David' 179). Furthermore, as in Rhys's *Voyage in the Dark* and Riley's *Waiting in the Twilight*, Dabydeen's non-linear narrative supports this mutual worlding, moving fluidly within paragraphs – even within a single sentence – between London at various times and Guyana in the past. As Charles Sarvan writes, its overlapping of pasts, presents and futures makes *The Intended* a 'novel of imbrication' (58); but as it imbricates different times it also correlates different places and the small worlds they contain. The narrative extends beyond the narrator's London adolescence to subsume and richly integrate the spaces and defining images of his Guyana boyhood, just as the British imperial narrative extended Britain and Britishness across the world's oceans and joined diverse lands and peoples into the vast, messy project of empire.

Messing with Identity

In the words of Gayatri Spivak, 'empire messes with identity' (226). The *Bildungsroman* narrative of *The Intended* carries its unnamed protagonist towards recognition of his own messy identity and a degree of ambivalent acceptance of it. His desire for assimilation into British society is demonstrated in part by his attraction to the stability and order evident in his white girlfriend's images of home. He juxtaposes the continuity and tradition on display in Janet's photographs with the untidy dislocations of diasporic Indians:

> Our lives were messy by contrast: families scattered across the West, settling in one country or another depending on the availability of visas; we lived from hand to mouth, hustling or thieving or working nightshifts and sleeping daytime; we were ashamed of our past, frightened of the present and not daring to think of the future. When I looked at the images of her mother and father in their neat house and manicured garden the first instinct was to inflict pain, to shatter the security of their lives, for in some vague way I felt they were responsible for my own disordered existence. (168)

It is not surprising that the narrator later deconstructs this opposition between English order and diasporic mess. As Dabydeen says in an interview, 'It's not enough to continue to blame whites for messing up our society. They may have introduced elements of the mess, but we completed that job with superb finality: that is why everyone in Guyana wants to leave' (Birbalsingh, 'David' 178). The mess that he here locates in Guyana he also finds, towards the end of *The Intended*, in England – the place for which many Guyanese and other 'New Commonwealth' migrants left. On the eve of Janet's trip to Australia and his own departure for Oxford, the narrator envies her voyage to 'a new beginning, ... a new, clean country. England is so messy and violent and drugged up, everything is going to pot' (242). He would probably find Australia (itself hardly untouched by empire and messy migrations) to be not so 'clean' on closer inspection; the narrator's consistent use of a retrospective irony *vis-à-vis* his younger self encourages the reader to regard this youthful grass-is-greenerism less than seriously. After all, the larger point Dabydeen is making with these metaphoric messes is that imperialism makes a mess – of identities, of cultures, of societies, of places – wherever it goes. Unlike the messy pink spots Dr Seuss's imperious Cat in the Hat spreads around the property he takes over, the pink blotches the British Empire scattered over the map of the world cannot be magically removed.[43] The Cat and the clean-up crew of miniature A–Z cats he keeps in his hat can zap their collective mess with a simple 'Voom,' but the stains of imperial history, however mutually created, are permanent. Moreover, those stains mark the map of 'messy' London – the streets of its famous 'A–Z' pocketbooks, as it were – as much as any maps of its distant colonies. Whether as empire's point of origin or as a final destination for diasporic peoples whose identities were messed with by imperial history, London proves as complicatedly untidy as any of its (former) colonies. Just as Joseph messes with the idealized paintings through which the World Cruise brings an A–Z world into London, the Commonwealth migrants who are transforming the (post)imperial metropolis and bringing 'the world' inside it are reimagining its stereotyped images and making it increasingly hard to see London (or England, or Britain) as an idealized location of stability, order, or clear-cut national identity.

At the end of *The Intended*, on the Oxford Street bus with Janet just before she leaves for Australia and he begins studies at Oxford University, the narrator still longs to escape his messy identity: 'I suddenly felt old and tired and done for. I wanted the bus to stop. I wanted to get off. All the stopping and starting was making me sick. I wanted to stop moving. I didn't want to go anywhere anymore. I didn't want to be born time and again. I didn't want to be an eternal, indefinite immigrant. I wanted to get off' (243). This bus trip in London signifies a larger legacy of diasporic journeys, just as the novel's other bus and train trips do: the first Guyana memory of Kumar's speedy bus, whose messy 'red and black dust, like a memory of its rage, ... slowly spread against the sky, but could barely stain it, the blueness from one end of the earth to the other absorbing and neutralising all' (18); the later memory of Kumar's bus crashing (like the leaf-borne wasp, like a latter-day slave ship) into the canal and drowning three people (see 56); the diasporic consciousness anxiously formed among South Asians reliving transcontinental journeys on the London Underground. With this final bus trip in London, the narrator's wish to get off the bus may be granted literally, but as a microcosmic metaphor it is misleading. The immigrant's journey can never be stopped; the legacy of history cannot be discarded like so much luggage abandoned or lost in transit. No trip to Oxford Street, to Oxford University, or to Australia can erase the diasporic immigrant's messy inheritances.

The novel's dishevelled chronology and perpetual narrative motion can make it seem random and messy – 'analogous,' as Margery Fee notes, to the collage structure of Joseph's documentary film (108). Nonetheless, the criss-crossing of images across times and places reveals *The Intended* to be an intricately unified narrative of interconnected worlds that reverberate within each other just as empire's distant worlds did. This novel of emergent cultural identity enacts formally the untidy but worldly identity the narrator gradually and ambivalently comes to understand, though not to embrace. Stuart Hall writes that Caribbean cultural identity 'belongs to the future as much to the past. ... Far from being eternally fixed in some essentialized past, [cultural identities] are subject to the continuous "play" of history, culture, and power' ('Cultural' 212–13). They are, he adds, 'constructed through memory, fantasy, narrative, and myth ... within the discourses of history and culture' and 'framed' by 'two axes or vectors, simultaneously operative: the vector of similarity and continuity and the vector of difference and rupture' (213). Dabydeen's narrator comes to understand these principles; his key microcosmic images, together with the remarkably rich metaphor of the transnational, transhistorical mess, bring them vividly to life.

Like the many West Indian writers of metropolitan novels who preceded him, Dabydeen sees London as a place where personal and collective identity can be productively interrogated. The individual's links to

larger entities and phenomena – geographical, historical, national, eth-
nic/racial – are brought into focus by London's role as central node in a
(post)imperial network that sprawls messily across time and space.
Through the recurring motifs of microcosmic worlds, oceans, twilight,
houses, perception, and of the real or imagined journeys that seem to
collapse the boundaries of time and space, West Indian novelists present
London as an increasingly borderless and global space. However bleak
many of these novels are, their narratives of metropolitan life lead
without exception to an enlarged conception of self and of West Indian
identity. They also lead to an enlarged conception of London; they
contest the city's physical and metaphorical restrictions – its sometimes
small, mean self-image as a place of exclusive white Britishness – with
reminders that imperialism's opening-out to the world has its oceanic
echoes in the postimperial migration that has made the metropolis an
ever more fluid, worldly space.

chapter four

London South-East: Metropolitan (Un)realities in Indian Fiction

The city, then, is above all a representation. But what sort of representation? By analogy with the now familiar idea that the nation provides us with an 'imagined community,' I would argue that the city constitutes an *imagined environment.*

James Donald

Urban Prospects

In the first chapter of *A Passage to India* (1924), the most famous English novel to contemplate the Indian subcontinent, E.M. Forster presents a meticulous depiction of urban social space. He divides his fictitious city of Chandrapore into three geographically and socially distinct zones: a riverside area inhabited by colonized Indians and characterized by rubbish, rot, and visual monotony; high ground near the railway station where the racially in-between Eurasians live; and the more distant heights of the nondescript British civil station, which unlike the city below 'provokes no emotion' and 'has nothing hideous in it.' The station is quite separate from the rest: it 'shares nothing with the city except the overarching sky' (10). In this scene-setting passage Forster not only wants to establish the way racialized power relations are inscribed and made starkly visible on the colonial landscape – this was a given in India, and his novel goes on to scrutinize those relations with much greater subtlety than these spatial divisions imply. He also, more importantly, wants to emphasize perspective: how the prospect the city presents radically alters when it is viewed from the station. From that high point the abject scene of mud and mean streets is hidden, and Chandrapore appears to be 'a city of gardens,' 'a forest lightly scattered with huts,' 'a tropical pleasaunce washed by a noble river' (9). The greenery that dominates the view serves to 'glorify the city to the English people who inhabit the rise, so that newcomers cannot believe it to be as meagre as it is described, and have to be driven down to acquire disillusionment' (10). As these new arrivals descend from their elevated domain to street level, Forster implies, Chandrapore comes into focus as the time-bound colonial city it really is, rather than as the picturesque, ahistorical village it appears to be.

When Mahatma Gandhi campaigned against colonial rule in the years between the publication of Forster's novel and India's independence in 1947, he increasingly, despite his urban background, came to identify the land he wanted to liberate as a nation of villages. In the words of Ashis Nandy, Gandhi 'thought of the village as the basic unit of Indian civilization; and he envisioned the future of India around that of the village' (*Journey* 16). If this alignment of time and place seems counter-intuitive, it is. Western culture has a long tradition of associating cities with the future and locating villages and the countryside in a figurative past, as Raymond Williams shows in *The Country and the City*. Nandy's *An Ambiguous Journey to the City* – which does for India's literary and cultural history something like what Williams does for England's – demonstrates that these dichotomous alignments have a purchase in India too, though they are complicated in uniquely Indian ways. In India, where 'the cultural psychology of space usually ends up as a political psychology of time,' the rural village is often identified with the past as 'a change-resisting depot of popular superstitions' (xi, 16). If the imagined village is 'the subaltern that cannot speak,' the colonial city is valorized as 'the new self, identified with history, progress, becoming' (13). By a different reckoning, however, the village is a positive counterpoint to the corrupting, atomizing city. It is constructed as a paradise, 'the depository of traditional wisdom and spirituality, and of the harmony of nature, intact community life and environmental sagacity – perhaps even a statement of Gandhian austerity, limits to want, and anti-consumerism' (13). Since cities like Bombay, Madras, and Forster's Chandrapore were the primary staging-grounds of colonialism – the places where Britain's trading activities, public buildings, and people made its power most visible – Gandhi's preference for villages can be seen not just as a backward-looking anachronism; it was also a strategic turning-away from the cosmopolitan spaces that represented the Raj's public face and the European narrative of historical progress that undergirded them. The city Forster's Britons find so disenchanting is a place they helped create.

The journey from village to city, whether one-way or return, has a long tradition in Indian writing from antiquity through postcolonial times. The earliest text Nandy examines is the *Mahabharata*, and while most of his examples are from twentieth-century literature and film, journeys beyond India fall outside his focus. When Indian novelists depict international journeys to London, whether from an Indian village or city, the metropolis prompts many of the same ambivalent responses that Nandy shows the Indian city generating.[1] Moreover, as the London novels of Kamala Markandaya, Anita Desai, Salman Rushdie, and Amitav Ghosh portray a white city 'through brown eyes'[2] – as they reverse and expand Forster's gaze – the spatial themes that inaugurate *A Passage to India*'s narrative resurface. Their migrant characters also discover a city in which racial divisions are spatially inscribed, despite the mobility urban space enables and the mingling of differences it necessitates. They too find the city more enchanting and comprehensible from a distance – as dreamed of from India or as viewed from above – than it proves to be up close. What is known of any place is a function of how, from where, and by whom it is perceived, and street-level London often prompts disillusionment, in large measure because it manifests more continuity than discontinuity with the colonial past and colonial Indian cities. As Indian writers and their protagonists articulate the disjunction between an imagined, desired, liberating London and a material, constraining London, they are often inspired to question its reality. Even as it presents concrete obstacles and barriers, the metropolis in Indian fiction is repeatedly figured as a place of unreality and artifice, a world characterized by the ephemeral, the metamorphic, and the immaterial.[3]

While such themes pervade urban discourses and narratives in general and are seen in many novels discussed elsewhere in this book, Indian culture provides special contexts for interpreting them in Indian novels. Cities in India can be highly segregated and stratified. The colonial divisions of space Forster observes may have dissolved (though their architectural legacy remains), but the Hindu caste system continues to influence the demarcation of urban territory. From the premise that the organization of space in a city is a 'cultural manifesto' that reflects its inhabitants' historical, cultural, and social experiences, Leighton Hazlehurst examines the ways one Indian city, Puranapur, spatializes caste divisions and groupings through its unofficial apportioning of 'economic,' 'ritually pure,' and 'ritually polluting' areas (186, 189). But while differentiated residential space 'keeps inviolate the corporate status and fundamental "sameness" of persons ... who occupy a common space' (189), city life requires mobility and economic interaction among different peoples. The result, Hazlehurst argues, is a discrepancy between 'space' and 'activities':

> While space defines and separates the urban landscape into distinct areas of 'status equivalence' (e.g. economic, residentially pure and polluting), activities do just the opposite. That is, activities 'link together' the urban landscape by 'violating' the very basis of spatial distinctions and separation. By the very nature of their exclusiveness, groups associated with each space are unable to remain self-sustaining. In fact, it is the economic and ritual interdependence of persons of different status which is, as we all recognize, a basic element of the caste system. From this perspective the organization of urban space in Puranapur may be likened to a facade, an 'as if' counterpart of the activities which force persons of different status into complementary relationships and violation of the exclusiveness of space. (190)

The caste separations materially inscribed on the landscape, in other words, turn out to be as immaterial as the invisible walls that mark off domains; they dissolve every time they are transgressed in the practice of everyday life.

These aspects of urban India provide one set of contexts through which city space has an ontological status that is paradoxically both real and unreal, bounded and transgressable, material and immaterial; Indian philosophy provides another. All indigenous schools of Indian thought maintain that reality cannot be apprehended through the senses or intellect.[4] In the most influential tradition, the Vedantic non-dualism of Samkara, 'reality' is identified solely with Brahman, an eternal, indescribable power that pervades and underlies all of sensible existence. Reality is that which cannot be sublated, with sublation defined as 'the mental process of correcting and rectifying ... a previously held judgment ... in the light of a new experience which contradicts it' (Puligandla 211). The unsublatable reality of Brahman, which can only be apprehended through non-perceptual, mystical insight, is extended in space and made accessible to the senses as 'appearance,' which because it is illusory – because it is not true reality – can always be sublated by other experiences. 'Unreality,' by contrast, is a term reserved for self-contradictory concepts such as square circles or married bachelors that by definition cannot become objects of sense-perception; unreality therefore 'neither can nor cannot be sublated' (214). The oscillation between reality and unreality that pervades Indian fictions of London is therefore best understood philosophically as a response to the world of 'appearance'; it has nothing to do with Samkara's 'unreality' and everything to do with *maya*. Often invoked as a shorthand for 'illusion,' *maya* in Vedantic thought is most usefully translated as 'our persistent *tendency* to regard appearances as reality,' 'our constant *propensity* to regard the sublatable as the unsublatable,' and 'our *ignorance* (*avidya*) as to the difference between appearance and reality' (217).

These and other Indian contexts can enrich the reading of Indian novels of London that, because of their genre, their setting, and the affiliations of their authors, are usually interpreted through Western literary paradigms. When the artist Valmiki in Markandaya's *Possession* (1963) turns his back on London and moves back to his Indian village, is he retreating to the past or embracing a brave new future – the 'alternative cosmopolitanism' Nandy associates with such journeys of return (*Journey* ix)? When the beleaguered Brahman Srinivas in Markandaya's *The Nowhere Man* (1972) finds his London doorstep smeared with feces, has his racist neighbour ironically performed an act of ritual caste pollution? When Dev in Desai's *Bye-Bye Blackbird* (1971) imagines the Battersea Power Station transformed into an Indian temple where *puja* is performed, is he seeking a ritually pure space in the metropolis? When Rushdie mentions the 'artificial' and 'fantastic nature' of cities in connection with *The Satanic Verses* (1988) – 'They're spaces which look very permanent, solid, but which in fact are extremely ephemeral and transitory, and huge buildings can fall overnight' (Ball, 'Interview' 32–3) – he may echo postmodernist thought on the city (not to mention Karl Marx's 'all that is solid melts into air'). But he may also be applying the concept of *maya* to a world of deceptive appearances, as may Amitav Ghosh when he stresses the sublatability of national borders and questions the materiality of London in *The Shadow Lines* (1988). When Indian writers and their characters journey to the metropolis, they reterritorialize it as literary terrain and lived space, but they also reimagine metropolitan life through Indian sensibilities.

Exhibiting the Exotic

Kamala Markandaya's *Possession* starkly foregrounds differences between 'Western' and 'Eastern' sensibilities, clearly inviting the allegorical reading it often receives.[5] When Caroline Bell takes a promising teenaged artist away from his Indian village to develop under her patronage in 1950s London, her plan is called 'imperial in its presumption' and she herself is repeatedly deemed 'imperious' (63, 12). Daughter of a wealthy Raj family, Lady Caroline first appears as a kind of angel with a cloud-like 'gown,' 'dazzling white' skin, and 'spun-silk hair, between silver and pale gold' (7). Meeting Valmiki by chance shortly after independence and becoming enthralled with his paintings, she feels free to make unilateral decisions about his future. As the narrator, Anasuya, notes with irony, Caroline 'was supremely confident, born and brought up to be so, with as little thought of fallibility as a colonial in the first flush of empire, as a missionary in the full armour of his mission, dogged by none of the hesitancies that handicap lesser breeds' (20). Alternately sceptical and supportive of Caroline's project, the ambivalent Anasuya has a 'love-hate relationship' with her, 'like the kind Britain and India used to have' (69). With all this interpretive cueing, a reader need not subscribe to Fredric Jameson's view that 'all third-world texts are necessarily ... national allegories' to see Markandaya's text as one ('Third-World' 69). In the tradition of distilling colonial encounters into the relationship of two male individuals (as in the theories of Albert Memmi and others), but with a gender twist, *Possession* positions Valmiki as India and Caroline as Britain. Initially cooperative, Valmiki learns from his patron, absorbs much from her strong personality, and is refashioned; over time, however, he resists her influence and finally rejects her and England to resume the authentic life he associates with his village. The narrative thus allegorizes the broad strokes of India's colonial history and emergence into nationhood. And while its presiding scepticism and irony may gently critique the ideological presumptions behind the allegory, the validity of the basic allegorical significations – colonizer and colonized, West and East – is never in doubt.

The central relationship subsumes a host of stereotypes: Valmiki is the creative, spiritual, illiterate, poverty-stricken villager whose natural resources will be 'wasted' unless developed by the metropolitan power (15). When Valmiki first meets Caroline, he lays his cheek against her hand 'the way a dog will sometimes thrust its muzzle into your palm' (17). Markandaya returns to this image in a later passage that depicts Valmiki's transformation after four years in London and generalizes him into a representative 'East':

His English was good, the accent cultivated – Caroline had clearly made him work at it. Most of the uncouthness was gone, and some of the honesty. Did it make him more acceptable? In this polished Western world, obviously yes. The East was too strident, too dissonant, too austere, too raw; it

had to be muted, toned down, tarted up ... before a measure of acceptance
came. Undilute East had always been too much for the West; and soulful
East always came lap-dog fashion to the West, mutely asking to be not too
little and not too much, but just right. (106–7)

This passage also reinforces a Pygmalion intertext that infiltrates the
novel in tandem with the colonial-national allegory. Valmiki is not only
Caroline's possession but her 'creation,' the jewel in her crown, 'clay she
had moulded and caressed to an image she could love' (40, 139). Like
Eliza Doolittle in Bernard Shaw's play, he must refine his speech to
improve himself and reflect well on a 'creator' whose patronage and
tutelage are motivated by capricious benevolence mixed with self-ag-
grandizement, and against whom he will eventually rebel. In both narratives, the human 'creation' is developed only in ways and to an extent
considered useful to the developer – like India under imperial rule. Eliza
is taught speech, manners, and codes of dress, but not much else;
Valmiki is refused formal education, and although he is expected to
produce art, he receives no artistic training. In contrast to Robertson
Davies's Pygmalionesque *A Mixture of Frailties*, which also portrays a
talented young colonial plucked from a supposedly disadvantageous
environment to launch an artistic career in London, a full education
isn't part of the plan.[6] Valmiki is expected to cultivate his talent innately,
simply by being in the right place and among inspiring people. To win
admiration for himself and his patron, he is not required to become a
complete adult much more than a showy lapdog would.

   One danger of allegory, even as overtly flagged as this one, is that
interpretation may too easily bypass primary referents – Caroline and
Valmiki as individuals, the village and London as specific places in
postcolonial time – en route to secondary ones – Britain and India, or
West and East, in a generic 'colonial' time-space. The fact that Valmiki is
a painter, together with the element of display and exhibition associated
with him and his work, implicitly draws on historical associations particular to London that complicate and enrich the allegorical significations.
In 1851, exactly a century before Valmiki's stay in London, the enor-
mously successful Great Exhibition of the Works of Industry of all Nations displayed the industrial and artistic achievements of Britain and its
Empire in the newly built Crystal Palace. Half of the fourteen thousand
exhibitors came from abroad, and over six million visitors took in their
displays (see Inwood 669). This much-vaunted collection of artifacts
positioned London as a site of accumulation and served as a forerunner

of the image of the metropolis as global microcosm so prevalent in postcolonial London narratives. As Anne McClintock notes, 'the Great Exhibition embodied the hope that all the world's cultures could be gathered under one roof' (57).[7] Arts and crafts collected by the East India Company were featured prominently, exhibiting India's artistic achievements to the British public for the first time. Thomas Metcalf, a historian of Indian art and architecture, summarizes the response: 'Startled by the "beauty, directness, and variety of form" of the objects displayed, the British art world was forced to acknowledge the "high perfection," as Professor J. Forbes Royle declared, to which the arts had been carried among "our fellow-subjects of the East, whom many of us had been in the habit of considering as barbarians"' (142–3).

The popularity of this exhibition, and one in Paris four years later, started a vogue for Indian art throughout the rest of the nineteenth century. A new museum of Indian art and cultural artifacts opened in London in 1858, and later exhibitions opened in Paris (1878) and London (1886). Collectively, these events nurtured public awareness of imperial activity, emphasizing Europe's power to order, preserve, classify, and symbolically possess the cultural diversity of an exoticized East. As *The Times* described the 1886 Colonial and Indian Exhibition, which featured replicas of Indian buildings and bazaars, 'the visitor is carried from the wild, mad whirl of the individual competitive struggle for existence to which civilization has been reduced in the ever changing West, into the stately splendour of that unchanging antique life of the East, the tradition of which has been preserved in pristine purity only in India' (qtd. in Metcalf 146). This write-up captures a characteristic ideological ambivalence. Europe may be the site of history, progress, and mastery, but the passive, timeless Orient nonetheless offers a seductive escape from modernity's harsher byproducts. Moreover, while the ex-hibit is created by Europeans, its contents are not; they are placed outside European artistic traditions and the temporality of European imperial history (since these 'antique' creations are both prior to and contemporaneous with the British Empire).[8]

A similar ambivalence is evident in *Possession*. When Caroline swoops Valmiki away from his village to London, he becomes both creator and creation, exhibitor and exhibit: he will create and exhibit paintings, and Caroline will create and exhibit him. In this latter role, he is to become assimilated enough to function in London society but not so much that he loses his exotic appeal; he is to Caroline what Minou, the pet monkey that becomes his accessory, is to him. At his first opening, both patron

and artist evoke theatrical splendour in their 'dazzling' white clothes
(105). Leading an equally well dressed Minou on a chain, Valmiki is self-
consciously attired in clothes that 'seemed designed for floating – pants
that ballooned prettily about his legs, gauzy white draperies only re-
motely related to anything worn in India, the ensemble highly reminiscent of ballet with an Oriental theme' (106). Although Anasuya comments
'acidly' on this apparel, Valmiki is sanguine about its inauthenticity: 'My
dear, you know and I know. But how many of the people here can tell
sheep from goat?' (106). Anasuya is more impressed by his art: 'six
splendid paintings of an India lovingly remembered and scrupulously
represented, a combination of passion and austerity that kept everyone
silent, momentarily, until release came in a spate of admiration and
congratulation, voiced in an audible and unfortunate but unembar-
rassed cascade of cliché' (107). With the enthusiastic reception of his
one-man show, Valmiki's art, like that of his nineteenth-century forebears, becomes 'fashionable'; indeed, it becomes part of a larger obsession with Indian culture from which 'Valmiki benefited. He did not
suspect that his success might be due to the turning of the great political
wheel that had put India on the map; or that he had come in at the
beginning of a cult. He thought, blithely and charmingly, that it was due
to his talent and industry and good public relationship, and so perhaps
in the main it was' (121).

Anasuya's guarded endorsement of his work leaves unexplored the
question of its authenticity and quality. Indeed, her narrative as a whole
rather surprisingly avoids the question of whether Valmiki paints in
Indian or European styles, or whether being in London changes his
work significantly. She mentions the subjects of his canvases but rarely
describes them in detail and never speaks to his influences or technique.
Since she does not hesitate to comment on the fraudulent exoticism of
his personal appearance, the reader is left to conclude that his work is at
least not blatantly hollow or opportunistic. Even as his paintings give
London's art crowd what it wants from an Indian artist, they stand up
as art, not just cultural tourism or populist exotica. However, though
his work may be the real thing, the inauthenticity of his appearance
increases. Valmiki takes to wearing a jewel-studded turban and self-
consciously displaying 'the Oriental extravagance that had come to be
expected of him' (116). When he dines at the Savoy with Jumbo, an
Indian prince, 'the waiters naturally took the gorgeous commoner for
the prince and the prince as another Indian-in-a-suit' (122). The faux-
Indian, Orientalist stereotypes to which Valmiki's persona appeals clearly

attract attention to his art, but as in the nineteenth-century exhibitions, it is the packaging of the work – how it is contextualized, commodified, and fetishized in London – more than the work itself that exploits European desires for an India of pleasurable alterity. In both centuries – whether the Raj is optimistically ascendant or fading nostalgically into the past – the curatorial scouting, transport, and exhibition of Indian art by Londoners and for Londoners turns it into an aesthetically and ideologically overdetermined spectacle. Through that packaging, London takes enthusiastic possession of India in the form of a simulacrum of its culture, and those who oversee the value-added package emerge as masters of that virtual India. Valmiki creates his art, but Caroline creates and markets the raw material that is Valmiki. When he and his work are well received it is not just he but also Caroline who is 'transfigured, uplifted by triumph' (107).

Charles Molesworth describes the London of Wordsworth's *The Prelude* as a place of 'spectacle' in which 'the particularity of individual human existence is distorted into an objectified world of display and proclamation whose rules are ultimately those of the market and the theatre' (17). Markandaya's London fits this description too, indirectly drawing as it does on the city's history as a place where the industrial and cultural wares of empire were gathered, brought to market, and theatrically exhibited. Indeed, one can even see Valmiki as a typological descendant of those unfortunate colonial 'others' taken to nineteenth- and early twentieth-century London to be exhibited as human curiosities.[9] The Canadian writer John Steffler, in his historical novel *The Afterlife of George Cartwright* (1992), tells the story of five Inuit transported to London from Labrador. All but one die – a common fate of indigenes wrenched away from their familiar climate, diet, and immunities. Valmiki is never in danger of not surviving, but he does fail to thrive artistically in his early metropolitan years. Away from the hardscrabble village life that fed his talent, ensconced in a comfortable London room, he stops painting for two years. Caroline is baffled by this: 'He has everything he needs, and nothing has come of it,' she frets (48). Her 'everything' includes food, space, materials, and freedom from quotidian distractions, but Anasuya recognizes that such unfamiliar luxuries are themselves the problem:

> I looked around the ordered room again, and all the painstaking provision that had been made, and thought about India – not mine, but his – and its extraordinary confusion, the passionate agglomeration of colour with which he had surrounded himself, the strange flotilla of basins and bowls as-

sembled with hard labour, the squelchy dyes, the fruit for which he had to
search, the gold-leaf for which he had had no money, the knowledge he
had garnered from infrequent excursions on foot to the nearest town, the
goats whose wanderings must have driven him frantic; thought of it, and it
needed no great imaginative effort to guess that the lifting of these pressures might have left him dizzy, in an atmosphere so weightless it might
have been a new element, which he had yet to learn to manipulate. (48–9)

Caroline solves the problem of Valmiki's displacement by generating
fake correspondence from the Swamy, his spiritual guide, surrogate
father, and mentor. Thus reconnected to home, Valmiki is able to get his
art (and his act) together, making his triumphant début two years later.
But the epistolary link is as fraudulent as the image he will later cultivate.
When the Swamy visits London and Valmiki discovers that Caroline's
Tamil cook actually wrote the letters, he is devastated. His commitment
to his London self temporarily unravels and he rejects Caroline for a
time. Markandaya describes the scattering of characters that follows in a
memorable image of London as a kind of laboratory experiment that
combines differences under intense and unstable pressure: 'It was as if a
sealed capsule had exploded, distributing its forcibly assembled compo-
nents over the globe' (153). Valmiki rejoins Caroline long enough to
accompany her and her paintings on an American tour, but he increasingly pulls out of her orbit and, in Anasuya's appraisal, becomes detached from his own 'facile' public 'postures,' although the 'austerity
and integrity' of his art does not suffer (155, 154, 155). He moves in with
another woman, and Anasuya wonders if his benefactor has finally recognized that her hand is 'played out' – 'that not everything can be bent or
bamboozled into compliance' (194). But Caroline reasserts herself
enough to destroy his relationship with Annabel; after further withdrawal and the death of his monkey, he is ready to leave. His parting
comment, as Minou lies dying, makes clear his cynical detachment from
his London identity: '"Monkey on my shoulder," he said, smiling grotesquely. "Am I worth an extra sixpence for the monkey on my shoulder?"' (214). Anasuya, who sails to India with him, wonders if he shares
her 'love for London': 'had this beautiful alien city, cold and warm in
turn like its people, the same kind of hold on him as it had on me so that
going away always became a kind of small death?' (214). Apparently not:
once back in his village Valmiki shows no interest in returning, despite a
final attempt by Caroline to once more remove him from the 'wasteland'
of his cave, away from the influence of the ascetic, Gandhi-like Swamy

(220). Valmiki seems content to paint in obscurity 'to glorify his god' rather than to exoticize himself and commodify India for Western markets (223). He even makes 'exhibits' of Caroline's uncashed cheques as a statement of renunciation (222).

Again, while a general if idealized allegory of colonial India moving towards a Gandhian, village-based nationhood can be seen in this narrative, the history of Indian arts particularizes it in important ways. With India's successful presence at the 1851 Great Exhibition, two parallel movements were inspired to valorize its traditional arts towards different social and cultural goals. The English arts and crafts movement saw in Indian artisans an echo of England's own medieval past, a tradition of individual labour to be embraced as a corrective model in their fight against dehumanizing, mechanized industrial production. Even so, William Morris and others worried that India's village artisans were imperilled by social and economic changes brought about by the Raj, particularly increases in European imports. But although there was a desire to retool the empire as a force for the preservation rather than the destruction of Indian village culture, it was recognized that changes could occur only 'when a wholesale alteration in their attitude toward work, greed, and art had taken hold of the British people. Hence the leaders of the English crafts movement found their appointed tasks at home' (Metcalf 153–4).

A second, contemporaneous movement did aspire to help traditional arts and crafts flourish in India. Its goal was preservation through training, and art schools were established in Madras, Bombay, Calcutta, and Lahore. But debates soon arose over the influence of European artistic traditions and their incompatibility with Indian ones. Drawing and painting instructors in the Madras School of Art, for instance, borrowed their curriculum from London's South Kensington School of Art. While this practice might be commensurate with Thomas Macaulay's famous Minute on Education, which sought to develop a class of Indians who were 'English in taste, in opinions, in morals, and in intellect' (Macaulay 249), European training undercut the mission of preserving traditional arts. As the British head of the Madras school worried in the 1870s, teaching students the anatomically accurate figure drawing of Europe could make them unable to then 'draw six arms on a single body, or to study flesh tones in the green or pink incarnations of Vishnu' (qtd. in Metcalf 156). Further contradictions in this largely English movement to train Indian artists and craftspeople developed around government pressures to commercialize Indian wares and develop overseas markets. Crafts enthusiasts argued that commercialization would lead to 'imitative copying, cheapening of workmanship, and eclecticism of design that were destroying precisely the "traditional" styles ... they wished to preserve' (157).

When Caroline first articulates her imperious plan for Valmiki – 'He must come away with us now, at once' – Anasuya replies, '"Do you mean to Madras?" – for that was as far as my imagination would carry me.' Caroline replies, 'God no. To Paris. Either Paris or London, I can't quite decide which' (15). Madras is the nearest big city; it is also home of the School of Art, which may be what Anasuya has in mind as she guesses Caroline's intention. But Caroline is no twentieth-century Macaulay Minuteman. As her laissez-faire approach to his creativity will make clear, she considers Valmiki a fully formed talent who needs no training in European or Indian artistic styles, just space, support, and access to a metropolitan art world. Her indecision about Paris or London is significant – these are the two cities that housed the great nineteenth-century exhibitions of Indian art. Her impetus is towards connoisseurship and display, not pedagogy; as noted above, her own added value, like the Victorian curators, consists in helping Valmiki most beneficially present his work to a responsive market – a market that eventually includes India, but only after Europe has endorsed his work.

Valmiki's inability to paint without a lifeline to the Swamy, his gradual disenchantment with Caroline and his metropolitan career, and his final retreat to a simpler, more authentic way of living and art-making all suggest that *Possession* allegorizes India's political history through specific reference to the place of its arts. Markandaya portrays the village as the site of innate, traditional, 'austere' art grounded in a simple, 'real' life of the spirit. While that art is strong enough to withstand dilution in the metropolis, its creator may not be; as in the exhibitions a century earlier, he and his work are framed and refashioned by forces of commercialization, exoticism, and false appearance associated with metropolitan culture. London becomes a place of *maya* that must be rejected in favour of a return to what Nandy calls the 'alternative cosmopolitanism' of the village – one that accommodates 'the humble vernacular' and rejects 'the compulsions of a global market' (*Journey* ix). The village in this case also represents a version of what Nandy calls elsewhere the 'spiritual India' often hailed as the 'real India' – an India that contrasts with 'the materialism of the modern West, ... providing an axis for a dissenting global consciousness. The West, according to this view, is already defeated by the superior Eastern civilizations; it only obstinately refuses to admit the fact' (*Intimate* 80). At the end of Markandaya's novel, it is the Swamy's and the village's spiritual 'East' that has triumphed over

Caroline's and London's materialistic 'West,' though Caroline, who 'came of a breed that never admitted defeat,' asserts her vision to the end (224). The Swamy prevails, despite her strong will, and with him a non-commercial, spiritual, and highly traditional view of art made for the glory of a god rather than any careerist or economic motive. The novel concludes with a triumph of Eastern 'tradition' over Western 'progress,' of artistic purity and authenticity over the distortion of Indian art and culture. With that triumph, a self-sufficient, non-materialistic India is thematically affirmed, though it is also clear that in these early years of India's independence, as under the Raj, that idealistic conception of the nation will be under continual pressure from countervailing Western views.

Nowhere City

London in *Possession* is a stage where old imperial tensions are played out in new contexts. The novel's referential and allegorical richness enables its London to represent aspects of the postimperial metropolis of the 1950s, the ascendant imperial city of the 1850s, and a more general transhistorical and transnational space in which 'Britain' endeavours to 'possess' 'India.' Markandaya's other London novel, *The Nowhere Man* (1972), presents a more referentially specific London – the city that experienced the racist upswings of the 1960s. Although its narrative covers fifty years of the immigrant Srinivas's life in London and includes a long flashback recalling his youth in colonial India, this period dominates. The novel opens in 1968, the year Enoch Powell made his infamous 'Rivers of Blood' speech, which crystallized and further aggravated Britons' growing hostility to 'New Commonwealth' immigrants over the postwar decades. Speaking in Birmingham, the Conservative member of parliament conveyed his 'foreboding' at the growth of 'dangerous and divisive' immigrant communities in Britain: 'Like the Roman,' he portentously said, 'I seem to see "the River Tiber foaming with much blood"' (qtd. in Layton-Henry 71). As Simon Gikandi and Ian Baucom have shown, Powell and the newly restrictive nationality legislation he helped bring about severed 'Englishness' and 'Britishness' from an empire with which they had once been seen as coterminous. Race and place of birth became the new criteria of belonging. Gikandi argues that in the imperial period 'the essence of a British identity was derived from the totality of all the people brought together by empire; in the postimperial period, in contrast, we find a calculated attempt to configure Englishness as

exclusionary of its colonial wards' (*Maps* 71). These changes were a
direct response to postwar migration; as Baucom writes, traditional ideas
of an empire-wide Britishness were seen to be too inclusive 'once the
"fantastic structure" of empire collapses in on itself, once the postimperial
frontier is drawn in Bristol or London, once white Britons can no longer
ignore the fact that they share their streets with the "strange races" of the
empire' (23).

Although Markandaya never mentions Powell, the exclusive racial
thinking he made respectable is embraced by Srinivas's antagonistic
neighbour, Fred Fletcher. And an early riverside scene provides an oblique but significant echo. After the death of his Indian wife, Vasantha,
Srinivas tips her ashes, along with earth and some water from the Ganges
River, off London Bridge into the Thames. Vasantha, who remained
'wholly Indian' throughout many years in London, would have preferred an Indian river, and her husband regrets 'consigning [her ashes]
to these alien waters' (40, 41). A passing policeman further diminishes
the ritual meaning of his act, reproving him for tipping 'household
rubbish' into the Thames: 'If everyone carried on the same,' he says, 'the
river would soon be polluted' (41). Although he does not initially realize
what the 'rubbish' is, the policeman imagines the river tainted by the
bodily materials of an immigrant; ashes, like the blood of Powell's metaphor, represent the black or brown-skinned migrants who would pollute
and dilute Englishness. In fact, the Brahman Srinivas is enacting a rite of
purification; for Hindus, fire and water are purifying elements, and
cremation rituals ensure safe passage of the departed to the land of the
ancestors.[10] Any pollution would therefore occur in reverse – Vasantha's
ashes and, symbolically, her Indianness being polluted and diluted to a
degree by 'alien waters,' though the Ganges water establishes a virtual
and ritual link to India's holiest river. As in Conrad's *Heart of Darkness*,
the Thames takes on aspects of the identity of a great river of empire and
thereby signifies the fluid, intimate relations between distant places that
imperialism brought about. When Powell sought to racially purify the
British Isles through the erection of ideological walls, he was responding
to the migrancy and presumed belonging that empire had engendered –
the fact that, as Kobena Mercer has pithily explained, 'We are here
because you were there' (7). If a metaphor is etymologically a bearing
across, a bridging of differences in meaning, Powell's river of blood
metaphor, however unwittingly, acknowledges the ways imperial history
bridges distances and differences between people and places. Powell
invokes Rome's Tiber River, and therefore the Romans who once con-

quered and occupied Britain, to analogize London and British space. And as a metaphor 'blood' can signify racial hybridity (or impurity) as strongly as 'river' signifies geographical and spatial fluidity, especially when different bloods are imagined combining in one river.

The Nowhere Man focuses more on conditions of immigrant dwelling than *Possession*, and the documentary realism of its narrative repeatedly relates Srinivas's difficulties in London to aspects of India's colonial history. Fred Fletcher blends archetypal racism against brown and black Londoners with fanciful 'daydreams' of himself as an imperial 'top man. The Governor. Governor-General. His Excellency the viceroy ... acknowledging the homage of dark millions' (244). In the pub, he and his friends see Srinivas's supposed crime of dispossession – evicting white tenants at a time of housing shortages – as creating a London equivalent to 'one of them slums in Calcutta' (214). When an ousted tenant's mother curses Srinivas for 'coming to this country, ... acting as if you owned it, oppressing *us*,' his son Laxman defends him by saying, 'If we do, we have learned from our masters, madam' (273). Srinivas's house, as in some West Indian novels of London, becomes the microcosmic site where tensions of national belonging are worked out under the shadow of a past imperial era. Purchased in the 1930s and named *Chandraprasad* after his and Vasantha's former Indian house, though 'it never took to its name,' the 'gaunt old building in South London' shelters grateful neighbours in its basement during wartime air raids (22, 19). Domestic space here represents the Indian couple's relative acceptance by the English at this time, which is 'perhaps because of the bombing which ripped away veils, not to say whole walls, revealing weeping surfaces and intimate interiors, and making it difficult for conventions to rule with their previous inflexible rod' (22). By the time Srinivas is forced in the 1960s to evict his white tenants (not telling them it is to protect them from his leprosy), xenophobic conventions and metaphorical walls between peoples have been made stronger than ever. The house becomes a neighbourhood *cause célèbre*, representing to the English Indians' lack of 'gratitude ... after all we've done for them' (274). If the eviction echoes Indian nationalists' insistence before 1947 that Britons living in their space leave, the very different Indian and British perspectives on that event correspond to the divided interpretations of this one in 1960s London.

Most importantly, the house comes to symbolize the impermanence and unreality of the tenuous sense of belonging Srinivas achieves in his early London years. The Indian *Chandraprasad* provides a precedent:

though it was seen by young Srinivas as a 'solid construction ... which would outlast them all,' after a top-to-bottom 'violation' of its interior by English police searching for anti-imperialists, Srinivas repaired the house but no longer felt attached to its material essence (137, 140). He resolved not to 'allow himself to be bound to, or feel for, possessions: for bits of wood, glass, beads, baubles, metals – even land – all those compositions of matter that would, ironically, outlast the human frame, but in turn be eclipsed by the indestructible spirit that informed it' (145). In London, he initially has misgivings about 'shackling himself to bricks and mortar': 'He did not feel like a founding father' (21). Nonetheless, over time he calls England 'my country now': 'I feel at home in it, more so than I would in my own' (60, 61). After incurring the racist animosity of Fred Fletcher and other neighbours, however, that sense of belonging erodes, and Markandaya captures his alienation in a vivid image of his house dematerializing:

> His mind ... considered illusions, of men and the castles they built, himself in particular, and the houses on two continents in which he had lodged, which each when the time was ripe had repudiated the contracts of security to which it had not in the first place been signatory.... He sighed, and looked about him at the attic, which had once presented aspects of solidity. Its walls were fragile now, reduced by the general paring away that was taking place. Was it really here, he asked himself, that he had sought and found refuge? He pondered, and was lost in wonder that these rafters and laths, which were so patently made of paper, could ever have seemed to promise him more than the flimsiest physical shelter. (225)

The long arm of empire has reached transhistorically across the ocean to taint Srinivas's life in London; this *Chandraprasad*, like the Indian one, no longer represents solidity and permanence but insecurity and dispossession.

Architecture, says Donatella Mazzoleni, is an extension and a metaphor of the body. Our built space represents 'the totality of the integuments and exoskeletons of our individual and collective body': 'A replica – and a double' (289). It appropriates and transforms 'the first space perceived as ... external to the body: the surface of the skin' (290). Srinivas's deteriorating house doubles his aging individual body and in doing so functions as a metaphor for his abjection from the collective, national body – a racialized body politic to which he is increasingly seen not to belong. His skin and his 'other' national identity define him as external to the English homeland; the spaces of nation, house, and body metaphorically coalesce. Shortly before he emigrated to England, feeling there was no future for him in British India, Srinivas was asked by his mother, 'If they are bad to you here, what makes you think they will be good to you there?' (156). After fifty years in London, he is increasingly forced to recognize and regret the links between 'India, an occupied country, a half-century ago, at a time of inflamed emotions' and 'England.... As it was now' (194, 195). Threatened with non-belonging by the English here now just as he was there then, he sees his own place-identity evaporating into immaterial non-existence, redefining him as 'a nowhere man looking for a nowhere city' (174).

In the climactic blaze with which Fred Fletcher tries to literally dematerialize the London *Chandraprasad*, Markandaya invokes the novel's key image of fire, which in various forms has become a symbol of ambivalent belonging. As noted above, the ashes of Vasantha's cremated body signify both connection to and disconnection from an India that she never left psychologically or spiritually despite decades in London. On the ship that took her and her husband to England, the last thing Srinivas saw as he left India was a 'galaxy of fireflies ... dancing along with the ship': 'It was a long time before they gave up and their light trails faded away' (158). The memory of this sight begins and ends the long flashback to India, and the fireflies themselves signify both connection and disconnection. They prompt a link through memory, and by following the ship for so long they suggest continuity: an India that will, in however fragile a form, follow Srinivas across the ocean. But they do eventually 'fade away,' and in introducing this image Srinivas has already noted their absence in London: they were 'extinguished in the gray vapors of colder seas. Of England, he said to himself: I am in England. Suddenly a gust of unreality swamped him' (100). Complexities of attachment and detachment are also related to fire imagery in the novel's wartime scenes. Srinivas's rooftop duties as neighbourhood 'fire watcher' contribute directly to his feeling that 'England was becoming his country' (30). But he and Vasantha cannot endorse the war effort the way their neighbours can because as Hindus they oppose killing; nonetheless, they suppress their beliefs, 'knowing what fiery coals could be heaped upon dissenting heads' (25). They are pleased when their son Seshu leaves bomber-pilot training as a conscientious objector, but shortly after he begins driving ambulances past 'the burning citadels of London,' he dies by a bomb (30). With this loss and the marriage of Laxman to a 'pale pink wife' (34), Vasantha must give up her vision of the three-storey house as a place where she and Srinivas can make a traditional Indian home with a floor for each son and his family. This vision has been the basis of what attachment to London she possessed.

Long after Vasantha dies and Srinivas begins living with Mrs Pickering, Fred Fletcher's fire consolidates the themes of national belonging and detachment associated with those earlier images of fire. Ironically (and rather grotesquely) is it Fred's fire that draws most fully on Hindu associations with the element. For Hindus, fire is variously destructive, useful, and comforting, but most importantly it is divine – venerated and worshipped through the fire-god Agni. One of the five great elements (with space, air, water, and earth), fire can purify the environment, remove poisons, act as a messenger to the gods, and protect the devout against evil spirits, particularly when used for sacrifice.[11] As in ancient Roman culture, the hearth is the holiest feature of the home; for Hindus, constant maintenance of the household fire by the householder is 'a strict religious obligation' (Chaudhuri 78). The fire Fred lights in Srinivas's basement, the acme of his campaign of racist confrontation, is a destructive and distorted version of a hearth fire. It is lit in a building that has come to symbolize for Fred a contaminated nation-space that he, as self-appointed protector and rightful occupant of the national household, wants to purify through an act of human sacrifice. As he stokes 'the wretched heap of kindling flickering weakly in the moldy basement,' his local act feeds delusions of national grandeur: 'In his mind's eye bonfires were blazing, great warning beacons lit at the summits of hills, answered in kind from mountain to mountain, a ring of fire, protecting the beloved coast' (300). But when his cross-belt gets entangled in the furnace, Fred inadvertently sacrifices himself, dying trapped and 'calling on God and man' to rescue him from 'his golden temple' (303, 302). Laxman sees the flames as a potential 'final purification by fire' as he rushes to rescue his father from the attic (310). This architectural high point does not become Srinivas's funeral pyre as the lowly basement does for Fred, but he dies nonetheless. Laxman – the son who in Hindu tradition would perform the cremation rites that usher the soul to heaven – finds Srinivas's body 'so light' that when he braces himself to lift it up, he 'nearly hit the ceiling' (310).

Fred's attempt to erect a figurative wall of fire around England – to protect the coast from non-white migrants and thus racially purify the nation – unintentionally achieves the reverse: it uses fire's destructive qualities to protect London from his own poisonous racism through an act of self-sacrifice. His death adds a grim retrospective irony to Srinivas's remark just before the fire that 'evil' of the sort the racist protestors represent 'burns itself out, eventually' (296). Markandaya gives the event attributes of a spectacle. Before he knows of the fire, Laxman hopes 'there won't be any fireworks' from his father's angry neighbours (307). Fred dresses in a faux-imperial costume to light the fire, and the space where the protestors gather (and later watch the blaze) is described as a theatrical stage:

> For, clearly, pavements, like people, were more than they appeared to be, whatever their surface guise. This gray stretch, for example, laid placidly along frontages and forecourts of houses, had been transformed into a theater, the ringing flagstones might have been boards under actors' feet, on which players were acting out their parts. The woman, for instance, who had come to support her [evicted] daughter, was playing the part of Mother – suffering, enduring, universal Mother figure she might have been, a madonna of the ages. (297)

Like a piece of tragic theatre, the fire and its aftermath result in a kind of catharsis, though Markandaya stops well short of suggesting that racism has been purged from the survivors who have witnessed its deadly potential. The implication that racial attitudes are a form of role-playing – that, as Srinivas's half-century in London shows, tolerance or hostility towards racial others is as mutable as the donning or doffing of a mask – offers small consolation. Whether deep-rooted or opportunistically superficial, 'real' or apparent, an exclusive equation of place with race is easily ignited, its mantle readily assumed, at the smallest spark of a pretext.

Originals and Replicas

Several times in *The Nowhere Man* Srinivas states that England is his country and home, but once he attracts racial resentment, he feels he has been 'transformed into a stranger,' an 'unwanted man,' an 'alien' (241). He starts wearing Indian clothes he had stored since his arrival, insisting to Mrs Pickering that 'I am, of course, an Indian' (243). In the absence of India or plans to return, this sudden embrace of Indianness is unconvincing, and Mrs Pickering seems to recognize it as a desperate nostalgia for certainties. Earlier, Srinivas has embraced a 'wider citizenship' freed of 'the fetters which tied him to any one country,' but the transnational identification he arrives at by the end is characterized by subtraction, not addition – neither/nor rather than both/and (40).

With two national identities withdrawn, Srinivas becomes an attenuated, weightless man belonging to a liminal 'nowhere.' His transcendence of earthly space (and apparent release from gravity) seems a fitting end to a pessimistic narrative. Later novels by Salman Rushdie and Amitav Ghosh will articulate more inclusive and enabling transnationalisms for Indians in London – anti-essentialist, boundary-hopping accumulations of place-identities in which the whole can be more, not less, than the sum of national parts. Their novels take to an extreme the connections between place, identity, and unreality that Markandaya introduces, with Rushdie's incorporating heady amounts of theatrical spectacle as well. Anita Desai's *Bye-Bye Blackbird* offers a crucial link between Markandaya's displaced, reality-challenged migrants and the outsized, theatrical protagonists of that most famous of postcolonial London novels, *The Satanic Verses*. As Desai's two Indian Londoners, Dev and Adit, probe their changing national attachments in an often unreal, theatrical, Indianized metropolis, her London anticipates key aspects of Rushdie's.

In *Bye-Bye Blackbird*, London's material surfaces are steeped in reminders of India and of an England that was well known in India before the journey to the actual place. It was known because the imperial project gave it such a weighty presence in the subcontinent. Even after independence that presence continues: culturally through literature and physically through architecture. These two legacies focus Desai's exploration of London's connectedness to India and the complex effect it has on migrants' evolving place-identities and sense of reality. Dev arrives in London in 1965 full of images derived from his colonial-style schooling in English literature. He can recognize metropolitan scenes and objects based on this imaginative preparedness: 'he had met them before, in the pages of Dickens and Lamb, Addison and Boswell ... ; not in colour and in three dimensions as he now encountered them, but in black and white and made of paper' (10). He marvels at 'how exact the reproductions had been, how accurate,' so that although he had never experienced 'this world' before, it was still 'known, familiar, easy to touch, enjoy and accept because he was so well prepared to enter it' (10, 11). He feels empowered by the materialization of what he knew as a 'paper replica' because that image seemed 'larger than life,' whereas 'what he now saw and touched and breathed was recognisably the original, but an original cut down to size, under control, concrete, so that it no longer flew out of his mind and hovered above him like some incorporeal, winged creature' (11). This passage is intriguing in many ways. In appropriating and subsuming London to his own experience and perspective, Dev begins to take possession of it. But he does so by establishing a line of temporal continuity between past and present (and between a textual image and an actual site) in a contained space – the scene takes place in a pub – where the differences between Britain's postcolonial present and its imperial past are papered over by a nostalgic traditionalism. The pub is an artifice, a rose-tinted replica of a former reality. The time with which it is infused denies time: fossilized history trumps dynamic change. If Dev can paradoxically figure the actual city as smaller than literary representations of it, and therefore as under his control, this is because he is constructing a false synecdoche between London and an unreal, packaged space within it.

Besides his literary reading, Dev is prepared for the metropolis through his experience of colonial architecture in India. Buildings and planning in colonial cities often 'mimicked' European designs (Jacobs, *Edge* 20); this was one way imperial powers reterritorialized alien space. In the heyday of colonialism, Thomas Metcalf writes, Britain's 'political authority took shape in stone'; 'to study colonial architecture is therefore to study the allocation of power, and the relationships of knowledge and power, that made up the colonial order' (xi). Under the influence of John Ruskin, English architecture was seen by Victorians to possess an 'identity-forming and reforming power' that could – unlike England's natural spaces – be exported to the colonies, where it would support the Englishness of colonizers abroad and, at the same time, impress that Englishness upon colonial subjects (Baucom 20). As education and literature were to Macaulay, cultural artifacts and architecture were regarded as transferable forces by which English identities could be produced abroad. Ruskin's valorizing of Gothic architecture, combined with 'his belief in the power of architecture to shape individual and collective identity,' influenced the design of public buildings in Indian cities, and the late nineteenth century saw the construction of numerous Gothic structures throughout the subcontinent (Baucom 78). This is why Dev finds the Albert Memorial in Hyde Park – which looks 'like a piece of architecture having a nightmare following an ample Victorian repast' – so familiar-looking. Its shapes 'recall to him similar nightmares of stone and marble in India' such as Bombay's Victoria railway terminus, Calcutta's Victoria Memorial, and the statue of Victoria outside Delhi's railway station (83). For Dev, these monuments represent those 'pockets and stretches of Victorian India which continue to have a life of their own, a dream life out of touch with the present' (84). Yet he finds the Albert Memorial oddly compelling:

Dev is not sure whether he comes to it, again and again, in order to look
upon the face of England as it had existed in his imagination when he was a
child ... or because it reminds him of that Victorian India that formed a
part – unreal and, therefore, all the more haunting, omnipresent and
subliminal – of the India he had known. (84)

Parts of London and of India's big cities make them seem like simulacra
of each other – unreal, temporally disjointed, and mutually reflective.
The reciprocal echoes are so strong that while Dev finds St Paul's Cathedral and Westminster Abbey 'awesome' and 'overpowering' (67), he
cannot see them as religious expressions but only as 'temples dedicated
to the British Empire' (68). This is, of course, anachronistic: the medieval abbey predates the empire by hundreds of years, and Christopher
Wren's cathedral was begun in 1675. But for Dev, the monumental
architecture of England is irrevocably linked with its imperial presence
abroad.

Monuments, like literary texts, always signify something beyond their
explicit referents or uses, but that greater signified is unstable; it shifts
over time and at any given moment varies from one viewer (or reader) to
another. As Henri Lefebvre writes, 'Monumental space offered each
member of a society an image of that membership, an image of his or her
social visage. It thus constituted a collective mirror more faithful than
any personal one' (*Production* 220). Monuments can become anachronistic, however, when the societal consensus they originally expressed no
longer holds. In the words of Yi-Fu Tuan, 'Most monuments cannot
survive the decay of their cultural matrix. The more specific and representational the object the less it is likely to survive: since the end of
British imperialism in Egypt, the statues of Queen Victoria no longer
command worlds but merely stand in the way of traffic. In the course of
time, most public symbols lose their status as places and merely clutter
up space' (164). Dev's confusion about what certain monuments are
monumentalizing, and whether familiar-seeming sites in London are
real or unreal, originals or replicas, evocatively captures the uncertain-
ties of knowing and belonging engendered by his colonial upbringing.
Empire and its institutions have affirmed his membership in English
society up to a point and saturated his consciousness with images and
knowledge of England. But the cultural matrix of empire has disappeared, and with it any clarity he might have felt about his attachment to
the imperial motherland.

Nonetheless, although he experiences the reality check of racial slurs and difficulties getting a job, Dev tends to see London in idealized, even deluded ways. He is most enthused about London when it seems least touched by time. Standing on a high hill from which he can see the city in a glance, he reverentially 'observes that the English have a genius for preserving beauty ... from the ravages of time and decay, so that it affects generation after generation in precisely the same manner' (82–3). The scene he describes, featuring churches, flowers, tufted grass, the ghost of Byron, and 'the sunlit city of London lying far below' (83), is a romantic escape from alienating street-level reality. The hilltop setting enables this; as Michel de Certeau observes, to look down at a city from above 'transforms the bewitching world by which one was "possessed" into a text that lies before one's eyes. It allows one to read it, ... looking down like a god' (92). Richard Sennett also shows how a choice of perspective can make a city 'cohere,' often with 'an undertone of possessive domination' (*Conscience* 155, 156) – as the hillside view of Forster's Chandrapore clearly does. When Desai's Dev admires the 'space and depth' of London's 'vistas' (which he contrasts with the 'tight, insular clusters' of Indian cities), he has the empowering 'sensation of an explorer on the verge of discovery' (70, 69, 70). This perception of London as a containable, legible, imageable urban scene comprehended from above may be familiar – English painting is full of such images – and it may be reassuring, but it is a fantasy. Such power and readability do not exist at street level; there the defining image is 'the green door of London itself slamming shut – briskly, decisively, as British doors do slam' (120). The London Dev experiences as 'a place of shut doors and curtained windows' may invite 'courtship,' but it 'would not be conquered' (55, 120). Below ground is no better: Clapham tube station is vividly portrayed as an 'unearthly,' 'menacing' 'labyrinth' that makes a panicky Dev think of Kafka, Alice in Wonderland, Martians, and tombs (57).[12] If such images of underground unreality draw on literary conventions, what Dev 'sees' from above, which feels so liberating, is also what he has been trained and predisposed to see. He finds security in a textual city untouched by time – known because read about, but ultimately unreal.

Wavering ambivalently between an empowering nostalgic unreality and an excluding present-tense reality, Dev's metropolitan mappings include one memorable imaginative flight that re-orients a monumental London building through an Indianizing vision. Dev sees the Battersea Power Station, predictably, as a shrine to British power, but he playfully counters that vision by imagining an alternative Hindu identity:

Look at those vast blank walls – like those of a secret vault of mighty
emperors. Look at those towering chimney-stacks sending out the smoke of
sacrificial fires. Can't you see the *puja* being conducted in its locked
chambers, by priests in saffron robes and vestal maidens in white? Can't you
see the great bonfire they've built inside and the herbs, the spices and
magic potions they hurl into it? Can't you hear the clanging of great gongs
and the blowing of long horns and singing of sweet hymns? I believe the
electricity of London is generated by that sacrificial bonfire, right in the
innermost heart of the temple. We ought to bow, Adit. We ought to kneel
down and pray. (54)

In this scene, as in the Victorian architectural links he sees, and as in an
equally ebullient fancy of Indian traders and armies invading London
on camels and elephants, building forts and temples in order to 'turn
the tables' on imperial history (61), Dev recognizes that the imperial
might represented by London's spatial monumentality is inseparable
from the energy and resources of the colonies that propped it up. Dev
acknowledges the empire's contribution to London by seeing some of
the city's most stubbornly concrete sites as infused or overlaid with India.

This act of imaginative reclamation and reterritorialization offers a
more promising coming-to-terms with England for Dev than his climactic countryside epiphany. This later experience finally prompts him to
see England not as an imperial 'aggressor' but as 'something quite small
and soft' that he can 'hold and tame and even love' (229). In a little rural
church he finds a 'natural simplicity and muteness' that appeal to him
much more than London's grand cathedrals (171). In a moment of what
Tony Hiss would call 'simultaneous perception' (3), Dev recognizes a
pastoral idyll that confirms that his dreams of England back home
(again, derived from nineteenth-century literature) were 'an exact, a
detailed, a brilliant and mirrorlike reflection of reality' (Desai 170). The
ecstasy caused by this discovery, which gives him the feeling of being
suspended in the air with 'a bird's eye view of an idyllic land,' bonds him
to England (169). The location of this epiphany is significant: David
Sibley argues that because the countryside is traditionally stereotyped as
the essence of timeless pure England, in contrast to the fluid cosmopolitan space of the city, it is an 'exclusionary' space that 'cannot accommodate difference' (107, 108). But overcoming this exclusiveness with
Romantic-Victorian nostalgia, as Dev does, does not affiliate his appropriation of English space, rural or urban, with a progressive postcolonial
politics. Indeed, his epiphany is a version of what Raymond Williams

calls a historically persistent 'structure of feeling' in which a rural golden age that never actually existed is idealized in 'reaction to the fact of change' associated with the city (35). As in Dev's earlier visions of London vistas and pubs, present-tense England is brought down to size, made visually and epistemologically containable, when it is perceived as continuous with a fossilized past that was always only an illusory object of desire. The psychological comfort Dev finds in the countryside is therefore based on a kind of willed self-deception and will have limited application in the city.

By contrast, his friend Adit, a former anglophile, does find the countryside exclusionary: visiting it catalyses an unexpected feeling of alienation from England and London. The 'sweet, sap-filled' Hampshire landscape becomes displaced in his mind by images of India's 'vast moonscape of dust, rock and barren earth' (177). When he looks at English animals or birds or rivers, he sees Indian ones; 'the insane spectacles on his eyes' superimpose one reality on the other (177). His sudden shift in perceptions irrevocably corrupts his image of London as a 'once-golden Mecca' (181). He now feels like a stranger and cannot recognize favourite streets and landmarks. Like his English wife Sarah – who privately already feels herself to be a 'fraud,' an 'impostor ... playing a part' on stage (34) – Adit starts considering his metropolitan life 'unreal' and London a place of inauthenticity and theatrical falseness (204). The last chapters of the book are permeated with negative references to role-playing, artifice, gaudy surfaces, and the theatre. Adit's antipathy to London is accentuated by news of India's war with Pakistan, which rouses his dormant nationalism and makes him feel increasingly out of place. But his response – to return to India and 'start living a real life' (204) – is no less beholden to imaginary geographies than Dev's fantasies. Just before leaving, Adit and Sarah imagine their London flat infiltrated, as their own consciousnesses now are, by Indian space. They feel Bengal and 'India sweep into their room like a flooded river, drowning all that had been English in it, all that had been theirs, friendly and private and comfortable, drowning it all and replacing it with the emptiness and sorrow, the despair and rage, the flat grey melancholy and the black glamour of India' (224). The Adit who begins the novel talking of his 'love' for an England of tweed, thatched cottages, and 'steamed pudding with treacle,' and who leaves feeling like a 'retiring ambassador bidding farewell to his faithful staff,' has traded one unreal object of desire for another (17, 18, 225). In the process, he has switched roles and traded places with Dev.

The novel's complex, obsessive treatment of these questions of the reality and authenticity of London and the Indian migrant's life there is crystallized in a late scene at an Indian restaurant. The atmosphere reminds Dev of provincial clubs in India that are 'years behind the times, so that there is still something of the British Raj left about them' (194). But there is a difference, he says: 'In those district clubs in India, it is only a ghost of the Raj that one sees lingering on, all dusty and cob-webbed and sad. Here you have the real thing – the very essence of the Raj, of the role of the *sahib log* – in its fullest bloom' (195). As with his other time-warped visions of England, Dev sees the restaurant as the original 'real' of something he knew as a replica, a second-generation image, in India. But this perception makes no allowance for time – for the fact that, in 1965, this restaurant too can only simulate the Raj. Sarah does seem to acknowledge its artifice when she sees the restaurant's 'exotic' accoutrements as 'all a bit outsize, more brilliant than they had been in real life, in India, for here there was no clammy tropical heat, no insidious dust, no insecurity, no shadow of history to shake or darken or wilt them.' To her, the waiters seem 'a little more theatrical than they would have been in India. Everyone seemed to be playing a part in a technicoloured film about the East' (195). After deciding that the food is more 'authentically Anglo-Indian' than Indian, Dev and his friends amuse each other by casting the staff and patrons as stereotyped players in the costume drama of colonial history (195–6). As in *The Nowhere Man*, theatricality serves as a metaphor for the fraudulent and superficial behaviour the legacy of empire continues to produce in London.

Desai, however, treats her metaphysical themes with more persistence, complexity, and scepticism than Markandaya. While Valmiki in *Possession* can reject London's unreality for an Indian life whose authenticity is taken for granted, Desai disavows any easy binaries. She places her migrants in a figurative hall of mirrors where such concepts as original and replica, source and reflection, authentic and inauthentic, real and unreal cease to have meaning. The India and London of her migrants' perceptions are both, in various ways, unreal spaces, made especially so because of their historical and ongoing involvement with each other and the continuous circulation of images back and forth. The forms of Englishness imposed on Indians materially through architecture and immaterially through images and texts become the filters through which London is perceived paradoxically as both an original and a second-generation copy. Images, knowledge, and memories of India become distorted, in turn, by the migrant's experience of a postimperial London saturated with 'almost-the-same-but-not-quite' reminders of India as it is and as England once perceived it. Both during and after the Raj, then, London constructs imaginary Indias and imaginary Londons that circulate in both places, and India does the same. From the Hindu perspective of Desai and her characters, all this image-mongering may simply be a version of *maya*: the illusory world of appearances that constitutes the only visible and tangible manifestation of a reality that eludes sensory knowing. In the language of Western postmodernism, it is a version of Jean Baudrillard's simulacrum – the proliferating replicas that substitute for a vanishing 'real' – and Fredric Jameson's 'depthless' late-capitalist city of surfaces and artifice.[13] What *Bye-Bye Blackbird* suggests is that the grand experiment in mutual construction and transformation that was imperialism, along with its messy aftermath, is just as implicated as late capitalism in the proliferation of bewildering, misleading images and disorienting, distorting (un)realities.

Ellowen Deeowen: Dog-Eared, Tortured, Reborn

Desai's vision of London and India sets the stage, so to speak, for Rushdie's. *The Satanic Verses*, the story of two Indian migrants who foil each other and finally switch roles, has much in common with Desai's, which can be seen, along with William Blake's *The Marriage of Heaven and Hell* and Mikhail Bulgakov's *The Master and Margarita*, as one of its important intertexts. Both novels portray men who would 'possess' or 'conquer' London developing ambivalent relationships with it. Both begin with arrivals, end with departures, and set pivotal late scenes in the countryside. Each novel strongly relates what can be known of the city with what the seeing eye perceives and what the imagination makes of this perception – the qualities of clarity, coherence, and orientation that define what Kevin Lynch calls a city's 'imageability' (9). For instance, both authors make much of the different ways the city appears from various heights: knowable and empowering from above, alienating and disempowering at street level, unearthly and deathly underground. Indeed, while Desai's Dev feels 'like Alice falling, falling down the rabbit hole' when he descends into a 'menacing' Underground station that resembles 'the dark labyrinth of a prison,' Rushdie begins *The Satanic Verses* by dropping his protagonists from an exploded airplane 'all the way down and along the hole that went to Wonderland' – which in this novel will turn out to be the phantasmagoric, metamorphic, labyrinthine, nightmarish world of London as a whole (*Blackbird* 57; *Verses* 6).[14]

Rushdie's Saladin and Gibreel are both actors, and it is in the theatrical realm – a specific manifestation of the visual imagination – that some
of the differences between Desai's London and Rushdie's are most
evident. For Desai's mid-1960s migrants, theatricality connotes excluding and misleading artifice more than transformation and play with the
apparently real; it is identified more with the burden of history than the
promise of the future. Moreover, for Dev, perceptions of London's 'unreality' are driven by an anxious fascination with imperialism's spatial
symbols, together with a tentative will-to-power over them that may
involve overlaying them with Indian realities, but most often means
identifying London as a version of its own historical self-representations
abroad. Desai's immigrants are still reacting to the city, responding to it
largely on its own terms; although it changes them, they do not transform or significantly reterritorialize it. Written in the mode of literary
realism, *Bye-Bye Blackbird* constructs a spatially imposing metropolis still
best understood through the filters of the imperial past. The material
and sociopolitical remnants of empire are visible in Rushdie's mid-1980s
London as well, but they represent transitory realities. Through a combination of magic and realism Rushdie portrays a city lurching through a
painful process of renewal and transformation that will inaugurate a
future in which the spatial and racial geopolitics of the past can become
obsolete, melted down like the wax effigies of 'History' in Pinkwalla's
nightclub (292). The process by which that future may be achieved is
illustrated through individual lives that exemplify the role-playing, shape-
shifting, and spectacle of the theatre as well as its endless project of
transforming and inventively redefining space.

The city that materially embodies those shape-shifting qualities most
vividly is Jahilia, a version of Mecca circa 600 AD that exists only in
Gibreel's schizophrenic dreams and becomes a metaphor for London.
As a city 'built entirely of sand,' it is a paradoxical place: its 'newly
invented permanence' is fabricated with 'the very stuff of inconstancy, –
the quintessence of unsettlement, shifting, treachery, lack-of-form' (93,
94). The other key spaces on which Rushdie figures London as a seemingly solid but actually 'most protean and chameleon of cities' (201) are
those of the human body and psyche. The unstable, reclaimable city and
the mutable, grotesque body function as metaphors for each other and
for a process of migrant self-fashioning that Rushdie constantly associates with hybridity, fluidity, and change. His central thematic question,
asked by the narrator in the opening scene, encapsulates the novel's
obsession with mutability and its vision of London: 'How does newness

come into the world? How is it born? Of what fusions, translations, conjoinings is it made?' (8). Newness so defined is never completely new; it is generated by combining and transforming that which already exists – just as sand, whose raw materiality goes back billions of years, is continually reshaped into new forms by natural and human forces.

The future, in other words, is born of the past, and the most complete, hopeful, and future-oriented process of self-fashioning the novel traces is the one that is initially most stuck in an unreconstructed past. The anglophile Saladin holds comfortable delusions of '*Ellowen deeowen London*' as a 'dream-city' of 'poise and moderation' that he contrasts with Bombay's 'confusion and superabundance' (37). As a boy,

> He dreamed of flying out of his bedroom window to discover that there, below him, was – not Bombay – but Proper London itself, Bigben Nelsonscolumn Lordstavern Bloodytower Queen. But as he floated out over the great metropolis he felt himself beginning to lose height, and no matter how hard he struggled kicked swam-in-air he continued to spiral slowly downwards to earth, then faster, then faster still, until he was screaming headfirst down towards the city, Saintpauls, Puddinglane, Threadneedlestreet, zeroing in on London like a bomb. (38–9)

This scene not only foreshadows (and echoes) his headfirst descent with Gibreel;[15] it also anticipates the project of street-level reclamation that Saladin, like London itself, will undergo. His notion of 'Proper London,' a historical city given illusory permanence by its monuments, relies on its temporal and spatial distance from Saladin (whether he is 'seeing' it from Bombay, from the air above London, or, as in this imaginative flight, both). To a greater degree than either of Desai's protagonists, however, Saladin moves convincingly beyond his attachment to this image of London – and beyond a related image of himself as 'a goodandproper Englishman' – as a result of street-level experiences (43). Through a kind of magical reality check he is jolted out of his anachronistic and isolationist modes of metropolitan dwelling: his belief that being 'a neat man in a buttoned suit' living 'an ordered, contented life' in London makes him 'a member of the real world' (74). Through the mutation of his body into a goatish beast, he is forced to join the crowd – a visibly different crowd now from the one in T.S. Eliot's 'Unreal City' (65). His Englishness aggressively challenged by immigration officers, his former career and love-life suddenly beyond reach, Saladin is compelled to seek refuge with the Bangladeshi Sufyans, people of his 'own kind' that he had formerly avoided (253). His education involves dissolving 'his old certainties' and finding himself not in his dream-London – he's been 'cast from the gates' of that city – but in the multiplicitous newness of a city that, like his out-of-control body, is continually becoming (259, 257).

What Saladin discovers is not a uniquely Indian or postcolonial or migrant insight; it is something all city-dwellers come to know. Elizabeth Wilson is one of many theorists to articulate the ways the city's transitoriness can make urban life unnervingly 'dreamlike and magical, yet also terrifying': 'Life and its certainties slither away underfoot. The continual flux and change is one of the most disquieting aspects of the modern city. We expect permanence and stability from the city. Its monuments are solid stone and embody a history that goes back many generations' (*Sphinx* 3–4). Nonetheless, Saladin's particular experience of this urban flux and change, like Dev's, is overdetermined by the fact of empire – by the ways his undesired (but inescapable) Indianness inter-sects with his desired (and officially recognized) Englishness. As Simon Gikandi has written, 'the resonance of empire lay in its ability to evoke a horizontal identity for both the colonizer and the colonized even when they were imprisoned in strict racial and economic hierarchies' (*Maps* 192). One legacy of this paradoxical similarity-with-difference is that the migrant to postimperial England is located both 'inside and outside Englishness' (205). As the cultural matrix nurtured by empire fades into the sunset, both urban space and the Englishness that it accommodates are destabilized. Cities are transformed by Commonwealth migration, and national identity is unsettled by legislative changes that react to the migrants' increased visibility and to the racially exclusive attitudes such visibility engenders.

As Saladin reluctantly acknowledges his South Asian affiliations and discovers that his devilish, horned new body has become an icon of interracial solidarity, he begins to reconcile himself to the fluid space of this demographically transformed metropolis. He is forced into the sorts of encounters across race, space, and class divides that metropolitan life constantly promotes and that make cities places 'saturated with possibili-ties for the destabilization of imperial arrangements' (Jacobs, *Edge* 4). Baucom, in a notable reading, observes that while Saladin has tried to redeem himself by abandoning his Indian self for a 'false,' 'museum' Englishness (complete with bowler hat), Gibreel perceives that 'it is England that requires redemption in order that the nation might be reconciled to its migrants' (203, 202). Gibreel's approach is preferable,

Baucom argues, but only up to a point; despite his spectacular efforts at redeeming the city 'Gibreel learns that the city has anticipated his arrival, that it has already begun to divert itself, that it is its own redeeming angel' (209–10). Baucom's learned and largely convincing reading nonetheless undervalues the changes Saladin goes through and the ways his experience throughout the narrative comes to exemplify, much more than Gibreel's, the kinds of redemption and transformation Rushdie favours.[16]

Rushdie envisions London's postcolonial renewal occurring through the collectivity and street-level action in which Saladin, however unwittingly, becomes involved, not through the literally top-down fantasies of a tropicalized metropolis imagined by a deluded monomaniac. Gibreel's vision of a London enlivened by the extremes of an Indian climate – with attendant benefits including 'increased moral definition,' 'better cricketers,' 'spicier food,' 'improved street life' and 'no more British reserve' – makes for a playful blending of stereotypes (354, 355). But for Rushdie, social transformation happens gradually and communally, not instantly and unilaterally as Gibreel, in his attempts to redeem London by angelic imperative, would have it. The activist politics represented in the novel, which Saladin is forced to experience, are messy, discordant, and even factionalizing as old racial hierarchies and divisions are challenged. And if the collectivities are grounded in the neighbourhood and ghetto spaces that are a local legacy of imperialism's global segregation of peoples, the transgressions of boundaries endemic to riots aim at the larger obliteration of segregating borders. As Malcolm Cross writes, racial segregation in large, first-world cities perpetuates social inequities by making deprivation and differentiation seem natural or commonsensical (see 111). In Indian cities, as noted above, spatial divisions based on caste identities perform a similar function. For Rushdie, the reclaiming of London by immigrants is all about erasing borders and renovating material reality. In some discourses of urban design, weak or transgressible borders are favoured for encouraging 'the narrative use of places' (Sennett, *Conscience* 196); Rushdie's narrative valorizes the gathering of different realities and stories in order to facilitate the city's endless generation of 'newness' through hybrid combinations. As he has Otto Cone say in the novel, 'The modern city ... is the locus classicus of incompatible realities. Lives that have no business mingling with one another sit side by side upon the omnibus' (314). Or, as Rushdie himself has said, the city constantly brings into the same narrative people who seem to 'belong in different kinds of story' (Ball, 'Interview' 33).

In other words, cities not only accommodate but are constantly renovated and redefined by the variegated uses their inhabitants make of them and the different narratives those uses generate. An emphasis on fluid, street-level use as a corrective to the often rigid spatial and sociopolitical prescriptions of plans, grids, buildings, or custom and tradition appear in a range of urban discourses – from Leighton Hazlehurst's distinction between ritually pure caste 'spaces' and the 'activities' that transgress spatial boundaries in urban India to Michel de Certeau's theory of walking as an appropriative practice that transgresses totalizing boundaries to rewrite city-space via individual itineraries and 'spatial stories.'[17] Homi Bhabha's distinction between the 'pedagogical' and the 'performative' also negotiates a version of this contrast between the top-down prescriptions of history, precedent, and authority on the one hand and emergent, bottom-up use on the other. As he writes in 'DissemiNation,' the narrative of the nation is 'split between the continuist, accumulative temporality of the pedagogical, and the repetitious, recursive strategy of the performative' (145). Whereas the pedagogical narrative is 'homogeneous, consensual' and 'totalizing,' the performative signifies 'the more specific address to contentious, unequal interests and identities within the population' (146). 'The people,' Bhabha notes, represent the 'cutting edge' where the pedagogical and performative are continuously negotiated (146). Rushdie's Saladin is initially affiliated with a London that exemplifies a pedagogical version of England and Englishness. Once he finds himself excluded from that national narrative, he reorients himself towards the emergent, street-level activity of the performative user who can, with a crowd of others, begin transforming the spaces and narratives of the city and the nation.

Theatrical performance is all about the design, transformation, and occupation of space; it is also about erecting and interrogating borders – between reality and illusion, on-stage and off-, actors and audience. One model of transgressive performance with particular applicability to Rushdie's vision of city-space is Mikhail Bakhtin's concept of 'carnival.' While the theories of the grotesque body and Menippean satire that Bakhtin develops from carnival are very applicable to *The Satanic Verses*,[18] the aspect of carnival itself of greatest interest here is its sociopolitical capacity to destabilize official orders and hierarchies. For Bakhtin, carnival is a participatory performance involving spectacle and play and affiliated with 'becoming, change, and renewal' (*Rabelais* 10). Located on 'the borderline between art and life,' carnival suspends established norms and social boundaries; it 'does not acknowledge any division between actors and spectators' (10, 7). Although culturally its world is far from the medieval and Renaissance Europe in which Bakhtin's theory originates, Rushdie's Rabelaisian novel is nonetheless infused with the revolutionary spirit of the carnivalesque. Saladin's old image of London is carnivalized, made topsy-turvy, as he is jolted out of ossified views into the recognition of an urban world characterized by transition, transformation, and uncertainty. His view of London is literally and metaphorically brought down to earth: he replaces the totalizing vision of a spectator located in the upper stratosphere with a partial, participatory, and performative experience grounded in the immigrant neighbourhood of Brickhall. He discovers for himself what Jonathan Raban calls the 'intrinsic theatricality of city life' – in which everyone is an actor performing the self and the city together for an audience composed of everyone else (34).

Both Saladin and Gibreel, like Desai's Dev and Adit, undergo processes of radical reorientation towards metropolitan London. All four men find their views of the city transformed, but Saladin's is the most promising postcolonial re-vision because, despite its elements of surreal fantasy, his experience is grounded in social reality. The limitations of Dev's and Adit's final comings-to-terms with London are partly a function of the solitary detachment and myopia of both men's urban experiences. Their attitudes to London are formed not through community involvement but internally and unilaterally: in the mental and imaginary realms, and through literary and theatrical models. Even *Bye-Bye Blackbird*'s most promising postcolonial images of London – Dev's fantasies of the Battersea Power Station as a Hindu temple and of England infiltrated by Indian social space – seem merely idiosyncratic, without social or political valence. Perhaps they can be no more than delightfully incongruous fancies in a London so demographically and spatially linked to its imperial past: a city where Indian communities are still at an early stage of formation, still mostly spectators or witnesses to the occupation and transformation of urban space.

Two decades later, when Gibreel has his similar fancy of a 'tropicalized' London, it is as both spectator and actor: he imagines himself to have the power of the Angel Azraeel to dramatically transform the metropolis from on high. The possibilities for empowering agency are certainly stronger in 1980s London, which has larger and more defined and rooted Indian communities than it did in the 1960s. But Gibreel's model of top-down, unilateral urban renewal proves a negative foil to that of Saladin. It is a migrant version of what Ashis Nandy describes as the 'magical feelings of omnipotence' that British colonizers imputed to themselves in India (*Intimate* 35). Not only do his proposals to achieve increased definition by obliterating shades of grey and reinforcing binaries sound regressive, but Gibreel himself is a deluded man whose grip on reality is tenuous. He is also a largely isolated figure in the novel; his megalomania originates in extended dreams and misapprehensions about the nature of social change. His effect on the masses as a screen idol, in the realm of theatrical fantasy, does not translate to street-level reality. Saladin's preferable experience of community entanglements is inaugurated by his bodily transformation, which is much more real in its way than Gibreel's. The latter may have a halo, but every time he attempts to do something angelic, he is humbled by his 'real' humanity and his illusory empowerment evaporates. Saladin's goat-body is clearly not illusory: the Sufyan girls may wonder if it is 'a trick, ... make-up or something theatrical,' but his metamorphic eight-foot-high beast-self is a material (if temporary) fact (257). And this change prompts the kinds of grassroots community identifications that, in a London increasingly occupied by people of colour, can lead to real, material transformations of urban social space. Through the recognitions of Saladin, Rushdie posits a London-to-be in which the spectator-actor divisions of personal fancy or conventional theatrics give way to the participatory tradition of carnival. He envisions an inclusive, hybridized, and revolutionary urban space in which old rigid realities can be played with and changed. His London is a usable, malleable city in which the postcolonial migrant is not just a spectator responding to and influenced by the city, but an actor on stage imagining, performing, and designing its new realities.

However, while Rushdie implicitly echoes Lewis Mumford's view of the city as 'a theater of social action' ('What' 185),[19] he is under no illusions that the renewal he advocates will be as pleasurable or fun as a carnival or a turn on the stage. The novel's chief events and symbols of street-level renewal are violent riots and destructive fires, and Saladin, like the city itself, is pulled kicking and screaming towards recognition of the change he is already going through and the newness his metamorphosis foists upon him. Such ambivalence is expressed by the diverse epithets attached to London throughout the novel. It is a 'tormented' and 'tortured metropolis whose fabric was now utterly transformed' (320). The fall of 'Proper London' from imperial greatness, together with the 'confusion of languages' its new migrants introduce, earns the now 'improper city' the name 'Babylondon' (459). But just as Saladin undergoes a form of rebirth, the 'dog-eared metropolis' will, by being well used in new ways by emergent communities, become a 'reborn city' (156, 422). Interestingly these last two adjectives, though equally serviceable as metaphors for the 'real' city, appear in relation to miniature representations of London whose use-value is clearly limited. The 'dog-eared metropolis' is 'Geographers' London,' the 'A to Z' book of maps Gibreel carries in his pocket as he leaves Rosa Diamond's Hastings abode for London (156); he will later mistake this set of flat cartographic images for the living, breathing city he wishes to 'redeem ... square by square' (326). His empowerment over the pocketbook metropolis will prove as temporary and illusory as the totalizing on-high view its maps replicate – 'the city in its corruption refused to submit to the dominion of the cartographers, changing shape at will' (327) – and Gibreel will later abandon the misleading maps. The second adjective, 'reborn,' describes a '*condensed*' replica of London built for a film production of the Dickensian musical *Friend!* This 'abridged metropolis' is the rebirth of a Victorian literary city, not of contemporary London (422). At a party on the film set, Saladin encounters an even smaller representation: a map of London magic-markered on an actress's breast. Parodically recalling prior equations of the conquest of London with the conquest of English women – Saladin's of Pamela, Gibreel's of Alleluia – this third image of a miniaturized city is, like the A–Z pocket-map and the film set, no substitute for the real one. Although the mammary metropolis 'summons him,' Saladin flees it and the sound-stage simulacrum for 'the madness of the street' (424).

Rushdie clearly prefers the mutable, material 'reality' found on (and metonymically symbolized by) the street over static representations of the city available in maps, replicas, pictures, texts, or bird's-eye views. The unstable city is best known and (re)claimed through mobile, interactive inhabitation at ground level, even if such local engagements can only ever be with a small part of the whole metropolis. Moreover, because cities constantly *do* change, Rushdie implies, they can *be* changed: like the people who inhabit them, they are inherently metamorphic and open to improvement. This quality is vividly conveyed through the image of Jahilia, the city of sand. What Mahound fails to see in Jahilia is what Gibreel fails to see in London: that the renewal of urban space and society is best achieved gradually and organically, through accretion and adaptation, not by obliterating and starting again in the name of a monologic attempt at redemption. The novel ends in a third city, Bombay, where Zeeny Vakil, the only character consistently in synch with the novel's value system, seems destined to finally succeed in the 'reclamation' of Saladin that she long ago made 'her project' (52). Her success is evident not only in his renewed romantic interest but in her enlistment of him in a street-level demonstration advocating urban renewal – an event he would previously have spurned. 'Try and embrace the city,' she encourages him, 'as it is, not some childhood memory that makes you both nostalgic and sick. Draw it close. The actually existing place. Make its faults your own. Become its creature; belong' (541). Having survived a final confrontation with Gibreel, who instead of killing him commits suicide, Saladin at the end seems committed to personal and urban reclamation. If he is 'getting another chance,' so is the city (547). But this reclamation involves equal measures of the past and the future. As he resumes his former name and his old idea of where 'home' is, he also endorses urban renewal in the sociopolitical and physical realms. 'Let the bulldozers come,' he thinks on the final page: 'If the old refused to die, the new could not be born' (547).

Lines across Space and Time

The turn to Bombay and a renewed version of Saladin's former self in the final chapter of *The Satanic Verses* is surprising. It can seem uncharacteristically sentimental in its portrayal of rejuvenated familial love and essentializing in its portrayal of the new/old Salahuddin Chamchawala reacquainting himself with his estranged father and his former self and home. Psychologically it may be understandable after his London experiences, but as Simon Gikandi observes, it appears to betray or reverse Rushdie's 'earlier critique of the *Heimat*' – the idea of the national homeland and essential belonging that his vision of migrancy and his commitment to newness would seem to reject (*Maps* 223). Certainly the final chapter grounds identity in place of origin to a degree unmatched elsewhere in this kinetic novel of global movement, which begins in the 'planet-shrinker,' the 'air-space ... that made the century possible, becoming one of its defining locations' (5), and which emphasizes displacement over emplacement throughout its interlocking narratives. But if, as Gayatri Spivak says, the 'central theme' of *The Satanic Verses* is 'the postcolonial divided between two identities: migrant and national' (219), it is important to remember that the novel explores such divides (and related splits such as spectator/actor, global/local, and pedagogical/performative) in three carefully described urban settings. This story of two men is also a tale of three cities – London, Jahilia, and Bombay – that exemplify similar characteristics and similar tensions between the multiplicitous and the unitary, between communal and authoritarian forces.[20] In each city Rushdie demonstrates that totalization, unilateralism, and monomania are unsuited to the diversity and flux of urban life. In all three settings identity is woven into the fabric of the city even as more transnational perspectives contribute to the renewal of place and self. Saladin's journey from beginning to end is exemplary. He descends from global airspace to a 'not-England' that feels like 'a transit lounge' more than a place (132); he then undergoes an enforced immersion in a performative England located on London's streets; finally, in Bombay, he achieves a renewed perspective on self and city as complex combinations of the inherited given and the emergent new.

The transnationalism of *The Satanic Verses* is not a free-floating, rootless global migrancy, but one that, as in Michael Peter Smith's model of transnational urbanism, fully accommodates and commits to the local.[21] Amitav Ghosh offers a comparable vision of transnationalism in *The Shadow Lines*; published the same year as *The Satanic Verses*, it too locates the quest for postcolonial identity in and between three distant-but-similar cities – in this case Calcutta, London, and Dhaka.[22] Ghosh's radically non-linear *Bildungsroman* spans two continents and forty years (1939 to the early 1980s), shuttling back and forth among memories and events distant in time and space. The integrating consciousness of its unnamed first-person narrator establishes a transnational perspective from which the three cities mirror each other and their relatedness is emphasized over their differences. The many lines that fluidly connect geographically and temporally disparate 'worlds' in his novel can resemble a narrative version of the emergent space of globalized 'flows' that Manuel Castells sees 'superseding the meaning of the space of places' (348). But Ghosh qualifies what some critics sees as the novel's privileged, universalizing vision of a world of borderless travel and metropolitan mutuality. His articulation of transnational identity and community, like Rushdie's, does not entirely dissolve the material and local in the face of the planet-shrinking, dematerializing spatial logic of the virtual and global. However, in its geographical imaginings this self-consciously cartographic novel undoubtedly comes close.

In the nineteenth century, Joseph McLaughlin writes, 'metropolitan London and Londoners, far from being the antithesis of those colonial and imperial places and peoples that comprised the British Empire, were actually their curious doubles. London was just as much an imperial stage as India or Africa ... ; it was an amalgam of multiple frontiers' (4). The twentieth-century legacy of such doubling is a theme of many postcolonial London novels, including the four discussed above. But *The Shadow Lines* is the most forthright of them all in exploring London cityscapes and peoples as 'doubles' or 'mirror images' of those in (post)colonial cities. In his essay 'The Diaspora in Indian Culture,' Ghosh writes, 'Just as the spaces of India travel with the migrant, India too has no vocabulary for separating the migrant from India': its diaspora 'is the mirror in which modern India seeks to know itself' (77, 78). His novel is an elaborate, baroque illustration of these principles of insepara-bility and reciprocity. London is a distant place the narrator, as a boy in Calcutta, comes to know through the stories and mappings of family members. His cousin Tridib, who has been called the novel's '*ur*-imagina-tion' (A.N. Kaul 307), influentially tells him 'that one could never know anything except through desire, ... a longing for everything that was not in oneself ... that carried one beyond the limits of one's mind to other times and other places, and even, if one was lucky, to a place where there was no border between oneself and one's image in the mirror' (29). The English boy Nick Price is one such image; after Ila first describes him to the narrator, Nick 'became a spectral presence beside me in my looking glass; growing with me, but always bigger and better, and in some ways more desirable' (49). In a novel replete with pairs of Indian relatives whose resemblance is asserted only to be denied,[23] this purely subjective and imaginative mirroring of boys from two unrelated families is more adventurous in its claims of transoceanic, transcultural similarity. The self-projection of the Bengali narrator into the older, blond, English Nick has no basis other than desire.

This superseding of real difference by desired similarity, of distance by proximity, is characteristic of a narrative that constantly places invented likeness and imagined or remembered knowledge in tension with visible, empirical, or official facts. Such desire is a legacy of colonialist discourses that circulated contradictory signals regarding the Britishness of Indians and the alterity of colonial subjects *vis-à-vis* their rulers. Indians under imperial rule were variously elevated and oppressed, anglicized and patronized, redeemed and seen as irredeemable, included and excluded from English power and an English culture and landscape they were encouraged to know well, but to know entirely through representations: texts and images of faraway realities. These contradictory dynamics of identification and disidentification, avowal and disavowal, find expres-sion in Ila's story of her blue-eyed, pink-skinned doll Magda being rescued from nasty London classmates by Nick. This fantasy turns out to be the more desirable version of Ila's own experience of racist taunting, to which the real Nick turned a blind eye. Similar disjunctions between desired and actual versions of metropolitan life and belonging inform the narrator's knowledge of London. On one hand he can navigate parts of the city expertly based purely on maps he memorized as a child in Calcutta. He knows the layout of Mrs Price's house on Lymington Road based on what Ila drew in the dust under a table in Calcutta, and after listening to Tridib's stories of his childhood stay in wartime London he knows parts of 'the A to Z street atlas of London ... by heart' (57). But when he demonstrates his acquaintance with the Solent Road neighbourhood to Nick and Robi, he continues to privilege the 'truth' of his imaginings of it as a wartime bomb site over the placid scene he observes in the 1970s:

> I had known that I would not see uprooted trees or splintered windows.... But despite that, I still could not believe in the truth of what I did see: the gold-green trees, the old lady walking her Pekinese, the children.... I could see all of that, and yet, despite the clear testimony of my eyes, it seemed to me still that Tridib had shown me something truer about Solent Road a long time ago in Calcutta, something I could not have seen had I waited at that corner for years.... I wanted to know England not as *I* saw her, but in her finest hour – every place chooses its own, and to me it did not seem an accident that England had chosen hers in a war. (56–7)

Like Dev in *Bye-Bye Blackbird*, Ghosh's narrator overlays visible, present-tense London with representations of the city's past internalized in India, though in this case the source of the knowledge is familial and oral rather than institutional and literary. In a novel obsessed with simultaneity and overlappings – of different times and distant places, of borders crossed, of realities remembered, imagined, and experienced – Ghosh asserts that what is 'true' or 'real' may exceed what the senses can apprehend. The city is a palimpsest: its present spaces are layered with local and global pasts that take both material and immaterial form – as built space and texts on the one hand, as memory and oral history on the other. Because it is important to see 'that a place does not merely exist, that it has to be invented in one's imagination' (21), present-day London must be seen to reveal the spectre of previous realities, alternative possibilities, worldly connections. When the narrator visits the Victor Gollancz bookshop, he tries to reconcile what he sees with Tridib's stories about Alan Tresawsen working for the Left Book Club before the war. In contrast to Ila, to whom only 'the current was the real' and the bookshop looks 'like any musty old office,' the narrator has 'seen it first through Tridib's eyes' and so 'its past seemed concurrent with its present' (30, 31). Philosophically speaking, the narrator presumes that reality, as the senses apprehend it, can always be sublated. And while in Hinduism, the unsublatable Brahman (the ultimate reality) is only accessible through transcendent, non-sensory insight, for Ghosh the truth of a place is apparent only by using the imagination to see beyond its temporal and material manifestations.

The narrator's reinscription of London through the lens of memory and imagination is politically ambiguous. As it appropriates the metropolis to Indian experiences and sensibilities, his narrative privileges imperial over postimperial London. The metropolis 'in her finest hour' is the one that existed before India's independence and before Commonwealth migrants thoroughly transformed and reterritorialized it. This is also an inaccessible London 'known' from afar and removed in time; like the only 'London' most colonized Indians ever knew, it is a representation rather than an inhabited place. The knowledge by which the narrator expertly navigates metropolitan neighbourhoods brings the all-inclusive cartographic knowledge associated with totalizing power together with the itinerary-knowledge by which an individual walker practises place, appropriating it to a personal narrative and thereby resisting that power. Ghosh's narrator deconstructs de Certeau's binary: the maps by which he orients himself to London combine the A–Z variety with those drawn in his head from stories told by Indians in India, translated seamlessly from and back into itineraries.

Ghosh likewise breaks down temporal boundaries between London past and present, imperial and postimperial, perceiving both simultaneously in the contemporary scene. If the past seems somehow 'truer' than the present, the novel does not (as some critics argue) elide the dynamic, contemporary city in order to resurrect a 'petrified' metropolis (Sen 50). The narrator – who marvels at 'the experience of hearing Bengali dialects which I had never heard in Calcutta being spoken in the streets of London' (236) – has lived in the city as an adult and come face to face with its migrant communities, including the hostile proprietor of the Taj Travel Agency who refuses to speak Bengali and has no patience for the narrator's attempts to confirm the building's history. The narrator's determination to layer the past over the present is an expression of his desire to maintain lines of temporal and geographical continuity. Like Desai's Dev, but for different reasons, he insists on seeing London's present through the filter of representations of it located in the Indian past. To Ila's suggestion that he 'just take the world as it is,' he advocates 'inventing what we saw'; otherwise 'we would never be free of other people's inventions' (31). He implies that as a result of the claims England made on Calcutta and on Indian spaces and peoples – claims which included the invention of an India that suited England's desires – India is entitled to its own invention or representation of London, Londoners, and English history. England and India, like the Datta-Chaudhuri and Price/Tresawsen families, have achieved a mutual intimacy over many years, which the novel renders figuratively as lines of connection that cross boundaries of spatial, temporal, national, and racial difference.

The larger political themes of the book – its meditations on nationalism and national identity in postcolonial South Asia – are also articulated through the metaphors of border-crossing lines and distance-shrinking mirror images. But Ghosh first lays the foundation for these rather abstract metaphors in his deployment of the more concrete and tangible metaphor of the house.[24] As noted above, the narrator's foreknowledge of London houses draws on Tridib's stories and on lines Ila draws in the dust to map metropolitan room arrangements when she and the narrator play 'houses' in a cellar in Raibajar, near Calcutta. The two children play under a large table bought at the Crystal Palace in the 1890s by their great-grandfather. The space beneath this migrant table emerges over the course of the novel as a powerful microcosm of transnational dwelling, remembering, and imagining. After the narrator describes his childhood visits there with Ila and May Price, the Raibajar cellar becomes conflated with Mrs Price's London cellar, where the adult Ila discovers the narrator's longing for her and sleeps with Nick instead. When the two cousins revisit the London cellar some time later, Ila says, 'So here we are.... Back in Raibajar' – the faraway place where she first introduced the narrator (imaginatively) to Nick and to the house they are now physically within (177). Referent is transformed into the distant space of its prior representation, and her remark sets the tone for two sequences in which the narrator is transported into memories of all the scenes and 'ghosts' he associates with these two underground spaces on different continents (178, 182). Pushing his technique of narrative interpellation to a dizzying extreme, Ghosh conflates moments, selves, and others separated in time and space: 'They were all around me, we were together at last, not ghosts at all: the ghostliness was merely the absence of time and distance' (178). Houses in London and Raibajar, and the various people and memories associated with them, are reflected through the

narrator's looking-glass consciousness and gathered into an imagined
and desired continuum.

Ghosh's exploration of national and transnational identity in a parti-
tioned subcontinent also begins in domestic space. The narrator's grandmother, Tha'mma, and her sister, Mayadebi, grew up in a house in
Dhaka that became absurdly divided after a family feud. In their childish
fancies, their uncle's off-limits half of the house became a place where
everything was imagined to be upside-down and backwards. The residential divide figuratively mirrors the partition of India and Pakistan, and
the relative upside-downness of the two halves is echoed in the narrator's
later remark that Dhaka and Calcutta were 'more closely bound to each
other' at a moment in 1964, long after partition, than ever before – 'so
closely that I, in Calcutta, had only to look into the mirror to be in
Dhaka; a moment when each city was the inverted image of the other,
locked into an irreversible symmetry by the line that was to set us free –
our looking-glass border' (228). The moment in question is a sequence
of riots that occurred in both Calcutta and Dhaka in January, 1964, one
of which killed Tridib as he accompanied Tha'mma in her quixotic
effort to relocate her ancient uncle from the upside-down house in
Dhaka to hers in Calcutta. The narrator's realization that the riot in
Dhaka that claimed Tridib is intimately connected with one he experienced as a schoolboy in Calcutta, and that both were started by an event
in Kashmir, prompts his meditation on the primacy of border-crossing
lines of transnational connection over the shadow lines of national
boundaries. Perhaps recalling that partition was accompanied by devas-
tating riots on both sides, he describes how terrifying these border-
hopping connections between distant realities can be:

> It is a fear that comes of the knowledge that normalcy is utterly contingent,
> that the spaces that surround one, the streets that one inhabits, can be-
> come, suddenly and without warning, as hostile as a desert in a flash flood.
> It is this that sets apart the thousand million people who inhabit the
> subcontinent from the rest of the world – not language, not food, not
> music – it is the special quality of loneliness that grows out of the fear of the
> war between oneself and one's image in the mirror. (200)

Tha'mma, whose family reunification scheme begins the chain of events
and responses that will later lead the narrator to these thoughts, has
been characterized in criticism as representing a 'militant' and 'essen-
tialist nationalism' that becomes the rejected obverse of the narrator's

privileged transnationalism (S. Kaul 134; Anjali Roy 37). And indeed, there are aspects of her character and her past that fit this description: her expression of support for a terrorist classmate, her ferocious attack on Ila for living in Britain, which in her view properly belongs to the British. And while it is true that, as Anjali Roy states, 'Tha'mma, as part of the generation which agreed to "dream" a new nation, must perforce believe in "the reality of nations and borders," beyond which "existed another reality," permitting only relationships of war and friendship "between those separate realities"' (37), in the novel these quoted beliefs are attributed to the narrator as a boy, not to Tha'mma (see 214). Indeed, Tha'mma is quite happy to extend her influence across the ocean to disrupt her grandson's life in London with an incriminating letter and, more significantly, to cross a national boundary in order to reunite with an uncle estranged by the family feud and the partition it symbolizes. Tha'mma may express surprise that the India–East Pakistan border is invisible and that Dhaka looks different from before, but in her defining act she endeavours to figuratively erase divisions of time and national space. It may be a kind of nationalism (in the form of riots) that prevents her from succeeding, causing the deaths of her uncle and nephew, but what she fails in is a border-defying act as profound in its way as any her grandson performs.

He is no less contradictory. As a boy the narrator conflates distant times, places, and people, freely trades reality for remembered or imagined representations of it; as a young man he brings the novel to a thematic culmination that draws lines of transnational connection as an ontological antidote to the harmful shadow lines of national boundaries. But he also says that it is he who, as a boy, 'believed that distance separates,' 'believed that across the border there existed another reality' (214). And as an adult he critiques what he sees as Ila's shallow cosmopolitanism. When she compares her pleasure at communal living with that of her uncles during the war, he is dismayed by her arrogant assumption 'that her experience could encompass other moments simply because it had come later; that times and places are the same because they happen to look alike, like airport lounges' (101). The link Ila makes here is no different from the ones the narrator makes repeatedly. The novel, for better or worse, seems content to leave these apparent contradictions unresolved; the result is to complicate and ultimately enrich its overall thematic trajectory.

That overall thrust has been critiqued on ideological grounds: A.N. Kaul, for instance, sees the novel as advocating a reality-free globalism –

as a 'wishing away of troublesome realities' such as national borders from
a vantage point of privileged, middle-class mobility (303). Ghosh, Kaul
argues, 'acknowledges no separate national or cultural realities': 'Despite its careful chronology and topography, *The Shadow Lines* may be
said to "happen" in all places at once. Every corner of it involves all its
space and every moment all its moments. There are no isolated or
isolable spots of time or place' (300, 305). Kaul's materialist reading
makes some strong points, but while it applies to passages such as the
cellar scenes discussed above, it exaggerates the placelessness of the
novel as a whole, which qualifies its dematerializing enthusiasms with a
countervailing commitment to the specificity of the local. For Ghosh,
similarity can coexist with difference. The mirror, as he figuratively
deploys it, both connects and divides separate realities; it is both a
border-crosser and a borderline. Distant realities may mirror each other
and defy gaps of time and space, but they retain their distinctiveness –
just as the people who are thought to look alike inevitably retain theirs
upon closer inspection.[25] This paradoxical difference-despite-similarity
is casually but tellingly demonstrated when Ila sees the narrator 'gazing'
at a London sweet-shop:

> Exactly like that sweet-shop at the corner of Gole Park, she said, isn't it.
> And so it was, with exactly the same laminated counters and plastic tables;
> exactly the same except that it was built into a terrace of derelict eigh-
> teenth-century London houses, and there was no paan-shop at the corner,
> and no Nathu Chaubey, but instead, as Nick pointed out, hanging over it
> was the great steeple of Hawksmoor's Christchurch Spitalfields. (98)

'Exactly the same except that' is the logic of all the novel's resemblances.
It applies to places separated by geographical gaps (as here), temporal
ones (as when Tha'mma marvels at the changes her old Dhaka
neighbourhood has undergone), or both (as when the narrator measures contemporary Solent Road against the war-time cityscape Tridib
'showed' him long ago in Calcutta). If, as discussed above, the Solent
Road scene favours imagined over visible reality, it also privileges history:
the city as a palimpsest whose 'reality' is by definition much deeper than
its material surfaces show. History is essential context for perceiving the
differentness of places separated in time, just as the sweet-shop passage
shows how the cultural and geographical differences inscribed on urban
landscapes provide the contexts – the 'except thats' – through which
apparently identical spaces are revealed to be entirely different.

The Shadow Lines commits to both the global and the local. Ghosh's strategy is not to dissolve borders and differences before a reality-defying, globalizing imagination, but rather to explore and negotiate the dense relations of similarity and difference that straddle the gaps of history, geography, and nationality. His preoccupation with travel, together with the mobility of his narrative, may suggest that the novel's true location is Castells's space of placeless flows, or the 'borderless world' of some globalization discourses (Miyoshi 78), or David Harvey's 'disorienting' space of postmodern 'time-space compression' (*Condition* 284). James Clifford, in an article partly concerned with Ghosh's writing, identifies him as an opponent of 'the classic anthropological quest for discrete traditions and cultural differences'; his theme of 'dwelling-in-travel' is best characterized, Clifford says, by the metaphor of the 'transit lounge. It's hard to imagine a better figure for postmodernity, the brave new world order of disorder, of rootless histories and selves' ('Transit' 7). Marc Augé identifies the 'airport lounge' and other spaces of transport as 'non-places' (96). As opposed to a traditional 'anthropological place,' which is occupied and given identity-enhancing meaning by its inhabitants, a non-place generates only 'the passive joys of identity-loss' and 'role-playing' (42, 103); it 'puts the individual in contact only with another image of himself' (79). *The Shadow Lines* may seem to favour such spaces of postmodernity or what Augé calls 'supermodernity' (78), but its immersion in history counterbalances and qualifies its privileging of geographical, imaginative, and narrative *routes* by attending equally to *roots*. While obsessed with mutual reflection and connection, Ghosh insists on the integrity of what he connects, locating the search for identity in specific locales as well as in the relations between them. As presiding consciousness, his narrator sets himself explicitly against a free-floating sense of perennially mobile, infinitely substitutable, homogenized space (as in the transit lounge), preferring to comb the surfaces and depths of multiple international locales for unexpected relations.

Ghosh's understanding of place is most compatible with that of Doreen Massey, who argues against postmodern geographers' anxieties about the vertiginous effects of 'fragmentation, depthlessness and instantaneity' and the resultant loss of a firm sense of place (*Space* 162). For Massey, the identities of all places or locales are 'porous' and 'unfixed' both spatially and temporally (5, 169). They are defined not by what they contain or what they historically have been but by their dynamic social interrelations. Some of these interrelations occur within their putative boundaries, but many extend beyond them to various elsewheres. Similarly, the identity of a place is conditioned but not predetermined by its history; that identity, and the use it makes of its history, is constantly changing. Those who attempt to fix the essence of a place, Massey says, are usually 'laying claim to some particular moment/location in time-space when the definition of the area and the social relations dominant within it were to the advantage of that particular claimant group' (169). When Ghosh's narrator claims that his imagined versions of metropoli-tan locales as they were during the war seem 'truer' than what he sees, he is not so much trying to fix an imperial, ethnically more 'English' London as individualizing it through his family connections to it. He thereby recognizes that any postcolonial encounter with London must negotiate not only the present reality – however tantalizingly familiar its Bengali dialects and shops may make it seem – but the previous Londons that have been important (as images and realities) for Indians. The former heart of empire may have been reterritorialized to a degree by 'New Commonwealth' immigration, but its historical social realities re-main inscribed in its built space and in the social structures those spaces have housed over time. For Ghosh, as for Massey, not only does space involve 'networks of relations at every scale from local to global,' but because those relations can only ever be fixed as 'simultaneity,' not stasis, the spatial is also irrevocably entangled with the temporal (*Space* 265).

The London of *The Shadow Lines* exemplifies Massey's relational mod-els of place, locale, and space-time. It also, like Rushdie's 'Ellowen Deeowen,' accommodates Smith's concept of a transnational city. Smith, like Massey, insists that cities be understood 'in the fullness of their particular linkages with the worlds outside their boundaries' (71), and his concept of 'transnational urbanism' aims to correct what he sees as a prevailing tendency among urban theorists (other than Massey) to sepa-rate the local 'inside' from the global 'outside' (101). Urban life, in Smith's view, is interpellated in multiple spatial scales that globalize the local and localize the global. His 'optic' of transnational urbanism ac-commodates a notion of human agency compatible with 'the messiness of living and acting in the mediated world of today': an agency that 'concretely connects macro-economic and geopolitical transformations to the micro-networks of social action that people create, move in, and act upon in their daily lives' (182, 6). Rushdie's Saladin, with some prodding, stumbles towards this kind of transnational agency, but Ghosh's narrator emphasizes transnational awareness more than agency. His cerebral narrative tells us little of his daily life and activities as an adult in London; the Londoner who best exemplifies Smith's urban transnational agency is the activist May Price, who, as Zeeny does to Saladin, induces the narrator to join her on a street-level mission of global-local betterment. The narrator's preference for meditating rather than acting upon his intricately networked transnationalism may be one reason why some critics see the novel's conjoining, dematerializing, border-dissolving ethos as mere wishful thinking by the privileged. Nonetheless, in its quieter way, Ghosh's self-consciously intellectual novel sets out the conceptual foundations by which London's local realities can be seen on the same level as Indian realities and subordinated to Indian experiences and narratives.

Both Ghosh's novel and Rushdie's go beyond the more negative versions of transnational identity explored in the earlier London narratives of Markandaya and Desai. Smith's view of 'subaltern identity formation' in the transnational city applies to all five texts in different ways. In subaltern 'narratives of belonging, resistance, or escape,' Smith writes, 'the spaces available for forming non-essentialist identities are *interstitial*, i.e. they open up between such dominant discursive venues as the "nation-state," the "local community," the "ethnoracial formation," and the "new world order"' (142). But while for Markandaya's and Desai's characters such in-betweenness leads variously to inauthenticity, artifice, unhousing, identity loss, and a grasping at illusory fantasies, both *The Satanic Verses* and *The Shadow Lines* move towards an additive transnational interstitiality. As London's social spaces become ever more Indianized and transnationalized, these more recent novels by Indian writers move towards what Smith calls 'life-worlds [which] are neither "here" nor "there," but at once *both* "here" and "there"' (151). (In Ghosh's case, one might add 'now' and 'then' to these conjoined binaries.) Both novels, in very different ways, open up the space of transnational migrant consciousness to a more enabling subjectivity and agency and a more celebratory (if also melancholic and nostalgic) view of migrancy. Rushdie, whose fictional and nonfictional writings consistently valorize the act of migration, writes in *Imaginary Homelands* that migrants are 'radically new types of human being: people who root themselves in ideas rather than places, in memories as much as material things. ... The migrant suspects reality: having experienced several ways of being, he understands their illusory nature. To see things plainly, you have to cross a frontier' (124–5). All five novels discussed in this chapter illustrate this view by explicitly thematizing the ways migrants are forced to question metropolitan realities and come to terms with perceived illusions by crossing temporal, spatial, metaphysical, and epistemological frontiers.

chapter five

London Centre:
The Familial Urban World
of Recent 'Black British' Writing

It is only in the last phase of British imperialism that the labouring classes of the satellites and the labouring classes of the metropolis have confronted one another directly 'on native ground.' But their fates have long been indelibly intertwined. The very definition of 'what it is to be British' – the centrepiece of that culture now to be preserved from racial dilution – has been articulated around this absent/present centre.

Stuart Hall

The Other No. 10

In her novel *Transmission* (1992), Atima Srivastava tells the story of a twentysomething Londoner who, like herself, migrated from India as a small girl. Angie is a contemporary woman working in the media and romantically involved with a young white man; despite occasional encounters with racists, she moves about London with the confident ease of the native she almost is. Contrasting the worldly ambitions and urban street smarts of Angie and her wheeler-dealer brother are her unacculturated parents, who irritate her by continuing to behave 'as if we were not living in a different country, in a different world'; indeed, they keep the heat turned up 'full blast' in the Finchley house they never seem to leave, 'as if the *desi* vegetables, Indian videos of trashy films, Indian friends were not enough of a re-creation of the life in Delhi' (19). This torrid dwelling is located in Margaret Thatcher's constituency and happens to be number 10 on its street, leading family members to joke that they live at 'the "other" No. 10' (18). But if the resemblance to the prime minister's Downing Street address playfully signifies a newly won immigrant power base, Srivastava ironically complicates the number's metonymic potential at its very first mention: 'The 10 was hanging off the door. No one had bothered to fix it' (18).

With this image, Srivastava deftly crystallizes the precarious history of postwar 'black British' settlement – the mass migration of West Indians, South Asians, and (to a lesser extent) Africans inaugurated by the SS *Windrush* and the 1948 Nationality Bill. In its policies and its social discourses, Britain has responded to 'New Commonwealth' arrivals with a confusing mix of open-armed welcome and racist marginalization, leading many black Britons to feel that they were invited to inhabit the seat of power only to be left hanging, outside the door as it were, by an exclusionary national ethos that no one will bother (or knows how) to fix. While the 1948 Bill conferred British citizenship upon all Commonwealth peoples, a series of restrictive legislative measures – the 1962 Commonwealth Immigration Act, the 1971 Immigration Act, and the 1981 Nationality Act – increasingly limited those rights in response to anxieties about white Britain being 'swamped' or 'flooded' by its dusky (post)colonial brethren. The so-called 'colour bar' erected *ad-hoc* barriers to equal treatment in areas such as employment, schooling, and housing, and both major political parties, in policies and public statements, played the race card in ways that aggravated interracial tensions. Discriminatory policing, the right-wing National Front, the 1958 Notting Hill riots, Enoch Powell's fear-mongering speeches and writings, and plain old xenophobic insularity: a host of factors contributed to a half-century of what most serious analysts conclude was a failure of popular and political will to incorporate darker-skinned immigrants fully into the body politic.[1] As Harry Goulbourne writes, 'the most powerful and influential of the attempts to redefine the post-imperial British national community is such that membership excludes non-white minorities who have settled on these shores since the Second World War' (1). The influence of an ethnically based nationalism has 'encouraged leaders at all levels of society to side-step the fundamental question of how a new national community may peacefully emerge in post-imperial Britain' (215). The legacy of missed opportunities and narrow-mindedness is that, as the title of Paul Gilroy's 1987 book proclaimed, *'There Ain't No Black in the Union Jack.'*

Even so, there are now two generations of adults who were born or grew up in Britain as the children of 'New Commonwealth' migrants. Those who have always called London home have a very different relationship to Britain and the capital than do (or did) their parents. For many, the ex-colonial homeland is a distant world to which they have never been: a land whose languages are unfamiliar and whose culture is known only as it has been sustained and mediated by parents and others in their community. For these young black Londoners, the metropolis is their familiar landscape and cultural environment – one that is only weakly and indirectly filtered through the memories of another place. The novels of contemporary London that began to appear in the 1990s from young authors of Caribbean, African, or Asian descent frequently reflect this generational difference – and a difference from the narratives of first-generation immigrants discussed in the previous chapters – in the ways they portray the city as an inhabited space. To state the obvious, these recent novels are distinguished by the fact that their young protagonists' parents are present in London at all; although most of the first-generation authors also centre their narratives on young people, parents are either unrepresented entirely or at least absent from London – back home in the (post)colony. However, as in Srivastava's *Transmission*, novels of the 1990s by writers born in the 1950s, 1960s, and 1970s frequently confine the parents they do include to a lesser narrative status that baldly emphasizes intergenerational difference.

Specifically, while young protagonists are shown on the move and on the make in the metropolitan cityscape – dynamically interacting in the public spaces of streets, clubs, schools, or workplaces – the parents are often, like Angie's, relegated to private, domestic space as the comparatively static representatives of cultural tradition. In Diran Adebayo's *Some Kind of Black* (1996), for instance, the protagonist is 'a Londoner yet to set foot in his home country' of Nigeria (29). At Oxford and then on the streets of a multicultural London that seems 'more tribalistic than it used to be' (104), Dele embarks on a complex process of exploring his black British identity through interactions with racist police, black activists and schemers, and various white and black sexual partners. His parents, worn out after years in London by 'the toll of the struggle,' are always seen at home except when they visit his sister in hospital, and 'whenever Dele returned home, it seemed that time had stood still' (42). The autocratic, Bible-thumping father, with his 'implicit regard for authority' (80), is a virtual caricature of the paterfamilias as blocking figure. He angrily and sometimes violently (but ultimately ineffectually) challenges Dele's every deviation from what his Nigerian values and metropolitan hard knocks have taught him is the route to a success and happiness he himself could never achieve. As a foil to Dele's more fluid identity, the father is saved from rigid two-dimensionality only by the memories of

Nigerian 'triumphs' and London 'indignit[ies]' he shares as 'inchoate intimacies' while Dele pulls out his grey hairs (44).

Both of these first novels by young writers establish a gulf between generations that corresponds to a set of interrelated binaries. The stay-at-home parents represent tradition and the past; their house is the familiar but unchanging *place* from which the younger generation, without severing ties completely, must escape in favour of the street – the liberation into future opportunities available in and represented by the city as fluid, transformative *space*. Members of the parental first generation, for whom the promise of an open and accommodating Britain was largely betrayed, are shown in a kind of spatial and psychological retreat. They are nostalgic, cautious voices newly (if shallowly) rooted in the metropolitan dwelling that represents their only site of continuity and control, a fortress against the affronts to cultural identity and dignity they constantly endure as a function of their precarious perches on the nation's margin. The more assimilated second generation, raised in the metropolis, are the objects of greater narrative interest because they are the ones with stories to tell. Their urban existence involves not a hardening around the past but rather discovery, emergence, risk, and real-world conflict. In addition to *Transmission* and *Some Kind of Black*, a version of this binary can also be found in Courttia Newland's first novel, *The Scholar* (1997), in which two black teenaged cousins are drawn into a bleak street-scene of drugs, guns, and crime while the well-meaning single mother who looks after them plays a small, home-bound role characterized by mounting poverty and obliviousness to the boys' dangerous entanglements. It can also be found in Andrea Levy's *Never Far from Nowhere* (1996), where the Jamaican single mother of two teenaged girls is an increasingly shrill voice chastising them (from the security of her kitchen) for their reckless adventures and social mistakes. In both books, the minimal claim to the city to which the older generation seems resigned is once again conveyed both socially and spatially; any hope (even when it is tragically wasted), and any real sense of engaged metropolitan belonging, are with the mobile young.

These fast-paced narratives of young black Londoners – and subsequent novels by the same authors as well as Meera Syal, Alex Wheatle, and others[2] – make for compelling reading and provide some fascinating insights into urban subcultures. But their London, for all its social complexity, is typically not the transnational city – the temporally and spatially relational space – that their Commonwealth predecessors discovered and novelized. Sidelining the world outside London as much as (or more than) they sideline the parental generation that represents it, focused on the present tenses of young characters swept up in the tense present, many of these novels correspondingly neglect to examine the contexts – historical, geographical, political, psychological – behind the racial and cultural themes they raise. As Kwame Dawes writes in connection with Newland's and Adebayo's first books, they show 'a strange uncertainty about how to locate this black British experience in the larger British world'; they lack 'any critical exploration of why things are as they are' (23, 22). Despite the confidence with which such narratives lay claim to a transforming urban landscape and society, they do so with temporal and spatial blinkers.

It is notable, then, that the two most celebrated and important 'black British' novels from the late twentieth century do reach out to the world in a way that contextualizes and complicates their young protagonists' stories. The London of Hanif Kureishi's *The Buddha of Suburbia* (1990) and Zadie Smith's *White Teeth* (2000) is transnational in large measure because the narratives are multigenerational. These first novels are as fully and sympathetically engaged with the metropolitan experiences of the parents' generation as with those of the younger characters. Both writers were born in London – Kureishi in 1954, Smith in 1975 – and have one white British parent and one 'New Commonwealth' parent: Kureishi's father is Pakistani, Smith's mother is Jamaican. Each novel features a young character with a corresponding family, and it is through the detailed scrutiny of familial relations that these narratives portray London as both familiar and unfamiliar. It emerges as a city whose transnational dimensions and transhistorical connections are woven, in varied and surprising ways, into the fabric of its residents' lives, whether first- or second-generation, 'black British' or white.[3]

The Semi-Detached Metropolis

Before he published *The Buddha of Suburbia*, Hanif Kureishi's screenplays for the films *My Beautiful Laundrette* (1986) and *Sammy and Rosie Get Laid* (1988) established his thematic preoccupations. All three narratives dramatize contradictory images of London through conflicts among racial groups and among different generations and economic classes within the same group. All three, in different ways, display the gaps opened up by perceptions of London as both a local and a transnational space. Taken together, they render a metropolis of increasing spatial, racial, and intergenerational complexity. Indeed, like the houses of the

South London suburbs in which Kureishi grew up and in which his novel is partly set, this London is semi-detached (which means it is also semi-attached) – from the nation and its ideas of Britishness, and from the global space beyond. 'I'm no Britisher, but a Londoner,' writes Kureishi in a published diary ('Some' 133); 'Neither of us are English, we're Londoners you see,' says Sammy in *Sammy and Rosie Get Laid* (234). And when Kureishi revises T.S. Eliot's famous catalogue of British culture[4] to include 'yoga exercises, going to Indian restaurants, the music of Bob Marley, the novels of Salman Rushdie, Zen Buddhism, the Hare Krishna Temple, as well as the films of Sylvester Stallone, therapy, hamburgers, visits to gay bars, the dole office and the taking of drugs' ('Bradford' 168–9), what he calls 'British people' (168) sound closer to Londoners than to Welsh miners or Norfolk farmers. Kureishi's London is a cosmopolitan space not fully attached to or detached from either British nation-space or transnational world-space. It hovers interstitially between the two.

Moose and Genghis, the disenfranchised and reactionary white louts of *My Beautiful Laundrette*, articulate a rough version of postimperial Britain's anxieties about immigrants. The film's central conflict pits these thugs against Omar, the Indian-English entrepreneur. Unemployed and feeling threatened by peoples who once came to Britain 'to work for us' (73), Genghis conflates race and class when he rejects the idea of a white boy (one of 'us') working under an upwardly mobile South Asian (one of 'them'). He furthermore conflates race and nation in his assumption of an England that properly belongs to whites: 'Get back to the jungle, wog boy,' he snarls at Omar (62). But Omar's employment of Johnny as a white man Friday shows that, even in what Rushdie calls 'The New Empire within Britain' (*Imaginary* 129), the tables can be turned on the racialized hierarchies of labour that obtained in imperial space.

The London that Omar invents for himself mediates the polarized views of his uncle and his father, both first-generation immigrants. Uncle Nasser, the businessman, sees London as a space of opportunity, 'a little heaven' where 'you can get anything you want ... [if you] know how to squeeze the tits of the system' (106, 48). His pragmatism elides issues of racial identity; he says, 'There's no race question in the new enterprise culture' (77). This attitude ignores a racial element that did indeed accompany Margaret Thatcher's notion of the '"enterprise culture"': Dick Hebdige argues that the hard-working, decent, entrepreneurial Britain Thatcher envisaged was pitted explicitly against what she called '"enemies without and within,"' a broad category that included 'agitators,' lazy '"scroungers"' unwilling to work, and 'unassimilable ethnic minorities' (130). In contrast to the optimistic (and quite assimilated) Nasser, his brother Hussein, Omar's father, is a dissolute, disillusioned socialist who feels that 'we are under siege by the white man': 'this damn country has done us in' (50, 105). But his grumpy radicalism has some blind spots; in his disappointment at Omar the 'underpants cleaner' who will 'kiss their arses and think of yourself as a little Britisher' (90, 58), he appears not to grasp the significance of Omar's reclamation of Johnny. Like the Indians once recruited by British imperialist armies to keep order among their fellows and protect British institutions, Johnny is hired in part to shield Omar and his laundrette from hostile elements of London society. Omar takes on the mantle of Nasser's 'enterprise culture' with a social agenda worthy of his father: 'I want big money. I'm not gonna be beat down by this country. When we were at school, you and your lot kicked me all round the place. And what are you doing now? Washing my floor. That's how I like it' (88).

Omar may never lead the grand working-class revolution his father desires, but on a local level he successfully challenges the dominant social order. Kwame Anthony Appiah defines 'the *post-* in postcolonial' as a 'space-clearing gesture' (348); with his spruced-up laundrette, Omar clears and reinvents a postcolonial space in the middle (if not the centre) of the old imperial metropolis. At the end of the film this space is under siege, a sure sign of its significance. And if there is an ironic gap between the laundrette and an equivalent power-base in colonial time-space – say, a government house or regional headquarters – in a new world order that has cashed in 'political imperialism' for the 'economic, monetary and commercial controls' of neo-imperialism (Williams 283), it is fitting that the space of occupation be a small, coin-oriented business. The washing machine's process of cleansing by agitation is oddly suitable as well. Moreover, with Omar poised to take over more laundrettes, and with Johnny's crisis of loyalties resolved, the playful splashing of the final scene hints at a new order to come in this microeconomy – one that could replace the vengeful satisfaction of Omar as boss and Johnny as boy with a more equitable partnership inspired by the mutuality of erotic love.

Kureishi's first film delineates spatial boundaries that may be either transgressed or shored up in the name of urban resistance and transformation. Johnny's story represents both possibilities: from squatting on private property to helping Nasser turf out squatters and Omar secure his laundrette. David Harvey, after Henri Lefebvre, sees 'a permanent tension between the *appropriation* and use of space for individual and social purposes and the *domination* of space' by institutionalized forms of power (*Urban* 177). Kureishi uses a small number of very localized spaces to tip the balance implied in that binary towards the former. By 'using' London in Michel de Certeau's liberatory sense, Kureishi's characters support a vision of the city as a composite of individual actions and subcommunities. As Harvey notes, such uses allow disenfranchised or minority groups to establish power bases and so contribute to the building and changing of the city (see *Urban* 241).

While the visual mode of *My Beautiful Laundrette* is unadorned, low-budget naturalism, *Sammy and Rosie Get Laid* is more surreal and stylized, more given to spectacle and incongruity. In part this is a function of its opening out to a broader visual and spatial canvas, an expanded urban landscape. But it also seems to represent a shifting concept of place – of where and what 'London' *is*. In such big scenes as the riot, 'the "fuck" night' ('Some' 181), and the clearing of the waste ground, Kureishi (with the director, Stephen Frears) makes London a site of romanticized urban rituals and showy events; the central characters parade through these with an eerie detachment and sense of normality. Kureishi signals an awareness of the city as an enabling space for theatricality and artifice – a vision he develops further in *The Buddha of Suburbia*.

Thematically his second film, like his first, explores incompatible visions of London. The discrepancies between such visions are often grotesquely ironic. Sammy's description of metropolitan life as blissful weekend walks, bookshop browsing, and lectures on semiotics creates an idyllic image of freedom that seems almost vulgar beside the scenes of mob violence and police in riot gear. But it has precedents: colonial administrators often experienced a similarly disconnected lifestyle and sense of place. The film's central images of derelict neighbourhoods and homeless gypsies, of aggro and violence, revise the imperial metropolis remembered (or imagined) by Sammy's father. For Rafi, 'my beloved London ... is the centre of civilization – tolerant, intelligent and completely out of control now, I hear' (206). If that postscript implies some awareness that London is not what it purportedly was, Rafi's story in the film is still bound up with his mistaken belief that by migrating to London he can be as free as his son and can therefore escape the consequences of faraway political activities.

He is, inevitably, proved wrong. Like the narrator in Amitav Ghosh's *The Shadow Lines*, he is forced to abandon his faith in 'the reality of nations and borders' and the separateness of distant places (Ghosh 214).

Now that the old empire (the 'New Commonwealth') is compressed into London, how can the metropolis be a haven set apart from the forces that disturb his peace and threaten his life in the unnamed country (probably Pakistan) where he tortured and killed? In a city that has absorbed so many elements of his former nation, he must confront political enemies and endure haunting by ghosts from his past, almost as if he were back home. Distant places have become merged. Early on Rafi wittily acknowledges London as a transnational space: 'Is this world war typical of your streets?' (203); 'You can have the money provided you buy yourself a house in a part of England that hasn't been twinned with Beirut!' (213). At the end, the convergence of the world upon his metropolitan space of retreat hems him in and prompts his suicide. The space-clearing scene on the waste ground just before his death symbol-izes Rafi's homelessness in a London emptied out of the kind of neutral zones where he might live peacefully, suggestively connecting his plight with that of 'inner city' Londoners unhoused by Thatcher's government.

London in *Sammy and Rosie Get Laid* is a more spatially differentiated city than in *My Beautiful Laundrette.* The 'inner city' takes on special resonance as 'a mass of fascination' that Sammy and Rosie refuse to leave, even when Rafi offers financial incentive. 'It's cosmopolitan, Pop,' says Sammy, defending his choice: 'Leonardo da Vinci would have lived in the inner city' (211). Ironically, its cosmopolitanism makes the centre's centre especially detached from a traditional British ethnic-national space. As the geographer Anthony King observes, 'the closer one moves to the centre of Greater London, the smaller the proportion of the population born in the UK' (*Global* 141); these demographics cause the inner city to be stereotyped as a '*black* inner city, characterized by lawless-ness and vice' and contrasted with the mythic real England located in the 'pure space' of the countryside (Sibley 42, 108). In the inner city one encounters the 'London' that most resembles and includes the ethnic diversity of 'the world.' It is here – in Sammy and Rosie's home and among their cosmopolitan friends, down the street from a flat where a white policeman kills an innocent black woman – that London first disagrees with Rafi. The peaceful space he seeks is really more 'England' than 'London,' and his best chance of finding it would seem to be in the suburbs, at the home of his old lover, Alice.

In Kureishi's view, 'England is primarily a suburban country and English values are suburban values' ('Some' 163). Historically, modern suburbia began in London (see Fishman 18–72); it developed in the eighteenth century during the early stages of high imperialism. While

Britain's armies and capital were reaching out to the far corners of the earth, its cities expanded by what one historian calls 'colonizations of growing territories' (Thompson 11).[5] Suburbia became a hybrid space between nature and community, country and city; if the semi-detached house was invented 'to produce scaled down and watered down versions of aristocratic [country] housing arrangements suited to smaller incomes,' it was also an emblem of success for those who moved there from the city (9, 2). Suburbia's spatial in-betweenness has a temporal corollary: it can represent the 'undefined present' caught between 'an image of the past' that Raymond Williams identifies with the country and 'an image of the future' he associates with the city (297). Alice therefore belongs in suburban space: she is an apparently idle representative of a faded gentry, a child of the Raj in its twilight suspended between a past she cannot abandon and a future that passes her by. Hers is a space caught between 'country' and 'city' – where 'country' connotes the past, colonial India, 'old England,' Rafi as her lover; and 'city' connotes the future, the 'world metropolis,' Sammy and Rosie's new England, Rafi returning too late. Any hope Rafi has of finding sanctuary with her is based only on the first part of this binary. But finally Alice's accumulated bitterness ensures that Rafi's past private life will return just as his past public life does – not to comfort or accommodate him but to haunt him and displace him.

This complex spatial differentiation of the metropolis is elaborated further in *The Buddha of Suburbia*. Karim describes himself as 'an Englishman born and bred ..., from the South London suburbs and going somewhere' (3). To say this much is already to challenge the view of H.G. Wells (one of Karim's idols) that the unfinished space of suburbia is composed of 'roads that lead nowhere' (Wells 41). Of course, Wells tells only half the story: even where the physical roads are aimless dead-ends, suburbia since it began has been a place from which to commute into town every day. However, spatial-literal movement (travelling) is not the same as social mobility ('going somewhere'), which may or may not require a trip. When Karim insists that 'our suburbs were a leaving place' he means both, and has something grander in mind than a commute: namely, 'the start of a life' (117). His leaving is a one-way journey, a permanent relocation in a new and stimulating urban space. The city is a space of discovery, experience, indulgence, and consumption called 'London'; in this semiotic geography, Bromley and the other outer suburbs are not 'London' but the equivalent of Williams's 'country': the past one leaves behind, the 'birth' that gives way to the city's 'learning'

(Williams 7). Karim's move from the suburbs to 'London proper' becomes a local, miniaturized version of postcolonial migrancy and culture
shock – the move from ex-colony (country) to metropolis (city). This
London not only includes 'the world' in the sense of peoples, it also
(as 'Greater London') replicates within its borders the world's spatial
patterning.

The novel is full of remarks that reflect its overlaying of analogous
global space on local metropolitan space. Three examples will serve as
illustration. First, Karim's early impressions of London expose a gap of
difference that seems unbridgeable: 'In London the kids looked fabu-
lous; they dressed and walked and talked like little gods. We could have
been from Bombay. We'd never catch up' (127–8). Second, his and
Charlie's sense of inferiority is rooted in a centre-envy they felt in the
suburbs, where 'to have an elder brother who lived in London and
worked in fashion, music or advertising was an inestimable advantage at
school' (8). Third, when Eva, like Karim, journeys to inner London, she
seeks 'to scour that suburban stigma right off her body,' but Karim sees
through her: 'She didn't realize it was in the blood and not on the skin;
she didn't see there could be nothing more suburban than suburbanites
repudiating themselves' (134). Beneath the surface of each of these
passages lies a clever intercontinental analogy. And while each parallel
implies a spatial reduction – a squeezing of physical scale – there is a
corresponding reduction of dimension that generates irony. Dynamics
of difference that in contexts of colonialism and postcolonial migrancy
hinge on matters of race, hegemony, culture, and capital shrink down in
metropolitan space to the ephemeral realms of fashion and style, of pop
culture, image-making, and the abstractions of what Pierre Bourdieu
calls 'symbolic capital' (171). In the first passage, Karim's observation
recalls the colonialist's assertion of racial, cultural, and religious superiority, but dilutes it to an image of two impressionable teenagers admiring
the glittering surfaces of stylistic others who resemble 'gods.' The second
example implicitly takes colonial and postcolonial societies' awe of the
Oxbridge-educated 'been-to' and recasts it as the second-hand glory
reflected by a relative who works in trendy, image-driven professions in
town. And third, if Eva's desire to shed her suburban skin resembles
processes of acculturation, assimilation, or deracination that many immigrants undergo, Karim's claim that the suburbs are 'in the blood and not
on the skin' is a deliberately outrageous appropriation of race-politics
language to describe a bored suburbanite's makeover.

Bromley equals Bombay: such ironic conflations of spaces and processes are characteristic of London in at least one way. The city has become deindustrialized; where once it manufactured ships and telephones and clothing and food, London now orients its economy towards the intangible products and services of high finance, tourism, fashion, advertising, marketing, and culture. As King remarks, 'Increasingly, investment is put into changing consciousness rather than producing goods' (*Global* 119). This reorientation from solid thing to abstract image, from the spatially substantial to the spatially insubstantial, mirrors the direction of Kureishi's ironic translations. His 'London' thus becomes a site compatible with some influential concepts of postmodernity: Jean Baudrillard's 'simulacrum' as the replica of the vanishing 'real'; Fredric Jameson's 'depthlessness' as an aesthetic consequence of late capitalist commodification; David Harvey's 'time-space compression' as the annihilation of boundaries that technology and multinational capital can accomplish.[6] *The Buddha of Suburbia* is not a postmodern fiction, but it does depict the move downtown as a journey into postmodern space, and this generates important ironies between the local and transcontinental versions of migration the book depicts.

For instance, when Karim's father, Haroon, moved from Bombay to Greater London, he left a quasi-aristocratic freedom for a workaday prison: 'His life, once a cool river of balmy distraction, of beaches and cricket, ... was now a cage of umbrellas and steely regularity' (26). After adjusting to his reduced circumstances, Haroon 'spent years trying to be more of an Englishman, to be less risibly conspicuous' (21). Karim, by contrast, finds his small-scale migration from Bromley to London to be a release from imprisoning adolescence into adult freedom. And while his father became an acculturated Englishman, Karim the 'Englishman born and bred' gets in touch with his Indian origins. However, his embrace of an ethnicity that had been a childhood burden takes place on the level not of identity but of artifice and image – performing Kipling's Mowgli and his own imitation of Changez on stage. Likewise, Haroon's second 'migration' – also from the suburbs to downtown – corresponds with his metamorphosis into a 'Buddha' with an exaggerated Indian accent and a salmagundi of Eastern mystical platitudes. Father and son both become faux-Indians, successfully marketing back to the English warmed-over versions of their own popular appropriations of Indian culture. In this collapsed 'world' in downtown London – a world of parody, pastiche, simultaneity, and simulacrum – they are no more authentically Indian in their roles than Charlie is authentically punk or Eva authentically artsy. But when the image takes over from the actual, when notions of authenticity and inauthenticity fall by the wayside (see Jameson, 'Postmodernism' 62), the artificiality may not matter.

Or does it? Amid all this parodic duplication and reduplication, one important difference is preserved. Karim and Haroon pursue similar goals of freedom, education, fulfilment of desire, and exploitation of ethnic identity in their journeys to the postmodern world city, but elsewhere in the novel the first and second generations are not so easily synchronized. The standoff between the traditional father Anwar and his Westernized daughter Jamila may parodically mimic Gandhi, but Anwar's hunger strike is a sincere act. However absurd and dislocated it may look, it reflects the real pain and crisis of a physical migration that did not coincide with psychic migration. Anwar's return to his origins is of a different order from Karim's or Haroon's. Without leaving the suburbs, he returns 'internally to India' as a way of 'resisting the English here' (64). He does not want an actual trip home, but by imposing his traditional authority on Jamila he combats (successfully if only symbolically) his daughter's assimilation. However pathetic (and unsatisfying even to him) his coercion may be, its integrity and time-honoured cultural grounding give it an old-fashioned air of authenticity.

The man he insists his daughter marry, the hapless Changez, represents a different response to the crisis of first-generation migrancy. Changez, as his name suggests, changes his expectations of marriage and revises his performance of masculinity to suit the surprises metropolitan life has in store. But there is a pain underlying his comic transformations that bursts out on occasion and makes clear the degree to which his experience of migration – particularly the depth of feeling and self-examination it provokes – differs from that of his peer Karim. For all their surface resemblances (centre-to-margin trajectory, pursuit of sexual pleasure, challenge to conventional gender relations), there is a crucial difference: Karim has a freedom to make choices (including sleeping with Jamila) that Changez does not have. Once he arrives in London to the dismay of the family that invited him, Changez must either conform to or resist the limited options Anwar and Jamila resentfully place on his sloping shoulders. Though he cheerfully makes the most of his rejection, his liberty to satisfy desires and construct his own identity is vastly compromised by comparison with Karim, who is 'ready for anything' and good at getting it (3, 121).

Kureishi's multigenerational narrative therefore contrasts the intercontinental and the intra-urban migratory experiences that it so provocatively and playfully analogizes. The former, as exemplified by Anwar,

Changez, and the young Haroon, produce deep pain, confusion, and crises of identities. The latter, as performed by Karim, Charlie, Eva, and the older Haroon, result in sensual pleasures, cunning, and the exploitation of identity as a fabricated image. Through counterpoint and juxtaposition, each keeps the other in perspective, and dimensionality starts to look like a function of mileage. *The Buddha of Suburbia* therefore qualifies and ironizes the author's previous constructions of London as an enabling space inclusive of peoples and processes that represent 'the world.' However cosmopolitan it may seem, however demographically greater than Britain, Kureishi's 'London' may also flatten that world into a spectacle. Though seeming to compress world-space, it cannot substitute for the world since there will always be psychic and geographical gaps that only the real traversing of cultural and physical distance can overcome. Anwar's folly and Changez's pain could have been avoided if Anwar had made a real rather than imaginary journey home and met his prospective son-in-law first. And only in London does Haroon's Buddha routine have any exchange value; in Bombay he might trade on his Englishness, but not his self-help spiritualism.

Among the provocative images Karim uses to describe his London – a 'playground' (196); 'a house with five thousand rooms' in which 'the kick was to work out how they connected, and eventually to walk through all of them' (126) – is the comparison of the city to a shabby theatre: 'As your buttocks were being punished on steel and plastic chairs you'd look across grey floorboards at minimal scenery, maybe four chairs and a kitchen table set among a plain of broken bottles and bomb-sites, a boiling world with dry ice floating over the choking audience. London, in other words' (207). As seen in the previous chapter, South Asian writers regularly analogize the experience of London to that of the theatre, and in doing so they continue a long tradition. Peter Ackroyd lists a host of commentators from previous centuries (including Wordsworth, Lamb, Boswell, and Dickens) for whom 'the theatricality of London is its single most important characteristic' (152). *The Buddha of Suburbia*, with its various theatre scenes and people, its preoccupation with watching and being watched, and its potent contrasts between shrunk-down local and expansive global scales, imagined and actual journeys, performative and authentic identities, pleasurable and painful experiences, is a theatrical novel on many levels. Like the Dickensian film-set in *The Satanic Verses*, the theatre as artificial, miniaturized representation of the world is the presiding image that captures Kureishi's metropolis. His London is a theatrical space where value derives as much

from seeming as from being, where one can travel the world while sitting
still without ever quite forgetting that the 'real world' outside is a very
different and distant place.

Route Canals

In an article on Hanif Kureishi, Bart Moore-Gilbert writes, 'Insofar as the
nuclear family has been so often equated with the nation in earlier
discourses of "Englishness" – especially, perhaps, in the war-time films of
the 1940s – the fact that Kureishi characteristically represents it as dysfunctional, and sympathetically presents alternatives to it, such as Jamila's
commune, is highly significant' (194). Kureishi's models of the family
are more than simply 'alternative': his portraits of homosexual couples
(Omar and Johnny), childless interracial couples (Sammy and Rosie),
extramarital affairs (Haroun and Eva), unconsummated marriages
(Changez and Jamila), and bisexual pleasure-seeking (Karim, Charlie)
subvert all the conventions – what some discourses would call the moral
foundations – of the traditional British family. Even so, Kureishi's early
work is consistently focused on the family as a crucible in which the
explosive differences that animate the wider national society can be
isolated and combined. Using irony and humour to tease out the
points of connection and separation between different generations'
experiences of metropolitan life, he creates a richer social portrait of
the immigrants' London than do most of his 'black British' peers.
Without sacrificing their ability to convey the kinetic energy, confidence, and newness of the second generation, he casts the peripatetic
urban lives of young Londoners in sharp relief by showing the temporal, geographical, and psychological distance other family members
have journeyed.

Zadie Smith gives similar pride of place to families in *White Teeth*, her
ambitious exploration of late twentieth-century multicultural London.
Though largely set in the suburban North London where Smith herself
was born and raised – it ventures into central London only occasionally –
her novel nonetheless positions its families within an even wider spatial
and temporal field, contextualizing their metropolitan present through
narrative excursions in its three 'Root Canal' chapters to India (the 1857
mutiny), Jamaica (a 1907 earthquake), and Eastern Europe (1945 at the
end of the war). Indeed, of all the recent 'black British' novels, it makes
the most concerted effort to sympathetically represent the experiences
of characters from more than one generation and place of origin. A

novel of intricate and often surprising relations among white, brown, and black Londoners, *White Teeth* begins thematically from the concept of 'involvement': the entanglement of the English with specific groups of others that the British Empire inaugurated and the postimperial metropolis continues to effect. Like Kureishi, Smith generates a variety of different kinds of personal relations – emotional, sexual, familial, intellectual, friendly – spanning traditional divisions – race, culture, age. Through the interpersonal, she analogizes broader patterns of sociohistorical involvement.

The analogy is reinforced explicitly in several passages. At the end of 'the century of the great immigrant experiment,' she writes, 'despite all the mixing up, despite the fact that we have finally slipped into each other's lives with reasonable comfort (like a man returning to his lover's bed after a midnight walk), despite all this, it is still hard to admit sometimes that there is no one more English than the Indian, no one more Indian than the English' (281, 282). When Captain Durham fails to rescue his Jamaican lover Ambrosia from the 1907 earthquake, it is not because 'he doesn't love her (oh, he *loves* her; just as the English loved India and Africa and Ireland; it is the love that is the problem, people treat their lovers badly)' (311). And at one point Smith, through the consciousness of the Bengali immigrant Alsana Iqbal, performs an extended riff on the word 'involved':

> Sometimes, here in England, especially at bus-stops and on the daytime soaps, you heard people say 'We're *involved* with each other,' as if this were a most wonderful state to be in, as if one chose it and enjoyed it. Alsana never thought of it that way. *Involved* happened over a long period of time, pulling you in like quicksand. ... Involved is neither good, nor bad. It is just a consequence of living, a consequence of occupation and immigration, of empires and expansion, of living in each other's pockets ... one becomes involved and it is a long trek back to being uninvolved. ... [People] walk IN and they get trapped between the revolving doors of those two *v*'s. *Involved.* The years pass, and the mess accumulates and here we are. Your brother's sleeping with my ex-wife's niece's second cousin. *Involved.* Just a tired, inevitable fact. (376; second ellipsis in original)

The 'revolving doors of those two *v*'s' suggests that 'involved' may or may not include 'love' (i.e. as *invloved*), depending on which way the doors settle. With her next metaphor, the accumulated 'mess,' Smith implies that years of mutual involvement (romantic, colonial, metropolitan) have produced a legacy of heaped-up stuff – a history – so oppressively out of control and in the way that it should be swept up.

Indeed, an important thematic trajectory within the novel advocates exactly such space clearing. Seventeen-year-old Irie Jones, whose parentage and year of birth correspond to Zadie Smith's, rails against the Jones and Iqbal families' penchant for wallowing in history, which she sees as the main cause of their dysfunctionality. She longs to live, as she believes the Chalfen family does, in 'neutral spaces. And not this endless maze of present rooms and past rooms and all the things said in them years ago and everybody's old historical shit all over the place. ... And every single fucking day is not this huge battle between who they are and who they should be, what they were and what they will be. ... No shit in attics. No skeletons in cupboards. No great-grandfathers' (440). She rails, in other words, against allowing past involvements to overdetermine present and future ones. A review of *White Teeth* in the *Economist* claims that Smith herself, like Irie, 'can't wait to be shot of the past,' and therefore that 'the real spark of the book is not post-colonial, but post-post-colonial. The younger generation – which is where Ms Smith is – has had history; they couldn't give an f-word for it' ('Pulling'). But if Smith really wanted to clear away the messy legacy of history, she would have written a novel more like those of the majority of her 'black British' peers: enamoured of the contemporary, mostly empty of the parents and worldly contexts that can sociohistorically situate fin-de-millennium London lives.

Her novel, by contrast, is packed with history and geography, with time and space, with complexities and unlikely (often ironic) connections. Her suburban London is inescapably transnational and steeped in the history of its (now more than ever) multicultural people. Kwame Appiah, as noted above, calls 'the *post-* in postcolonial' a 'space-clearing gesture ... concerned with transcending, with going beyond, coloniality' (348); this is an accurate definition, but it is important to add that the space metaphorically cleared by postcolonial theorists (and in texts labelled postcolonial) is not a space outside history. On the contrary, it is a space that has been cleared of the old imperial-colonial ideologies and concepts of ethnic-racial entitlement through which history used to be framed. The postcolonial still, as the word suggests, includes and foregrounds the history and aftermath of colonialism, but it hopes to view that messy and complicated inheritance – the fact that, as Appiah goes on to write, 'we are all already contaminated by each other' (354) – from alternative perspectives. The *Economist* reviewer implies that there is an uncontaminated, history-free 'post-post-colonial' space to which Zadie

Smith points the way. But the novel routinely undercuts the hopes of its characters for a 'neutral' or 'final' space. It refuses to endorse the various impetuses within it towards liberation from history and mutual influence, even as it distances itself firmly from suggestions that history determines or controls the present – or that the present determines or controls the future. With these thematic cross-currents, Smith deftly negotiates a vision of London, and the diverse lives it includes, as laden with a history whose impact on the present and future is unavoidable but also unpredictable, capricious, even accidental. Just as the postcolonial cannot get completely outside colonialism's long shadow, Smith's narrative and its metropolitan setting can only comprehend any 'post-post-colonial' possibilities from amidst the cluttered relationality of a postcolonial perspective that is far from clear of 'historical shit.'

The novel's major events and motifs (including the ubiquitous shit) cumulatively support its vision of mutually contaminated lives intimately interwoven with each other and with the past. In the opening scene, when Archie tries to remove himself from history, to determine his absence from the future, his choice of location – a 'nasty urban street' rather than 'some pleasant, distant woodland' – thwarts his plan (3). He inhales carbon monoxide in what Marc Augé would call one of 'supermodernity''s quintessential 'non-places' (96). 'Squeezed between an almighty concrete cinema complex at one end and a giant intersection at the other,' Smith writes, 'Cricklewood Broadway was no kind of place. It was not a place a man came to die. It was a place a man came in order to go other places via the A41' (3). But if this site is more space than place, as such it points relationally to an infinite number of preferable elsewheres, which in turn imply a future in which they might be visited (via the A41). As Yi-Fu Tuan writes, space 'suggests the future and invites action' (54); Archie will unexpectedly gain the future his coin-toss had ruled out because even here, alone in his car, he is not removed from happenstance and serendipity – from connection. In Smith's rather cheeky explanation, 'Whilst he slipped in and out of consciousness, the position of the planets, the music of the spheres, the flap of a tiger-moth's diaphanous wings in Central Africa, and a whole bunch of other stuff that Makes Shit Happen had decided it was second-chance time for Archie' (4). The 'shit' in question is literal; it is the random placement of pigeon droppings on a nearby halal butcher's shop that saves Archie for a future in which he may not travel far, but he will be 'transformed' (20), and over time his actions (past, present, and future) will make a lot happen.

His unlikely relationship with Clara begins 'by accident' that same New Year's Day (20); he 'quite indiscriminately chooses a route' that leads to their meeting (16), and she too has entered a new future by breaking with Ryan Topps and the Jehovah's Witness faith whose end-of-the-world prophecy has just been disproved. Like the Jamaican earthquake, which felt like 'the world was ending that afternoon in Kingston' but which coincided with the birth of Clara's mother (311), the concatenation of Archie's and Clara's reprieved futures at the outset of her narrative establishes Smith's penchant for twisting endings into beginnings by fusing the planned-for (suicide, apocalypse, childbirth) to the arbitrary and accidental (where pigeons choose to defecate, where Archie randomly wanders, when an earthquake happens). She does it again at the end: Marcus and Magid's FutureMouse project is launched (fittingly, it turns out, on New Year's Eve) as the epitome of the hyper-planned and controlled future. Through genetic engineering, they have mapped out the next seven years of the mouse's development, which is to be closely studied. But here too the random human element throws a spanner in the works – this time through the confluence of Millat's deviation from KEVIN's protest plan and Archie's response to the surprise reappearance of 'Dr Sick.' The mouse escapes in the ensuing commotion, free to live its pre-programmed life where it will. An experiment in total planning and control – in the elimination of genes' unpredictable effects on biological outcomes – is contaminated and destroyed by unforeseeable external factors.

From another perspective, however, these same disruptive factors do have causes, and the causes are by definition located in the past, in history. But this (determining) history is itself defined by the arbitrary choice: Archie's 1945 coin-flip to decide Dr Sick's fate, and Samad's tortuous decision about which twin to keep and which to send to Bangladesh. Choices and actions have long-term consequences, as the doctor pleads with young Archie, but those consequences are infinite in their possibilities. As Samad tells Archie in 1945, 'Our children will be born of our actions. *Our accidents will become their destinies*' (88). Shortly thereafter, he urges Archie to kill the doctor – to intervene in history and the future – so the two men can have 'blood on [their] hands' and atone for their lacklustre contribution to the war (102). Samad seems oblivious to the vast contradiction between his desire to play God and both his Islamic beliefs – 'that essentially we are weak, that we are not in control, ... I surrender to God,' as he later declaims (249) – and his main objection to Dr Sick's eugenics: that 'he wants to control, to dictate the future' (102). Samad's belief that Archie did kill the scientist cements their friendship and leads to their later reunion in London and the mutual involvement of their wives and children. Their shared 'history,' of course, is false; its falseness is revealed only as a consequence of the unfolding history of the younger generation's interfamilial relations. And so the ironies proliferate.

Smith's densely intricate narrative interconnections work feverishly to simultaneously reinforce and ironically complicate the relations between history and destiny, choice and consequence, accident and design.[7] The Glenard School's Victorian origins as a workhouse in which its colonial benefactor's (ultimately failed) interracial educational experiments took place inspires its present-day headmaster to propose a similar interracial educational experiment; the resulting involvement of Irie and Millat with the Chalfens helps bring about the ultimate failure of Marcus's FutureMouse experiment. Samad's twin-splitting experiment also fails. His attempt to control the future – to guarantee Magid's development of a piously Islamic cultural identity (a scheme cooked up, ironically, in the time-storing, unchanging environs of O'Connell's) – backfires as Magid becomes 'a pukka Englishman' and Millat a 'fully paid-up, green bow-tie wearing fundamentalist terrorist' (349). Moreover, despite years of physical separation and cultural disentanglement, the twins' destinies continue to become interleaved so that when they are reunited in a neutral place, 'they make a mockery of that idea, a neutral place; instead they cover the room with history – past, present and future history (for there is such a thing) – they take what was blank and smear it with the stinking shit of the past like excitable, excremental children. They cover this neutral room in themselves. Every gripe, the earliest memories, every debated principle, every contested belief' (397). This messy outcome has been anticipated during the initial search for such a room; here the narrator extends the idea of the past's inescapability to the city as a whole:

> A neutral place. The chances of finding one these days are slim. ... The sheer *quantity* of shit that must be wiped off the slate if we are to start again as new. Race. Land. Ownership. Faith. Theft. Blood. And more blood. And more. And not only must the *place* be neutral, but the messenger who takes you to the place, and the messenger who sends the messenger. There are no people or places like that left in North London. (391–2)

By extension, the city itself can never be neutral, and so it is fitting that the sterile 'final space' near Trafalgar Square in which the FutureMouse is launched should become contaminated by the accidental consequences of history.

Through its heady meditations and plot machinations involving the caprices of history and time, *White Teeth* layers a original set of transgenerational contexts into its more familiar themes of immigrant identity and belonging. When Samad resists England's acculturating power and imposes homeland values on his children only to have his hopes dashed, his story recalls Kureishi's Anwar. When the narrator announces, 'This has been the century of strangers, brown, yellow and white[,] ... the century of the great immigrant experiment' (281), Salman Rushdie echoes clearly.[8] When Irie thinks of England as 'a giant mirror' in which she is 'without reflection' and longs to '*merge* with' the Chalfens' Englishness (230, 283), or when the culturally hybrid Millat experiences 'the feeling of belonging nowhere that comes to people who belong everywhere' and feels he has 'no face in this country' except the negative, stereotype-laden identity of 'Paki' (233, 202), Smith is on well-trodden immigrant-novel turf. Her obsession with 'roots' is also familiar, though her controlling metaphor of teeth is original; moreover, by naming her flashback chapters 'Root Canals,' she hints at the roots/routes duality of migrancy, since outside of dentistry a canal is a route. It is, notably, an inland waterway, a local route; Smith also links roots to oceanic, global routes when she extends Samad's belief that 'tradition was culture, and culture led to roots, and these were good' with the following metaphor: 'Roots were what saved, the ropes one throws out to rescue drowning men, to Save Their Souls. And the further Samad himself floated out to sea, ... the more determined he became to create for his boys roots on shore, deep roots that no storm or gale could displace' (168). Strong local roots, in other words, are a defence against the dangers of ocean-crossing routes.

Ultimately, however, the uniqueness of Smith's novel and its vision of London is found less in its geographical and spatial sensibility than in its thematic foregrounding of time, history, and causality. Whereas Kureishi locates two generations of metropolitan experience in a spatially nuanced but temporally uncomplicated London, Smith applies most of her nuance and intellectual energy towards teasing out the ironically unpredictable, generation-crossing relationships between past actions and future consequences. The London (and Britain) she implicitly constructs is a consequence of its history, including imperialism, but while it may be too layered with history's residue – its shit – ever to be wiped clean and made neutral, her thematics also imply that London's future possibilities need not be defined or limited by that excremental history. The city's future cannot be extrapolated or divined from its past because it is not a controlled experiment; it can always be transformed in unexpected ways by unforeseen choices, combinations, random happenings, or accidents. If London, like Samad and Archie, has 'one leg in the present, one in the past,' then by Smith's logic its 'roots will always be tangled' (70). And if the city is like Millat, who 'stood schizophrenic, one foot in Bengal and one in Willesden[,] ... as much there as he was here' (190), then its tangled roots will not just be growing under local ground. As cities have always done, London uproots people and brings them and their worlds together to encounter each other, create new entanglements on top of old ones, and produce new mixtures and identities. Always emergent and transformative, the metropolis can never be a neutral, final space.

Endings and Beginnings

White Teeth was published early in 2000, the year that technically ended the preceding millennium but was embraced worldwide as the *de facto* beginning of the new one. Indeed, the *Economist* reviewer called Smith's book, with its supposed impatience with the past, 'triumphantly *début de siècle*' ('Pulling'). But just as her narrative wallows in the very history it is supposedly eager to jettison, at the very end Smith metafictionally contemplates the fact that narrative, like a period of history, is never really over no matter how strong the desire to have it done with. '*But first the endgames*,' she writes: 'Because it seems no matter what you think of them, they must be played, even if, like the independence of India or Jamaica, like the signing of peace treaties or the docking of passenger boats, the end is simply the beginning of an even longer story' (461). As she proceeds to outline the directions her narrative could take after Millat shoots Archie and the FutureMouse escapes – the various options designed to please notional focus groups – what saves her ending-that-isn't from being a glibly cynical cop-out is that she has earned the right to it. Thematically her novel has been preoccupied with the yoking of endings to beginnings and with the inevitable (if unpredictable) ways the past erupts into the present and future. Her characters cannot put paid to their personal or collective histories, nor can they plan their own or each other's future development, any more than London can.

London's history is at once buried in layers of material remains, remembered through narratives and images, and visibly present in its people and spaces. As the postcolonial texts examined in this study have encountered London – which is to say, as characters have experienced it and authorial sensibilities have constructed it – the city has consistently been infused with local and global histories. These histories represent both a burden and a source of connection. History in its various forms has a habit of bursting forth unexpectedly, generating new and transforming stories for the city in the form of surfacing Roman baths or phantasmagoric dreams or *déjà-vu* architecture or grim race riots. And while these narratives are commonly about what Salman Rushdie calls 'newness' – the emergent future of migrant identities and their reclaimed, transformed urban worlds – they are unavoidably steeped in the past. It is notable that the central themes and motifs of Peter Ackroyd's 'biography' of London, published the same millennium-ending-and-beginning year as *White Teeth* and covering two thousand years of the city's history, are all drawn upon freely and frequently by the authors of postcolonial London novels. Ackroyd, for whom the city is 'a labyrinth, half of stone and half of flesh' (2), organizes his massive synchronic history around such recurring associations with London and Londoners as light and darkness, fire, the crowd, theatricality, housing, transport, time, death, the Thames, immigration, and suburban life. He discusses London as an unreal city, a world city, an imperial city, and an eternal city – a messy, chaotic perpetual-motion machine that never stops reinventing itself. As postcolonial writers appropriate these many time-honoured images in the service of their own narratives, they contribute to that ongoing project of reinvention.

The image with which Ackroyd begins his book is, as it happens, the one that emerges as the defining image of the transnational London of postcolonial fiction. 'In the beginning was the sea,' he intones: 'the site of the capital, fifty million before, was covered by great waters,' evidence of which can still be seen in the city's 'weathered stones' (7). Ackroyd is not insensitive to the figurative implications of this prehistorical fact, remarking that 'London has always been a vast ocean in which survival is not certain' (7), and, ominously, that 'like the sea and the gallows, London refuses nobody' (8). The narratives with which *Imagining London* has been concerned have been stories of survival by people who have crossed the sea, by boat or by air, to plunge into a 'metropolitan sea' where they hope not to drown but to stay afloat. What they discover there is a world in which personal and cultural identity are as fluid and in-between as the oceans that divide them from and connect them to their original homes. Water and the sea seep into many novels as explicit and sometimes controlling images for the transnational, relational metropolis, a place and a space defined by its intimate, weblike connections to other places, particularly those of the empire that the back-and-forth sea voyages of times past helped build. And if one meaning of 'oceanic' cited in the *OED* derives from 'a feeling as of something limitless, unbounded' sometimes associated with 'a tendency towards cosmic self-transcendence,'[9] then the colossal city that seems unlimited geographically, historically, demographically, and experientially is undoubtedly an oceanic space.

One way London's oceanic magnitude is made less daunting and more navigable is through fictional narrative's capacity for rendering the human experience of taking possession – of distilling the chaotic, boundless city down to what can be known, comprehended, and (re)claimed. Within those narrative representations there is a recurring impulse to create microcosmic images of a smaller, more manageable city, which take many metaphorically suggestive forms: a house, a club, a family, a community, a neighbourhood, a shop, a body of water, a ride on the tube. An extreme version of the reducing, shrinking impulse is the keepsake pens brought from London to India in Arundhati Roy's *The God of Small Things*, in which 'a cut-out collage of a London streetscape was suspended' in water (253). Invoked at the beginning of this book as a metonymic symbol of London's imperial power and quotidian presence in postcolonial lives and writings,[10] here at the end some further ramifications can be seen. As Roy briefly describes it, the streetscape contains famous landmarks of London's global reach ('Buckingham Palace and Big Ben') but it also includes more mundane 'shops and people' (253) – the stone and flesh that in equal parts comprise Ackroyd's London. While these elements of the urban scene are fixed in place, a bus moves 'up and down' the street, recalling in miniature the back-and-forth journeys of migration that typified empire and the transformations of the postimperial metropolis. It is fitting, moreover, that the entire scene is immersed in the water that once submerged London and across which those historical and contemporary journeys to and from the 'metropolitan sea' have occurred. And while the dark ink that flows past the streetscape may resemble a miniature Thames, more directly it represents the writing within, through, and outside London that the children in Roy's novel can symbolically perform when they take the pens in their hands. It is a miniature representation of the thousands of miles of ink writers have spilled – enough to go round the world many times, no doubt – placing postcolonial lives within, through, and outside the city they keep striving to get hold of and make their own.

Notes

Chapter 1: Introduction

1 The painting, by Neils M. Lund, renders a cityscape of monumental build-ings and teeming crowds at Bank Junction to portray London as hub of England's imperial power. 'Pink-stained' refers to the colour English maps traditionally used to mark imperial territories.

2 Hence the common usage of the word 'metropolis' (and cognates such as 'metropole' and 'metropolitan') to mean Europe, England, the West, and/ or the site of imperial power.

3 See Achebe's *No Longer at Ease* (1960) and *Anthills of the Savannah* (1987), Emecheta's *Kehinde* (1994), and Vassanji's 'The London-returned' in *Uhuru Street* (1993), for example. The endorsement London bestows may turn out to be a dubious benefit. Not all 'been-tos' are hoist with their metropolitan petard the way Achebe's tragically are, but their perceived specialness in-evitably puts them out of step with the societies that admire them. A West Indian example is Naipaul's portrait in *A House for Mr Biswas* of Owad, whose self-importance on returning to Trinidad from London looks in-creasingly ridiculous. And when the budding journalist Mr Biswas imitates London tabloids, the shoddy results critique London's self-projection as a cultural centre.

4 See Clifford, 'Traveling' and Pratt, *Imperial.*

5 See Richler, *Horseman* 221-32 and Selvon, *Housing* 103–28.

6 See Donald 14–17 and M. Smith 116–17.

7 Aijaz Ahmad has made related complaints about the evacuation of a real-world politics of resistance from 'Third World' and postcolonial literary studies. See *In Theory*, esp. 43–94.

8 See Jacobs, *Edge* 10 and King, *Global* 73 for statements of London as source of imperial power.

9 Examining the changing Londons described by tourist guidebooks between 1851 and 2000, David Gilbert and Fiona Henderson observe a similar polarity between 'an ancient city with its roots deep in the past' and one defined by 'global centrality' associated with imperial power and postimperial migration (125). In the 1930s, they note an emphasis on London as the 'domestic home' of an imperial family with siblings and children – 'a site of imperial unity rather than as the crucible of power' – particularly in a book entitled *The Empire Comes Home* (1937) that 'portrayed London as a kind of imperial front parlour, simultaneously a familiar part of the family home, but also the place where special occasions took place' (131). Recently, they note a shift in the recommended objects of tourist consumption from fixed architectural entities such as monuments and cathedrals to the spectacle of London's 'ethnic diversity' and 'globalized urban culture' (134).

10 These parallel developments in both postcolonial theory and London's identity may explain why London, despite its prevalence in postcolonial literature, has until recently been relatively neglected in postcolonial criticism and theory. The nationalist 'first moment' leads to a critical privileging of novels set on the colonial ground and embedded in local/ national cultures – in Africa, India, or Trinidad, for instance – rather than in a site so redolent of imperial power as London. The transnational 'second moment' leads to an interest in narratives of displacement and travel and set in various locations whose very multiplicity helps stress the complexity of cultural identities. One result of this latter focus on rootlessness is a disinclination to pay sustained attention to any one place – particularly, perhaps, a metropolitan one.

11 More recently, Edward Soja has reiterated this idea (see 165).

12 Cf. urban theorist Anthony King, who writes that 'In at least two senses, all cities can be described as colonial: at the local level, the powers that form them organize their hinterland and live off the surplus the non-urban realm provides. At the global level, existing cities organize the surplus both of their own society as well as that of others overseas' (*Urbanism* 15).

13 Such associations continue well beyond London's heyday as imperial centre. In his recent memoir *Bombay–London–New York* (2002), Amitava Kumar recalls how, as a young man in India in the mid-1980s, he nurtured a 'dream' of London as 'a bright place' (108). His belief in London as the desirable destination for a writer came from reading Naipaul's memoir 'Prologue to an Autobiography' (1984). As discussed in chapter 3, many of Naipaul's generation of West Indian literary aspirants moved to London to establish their careers; Kumar's response speaks to London's continuing hold on the postcolonial writerly imagination.

14 Pullinger's novel is discussed in chapter 2. In *Heart of Darkness*, Joseph Conrad's Marlow calls London a 'monstrous town' (7); while he does not connect this image overtly to imperialism, London is clearly positioned in the novel as an imperial headquarters.

15 See William Safran's seminal article (esp. 83–4) as well as the important critiques and extensions of his definition of diasporas by James Clifford ('Diasporas' 304–15) and Robin Cohen (21-9). See also Brah 178–81.

16 For instance, as in Hannerz's 'transnational management class,' mentioned above. Saskia Sassen, a leading theorist of the 'global city' as an economic construct, tends to treat 'global' and 'transnational' as synonymous, as in an article on identity in the global city: 'In the past cities were centers for imperial administration and international trade. Today they are transnational spaces for business and finance, where firms and governments from many different countries can transact with each other, increasingly bypassing the firms of the host country' (138).

17 Canada's membership in the 'postcolonial' embrace is controversial. The field's first primer, *The Empire Writes Back*, includes it and other 'settler colony' literatures, reflecting one strand of postcolonialism's origins, in Commonwealth literary studies. But many postcolonial theorists (including Edward Said, Homi Bhabha, and Gayatri Spivak) do not discuss Canadian, Australian, New Zealand, or white South African literatures. The ambiguous status of European settler-colony populations – who historically were colonizers of aboriginal peoples but culturally and geographically marginalized *vis-à-vis* their nations of origin, and who today wield disporportionate power in their increasingly multicultural and transnational societies – complicates their inclusion. Good discussions of Canada's postcolonial complexities can be found in articles by Donna Bennett, Linda Hutcheon ('Circling'), Stephen Slemon ('Unsettling'), and Cynthia Sugars, and books by Sylvia Söderlind, Marie Vautier, and Laura Moss, ed., among others (see Works Cited), as well as in *Testing the Limits*, a special issue of *Essays on Canadian Writing* edited by Diana Brydon. Chapter 2 of this study aims, among other things, to demonstrate the ways in which white Canadian authors and characters bring some of the same baggage to London, and see it as a similarly unique and important transnational space, as their Caribbean and South Asian counterparts – even if the postcolonial geography their presence implies is a notably uneven one because their difference from the English is more audible than visible, more cultural than ethnic or racial. As for other national and regional literatures, London has inspired an uncontainable plenitude. I can do no more than mention here a number of prominent postcolonial writers whose London novels I do not have

space to examine: Nigeria's Buchi Emecheta (*In the Ditch, Second Class Citizen,* and *Kehinde*) and Biyi Bandele (*The Street*); Ghana's Ama Ata Aidoo (*Our Sister Killjoy*); South Africa's Christopher Hope (*Serenity House*); Rhodesia/Zimbabwe's Doris Lessing (*The Good Terrorist*); Australia's Patrick White (*The Living and the Dead*) and Jessica Anderson (*Tirra Lirra by the River*); New Zealand's Janet Frame (*The Edge of the Alphabet*); and Hong Kong's Timothy Mo (*Sour Sweet*). Australia's Peter Carey offers fascinating renderings of nineteenth-century London in *Oscar and Lucinda* and *Jack Maggs*. Apart from the fact that some on this list focus on British rather than immigrant characters, no other nation or culturally coherent region has the critical mass of London novels that Canada, the West Indies, South Asia, and 'black Britain' have produced.

Chapter 2: London North-West

1 See Frye 227; Atwood, *Survival*; J. Moss, *Patterns*.
2 Of the many critics who have interrogated Frye's famous statement, two usefully supplement my own reformulation of it. Donna Pennee suggests that the concerns about representation, difference, and collective identity that recently dominated literary studies in Canada and abroad mean that 'the question of "where is here?" has been superseded by the question that Frye thought, at one point in his career, was less important, namely, "who am I?" Or rather, the question of "where is here?" has proved to be inseparable from the question "who am I?", for representation (the literary and the political, the literary as political) works from both the sites of individual subjectivity and place and context' (203). According to Diana Brydon, 'The question has never been "Where is here?" Not really. The question has always been "What are we doing here?" And that question inevitably breeds others. ... Who is included in that we, and who is included in that endeavour?' ('It's Time' 14). The continued relevance and resonance of this question are evident in a special issue of *Essays on Canadian Writing* published in 2000 under the title *Where Is Here Now?*; variations on Frye's question are addressed by many of the contributors. Frye's idea is also creatively revisited in Peter Dickinson's *Here Is Queer* (1999).
3 Novels by all of these authors are discussed in this chapter. One Canadian author not discussed here who has written interestingly (though very briefly) of London is Margaret Laurence, in *The Diviners* (1974).
4 Cf. McLuhan, who writes, 'Canadians never got "delivery" on their first national identity image in the nineteenth century and are the people who learned how to live without the bold accents of the national ego-trippers of other lands' ('Canada' 227).

5 In his book *Playing Dead*, Rudy Wiebe writes that he is 'convinced that the only natural human boundary is water,' and then contrasts Canada's oceanic and inland borders: 'The Great Lakes are there, yes, and the brief Niagara River, but so much of Canada's southern boundary is invisible from the air; too much of its southern edge was conceived in the imagination of officials who had never [seen] and had never intended to see it. ... And ... so much of what makes Canada geographically artificial as the nation of the northern half of North America is exactly that: its lack of definition by water' (9–10).

6 Indeed, in the aftermath of the terrorist attacks of 11 September 2001, the concept of a 'porous border' between Canada and the United States dominated the Canadian news. Now, however, the anxiety was apparently mutual: US officials worried that Canada might be an entry-point for terrorists heading south, and Canadians worried alternately that a tighter US border would disrupt trade and free movement, or that a new 'continental border' policy (allowing a more open US border) would require harmonized immigration policies and consequent loss of Canadian sovereignty.

7 See articles by Smaro Kamboureli, Christopher Gittings, Teresa Heffernan, and Stephen Slemon ('Monuments' 12), as well as books by Linda Hutcheon (*Canadian*, various pp.) and Frank Davey (182–94). Their collective lack of interest in Britain is exemplified by Davey's identification of the 'six major oppositions' that structure Anna's life: 'pastoral versus industrial, large versus small, women versus men, "freakish" versus "normal," the United States versus Canada, and Confederate South versus Yankee North' (182, 183). Canada versus Britain is notably absent.

8 See Bakhtin, *Rabelais* 303–436.

9 Anna does so in her opening monologue, where she announces that among the three spiels she has 'up my long sleeve' to present to the reader, one is 'what my hometown will say about me 100 years from now' (2). As Gittings notes, this bit of postmodern textual play gives Anna a 'doubled vision of a past and present' and places her text in 'an ontologically ambiguous and liminal zone that straddles 1877 and 1977, and invades the reader's present' (83).

10 Di Brandt writes that her students at the University of Windsor 'recently identified as the central motif of CanLit, "How can we get out of the small town to the big city?"' (107).

11 W.H. New writes in *Land Sliding* of a Canadian National Railways poster from the early twentieth century that sounds similar: it 'advertised Canada as "The Right Land for the Right Man" (the man in the poster wears a broad-brimmed hat and open-necked shirt, and holds in his hands a framed image of a productive farm with a train running past cultivated fields)'

(86). A copy of the poster is printed on the dustjacket of Jonathan Kertzer's *Worrying the Nation*.

12 Interviewed in 1968, Davies agrees with Gordon Roper's view that once Monica leaves Salterton 'the novel moves into another world and becomes another kind of fiction' (Roper 40). Davies says, 'I think I muddled that': 'what I really wanted to do was to put the world of Salterton into perspective and compare it to another world which has very different values. ... And it was an attempt to explore in some sense the awful provinciality which still prevails in Canada about the arts' (40–1).

13 In Patricia Monk's Jungian reading, Monica must abandon the delusions of her old 'mundane reality' and embrace a new 'transcendent reality'(61); this 'duality' corresponds to 'the dark and the light, the demonic and the celestial' (73).

14 This implied preference leads Michael Peterman to castigate Davies's 'excessive homage to artistic imperialism': 'He makes it clear that she couldn't receive an education of such quality except at the center – in England' (112).

15 See W.J. Keith's article on the novel's anti-romantic aspects.

16 Intriguingly, the next three novels examined herein also employ this motif: the first time Richler's Jake is shown returning to Montreal is for his father's funeral, and Pullinger's Audrey first goes back to Victoria when her mother is accidentally killed by her father. When Bush's Arcadia returns home, she discovers her father has cancer. This recurring narrative of the dead or dying parent reinforces the connections these novels make between their journeys of self-discovery and themes of nationality and place-identity.

17 Richler writes vividly of London in two essays, 'London Province' (1962) and 'London Then and Now' (1998). Many of Jake's responses to London echo Richler's; almost identical passages to most of those quoted above are found in 'London Province' (see esp. 40–2). In this essay Richler also mentions his friendship with George Lamming and their camaraderie with 'other discontented and disoriented colonials: Australians, more Canadians, and West Indians' (43). Richler lived mostly in London between 1951 and 1972.

18 Jake tells the American immigration officer that he is twenty (103), but since the scene takes place in the autumn of 1951 and Jake was seven in the summer of 1937 when he first met Joey (86, 111), he would be twenty-one at this time. The transitional nature of the time is more generally conveyed by the fact that Jake abandons his university degree before leaving for New York and by a passage describing him and his friends shortly after he returns to Montreal, before leaving for Toronto: 'No longer boys they were

but, mercifully, not yet full-grown men either, envy-ridden, harassed by mortgages and calorie intake and child education. Everything was still possible. Nobody had yet looked at himself maturely and settled for the workable marriage or the tolerable job' (134).

19 See J. Moss, 'Richler's'; Ramraj 92–106; Davidson 145–63; Brenner 85–110.

20 Richler reinforces Jake's identity as in between his two *alter egos* through their names: not only is Jake mistaken for Joey based on the shared initial J, but he affectionately calls Harry 'Herschel,' a diminutive version of his own surname. Moreover, it may also be telling that Jake Hersch's names begin with the J of Joey and the H of Harry, and that the letter alphabetically between H and J is the 'I' of the first-person subject; third-person narration notwithstanding, the 'I' through which Richler focalizes his narrative, Jake Hersch, is the pivot on either side of which Joey and Harry are located, and he is self-divided by his affiliations with both men.

21 Richler mentions 'swinging London' in a CBC Radio interview broadcast on 11 January 1969, comparing it to New York: 'I also prefer London as a city. On the other hand, New York and London are almost interchangeable now, which is like this whole myth of swinging London, [which] really means it got more like New York and New York approved. ... What happened is London, which was a flaking, dowdy city, became visibly, noticeably gayer and more prosperous, and rather like New York' (Watmough).

22 Richler repeats these passages in very similar wording later in the novel (288–9).

23 See Muuss (42–83), Marcia, and Baumeister for summaries of the influential theories of identity formation and crisis proposed by Erik Erikson, James Marcia, and others.

24 Richler's novel looks 'back' both in terms of the organization of this chapter and chronologically: the 1967 London of its main narrative is later than the Londons of Swan (1871), Davies (early-mid 1950s), and Atwood (early 1960s). It does not look back in terms of publication sequence, since Swan's and Atwood's novels were published later.

25 Arif Dirlik, for instance, concludes a detailed examination of 'place' in global/local debates by observing that 'modernity driven by capitalism has rendered places into inconveniences in the path of progress'; he wryly recommends resisting such antihuman forms of progress by 'questioning if capital, and the globalism off which it nourishes, are inconveniences on the way to places' ('Place-Based' 42).

26 Beyond the sources cited above, further reading on Canadian multiculturalism can be found in Hutcheon, Introduction; Bissoondath; Kamboureli, *Scandalous*; and Day.

27 See Pethick 9–10; D. Smith 12–13; and the two articles by Girard. Given Pullinger's preoccupation with water, the following passage from Dorothy Smith's account of Douglas's Scottish childhood is of interest: 'Over fifty years later he remembered vividly his first dip in the River Clyde, when his landlady's daughter plunged him "head over heels into the flowing stream. I was a very little fellow then," he adds, "and was, at least for a time, thoroughly cured ... of all longings for cold baths and deep water"' (12–13).

28 Arcadia says her name 'was assumed to be simply a sign of English eccentricity' (39). Her surname, Hearne, points to the eighteenth-century explorer of Arctic Canada, Samuel Hearne, and her first name, Hispanic in origin, means 'adventurous' (Parenthood.com). The psychological and ethical journey the novel narrates will enable Arcadia to more fully live up to these associations with her name. Furthermore, 'Arcadia' combines rural and urban associations with derivations from Arcadian (as in ideally rustic or pastoral) and arcadian (from arcade in its architectural sense as applied to arched buildings, shop-lined avenues, and places of amusement).

29 In a connected but reversed image, Arcadia says that in her childhood, 'The ravines were rooms, great green rooms expanding around us' (69). References to the sky, clouds, and the moon recur throughout the novel.

30 Cf. Jane Jacobs in *The Death and Life of Great American Cities*: 'Great cities are not like towns, only larger. They are not like suburbs, only denser. They differ from towns and suburbs in basic ways, and one of these is that cities are, by definition, full of strangers' ('Uses' 104).

31 Information about the station comes from the Battersea Power Station Community Group web site. The site contains, in its account of the building's history, details about an American-style theme park that was to be built inside it during the late 1980s but was abandoned in 1989, the year Pullinger's novel was published. On 12 December 2000, the BBC reported that the Canadian circus troupe Cirque du Soleil planned to build a two-thousand-seat theatre inside the power station, which would have become the group's first permanent home ('Battersea'). This plan, too, was subsequently abandoned.

32 The novel's ambiguous political themes may seem appropriate given the year it was published: 1989 marks not only the end of Canada's left-nationalist consensus, as Ian Angus notes, but the end of the Cold War. With the disappearance of what might be called an international 'consensus' (at least as far as where lines of disagreement and borders could be drawn), the US emerged as the world's only superpower. The confusions wrought by the period of transition into what then-president George Bush called the 'new world order' were arguably not unlike those of Pullinger's characters:

monumental changes were in the offing, but it was unclear what new states they heralded or how the US would wield its increased power.

Chapter 3: London South-West

1 All quotations from *Caribbean Voices* programs come from scripts held at the BBC Written Archives Centre in Caversham and are identified by broadcast date and box number; the accession number is 20946. Recordings of the broadcasts have not been preserved.

2 The first script in the BBC archive, entitled 'Calling the West Indies' (changed to 'Caribbean Voices' by the second), refers to the signature music in June Grimble's introductory remarks: 'Perhaps you recognized the opening music, West Indies? It was "Jam", an old West Indian lullaby. We have chosen it as a signature tune to this series of your own poems and stories, to which we turn again in our Sunday evening programmes' (11–12/3/45; Box 1).

3 All quotations from correspondence written by or to Henry Swanzy are taken from the Henry Swanzy Papers held at the University of Birmingham. Letters are identified by date; the accession number is 1997/18.

4 In an effort to be reasonably comprehensive, novels by all these authors are discussed in this chapter, though not all have been given extended analysis. Of the fifteen texts discussed, those receiving the fullest discussion are Lamming's *The Emigrants*, Rhys's *Voyage in the Dark*, Selvon's *The Lonely Londoners*, Naipaul's *The Mimic Men*, and Dabydeen's *The Intended*. Several novels have not been included. Caryl Phillips's *The Final Passage* (1985) and Neil Bissoondath's *The Worlds within Her* (1998) both contain notable London scenes, but while they return to the 1950s era so thoroughly examined in earlier novels, they do not augment their predecessors sufficiently to warrant inclusion in this already abundant chapter. By contrast, Naipaul's *Mr Stone and the Knights Companion* (1963) and E.R. Braithwaite's *Choice of Straws* (1965) have been left out because their lack of manifestly West Indian perspectives or referents places them outside this chapter's focus. Minor London novels by Selvon (*The Housing Lark*, 1965) and Salkey (*The Adventures of Catullus Kelly*, 1969) have been omitted in favour of the authors' more substantial fictions.

5 Lamming echoes this passage in a later autobiographical essay: 'I remember coming in on what was called the boat-train into Waterloo. You see these buildings, these sort of factories and men are telling each other: "Look, that is where we get the Bovril from", "Look, look that is where we get the Ovaltine from", "Look, look, look"; ('Coldest' 5).

6 Georg Simmel's classic essay 'The Metropolis and Mental Life' offered a
  compelling analysis of this urban fact in 1903, and Pierce Egan's *Life in
  London* spoke to it in 1821: 'The next door neighbour of a man in London
  is generally as great a stranger to him as if he lived at the distance of York'
  (qtd. in Raban 89). Cf. Wordsworth in Book VII of *The Prelude* on urban
  alienation: ' ... how men lived / Even next-door neighbours, as we say, yet
  still / Strangers, nor knowing each the other's name' (227; lines 116–18).

7 For example, see Paquet 31-4 and Gikandi, *Writing* 91-2.

8 For a discussion of this figure, see Pratt, 'Scratches' esp. 144.

9 Supriya Nair similarly sees *The Emigrants* and the later London novel *Water
  with Berries* as containing 'brief moments of productive resistance amidst
  the overpowering aridity, usually enacted in a subterranean space' (73).

10 Paul Gilroy notes the frequency of the rebirth motif in narratives of immigration to England from the New World; the radical journalist and political
   organizer Ida B. Wells, he says, is 'typical, describing her productive times
   in England as like "being born again in a new condition"' (*Black* 17–18).

11 The original ending of *Voyage in the Dark*, changed on the publisher's
   request, had Anna herself dying of complications from the abortion (see
   O'Connor 128–31)

12 I am indebted to O'Connor's fine, detailed reading of the novel, and particularly to her demonstration of the ways 'the very direct connection of
   place to feeling' in Rhys's writing is conveyed through the 'spatial dimension' and 'symbolic function' of the rooms in *Voyage in the Dark* (1, 105). At
   one point O'Connor positions the novel within a tradition of 'literature of
   enclosure,' with its 'womb-like' rooms suggesting both a Freudian notion
   of regression to a safer, infantile state and, more strongly, associations with
   death: 'the room finally provides not a refuge but a shroud' (105–6).

13 Elaine Savory offers an intriguing reading of the oppressive houses that
   dominate Anna's London: 'Anna also manages to "read" London as a series
   of black and white contrasting symbols, like a text. It is a great many white
   people and dark houses. It is the houses which seem to disapprove of her
   and not the people; the houses seem like characters, both human and in
   the sense of letters on a page. The pale people are backdrop and setting,
   the page on which the dark houses speak' (93). It is worth noting, furthermore, that the people Anna meets often prove indistinguishable; the two
   Miss Cohens have the same noses and eyes (see 24), and Walter Jeffries
   looks like a waiter who serves them: 'Their noses were exactly alike, their
   faces very solemn. The brothers Slick and Slack, the Brothers
   Pushmeofftheearth' (17–18).

14 Similarly worded passages can be found elsewhere in the novel: in

Newcastle she observes 'the rows of houses outside, gimcrack, rotten-looking, and all exactly alike' (26); in London 'the houses on either side of the street were small and dark and then they were big and dark but all exactly alike' (82). Rhys, who like Anna left the West Indies for London as a teenager, records her own similar responses to the city in *Smile Please*. On her first day, 'I wanted to see what London looked like,' but after walking around she concludes, 'It was all the same, long, straight, grey, a bit disappointing' (80). Regarding chorus girls, interestingly, she employs a now-familiar phrase only to qualify it: 'People talk about chorus girls as if they were all exactly alike, all immoral, all silly, all on the make. As a matter of fact, far from being all alike they were rather a strange mixture' (88).

15 Rhys's sense of disorientation contrasts markedly with a similar passage in Dorothy Richardson's earlier thirteen-volume novel *Pilgrimage*, which connotes a feeling of empowerment brought on by London's immense, multidirectional reach. Richardson's female character lies in her room 'tingling to the spread of London all about her, herself one with it, feeling her life flow outwards, north, south, east, and west, to all its margins' (qtd. in Donald 4).

16 In 1652, about forty Caribs were forced by French soldiers to the northern-most point of Grenada, where, as George Brizan writes, 'covering their eyes with their hands they plunged into the sea to meet what to them was a glorious end, compared to a base and shameful death at the hands of the Frenchman' (19). The site has become known as Le Morne des Sauteurs, or Leaper's Hill. Derek Walcott vividly renders this historical event in parts III and IV of chapter 11 of his autobiographical poem *Another Life* (*Collected* 212–14).

17 For a good discussion of theories regarding abortion and infanticide practised by Caribbean slave women, see Barbara Bush 137–42 and 147–9.

18 The word 'capsize' obliquely associates London's buses with the water across which Tanty migrated. In *The Rules of Engagement*, Catherine Bush uses a memorable simile to makes a similar association; in the heavy rain-storm that hinders Arcadia's passport-delivery mission, 'cars swam past' and on Oxford Street 'a row of buses inched along like lumbering bottom feeders' (130–1).

19 For an excellent overview of the complex phenomenon of *flânerie*, see Keith Tester's *The 'Flâneur'*, especially the essays by Tester, Ferguson, Mazlish, and Shields listed in Works Cited. See also Walter Benjamin's *Charles Baudelaire* (esp. 35–66 and 120–34) and Anke Gleber's *The Art of Taking a Walk* (esp. 3–60).

20 For a thorough examination of postmodernism's 'curious mixture of the

complicitous and the critical' (201), see Linda Hutcheon's *A Poetics of Postmodernism*, esp. 201-21.

21 In *Black Skin, White Masks*, Fanon describes the experience of being reminded of his 'physiological self' when a child repeatedly says, 'Look, a Negro!' and then adds, 'Mama, see the Negro! I'm frightened!' (111, 112).

22 In their reading of Selvon's later novel *Moses Ascending*, Keith Booker and Dubravka Juraga remark upon 'a motif that runs throughout Selvon's work, in which West Indian men, feminized by their subaltern positions within the colonial system, seek empowerment through sexual exploitation of women' (70).

23 Alfie's journey echoes Foster's in other ways: the narratives of both protagonists follow a Trinidad-London-return structure, though Alfie's return is to St Lucia. On his return, Alfie, like Foster, finds himself discussing big questions of nationalism and national identity, eventually articulating an antinationalist, global vision that is closer to where Foster begins than to where he ends: 'All this nationalism people keep getting fanatic about is nothing to be proud of, Constance. Why should I want to boast of being a Trinidadian, or a West Indian? Why not a man of the Earth? A civilised man of the Earth. That's something to boast about. Nationalism only leads to war, so why should we West Indians strive so hard to establish our identity in the world? ... Isn't it enough merely to be cultured in a world sense? Culture has no boundaries, really. A truly civilised man should embrace the culture of every part of the world and claim it as part of his own.' (290). Unlike Selvon, however, Mittelholzer does not trace this vision to his protagonist's London experience; Alfie says, 'I've always felt deep inside that it's stupid to get worked up about national pride and a chauvinistic love of one's own country. Since I was a boy I knew that the day would come when I'd run off and merge myself with the world at large, and be faithful to no particular area – no particular flag or government or political ideology. I was born that way' (326). In keeping with the novel's lack of interest in rendering a detailed or distinctive London, Mittelholzer misses an opportunity to tie Alfie's transnational views to London's identity as (post)imperial 'world city.'

24 *The Mimic Men* is Naipaul's second novel set in London – it was preceded by *Mr Stone and the Knights Companion* – but the first with West Indian characters.

25 Peter Ackroyd notes that London 'has always been a shadowy city' characterized by the crepuscular light that hangs under what Dickens called '"the leaden canopy of its sky"' (110; qtd. in 111). Conrad famously portrayed the Thames as a site of 'brooding gloom' and 'darkness' (*Heart* 5, 111), but

others have seen the heavy interiority of a London night more positively, including Virginia Woolf, who in Ackroyd's view conveys a 'sense of immensity' in her 'account of London as "a swarm of lights with a pale yellow canopy drooping above it. There were the lights of the great theatres, the lights of the long streets, lights which indicated huge squares of domestic comfort, lights that hung high in the air. No darkness would ever settle upon these lamps, as no darkness has settled upon them for hundreds of years"' (448). M.G. Vassanji's novel *The Book of Secrets* (1994) portrays a British administrator in rural Kenya in 1913 becoming homesick for metropolitan light and imagining his distance from it magically eliminated: 'The nights were cold and dry, the blackness so absolute, so palpably dense he felt that if he reached out a hand from where he slept he could pull it aside and let in the lighted world of London, Paris, and Hamburg' (52).

26 See, for example, Derrick 205 and Thieme 115, 135. In a memorable image, John Wain says that the novel's 'characters seem as if they had been through some refrigerating process' (qtd. in D. Hassan 259).

27 These ideas are repeated, with variations, throughout the novel's first London segment, as in the following passage: 'In the great city, so three-dimensional, so rooted in its soil, drawing colour from such depths, only the city was real. Those of us who came to it lost some of our solidity; we were trapped into fixed, flat postures' (27).

28 The first section of Walcott's essay, published in 1970, obliquely echoes Naipaul in several spots. Walcott refers to 'those who have been called not men but mimics' (5) and begins the essay with references to 'dusk' and 'cities' (3). His statement that 'if there was nothing, there was everything to be made' (4) responds to Naipaul's infamous claim in *The Middle Passage* that 'nothing was created in the British West Indies' (27).

29 See Achebe's 'An Image of Africa' (*Hopes* 1–13) and Said's *Culture and Imperialism* 19–31. Naipaul too has critiqued Conrad, though for more writerly reasons; see his essay 'Conrad's Darkness' (*Return* 221–45).

30 In content, structure, and tone much closer to a memoir than the 'novel in five sections' it proclaims itself to be (3), *The Enigma of Arrival* is narrated by an unnamed figure whose experiences correspond very closely to Naipaul's own. The narrator will henceforth be referred to simply as 'Naipaul.'

31 Two early stories by Naipaul, published in *A Flag on the Island* (1967) but written in 1957, are set in a London boarding house; in neither 'Greenie and Yellow' (74–84) nor 'The Perfect Tenants' (85–100) does a transnational community of tenants appear.

32 'Michael X and the Black Power Killings in Trinidad' is collected in *The Return of Eva Perón* 1–97; Jimmy Ahmed is a character based on Michael X in

his novel *Guerrillas* (1975). Migration to London is also a theme in
Naipaul's *Half a Life* (2001).

33 Lamming also uses the cartographic oceans in this scene to indicate an
equally foreboding proximity to the United States: 'But the ocean was too
narrow a stretch between San Cristobal and her northern neighbour. There
to the north, a nightmare away, the stupendous power of America sent a
shiver through every nerve; shut every eye with fear. The ocean was innocent, an amiable killer beside those urgent executioners who kept vigil
over the fortunes of that hemisphere. ... The island was smiling under the
monstrous shadow of its northern neighbour' (18–19). Though intriguing
in their uses of the ocean as a metaphor, these references to American neo-
imperial power are not connected to the events of the book, in which
London and the former British Empire remain the focus.

34 In an interview, Lamming says his final chapter is intended to suggest that
the Gathering members 'are not going to return [to San Cristobal]. What
they will have to deal with now is the new reality in the experience – that is,
the world of blacks in England, rather than what they propose to do about
the world on the island' (qtd. in Paquet 90). Peter Hulme offers a similar
reading of the novel's ending: 'If the work of the postcolonial writer involves, as Lamming suggests earlier in his interview with George Kent in
1974, a "shaping of the national consciousness," then, perhaps surprisingly,
this "nation" turns out the be Britain' ('Profit' 135). Interestingly, this final
chapter does not appear in the American edition of the novel published by
Holt, Rinehart, and Winston.

35 Lamming's and Salkey's yoking of theatricality to a racialized political
resistance, and to artifice and ephemerality observed in some aspects of
metropolitan life, is also a feature of novels by Kamala Markandaya, Anita
Desai, and Salman Rushdie discussed in chapter 4.

36 Cf. Kamala Markandaya's *The Nowhere Man*, discussed in chapter 4.

37 The fire, John McLeod notes, 'recalls the New Cross fire of 1981 in which
thirteen black Londoners were killed' (*Beginning* 233). The Nationality Act
that redefined citizenship to favour whites over blacks was legislated, as it
happens, the same year.

38 See Naipaul, *Loss* 371-4. Naipaul's view is corroborated by the historian
Gordon Lewis, who writes that after emancipation, the West Indies suffered
losses because 'having been originally cultivated by the British mercantilist
commercial capitalism as sources of capital accumulation they were abandoned by the new British laissez-faire industrial capitalism of the nineteenth century' (58).

39 The novel's intertextual nods to *Heart of Darkness* are the subject of an

article by Charles Sarvan. They are also dealt with in passing by Margery Fee and Karen McIntyre in their essays on *The Intended.*

40 See discussions of novels by Catherine Bush and Kate Pullinger in chapter 2 and by Hanif Kureishi in chapter 5, for instance.

41 E.g., Walcott's poem 'The Sea Is History' (*Collected* 364–7).

42 Dabydeen's second novel, *Disappearance* (1993), set on the southern shore of England near Hastings, is narrated by a Guyanese engineer working to reclaim eroded coastline. It makes the sea's elemental power a controlling metaphor for its complex exploration of empire, history, migration, and the relations between British and Guyanese spaces, and intertextually references Naipaul's *The Enigma of Arrival* and the early novels of Wilson Harris.

43 See Dr Seuss's *The Cat in the Hat Comes Back.* The analogy here is to the ubiquitous pink used on maps of the British Empire.

Chapter 4: London South-East

1 Nandy's book is the most recent and thorough discussion of the literary response to Indian cities; see also Apte and Zelliot.

2 Novels by all four authors are discussed in this chapter. *Through Brown Eyes* is the title of a fascinating memoir of migration from Bombay to London in the 1960s by the architect Prafulla Mohanti.

3 Although this chapter focuses on texts by Indian-born authors, representations of London as a place of unreality can be found in novels by diasporic Indians as well; see, for instance, Sam Selvon's *The Lonely Londoners* (7), V.S. Naipaul's *The Mimic Men* (18–19), and M.G. Vassanji's *The Book of Secrets* (290).

4 See Puligandla 25; 'Indian thought' in this context refers to Hindu, Jain, and Buddhist traditions; it excludes the minor materialist tradition. Complementary discussions of the philosophical traditions discussed in this paragraph can be found in books by Zimmer, Smart, and Hiriyanna.

5 Markandaya's publisher, Putnam, encouraged an allegorical reading in the first sentence of the flap copy for the first edition, calling *Possession* a 'dramatic novel of contemporary East and West.' Various critics have followed this lead. M. Joseph calls the novel 'a microcosmic rendering of England's possession of India' (qtd. in Jha 25); S.C. Harrex sees the Valmiki-Caroline relationship as 'symbolic of the historic relations between Britain and India' (qtd. in Afzal-Khan 119), while for Fawzia Afzal-Khan, *Possession* is 'about the struggle for supremacy between two modes of thought and being: the Indian mythic/spiritual mode, and the Western realistic/materialistic, aggressive mode' (118).

6 Davies's novel is discussed in chapter 2. His Monica, unlike Eliza and Valmiki, does not rebel against her creator(s).

7 A fanciful illustration of the event, with the caption 'ALL THE WORLD GOING TO SEE THE GREAT EXHIBITION OF 1851,' showed a globe with swarms of people converging on a London positioned, like some geographically anomalous magnetic pole, on top (McClintock 57). The Exhibition's success also supports London's 'claim to being a birthplace of tourism in its modern and commodified form' (Gilbert and Henderson 124).

8 Nandy sees the European museum as representing spatially the conquest of time and space: the triumph, via a European-dominated 'history,' over Europe's own less civilized pasts and over the spaces and peoples of far-flung lands. These two worlds of others became mutually associated as they were contained together under the museum's roof: distant colonial society could represent a version of Europe's past, and vice versa (see *Journey* 2–4).

9 In an article on this phenomenon, Brian Street writes, 'Members of "savage" countries were taken to England and other European societies in remarkable numbers to be viewed as specimens or zoo-like exhibits, to satisfy curiosity and to reinforce the confidence of the public in their own "progress"' (122). Some performed in London theatres such as the Hippodrome.

10 See K. Rao 28–32 and Klostermaier 189–91.

11 See K. Rao 31 and Patton 42–3.

12 Henri Lefebvre notes that in perceptions of space, 'Altitude and verticality are often invested with a special significance ..., but such meanings vary from one society or "culture" to the next. By and large, however, horizontal space symbolizes submission, vertical space power, and subterranean space death' (*Production* 236). Desai's use of perspective clearly presumes these symbolic associations.

13 See Jameson, 'Postmodernism' 60 and Baudrillard. Cf. the postmodern city of Hanif Kureishi's *The Buddha of Suburbia*, discussed in chapter 5.

14 (Excuse the pun.) Rushdie also represents London below street level as an especially labyrinthine and disorienting site; Gibreel experiences the Underground as 'that hellish maze, that labyrinth without a solution,' a map-defying 'subterranean world in which the laws of space and time had ceased to operate' (201).

15 This childhood memory precedes the airplane crash by many years, but is placed later in Rushdie's narrative as part of a flashback to Saladin's earlier life. The 'headfirst' position of both falls is significant: the fact that, in a novel concerned with the rebirth and renewal of individual identity and

urban space, it is Saladin who descends 'in the recommended position for babies entering the birth canal' while Gibreel is (to extend the analogy) a breech (re)birth, anticipates from the outset which of the two will most successfully be reborn (4).

16 Based on a number of 'parallels' between Saladin's experiences and Rushdie's own, Susheila Nasta reads the novel as containing a 'partially embedded ... autobiographical narrative' (*Home* 167).

17 See Hazlehurst 190 and de Certeau 91-130.

18 See Bakhtin, *Rabelais* (esp. 303–436) for carnival and the grotesque body; see his *Problems* (esp. 112–37) for carnival and Menippean satire. For a full discussion of what I call Rushdie's 'Menippean grotesque,' see Ball, *Satire* 115–63.

19 In 'What Is a City?' Mumford writes, 'The city in its complete sense, then, is a geographic plexus, an economic organization, an institutional process, a theater of social action, and an aesthetic symbol of collective unity. The city fosters art and is art; the city creates the theater and is the theater. It is in the city, the city as theater, that man's more purposive activities are focused, and work out, through conflicting and cooperating personalities, events, groups, into more significant culminations' (185).

20 In an interview, Rushdie says, 'the act of migrating from Bombay to London is perhaps not as far as to go from an English village to London, because these two cities have great things in common,' including their 'fantastic,' 'ephemeral and transitory' nature (Ball, 'Interview' 32). These remarks echo the narrator's description of Saladin's childhood journey from Bombay to London, 'from Indianness to Englishness,' as 'an immeasurable distance. Or, not very far at all, because they rose from one great city, fell to another. The distance between cities is always small; a villager, travelling a hundred miles to town, traverses emptier, darker, more terrifying space' (41). Scholarly support for this idea is provided by the urban geographer Anthony King, who notes that colonial port and industrial cities (including Bombay and many others) became 'part of an emerging British colonial urban system' in the eighteenth and nineteenth centuries. By the beginning of the twentieth, 'their built and spatial environments (as well as other phenomena) begin to have more in common with each other than each has with the economically, politically, and culturally very different environments of the interior of the countries and continents where such ports were located' (*Urbanism* 140).

21 Smith's ideas are discussed in earlier chapters and later in this one.

22 Some other recent novels by South Asian writers also involve non-linear narratives that shuttle between London and one or more other cities – most notably *Bombay Talkie* (1995) by Ameena Meer (set in London,

Bombay, and New York) and *The Sandglass* (1998) by Romesh Gunesekera (London and Colombo). While these two books could be fruitfully compared with *The Shadow Lines*, they have been omitted for reasons of space, and because neither thematizes metropolitan life with anything like Ghosh's fervent intellectualism and narrative panache.

23 For instance, as children the narrator and Ila 'were so alike that I could have been her twin' (31). As an adult he recalls Mayadebi and Tha'mma performing certain actions 'in exactly the same way, as though there was a mirror between them,' but Robi tells him that 'they hadn't looked at all like each other; they were completely different' (35). The narrator imagines Tridib as a child looking like himself, but Tha'mma corrects him: 'No, he looked *completely* different – not at all like you' (4).

24 For a discussion of the nation-as-house metaphor that complements what follows, see Anjali Roy's article.

25 Cf. Derek Walcott's use of the mirror to convey a false division between European and colonial worlds (see 'The Caribbean' 6–7), as discussed in chapter 3.

Chapter 5: London Centre

1 See, for instance, books by Fryer, Sivanandan, Layton-Henry, Gilroy (*There Ain't*), Goulbourne, and Alibhai-Brown.

2 See Srivastava's *Looking for Maya* (1999), Adebayo's *My Once upon a Time* (2000), Newland's *Society Within* (1999), Syal's *Life isn't all ha ha hee hee* (1999), and Wheatle's *Brixton Rock* (1999).

3 'Black British' has become well established in academic and literary circles as a category that includes British residents of South Asian as well as African or Caribbean origin, whether first-generation immigrants or their British-born offspring. James Procter, in the introduction to his anthology *Writing black Britain 1948–1998*, acknowledges that 'black British' is a 'vexed' grouping but defends its use to refer to 'an "imagined community" comprising Caribbean, African and South Asian experience in Britain' (5). He quotes Kobena Mercer's useful explanation of it as a label that emerged in late-1960s and 1970s Britain. In Mercer's words, '"When various peoples – of Asian, African, and Caribbean descent – interpellated themselves and each other as /black/ they invoked a collective identity predicated on political and not biological similarites. In other words, the naturalized connotations of the term /black/ were disarticulated out of the dominant codes of racial discourse, and rearticulated as signs of alliance and solidar-

ity among dispersed groups of people sharing common historical experience of British racism'" (Procter, 'General' 5). Even so, the continuing
racial connotations of 'black' (as distinct from Asian 'brown') can create
problems of (dis)identification; in a comic passage in Kureishi's *The Buddha
of Suburbia*, the theatre director Matthew Pyke asks Karim to create a character 'from your own background. ... Someone black,' to which Karim
replies that 'I didn't know anyone black, though I'd been at school with a
Nigerian' (170).

4 For Eliot, as quoted by Kureishi, culture '"includes all the characteristic
activities of the people: Derby Day, Henley regatta, Cowes, the Twelfth of
August, a cup final, the dog races, the pin-table, Wensleydale cheese, boiled
cabbage cut into sections, beetroot in vinegar, nineteenth-century gothic
churches and the music of Elgar'" ('Bradford' 168).

5 There are some fascinating parallels between the histories of suburbia and
of empire. Imperial and suburban expansion occurred not only simultaneously, but for some of the same reasons: the desire for economic growth
and investment of surplus capital and labour; a pioneering attraction to
spatial frontiers; a sense of race- or class-based superiority and exclusivity;
and, as a function of that sense, an evangelical moralism. The wealth that
funded suburbia in its birthplace (London) came from merchants profiting
from imperial trade. The nineteenth and early twentieth centuries saw both
suburbia and empire valorized and celebrated, while the eventual disenchantment with both after World War Two (though only the latter was
dismantled) has at least one cause in common: both 'peripheries' were
seen to be economic drains, in terms of lost tax base or high maintenance
costs respectively, on the 'centre.'

6 For discussions of these seminal concepts, see Baudrillard; Jameson,
'Postmodernism'; and Harvey, *Condition*.

7 In a lengthy review essay published in the *New Republic*, James Wood sees
White Teeth as an example of a plague of 'profusion' and overly contrived
interrelatedness afflicting some 'big' contemporary novels (42). His other
examples of 'excessively centripetal' narratives (41) include recent books
by Salman Rushdie, Don DeLillo, and Thomas Pynchon.

8 In *Imaginary Homelands*, Rushdie calls 'the migrant sensibility ... one of the
central themes of this century of displaced persons' and goes on to show
how the 'mass migrations' of the twentieth century have created 'radically
new types of human being' (124).

9 The first of these citations is from Sigmund Freud; the second is from
Arthur Koestler.

10 As she reduces the metropolis to a few decorative inches of pen bestowed
   upon Indians, Roy may be recalling an image in another famous Indian
   novel to which hers bears more than passing resemblance. In Salman
   Rushdie's *Midnight's Children*, Saleem remembers a toy he played with as a
   child: a tin globe on which the words 'MADE AS ENGLAND' were printed
   (259).

Works Cited

Achebe, Chinua. *Hopes and Impediments: Selected Essays 1965–1987*. Oxford: Heinemann, 1988.

– *Things Fall Apart*. 1958. Oxford: Heinemann, 1962.

Ackroyd, Peter. *London: The Biography*. London: Chatto and Windus, 2000.

Adebayo, Diran. *Some Kind of Black*. London: Virago, 1996.

Afzal-Khan, Fawzia. *Cultural Imperialism and the Indo-English Novel: Genre and Ideology in R.K. Narayan, Anita Desai, Kamala Markandaya, and Salman Rushdie*. University Park: Pennsylvania State UP, 1993.

Ahmad, Aijaz. *In Theory: Classes, Nations, Literatures*. London: Verso, 1992.

Aidoo, Ama Ata. *Our Sister Killjoy; or Reflections from a Black-eyed Squint*. 1977. London: Longman, 1988.

Alibhai-Brown, Yasmin. *Imagining the New Britain*. New York: Routledge, 2001.

Anderson, Benedict. *Imagined Communities: Reflections on the Origin and Spread of Nationalism*. 1983. Rev. ed. London: Verso, 1991.

Angus, Ian. *A Border Within: National Identity, Cultural Plurality, and Wilderness*. Montreal and Kingston: McGill-Queen's UP, 1997.

Appiah, Kwame Anthony. 'Is the Post- in Postmodernism the Post- in Post-colonial?' *Critical Inquiry* 17.2 (1991): 336–57.

Apte, Mahadeo L. 'Reflections of Urban Life in Marathi Literature.' Fox 199–214.

Ashcroft, Bill, Gareth Griffiths, and Helen Tiffin. *The Empire Writes Back: Theory and Practice in Post-Colonial Literatures*. London: Routledge, 1989.

Atwood, Margaret. *Lady Oracle*. 1976. Toronto: Seal, 1977.

– *Survival: A Thematic Guide to Canadian Literature*. Toronto: Anansi, 1972.

Augé, Marc. *Non-Places: Introduction to an Anthropology of Supermodernity*. Trans. John Howe. London: Verso, 1995.

Bachelard, Gaston. *The Poetics of Space*. Trans. Maria Jolas. 1964. Boston: Beacon, 1994.

Baker, Houston A., Jr, Manthia Diawara, and Ruth H. Lindeborg, eds. *Black British Cultural Studies: A Reader.* Chicago: U of Chicago P, 1996.

Baker, Houston A., Jr, Stephen Best, and Ruth H. Lindeborg. 'Representing Blackness/Representing Britain: Cultural Studies and the Politics of Knowledge.' Baker et al., eds. 1–15.

Bakhtin, Mikhail. *Problems of Dostoevsky's Poetics.* Ed. and trans. Caryl Emerson. Minneapolis: U of Minnesota P, 1984.

– *Rabelais and His World.* Trans. Hélène Iswolsky. Bloomington: Indiana UP, 1984.

Ball, John Clement. 'An Interview with Salman Rushdie.' *Toronto South Asian Review* 10.1 (1991): 30–7. Rpt. in Michael Reder, ed. *Conversations with Salman Rushdie.* Jackson: UP of Mississippi, 2000. 101–9.

– *Satire and the Postcolonial Novel.* New York: Routledge, 2003.

Battersea Power Station Community Group. *BPSCG web site.* 2 Oct. 2002 <http://www.batterseapowerstation.com/>.

'Battersea Revived by the Circus.' *BBC Homepage.* 12 Dec. 2000. 2 Oct. 2002 <http://news.bbc.co.uk/1/hi/entertainment/1066758.stm>.

Baucom, Ian. *Out of Place: Englishness, Empire, and the Locations of Identity.* Princeton: Princeton UP, 1999.

Baudrillard, Jean. *Simulacra and Simulation.* Trans. Sheila Faria Glaser. Ann Arbor: U of Michigan P, 1994.

Baumeister, Roy F. 'Identity Crisis.' *Encyclopedia of Adolescence.* Ed. Richard M. Lerner, Anne C. Petersen, and Jeanne Brooks-Gunn. New York: Garland, 1991. 518–21.

Benjamin, Walter. *Charles Baudelaire: A Lyric Poet in the Era of High Capitalism.* Trans. Harry Zohn. 1973. London: Verso, 1997.

Benko, Georges. 'Introduction: Modernity, Postmodernity and the Social Sciences.' *Space and Social Theory: Interpreting Modernity and Postmodernity.* Ed. Benko and Ulf Strohmayer. Oxford: Blackwell, 1997. 1–44.

Bennett, Donna. 'English Canada's Postcolonial Complexities.' *Essays on Canadian Writing* 51–2 (1993–4): 164–210.

Bennett, Louise. 'Colonization in Reverse.' *The Penguin Book of Caribbean Verse in English.* Ed. Paula Burnett. Harmondsworth: Penguin, 1986. 32–3.

Bhabha, Homi K. *The Location of Culture.* London: Routledge, 1994.

Birbalsingh, Frank. 'David Dabydeen: Coolie Odyssey' [interview]. Birbalsingh, *Frontiers* 167–82.

– 'Samuel Selvon and the West Indian Literary Renaissance.' Nasta, ed. 142–59.

Birbalsingh, Frank, ed. *Frontiers of Caribbean Literature in English.* New York: St Martin's, 1996.

Bissoondath, Neil. *Selling Illusions: The Cult of Multiculturalism in Canada.* Toronto: Penguin, 1994.

Blake, Ann, Leela Gandhi, and Sue Thomas. 'Introduction: "Mother Country."' *England through Colonial Eyes in Twentieth-Century Fiction.* Ed. Blake, Gandhi, and Thomas. Houndsmills, UK: Palgrave, 2001.

Boddy, Kasia. 'A Question of Race.' Rev. of *The Last Time I Saw Jane,* by Kate Pullinger. *Times Literary Supplement* 17 May 1996: 24.

Booker, M. Keith, and Dubravka Juraga. *The Caribbean Novel in English: An Introduction.* Portsmouth, NH: Heinemann, 2001.

Bourdieu, Pierre. *Outline of a Theory of Practice.* Trans. Richard Nice. Cambridge: Cambridge UP, 1977.

Bradbury, Malcolm. 'The Cities of Modernism.' *Modernism 1890–1930.* Ed. Bradbury and James McFarlane. 1974. Sussex: Harvester, 1978. 96–104.

Brah, Avtar. *Cartographies of Diaspora: Contesting Identities.* London: Routledge, 1996.

Brandt, Di. 'Going Global.' *Where Is Here Now?* Spec. issue of *Essays on Canadian Writing* 71 (2000): 106–13.

Brenner, Rachel Feldhay. *Assimilation and Assertion: The Response to the Holocaust in Mordecai Richler's Writing.* New York: Lang, 1989.

Brizan, George. *Grenada: Island of Conflict: From Amerindians to People's Revolution 1498–1979.* London: Zed, 1984.

Brydon, Diana. 'It's Time for a New Set of Questions.' *Where Is Here Now?* Spec. issue of *Essays on Canadian Writing* 71 (2000): 14–25.

Brydon, Diana, ed. *Testing the Limits: Postcolonial Theories and Canadian Literature.* Spec. issue of *Essays on Canadian Writing* 56 (1995).

Bullock, Alan. 'The Double Image.' *Modernism 1890–1930.* Ed. Malcolm Bradbury and James McFarlane. Harmondsworth: Penguin, 1976. 58–70.

Bush, Barbara. *Slave Women in Caribbean Society 1650–1838.* Kingston, Jamaica: Heinemann, 1990.

Bush, Catherine. *The Rules of Engagement.* Toronto: HarperFlamingo, 2000.

Carey, Barbara. 'Packed Agenda Fails in the End.' Rev. of *The Last Time I Saw Jane,* by Kate Pullinger. *Toronto Star* 25 Jan. 1997: J17.

Carter, Erica, James Donald, and Judith Squires. Introduction. Carter et al., eds. vii–xv.

Carter, Erica, James Donald, and Judith Squires, eds. *Space and Place: Theories of Identity and Location.* London: Lawrence and Wishart, 1993.

Castells, Manuel. *The Informational City: Information Technology, Economic Restructuring, and the Urban-Regional Process.* Oxford: Blackwell, 1989.

Cavell, Richard. 'Here Is Where Now.' *Where Is Here Now?* Spec. issue of *Essays on Canadian Writing* 71 (2000): 195–202.

Chambers, Iain. 'Cities without Maps.' *Mapping the Futures: Local Cultures, Global Change*. Ed. Jon Bird et al. London: Routledge, 1993. 188–98.

Chapple, Christopher Key, and Mary Evelyn Tucker. *Hinduism and Ecology: The Intersection of Earth, Sky, and Water*. Cambridge: Harvard U Center for the Study of World Religions, 2000.

Chaudhuri, Nirad C. *Hinduism: A Religion to Live By*. New York: Oxford UP, 1979.

Clarke, Austin. *A Passage Back Home: A Personal Reminiscence of Samuel Selvon*. Toronto: Exile, 1994.

Clifford, James. 'Diasporas.' *Cultural Anthropology* 9.3 (1994): 302–38.

– 'The Transit Lounge of Culture.' *Times Literary Supplement* 3 May 1991: 6–7.

– 'Traveling Cultures.' *Cultural Studies*. Ed. Lawrence Grossberg, Cary Nelson, and Paula Treichler. New York: Routledge, 1992. 96–112.

Cohen, Robin. *Global Diasporas: An Introduction*. Seattle: U of Washington P, 1997.

Conrad, Joseph. *Heart of Darkness*. 1902. Harmondsworth: Penguin, 1973.

Crang, Mike. *Cultural Geography*. London: Routledge, 1998.

Cross, Malcolm. 'Race and Ethnicity.' *The Crisis of London*. Ed. Andy Thornley. New York: Routledge, 1992. 103–18.

Dabydeen, David. *Disappearance*. London: Secker and Warburg, 1993.

– *A Harlot's Progress*. London: Cape, 1999.

– *The Intended*. 1991. London: Vintage, 2000.

Danahey, Martin A., ed. *The Strange Case of Dr Jekyll and Mr Hyde*. By Robert Louis Stevenson. 1886. Peterborough, ON: Broadview, 1999.

Daniels, S., and S. Rycroft. 'Mapping the Modern City: Alan Sillitoe's Nottingham Novels.' *Transactions of the Institute of British Geographers* 18.4 (1993): 460–80.

Dash, J. Michael. Introduction. Glissant xi–xlv.

Davey, Frank. *Post-National Arguments: The Politics of the Anglophone-Canadian Novel since 1967*. Toronto: U of Toronto P, 1993.

Davidson, Arnold E. *Mordecai Richler*. New York: Ungar, 1983.

Davies, Robertson. *A Mixture of Frailties*. 1958. Toronto: Penguin, 1997.

Dawes, Kwame. 'Negotiating the Ship on The Head: Black British Fiction.' *Wasafiri* 29 (1999): 18–24.

Day, Richard J.F. *Multiculturalism and the History of Canadian Diversity*. Toronto: U of Toronto P, 2000.

de Certeau, Michel. *The Practice of Everyday Life*. Trans. Stephen Rendall. Berkeley: U of California P, 1984.

Derrick, A.C. 'Naipaul's Technique as a Novelist.' *Critical Perspectives on V.S. Naipaul*. Ed. Robert D. Hamner. Washington: Three Continents, 1977. 194–206.

Desai, Anita. *Bye-Bye Blackbird*. [1971.] New Delhi: Orient, 1985.

Dhingra, Leena. *First Light*. 1988. Calcutta: Rupa, 1991.

Dickinson, Peter. *Here Is Queer: Nationalisms, Sexualities, and the Literatures of Canada*. Toronto: U of Toronto P, 1999.

Dirlik, Arif. 'The Global in the Local.' Wilson and Dissanayake 21–45.

– 'Place-Based Imagination: Globalism and the Politics of Place.' *Places and Politics in an Age of Globalization*. Ed. Roxann Prazniak and Dirlik. Landham, MD: Rowman, 2001. 15–51.

Donald, James. *Imagining the Modern City*. Minneapolis: U of Minnesota P, 1999.

Donnell, Alison, and Sarah Lawson Welsh. '1950–65[:] Introduction.' *The Routledge Reader in Caribbean Literature*. Ed. Donnell and Welsh. London: Routledge, 1996. 206–21.

'Dusk.' Def. 2a. *The Oxford English Dictionary*. 2nd ed. 1989.

Eliot, T.S. 'The Waste Land.' 1922. *Collected Poems 1909–1962*. 1963. London: Faber, 1974. 61–86.

Engels, Friedrich. 'The Great Towns.' 1845. *The City Reader*. Ed. Richard T. LeGates and Frederic Stout. London: Routledge, 1996. 47–55.

Evaristo, Bernardine. *The Emperor's Babe*. 2001. London: Penguin, 2002.

Fanon, Frantz. *Black Skin, White Masks*. Trans. Charles Lam Markmann. New York: Grove, 1967.

Fee, Margery. 'Resistance and Complicity in David Dabydeen's *The Intended*.' *ARIEL* 24.1 (1993): 107–26.

Ferguson, Priscilla Parkhurst. 'The *Flâneur* on and off the Streets of Paris.' Tester, ed. 22–42.

Fishman, Robert. *Bourgeois Utopias: The Rise and Fall of Suburbia*. New York: Basic, 1987.

Fogel, Stanley. *A Tale of Two Countries: Contemporary Fiction in Canada and the United States*. Toronto: ECW, 1984.

Forster, E.M. *A Passage to India*. 1924. Harmondsworth: Penguin, 1961.

Foucault, Michel. 'Of Other Spaces.' *Diacritics* 16.1 (1986): 22–7.

Fox, Richard G., ed. *Urban India: Society, Space and Image*. [Durham]: Duke U Program in Comparative Studies on Southern Asia, 1970.

Freud, Sigmund. *Civilization and Its Discontents*. Trans. Joan Rivière. 3rd ed. London: Hogarth/Institute of Psychoanalysis, 1946.

Friedmann, John. 'Where We Stand: A Decade of World City Research.' Knox and Taylor 21–47.

Frye, Northrop. 'Conclusion to a *Literary History of Canada*.' 1965. *The Bush Garden: Essays on the Canadian Imagination*. 2nd ed. Toronto: Anansi, 1995. 215–53.

Fryer, Peter. *Staying Power: The History of Black People in Britain*. London: Pluto, 1984.

Gandhi, Leela. *Postcolonial Theory: A Critical Introduction.* New York: Columbia UP, 1998.

George, Rosemary Marangoly. *The Politics of Home: Postcolonial Relocations and Twentieth-Century Fiction.* Cambridge: Cambridge UP, 1996.

Gerzina, Gretchen Holbrook. *Black London: Life before Emancipation.* New Brunswick: Rutgers UP, 1995.

Ghosh, Amitav. 'The Diaspora in Indian Culture.' *Public Culture* 2.1 (1989): 773–8.

– *The Shadow Lines.* 1988. New York: Penguin, 1990.

Gikandi, Simon. *Maps of Englishness: Writing Identity in the Culture of Colonialism.* New York: Columbia UP, 1996.

– *Writing in Limbo: Modernism and Caribbean Literature.* Ithaca: Cornell UP, 1992.

Gilbert, David, and Fiona Henderson. 'London and the Tourist Imagination.' *Imagined Londons.* Ed. Pamela K. Gilbert. Albany: State U of New York P, 2002.

Gilroy, Beryl. *Boy-Sandwich.* Oxford: Heinemann, 1989.

Gilroy, Paul. *The Black Atlantic: Modernity and Double Consciousness.* Cambridge: Harvard UP, 1993.

– *'There Ain't No Black in the Union Jack': The Cultural Politics of Race and Nation.* 1987. Chicago: U of Chicago P, 1991.

Girard, Charlotte S.M. 'Sir James Douglas' Mother and Grandmother.' *BC Studies* 44 (1979–80): 25–31.

– 'Some Further Notes on the Douglas Family.' *BC Studies* 72 (1986–7): 3–27.

Gittings, Christopher. 'A Collision of Discourse: Postmodernisms and Post-Colonialisms in *The Biggest Modern Woman of the World.*' *Journal of Commonwealth Literature* 29.1 (1994): 81–91.

Gleber, Anke. *The Art of Taking a Walk: Flanerie, Literature, and Film in Weimar Culture.* Princeton: Princeton UP, 1999.

Glissant, Edouard. *Caribbean Discourse: Selected Essays.* Trans. J. Michael Dash. Charlottesville: UP of Virginia, 1989.

Goulbourne, Harry. *Ethnicity and Nationalism in Post-Imperial Britain.* Cambridge: Cambridge UP, 1991.

Grant, Judith Skelton. *Robertson Davies: Man of Myth.* Toronto: Viking, 1994.

Gregory, Derek. *Geographical Imaginations.* Cambridge, MA: Blackwell, 1994.

Hall, Peter. *The World Cities.* 3rd ed. New York: St Martin's, 1984.

Hall, Stuart. 'Cultural Identity and Cinematic Representation.' 1989. Baker et al., eds. 210–22.

– 'Minimal Selves.' 1987. Baker et al., eds. 114–19.

Hall, Stuart, et al. 'Reinventing Britain: A Forum.' *Wasafiri* 29 (1999): 37–44.

Harris, Wilson. *The Angel at the Gate.* London: Faber, 1982.

Harvey, David. *The Condition of Postmodernity: An Enquiry into the Origins of Cultural Change.* Cambridge: Blackwell, 1990.

– *The Urban Experience.* Baltimore: Johns Hopkins UP, 1989.

Hassan, Dolly Zulakha. *V.S. Naipaul and the West Indies.* New York: Lang, 1989.

Hassan, Ihab. 'Cities of Mind, Urban Words: The Dematerialization of Metropolis in Contemporary American Fiction.' *Literature and the Urban Experience: Essays on the City and Literature.* Ed. Michael C. Jaye and Ann Chalmers Watts. New Brunswick: Rutgers UP, 1981. 93–112.

Hazlehurst, Leighton. 'Urban Space and Activities.' Fox 186–95.

Hebdige, Dick. 'Digging for Britain: An Excavation in Seven Parts.' 1987 rev. 1992. Baker et al., eds. 120–62.

Heffernan, Teresa. 'Tracing the Travesty: Constructing the Female Subject in Susan Swan's *The Biggest Modern Woman of the World.*' *Canadian Literature* 133 (1992): 24–37.

Hiriyanna, M. *The Essentials of Indian Philosophy.* London: Allen, 1949.

Hiss, Tony. *The Experience of Place.* 1990. New York: Vintage, 1991.

Howells, Coral Ann. *Private and Fictional Worlds: Canadian Women Novelists of the 1970s and 1980s.* London: Methuen, 1987.

Hulme, Peter. 'Including America.' *ARIEL* 26.1 (1995): 117–23.

– 'The Profit of Language: George Lamming and the Postcolonial Novel.' *Recasting the World: Writing after Colonialism.* Ed. Jonathan White. Baltimore: Johns Hopkins UP, 1993. 120–36.

Hutcheon, Linda. *The Canadian Postmodern: A Study of Contemporary English-Canadian Fiction.* Toronto: Oxford UP, 1988.

– '"Circling the Downspout of Empire": Post-Colonialism and Postmodernism.' *ARIEL* 20.4 (1989): 149–75.

– Introduction. *Other Solitudes: Canadian Multicultural Fictions.* Ed. Hutcheon and Marion Richmond. Toronto: Oxford UP, 1990. 1–16.

– *A Poetics of Postmodernism: History, Theory, Fiction.* New York: Routledge, 1988.

Inwood, Stephen. *A History of London.* New York: Carroll and Graf, 1998.

Jacobs, Jane. 'The Uses of Sidewalks: Safety.' 1961. *The City Reader.* Ed. Richard T. LeGates and Frederic Stout. London: Routledge, 1996. 104–8.

Jacobs, Jane M. *Edge of Empire: Postcolonialism and the City.* London: Routledge, 1996.

James, Louis. *Caribbean Literature in English.* London: Longman, 1999.

Jameson, Fredric. 'Postmodernism, or the Cultural Logic of Late Capitalism.' *New Left Review* 146 (1984): 53–92.

– 'Third-World Literature in the Era of Multinational Capitalism.' *Social Text* 15 (1986): 65–88.

Jha, Rekha. *The Novels of Kamala Markandaya and Ruth Jhabvala: A Study in East-West Encounter.* New Delhi: Prestige, 1990.

Kamboureli, Smaro. '*The Biggest Modern Woman of the World*: Canada as the Absent Spouse.' *Studies in Canadian Literature* 16.2 (1991): 1–16.

– *Scandalous Bodies: Diasporic Literature in English Canada.* Toronto: Oxford UP, 1999.

Kaul, A.N. 'A Reading of *The Shadow Lines*.' *The Shadow Lines*. By Amitav Ghosh. Delhi: Oxford UP, 1995. 299–309.

Kaul, Suvir. 'Separation Anxiety: Growing Up Inter/National in Amitav Ghosh's *The Shadow Lines*.' *Oxford Literary Review* 16.1–2 (1994): 125–45.

Keith, W.J. '*A Mixture of Frailties* and "Romance."' *Robertson Davies: An Appreciation*. Ed. Elspeth Cameron. Peterborough, ON: Broadview/Journal of Canadian Studies, 1991. 199–212.

Kertzer, Jonathan. *Worrying the Nation: Imagining a National Literature in English Canada.* Toronto: U of Toronto P, 1998.

Kincaid, Jamaica. *Annie John.* 1985. New York: Plume, 1986.

King, Anthony D. *Global Cities: Post-Imperialism and the Internationalization of London.* London: Routledge, 1990.

– 'Re-presenting World Cities: Cultural Theory/Social Practice.' Knox and Taylor 215–31.

– *Urbanism, Colonialism, and the World-Economy: Cultural and Spatial Foundations of the World Urban System.* London: Routledge, 1990.

Klostermaier, Klaus K. *A Survey of Hinduism.* 2nd ed. Albany: State U of New York P, 1994.

Knox, Paul L. 'World Cities in a World-System.' Knox and Taylor 3–20.

Knox, Paul L., and Peter J. Taylor, eds. *World Cities in a World-System.* Cambridge: Cambridge UP, 1995.

Krishnaswamy, Revathi. 'Mythologies of Migrancy: Postcolonialism, Postmodernism and the Politics of (Dis)location.' *ARIEL* 26.1 (1995): 125–46.

Kumar, Amitava. *Bombay–London–New York.* New York: Routledge, 2002.

Kureishi, Hanif. 'Bradford.' *Granta* 20 (1986): 147–70.

– *The Buddha of Suburbia.* 1990. New York: Penguin, 1991.

– *London Kills Me: Three Screenplays and Four Essays.* New York: Penguin, 1992.

– *My Beautiful Laundrette.* 1986. Kureishi, *London* 38–114.

– *Sammy and Rosie Get Laid.* 1988. Kureishi, *London* 195–264.

– 'Some Time with Stephen.' 1988. Kureishi, *London* 117–94.

Lamming, George. 'The Coldest Spring in Fifty Years: Thoughts on Sam Selvon and London.' *Kunapipi* 20.1 (1998): 4–10.

– 'Concepts of the Caribbean.' [1985.] Birbalsingh, *Frontiers* 1–14.

– *The Emigrants.* 1954. Ann Arbor: U of Michigan P, 1994.

– *The Pleasures of Exile.* London: Joseph, 1960.

– *Water with Berries.* London: Longman, 1971.

Layton-Henry, Zig. *The Politics of Race in Britain.* London: Allen and Unwin,1984.

Lefebvre, Henri. *The Production of Space.* 1974. Trans. Donald Nicholson-Smith. Oxford: Blackwell, 1991.

– *Writings on Cities.* Ed. and trans. Eleonore Kofman and Elizabeth Lebas. Oxford: Blackwell, 1996.

Levy, Andrea. *Never Far from Nowhere.* London: Review, 1996.

Lewis, Gordon K. *Slavery, Imperialism, and Freedom: Studies in English Radical Thought.* New York: Monthly Rev., 1978.

Lynch, Kevin. *The Image of the City.* Cambridge: MIT P, 1960.

Macaulay, Thomas Babington. *Selected Writings.* Ed. John Clive and Thomas Pinney. Chicago: U of Chicago P, 1972.

MacLulich, T.D. *Between Europe and America: The Canadian Tradition in Fiction.* Toronto: ECW, 1988.

Marcia, James E. 'Identity and Self-Development.' *Encyclopedia of Adolescence.* Ed. Richard M. Lerner, Anne C. Petersen, and Jeanne Brooks-Gunn. New York: Garland, 1991. 529–33.

Markandaya, Kamala. *The Nowhere Man.* New York: John Day, 1972.

– *Possession.* London: Putnam, 1963.

Martin, S.I. *Incomparable World.* London: Quartet, 1996.

Massey, Doreen. 'Power-Geometry and a Progressive Sense of Place.' *Mapping the Futures: Local Cultures, Global Change.* Ed. Jon Bird et al. London: Routledge, 1993. 59–69.

– *Space, Place, and Gender.* Minneapolis: U of Minnesota P, 1994.

Mazlish, Bruce. 'The *Flâneur*: From Spectator to Representation.' Tester, ed. 43–60.

Mazzoleni, Donatella. 'The City and the Imaginary.' Trans. John Koumantarakis. Carter et al., eds. 285–301.

McClintock, Anne. *Imperial Leather: Race, Gender and Sexuality in the Colonial Contest.* New York: Routledge, 1995.

McIntyre, Karen. '"A Different Kind of Book": Literary Decolonization in David Dabydeen's *The Intended.*' *ARIEL* 27.2 (1996): 151–75.

McLaughlin, Joseph. *Writing the Urban Jungle: Reading Empire in London from Doyle to Eliot.* Charlottesville: UP of Virginia, 2000.

McLeod, John. *Beginning Postcolonialism.* Manchester: Manchester UP, 2000.

– Rev. of *The Emperor's Babe,* by Bernardine Evaristo. *Wasafiri* 34 (2001): 60–1.

McLuhan, Marshall. 'Canada: The Borderline Case.' *The Canadian Imagination: Dimensions of a Literary Culture.* Ed. David Staines. Cambridge: Harvard UP, 1977. 226–48.

- *The Gutenberg Galaxy: The Making of Typographic Man.* Toronto: U of Toronto P, 1962.

Mercer, Kobena. *Welcome to the Jungle: New Positions in Black Cultural Studies.* London: Routledge, 1994.

Metcalf, Thomas R. *An Imperial Vision: Indian Architecture and Britain's Raj.* Berkeley: U of California P, 1989.

Miller, J. Hillis. *Topographies.* Stanford: Stanford UP, 1995.

Mishra, Vijay. 'Postcolonial Differend: Diasporic Narratives of Salman Rushdie.' *ARIEL* 26.3 (1995): 7–45.

Mittelholzer, Edgar. *A Tale of Three Places.* London: Secker and Warburg, 1957.

Miyoshi, Masao. 'A Borderless World? From Colonialism to Transnationalism and the Decline of the Nation-State.' Wilson and Dissanayake 78–106.

Mohanti, Prafulla. *Through Brown Eyes.* Oxford: Oxford UP, 1985.

Molesworth, Charles. 'The City: Some Classical Moments.' *City Images: Perspectives from Literature, Philosophy, and Film.* Ed. Mary Ann Caws. New York: Gordon, 1991. 13–23.

Monk, Patricia. *The Smaller Infinity: The Jungian Self in the Novels of Robertson Davies.* Toronto: U of Toronto P, 1982.

Moore-Gilbert, Bart. 'Hanif Kureishi's *The Buddha of Suburbia*: Hybridity in Contemporary Cultural Theory and Artistic Practice.' *QWERTY: Arts, Littératures et Civilisations du Monde Anglophone* 7 (1997): 191–207.

Moraru, Christian. 'Refiguring the Postcolonial: The Transnational Challenges.' *ARIEL* 28.4 (1997): 171–85.

Morley, David, and Kevin Robins. *Spaces of Identity: Global Media, Electronic Landscapes and Cultural Boundaries.* London: Routledge, 1995.

Moss, John. *Patterns of Isolation in English Canadian Fiction.* Toronto: McClelland and Stewart, 1974.

- 'Richler's Horseman.' *The Canadian Novel Here and Now.* Ed. Moss. Toronto: NC, 1978. 156–65.

Moss, Laura, ed. *Is Canada Postcolonial? Unsettling Canadian Literature.* Waterloo, ON: Wilfrid Laurier UP, 2003.

Mudrooroo. *Master of the Ghost Dreaming.* Sydney: Angus and Robertson, 1991.

Mukherjee, Arun. 'Whose Post-Colonialism and Whose Postmodernism?' *World Literature Written in English* 30.2 (1990): 1–9.

Mumford, Lewis. 'What Is a City?' 1937. *The City Reader.* Ed. Richard T. LeGates and Frederic Stout. London: Routledge, 1996. 184–8.

Muuss, Rolf E. *Theories of Adolescence.* 6th ed. New York: McGraw-Hill, 1996.

Naipaul, V.S. *The Enigma of Arrival: A Novel in Five Sections.* Harmondsworth: Penguin, 1987.

- *A Flag on the Island.* 1967. Harmondsworth: Penguin, 1969.

– 'London.' [1958.] *The Overcrowded Barracoon*. By Naipaul. 1972. Harmondsworth: Penguin, 1976. 9–17.

– *The Loss of El Dorado: A History*. 1969. Harmondsworth: Penguin, 1973.

– *The Middle Passage: Impressions of Five Societies – British, French and Dutch – in the West Indies and South America*. 1962. Harmondsworth: Penguin, 1969.

– *The Mimic Men*. 1967. Harmondsworth: Penguin, 1969.

– 'Prologue to an Autobiography.' *Finding the Centre: Two Narratives*. By Naipaul. 1984. Harmondsworth: Penguin, 1985. 13–72.

– *The Return of Eva Perón, with the Killings in Trinidad*. 1980. New York: Vintage 1981.

Nair, Supriya. *Caliban's Curse: George Lamming and the Revisioning of History*. Ann Arbor: U of Michigan P, 1996.

Nandy, Ashis. *An Ambiguous Journey to the City: The Village and Other Odd Ruins of the Self in the Indian Imagination*. New Delhi: Oxford UP, 2001.

– *The Intimate Enemy: Loss and Recovery of Self under Colonialism*. 1983. New Delhi: Oxford UP, 1988.

Nanton, Philip. 'What Does Mr Swanzy Want? Shaping or Reflecting? An Assessment of Henry Swanzy's Contribution to the Development of Caribbean Literature.' *Kunapipi* 20.1 (1998): 11–20.

Nasta, Susheila. *Home Truths: Fictions of the South Asian Diaspora in Britain*. Houndsmills, UK: Palgrave, 2002.

Nasta, Susheila, ed. *Critical Perspectives on Sam Selvon*. Washington: Three Continents, 1988.

Needham, Anuradha Dingwaney. *Using the Master's Tools: Resistance and the Literature of the African and South-Asian Diasporas*. New York: St Martin's, 2000.

New, W.H. *Borderlands: How We Talk about Canada*. Vancouver: UBC P, 1998.

– *Land Sliding: Imagining Space, Presence, and Power in Canadian Writing*. Toronto: U of Toronto P, 1997.

Newland, Courttia. *The Scholar: A West Side Story*. 1997. London: Abacus, 1998.

'Oceanic.' Def. 2b ['oceanic feeling']. *The Oxford English Dictionary*. 2nd ed. 1989.

O'Connor, Teresa F. *Jean Rhys: The West Indian Novels*. New York: New York UP, 1986.

Osachoff, Margaret Gail. 'Richler's Pastoral of the City Streets.' *Perspectives on Mordecai Richler*. Ed. Michael Darling. Toronto: ECW, 1986. 33–51.

Paquet, Sandra Pouchet. *The Novels of George Lamming*. London: Heinemann, 1982.

Parenthood.com. *Baby Names, Meanings of Names*. 7 Oct. 2002 <http://www.parenthood.com/parent_cfmfiles/babynames.cfm>.

Patton, Laurie L. 'Nature Romanticism and Sacrifice in Rgvedic Interpretation.' Chapple and Tucker 39–58.

Pennee, Donna Palmateer. '"Après Frye, rien"? Pas du tout! From *Contexts* to *New Contexts*.' *New Contexts of Canadian Criticism*. Ed. Ajay Heble, Pennee, and J.R. (Tim) Struthers. Peterborough, ON: Broadview, 1997. 202–19.

Peterman, Michael. *Robertson Davies*. Boston: Twayne, 1986.

Pethick, Derek. *James Douglas: Servant of Two Empires*. Vancouver: Mitchell, 1969.

Pike, Burton. *The Image of the City in Modern Literature*. Princeton: Princeton UP, 1981.

Porter, Roy. *London: A Social History*. London: Hamilton, 1994.

Pratt, Mary Louise. *Imperial Eyes: Travel Writing and Transculturation*. London: Routledge, 1992.

– 'Scratches on the Face of the Country; or, What Mr. Barrow Saw in the Land of the Bushmen.' *'Race,' Writing, and Difference*. Ed. Henry Louis Gates, Jr. Chicago: U of Chicago P, 1986. 138–62.

Procter, James. 'Descending the Stairwell: Dwelling Places and Doorways in Early Post-War Black British Writing.' *Kunapipi* 20.1 (1998): 21–31.

– 'General Introduction: "1948"/"1998" Periodising Postwar black Britain.' *Writing black Britain 1948–1998: An Interdisciplinary Anthology*. Ed. Procter. Manchester: Manchester UP, 2000. 1–12.

Pulingandla, R. *Fundamentals of Indian Philosophy*. Nashville: Abingdon, 1975.

'Pulling Teeth.' Rev. of *White Teeth*, by Zadie Smith. Review of Books. Spec. section of *The Economist* 19 Feb. 2000: 5.

Pullinger, Kate. Introduction. *Border Lines: Stories of Exile and Home*. Ed. Pullinger. London: Serpent's Tail, 1993. 7.

– *The Last Time I Saw Jane*. Toronto: Little, Brown, 1996.

– *When the Monster Dies*. London: Cape, 1989.

Quayson, Ato. *Postcolonialism: Theory, Practice or Process?* Cambridge: Polity, 2000.

Raban, Jonathan. *Soft City*. 1974. London: Flamingo, 1984.

Ramchand, Kenneth. Introduction. Selvon, *Island* v–xxv.

– 'Song of Innocence, Song of Experience: Samuel Selvon's *The Lonely Londoners* as a Literary Work.' Nasta, ed. 223–33.

– *The West Indian Novel and Its Background*. London: Faber, 1970.

Ramraj, Victor J. *Mordecai Richler*. Boston: Twayne, 1983.

Rao, K.L. Seshagiri. 'The Five Great Elements (*Pañamahabhuta*): An Ecological Perspective.' Chapple and Tucker 23–38.

Rao, Raja. Author's Foreword. 1938. *Kanthapura*. New York: New Directions, 1967. vii–viii.

Rhys, Jean. *Smile Please: An Unfinished Autobiography*. New York: Harper and Row, 1979.

– *Voyage in the Dark.* 1934. Harmondsworth: Penguin, 1969.

Richler, Mordecai. 'London Province.' *Encounter* 19 (July 1962): 40–4.

– 'London Then and Now.' *Belling the Cat: Essays, Reports, and Opinions.* Toronto: Knopf, 1998. 179–99.

– 'O Canada.' *Home Sweet Home.* 1984. Markham, ON: Penguin, 1985. 265–91.

– *St. Urbain's Horseman.* 1971. Toronto: Seal, 1978.

Rigelhof, T.F. 'Catherine Bush and the Other Talent in the Room.' *Essays on Canadian Writing* 73 (2001): 208–26.

Riley, Joan. *Waiting in the Twilight.* London: Women's, 1987.

Roper, Gordon. 'Conversations with Gordon Roper.' *Conversations with Robertson Davies.* Ed. J. Madison Davis. Jackson: UP of Mississippi, 1989. 9–61.

Roy, Anjali. '*Microstoria*: Indian Nationalism's "Little Stories" in Amitav Ghosh's *The Shadow Lines.*' *Journal of Commonwealth Literature* 35.2 (2000): 35–49.

Roy, Arundhati. *The God of Small Things.* Toronto: Random, 1997.

Rushdie, Salman. *Imaginary Homelands: Essays and Criticism 1981–1991.* 1991. London: Penguin, 1992.

– *Midnight's Children.* 1980. New York: Knopf, 1981.

– *The Satanic Verses.* London: Viking, 1988.

Sack, Robert David. *Conceptions of Space in Social Thought: A Geographic Perspective.* London: Macmillan, 1980.

Safran, William. 'Diasporas in Modern Societies: Myths of Homeland and Return.' *Diaspora* 1.1 (1991): 83–99.

Said, Edward W. *Culture and Imperialism.* New York: Knopf, 1993.

– *Orientalism.* 1978. New York, Vintage, 1979.

Salkey, Andrew. *Escape to an Autumn Pavement.* London: Hutchinson, 1960.

– *Come Home, Malcolm Heartland.* London: Hutchinson, 1976.

Sarvan, Charles. 'David Dabydeen's *The Intended*: A Parodic Intertextuality.' *International Fiction Review* 21.1–2 (1994): 58–61.

Sassen, Saskia. 'Identity in the Global City: Economic and Cultural Encasements.' *The Geography of Identity.* Ed. Patricia Yaeger. Ann Arbor: U of Michigan P, 1996. 131–51.

Savory, Elaine. *Jean Rhys.* Cambridge: Cambridge UP, 1998.

Scott, Jamie S., and Paul Simpson-Housley. 'Eden, Babylon, New Jerusalem: A Taxonomy for Writing the City.' *Writing the City: Eden, Babylon, and the New Jerusalem.* Ed. Peter Preston and Simpson-Housley. London: Routledge, 1994. 331–41.

Selvon, Samuel [Sam]. 'Finding West Indian Identity in London.' *Kunapipi* 9.3 (1987): 34–8.

– *The Housing Lark.* London: MacGibbon and Kee, 1965.

– *An Island Is a World.* 1955. Toronto: TSAR, 1993.

– *The Lonely Londoners.* 1956. Toronto: TSAR, 1991.

– *Moses Ascending.* 1975. London: Heinemann, 1984.

Sen, Asha. 'Crossing Boundaries in Amitav Ghosh's *The Shadow Lines.' Journal of Commonwealth and Postcolonial Studies* 5.1 (1997): 46–58.

Sennett, Richard. *The Conscience of the Eye: The Design and Social Life of Cities.* New York: Knopf, 1990.

– *The Uses of Disorder: Personal Identity and City Life.* New York: Knopf, 1970.

Seuss, Dr. *The Cat in the Hat Comes Back!* 1958. New York: Random, 1986.

Shields, Rob. 'Fancy Footwork: Walter Benjamin's Notes on *Flânerie.'* Tester, ed. 61–80.

– *Places on the Margin: Alternative Geographies of Modernity.* London: Routledge, 1991.

Sibley, David. *Geographies of Exclusion: Society and Difference in the West.* London: Routledge, 1995.

Simmel, Georg. 'The Metropolis and Mental Life.' 1903. *On Individuality and Social Forms: Selected Writings.* By Simmel. Ed. Donald N. Levine. Chicago: U of Chicago P, 1971. 324–39.

Sivanandan, A. *A Different Hunger: Writings on Black Resistance.* London: Pluto, 1982.

Slemon, Stephen. 'Monuments of Empire: Allegory/Counter-Discourse/Post-Colonial Writing.' *Kunapipi* 9.3 (1987): 1–16.

– 'Unsettling the Empire: Resistance Theory for the Second World.' *World Literature Written in English* 30.2 (1990): 30–41.

Smart, Ninian. *Doctrine and Argument in Indian Philosophy.* London: Allen and Unwin, 1964.

Smith, Dorothy Blakey. *James Douglas: Father of British Columbia.* Toronto: Oxford UP, 1971.

Smith, Michael Peter. *Transnational Urbanism: Locating Globalization.* Malden, MA: Blackwell, 2001.

Smith, Zadie. *White Teeth.* London: Hamilton, 2000.

Smollett, Tobias. *The Expedition of Humphry Clinker.* 1771. Ed. Angus Ross. Harmondsworth: Penguin, 1967.

Söderlind, Sylvia. *Margin/Alias: Language and Colonization in Canadian and Québécois Fiction.* Toronto: U of Toronto P, 1991.

Soja, Edward W. *Postmodern Geographies: The Reassertion of Space in Critical Social Theory.* London: Verso, 1989.

Spivak, Gayatri Chakravorty. *Outside in the Teaching Machine.* New York: Routledge, 1993.

Srivastava, Atima. *Transmission.* London: Serpent's Tail, 1992.

Stead, Kit. Rev. of *The Last Time I Saw Jane,* by Kate Pullinger. *Observer* 12 May 1996: D16.

Steffler, John. *The Afterlife of George Cartwright.* Toronto: McClelland and Stewart, 1992.

Street, Brian. 'British Popular Anthropology: Exhibiting and Photographing the Other.' *Anthropology and Photography 1860–1920.* Ed. Elizabeth Edwards. New Haven: Yale UP, 1992. 122–31.

Sugars, Cynthia. 'National Posts: Theorizing Canadian Postcolonialism.' *International Journal of Canadian Studies* 25 (2002): 41–67.

Swan, Susan. *The Biggest Modern Woman of the World.* Toronto: Lester and Orpen Dennys, 1983.

Swanzy, Henry. 'Caribbean Voices[:] Prolegomena to a West Indian Culture.' *Caribbean Quarterly* 1.2 (1949): 21–8.

– 'The Islands of Calypso.' *New Statesman* 10 Sept. 1960: 350–1.

Tajbakhsh, Kian. *The Promise of the City: Space, Identity, and Politics in Contemporary Social Thought.* Berkeley: U of California P, 2001.

Taylor, Charles. *Multiculturalism and 'The Politics of Recognition.'* Ed. Amy Gutmann. Princeton: Princeton UP, 1992.

Tester, Keith. Introduction. Tester, ed. 1–21.

Tester, Keith, ed. *The 'Flâneur.'* London: Routledge, 1994.

Thieme, John. *The Web of Tradition: Uses of Allusion in V.S. Naipaul's Fiction.* Aarhus, Denmark: Dangaroo, 1987.

Thomas, Clara. 'The Two Voices of *A Mixture of Frailties.*' *Robertson Davies: An Appreciation.* Ed. Elspeth Cameron. Peterborough, ON: Broadview, 1991. 182–98.

Thompson, F.M.L., ed. *The Rise of Suburbia.* Leicester: Leicester UP, 1982.

Thorsell, William. 'Manley: A Man with a Message.' *Globe and Mail* 15 Oct. 2001: A21.

Toronto Convention and Visitors Association. Home page. 23 Oct. 2003 <http://www.torontotourism.com/>.

Tuan, Yi-Fu. *Space and Place: The Perspective of Experience.* Minneapolis: U of Minnesota P, 1977.

Vassanji, M.G. *The Book of Secrets.* Toronto: McClelland and Stewart, 1994.

– *No New Land.* Toronto: McClelland and Stewart, 1991.

– *Uhuru Street.* Toronto: McClelland and Stewart, 1993.

Vautier, Marie. *New World Myth: Postmodernism and Postcolonialism in Canadian Fiction.* Montreal and Kingston: McGill-Queen's UP, 1998.

Walcott, Derek. 'The Caribbean: Culture or Mimicry?' *Journal of Interamerican Studies and World Affairs* 16.1 (1974): 3–13.

– *Collected Poems 1948–1984.* New York: Noonday, 1986.

– 'The Muse of History: An Essay.' *Is Massa Day Dead? Black Moods in the Caribbean.* Ed. Orde Coombs. Garden City, NY: Anchor, 1974. 1–27.

- 'What the Twilight Says: An Overture.' *Dream on Monkey Mountain and Other Plays.* New York: Farrar, 1970. 3–40.
Walmsley, Anne. *The Caribbean Artists Movement 1966–1972: A Literary and Cultural History.* London: New Beacon, 1992.
Watmough, David. Interview with Mordecai Richler. CBC Radio, 11 Jan. 1969.
Weinfeld, Morton. 'Social Identity in the 1990s.' *Clash of Identities: Media, Manipulation, and Politics of the Self.* Ed. James Littleton. Toronto: Prentice-Hall, 1996. 119–25.
Weiss, Timothy F. *On the Margins: The Art of Exile in V.S. Naipaul.* Amherst: U of Massachusetts P, 1992.
Wells, H.G. *The New Machiavelli.* 1910. New York: Dunfield, 1917.
'What Does Mr Swanzy Want?' By Philip Nanton. Prod. Matt Thompson. BBC Radio 4. 1998.
Whitaker, Reg. 'Sovereign Division: Quebec Nationalism between Liberalism and Ethnicity.' *Clash of Identities: Media, Manipulation, and Politics of the Self.* Ed. James Littleton. Toronto: Prentice-Hall, 1996. 73–87.
White, Landeg. *V.S. Naipaul: A Critical Introduction.* London: Macmillan, 1975.
Wiebe, Rudy. *Playing Dead: A Contemplation Concerning the Arctic.* Edmonton: NeWest, 1989.
Williams, Raymond. *The Country and the City.* 1973. London: Hogarth, 1993.
Wilson, Elizabeth. 'The Invisible *Flâneur.*' *Postmodern Cities and Spaces.* Ed. Sophie Watson and Katherine Gibson. Oxford: Blackwell, 1995. 59–79.
- *The Sphinx in the City: Urban Life, the Control of Disorder, and Women.* Berkeley: U of California P, 1991.
Wilson, Rob, and Wimal Dissanayake, eds. *Global/Local: Cultural Production and the Transnational Imaginary.* Durham: Duke UP, 1996.
Wood, James. 'Human, All Too Inhuman: The Smallness of the "Big" Novel.' *New Republic* 24 July 2000: 41–6.
Wordsworth, William. *The Prelude, or Growth of a Poet's Mind.* Ed. Ernest de Selincourt. 1926. 2nd ed. rev. Helen Darbishire. London: Oxford UP, 1959.
Wyke, Clement H. *Sam Selvon's Dialectical Style and Fictional Strategy.* Vancouver: UBC P, 1991.
Young, Robert J.C. *Colonial Desire: Hybridity in Theory, Culture, and Race.* London: Routledge, 1995.
Zelliot, Eleanor. 'Literary Images of the Modern Indian City.' Fox 215–23.
Zimmer, Heinrich. *Philosophies of India.* Ed. Joseph Campbell. Princeton: Princeton UP, 1951.

Index